Blue Studios

Poetry and Its Cultural Work

RACHEL BLAU DUPLESSIS

THE UNIVERSITY OF ALABAMA PRESS
Tuscaloosa

The University of Alabama Press
Tuscaloosa, Alabama 35487-0380

Manufactured in the United States of America

Typeface: Minion

∞

The paper on which this book is printed meets the minimum requirements of American National Standard for Information Sciences-Permanence of Paper for Printed Library Materials, ANSI Z39.48-1984.

Library of Congress Cataloging-in-Publication Data

DuPlessis, Rachel Blau.
Blue studios : poetry and its cultural work / Rachel Blau DuPlessis.
p. cm. — (Modern and contemporary poetics)
Includes bibliographical references and index.
ISBN-13: 978-0-8173-1508-5 (cloth : alk. paper)
ISBN-10: 0-8173-1508-X (cloth: alk. paper)
ISBN-13: 978-0-8173-5321-6 (pbk. : alk. paper)
ISBN-10: 0-8173-5321-6 (pbk. : alk. paper)
1. American poetry—20th century—History and criticism. 2. Feminism and literature—United States—History—20th century. 3. Poetry—Authorship—Sex differences—History—20th century. 4. Women and literature—United States—History—20th century. 5. American poetry—Women authors—History and criticism. 6. Feminist poetry, American—History and criticism. 7. Sex role in literature. I. Title. II. Series.
PS310.F45D87 2006
811′5093522—dc22

2005027020

Blue Studios

MODERN AND CONTEMPORARY POETICS

Poetry is related to
music and cadence and therefore to the
force of events
—George Oppen

The handle of it was blue.
—Lorine Niedecker

Contents

Acknowledgments ix

Introduction 1

I. Attitudes and Practices

1. Reader, I married me: Becoming a Feminist Critic 15

2. *f*-words: An Essay on the Essay 34

3. Blue Studio: Gender Arcades 48

II. Marble Paper

4. Manifests 73

5. Marble Paper: Toward a Feminist "History of Poetry" 96

6. Propounding Modernist Maleness: How Pound Managed a Muse 122

III. Urrealism

7. Lorine Niedecker, the Anonymous: Gender, Class, Genre, and Resistances 139

8. The Gendered Marvelous: Barbara Guest, Surrealism, and Feminist Reception 162

9. "Uncannily in the open": In Light of Oppen 186

IV. Migrated Into

10. On *Drafts*: A Memorandum of Understanding 209

11. Haibun: "Draw your Draft" 218

12. Inside the Middle of a Long Poem 236

Notes 253

References 279

Index 299

Acknowledgments

My deepest thanks go to Hank Lazer and Juliana Spahr—for the two probing nonanonymous readers' reports that helped me focus, cut, and mull this book as I was rewriting, remixing, and reconceptualizing it—and to Charles Bernstein for support. Dan Waterman, the Alabama editor, was terrific, both professional and adept. Joe Abbott was a stellar copy editor; Conna Clark, Philadelphia Museum, guided the choice of cover. My deepest institutional thanks go simultaneously to Temple University, for sabbaticals in both 2001–2 and 2004–5, and to the Pew Fellowship for Artists, for my 2002 grant (taken in 2004–5), which allowed me to complete this work, as well as to write poetry.

Most of these essays have been significantly revised for this volume. Many thanks to the following editors and publishers:

"Reader, I married me: A Polygynous Memoir." In *Changing Subjects: The Making of Feminist Literary Criticism,* ed. Gayle Greene and Coppélia Kahn. New York: Routledge, 1993. Additional material from "Circumscriptions: Assimilating T. S. Eliot's Sweeneys." In *People of the Book: Thirty Scholars Reflect on Their Jewish Identity,* ed. Jeffrey Rubin-Dorsky and Shelley Fisher Fishkin. Madison: University of Wisconsin Press, 1996.

"Lorine Niedecker, the Anonymous: Gender, Class, Genre, and Resistances." *Kenyon Review* 14, no. 2 (spring 1992), ed. Marilyn Hacker; repr. in *Lorine Niedecker: Woman and Poet,* ed. Jenny Penberthy. Orono, ME: National Poetry Foundation, 1996. Unpublished Lorine Niedecker material is cited with the generous permission of the late Cid Corman, her then literary executor; an unpublished LN letter by the kind permission of The Archive for New Poetry, Mandeville Department of Special Collections, University of California, San Diego; a letter by Carl Rakosi, courtesy of the late Carl Rakosi and The Archive for New Poetry.

"On Drafts: A Memorandum of Understanding." *TO:* 1, no. 1 (July 1992), ed. Andrew Mossin and Seth Fretchie; repr. in *Onward: Contemporary Poetry and Poetics,* ed. Peter Baker. New York: Peter Lang Publishing, 1996.

"The Gendered Marvelous: Barbara Guest, Surrealism, and Feminist Reception." In *The Scene of My Selves: New Work on New York School Poets,* ed. Terence Diggory and Stephen Paul Miller. Orono, ME: National Poetry Foundation, 2001.

"*f*-words: An Essay on the Essay." *American Literature* 68, no. 1 (March 1996), ed. Sharon O'Brien. Special issue on contemporary writing in the United States.

"Manifests." In "Poetry, Community, Movement," ed. Jonathan Monroe, special issue, *Diacritics* 26, no. 3 (fall-winter 1996).

"Haibun: Draw your / Draft." *Sulfur* 42 (April 1998), ed. Clayton Eshleman; repr. in *H.D. and Poets After,* ed. Donna Krolik Hollenberg. Iowa City: University of Iowa Press, 2000.

"Marble Paper: Toward a Feminist History of Poetry." *Modern Language Quarterly* 65, no. 1 (March 2004). Three people have given this essay interested support: Marshall Brown, Jeanne Heuving, and Jonathan Culler.

"Blue Studio: Gender Arcades." *Open Letter* (Canada), 11th ser., no. 4 (spring 2002), ed. Louis Cabri and Nicole Markotic. With many thanks to Barbara Cole as interlocutor.

"'Uncannily in the open': In Light of Oppen." Delivered October 2003 at the University of California, San Diego, for the Roy Harvey Pearce Archive for New Poetry Prize lecture. Excerpts delivered at the Modernist Studies Association, October 2003. An excerpt appears in *Poetry Project Newsletter* 201 (December/January 2004–5). The essay includes material from "The Topos of the 'Thing': Some Thoughts on 'Objectivist' Poetics." In *The Idea and the Thing in Modernist American Poetry,* ed. Cristina Giorcelli. Palermo: Renzo e Rean Mazzone Editori, 2001.

"Propounding Modernist Maleness: How Pound Managed a Muse." *Modernism/Modernity* 9, no. 3 (2002). With thanks to Cassandra Laity, editor.

Some material in the introduction from "Statement for PORES." PORES 2 (October 2003). Online journal journal@pores.bbk.ac.uk/2/index.htm (accessed June 17, 2005).

"Inside the Middle of a Long Poem," delivered at the Craft, Critique, Culture conference, University of Iowa, March 29, 2003.

Introduction

Blue means freshened, old-fashioned blueing in wash water; blue sky rounding from the horizon; blue evokes an ideal, like the famous Azure of symbolist poetics; blue is intense, the color of batik. Sometimes blue means moody, depressed, forsaken. A Blue Studio is a pensive work site where a new world is hoped and an old can interrupt this hope. Thus it is a place of conflict and cross motives. Blue Studio is particularly a metaphor for working through negativity, an idea that threads through this book. Most of the poets and works taken up here write from a horizon of hope—political hope, cultural hope, a sense of changed relations to the world—yet many also move into that space from a sense of desperation and desolation. This book creates a blue space for thinking about the terrain to traverse while watching a horizon for change. *Blue Studios* proposes cultural work that poetry does and could do and some work for a poet-critic, facing a practice involved with such a vulnerable mix of desolation and hope. Thus a Blue Studio takes its cue from Adorno, who rejects the purely "lamenting subject" and at the same time accepts that "there is no longer beauty or consolation except in the gaze falling on horror, withstanding it, and in unalleviated consciousness of negativity holding fast to the possibility of what is better" (Adorno 1974, 16, 25).

I started blue—as a *Blau.* This onomastic word offered me a talismanic color, and insofar as adults have such colors, it remains one. These essays negotiate a border between patriarchal culture and postpatriarchal culture—a utopian blueness in which the "blue" that is for "boys" crosses with my family name of origin.[1] But I am torquing the male-coded "blue" in my processing of its cultural claims. During the twentieth century our families were, our cultures were, our nations were in considerable flux around gender and power. And this remains true in the twenty-first. Under the regimes of heresy hunting, war economies, fundamentalist enormities of modernity and antimodernity, Woman is again deployed as a weapon against women (and often against men), a figure trundled back into her iconic position as controlled, unthinking, compliant, outside of history. Culturally and socially we are still knotted, loosely or tightly, into the patriarchal, and yet we hold a blue sign from the analytic formations of gender struggle and "oppositional poetics," blue threads in that labyrinth (Hunt 1990, 197).

This book discusses ways gender, poetry, and poetics intersect in the cultural work of one poet-critic. My focus on gender is more than a simple critical preference. Gender is both a sociohistorical phenomenon in the formation of subjectivity and social status and a set of discourses and modes central to poetry as a practice. Thus gender readings are central to sociopoesis, or the analysis of poetry by helixed social and aesthetic concerns. Gender operates here in the narratives of becoming a critic and of becoming a poet; gender is at work in mentor and "influence" relations, in the production of poetry, in choices of genre (essay and long poem). To analyze institutions of poetic practice like "the muse," to scrutinize manifestoes, to construct historical and theoretical observations on specific poets, to evaluate poetics and movements, gender is the focus.

In *The H.D. Book* Robert Duncan recalls "Kandinsky in *Concerning the Spiritual in Art* speaks theosophically as well as psychologically when he tells us that in the color blue 'We feel a call to the infinite, a desire for purity and transcendence. *Blue is the typical heavenly color;* the ultimate feeling it creates is one of rest' " (Duncan 1983, 49). But I want a blue of restless yearning, not rest; of earth, not "heaven"; of lucidity but not purity. Nonetheless, the emancipation of possibility is never limited by strict material conditions or political choices narrowly construed; there is a remainder of emotion, arousal, the sharp shift of realms. How to calibrate the political meanings and contributions of creative practices?[2] Sometimes events occur for reasons far beyond reason or self-interest; it is in this area of evocative signification that languages of poetry exfoliate.[3] In his magisterial *H.D. Book* that is a model in so much—in essay mode, in thinking through a full modernism, in trying to understand the gender struggles for cultural authority of the moderns and their political rage and yearning—Duncan has a transcendent approach to female figures. He deplores the fact that many male writers have difficulty acknowledging the Poetess (he uses this word positively), the Prophetess, the Great Mother; he is motivated to reverse the denial of female power by his sometime assent to Jungian soul-making. Duncan is subtle in his hypersaturated meditations: he comprehends perfectly how culture has difficulty with women seeking mastery, with women producing excess. Holding my suspicion of his transhistorical moments at bay, I want to acknowledge how much Duncan's passionate example of thinking in essays has affected this work.

For this scrutiny of culture and social life inside the language of poetry, let me borrow H.D.'s word *spectrum-blue,* a color that is a phantom, an image, and the blue light from prismatic diffusion (H.D. 1998a, 20). This is a sense of aura generated when material and ideal practices confront each other: material mystery. The presences and energies we feel are our struggling selves projected despite the inhumanities in which our culture is encouraged, despite the complex of controlling institutions that encourage plunder in the name of profit and consuming in the name of a hidden panic. The presences and energies are the deaths we walk upon, as we live marched and herded into what Erica Hunt has called the ongoing New War (Hunt 1990, 198). But blue is also the horizon of hope and resistance: in Hunt's words, an "oppositional poetics" of "speculative and liberatory" communities to which feminist thought is central (Hunt 1990, 197, 202).

In this book, as in *The Pink Guitar: Writing as Feminist Practice,* the essay is a method of writing "otherhow" rooted in cultural and political investigation and in resistance. The postpatriarchal essay offers a method of thought and an ethical attitude, not simply a style or a rhetorical choice. It is a method of the passionate, curious, multiple-vectored, personable, and invested discussion, as if a person thinking were simply talking in the studio of speculation, grief, and utopia. Essays can break the normalizing dichotomy between discursive and imaginative writing, between the analytic and the creative. In Teresa de Lauretis's words, this mix offers a "view from 'elsewhere'" (De Lauretis 1987, 25). In a recent anthology of feminist hopes for the future published in millennial 2000, Catherine Belsey calls for precisely the kind of "writing as a feminist" that has been, for many decades, practiced, precisely and decidedly, in work by Joan Retallack, for instance, by Kathleen Fraser, Carla Harryman, Anne Waldman, Caroline Bergvall or myself, and by other writers of gender-inflected essays such as Lyn Hejinian, Leslie Scalapino, and Susan Howe, not to speak of gender thinking by Charles Bernstein, Peter Middleton, and others—dialogic writing, laying bare the device, playful-intense, moving into different registers, offering pluralities of readings, asking unanswerable questions, frame-breaking, resisting grand theory, yet philosophical. Belsey closes her call with a Lacanian utopian flourish, proposing that "mastery proffered and then withheld, truth glimpsed and yet elusive," might make feminist writing "an object of desire, both as text and as politics" (Belsey 2000, 160–61). Well, we can hope. In her call for an engaged political-aesthetic-feminist writing that already exists, she could not have better illustrated the gap between the worlds of poetics and the worlds of feminist theory. *Blue Studios* throws itself into (or perhaps across) that gap. Here I speak as a poet-critic with an interest in creating a pensive, not an authoritative, space, one not only theoretical nor only practical but a thinking-in-writing with the goal of attentiveness to material mystery. My investment in the essay parallels my interest in an ethical dimension for writing. The essay as mode of thinking produces a utopian blueness because it invents an intersubjective relation between reader and text, between writer and reader, between author and evidence, between analysis and need, between theorizing and praxis. A book should be porous; it should have enough air and space, enough blue air, so that whoever enters it can breathe.

The book *Blue Studios* is a reflection, if inadequate, of a displacement and estrangement of cultural habits under the long, self-complicating (and perhaps bluish) "messianic light" of which Theodor Adorno speaks in *Minima Moralia: Reflections from Damaged Life:* "Perspectives must be fashioned that displace and estrange the world, reveal it to be, with its rifts and crevices, as indigent and distorted as it will appear one day in the messianic light" (Adorno 1974, 247). This transformative perspective is secular; it involves both social justice and a sense of cultural intricacy; it is skeptical and never fulfilled—on principle. In the works I talk about here poetry and poetics are not only literary and aesthetic, not only institutional practices or events in language, but events in consciousness, in collective understanding. Thus the interest of poetry as a writing practice that enters evocative realms in ways both beyond conventional reason and beyond fixity of identified message. We do not know how people might be inspired via "the cultural life of fantasy" to what Judith Butler calls "resignification of social bonds," but in a blue studio this is some cultural work that poetry may do (Butler 2004, 216). This book probes the perspectives of curiosity and practice that reveal the world to be a tiny bit hopeful amid depredation. This book is backlit by almost hopeless hope.

Talismanic blue is conventionally a color of haunting. I feel like the ghost of the future. Under one rubric that I chose and that historically chose me—the rubric of "feminism"—the whole of culture and cultural products would have to be reconceptualized. We have known that, and acted on it, for a longish time, but it has not yet been enough. The world is riddled by fundamentalisms of several varieties, many religiously based, our own U.S. homegrown kinds and those of others; central to these is the strong-arm mandate to control women physically, intellectually, and ideologically, even more so than the mandate to control other men. Thus it is vital to declare that the secular entrance of women in society, with coequal political, cultural, and legal stakes and coeval temporalities, is a test for modernization and modernity. Possibly also for modernism as a cultural movement.

Like its companion, *The Pink Guitar,* this work is constituted to resist, in Steve Evans's words, "an avant-garde without women, and a poetics without poetry," as well as resisting oversimplified notions of what gender analysis does in general, and around poetry in particular (Evans 2001, ii). Poetry as a mode of practice thus has a large, world-historical responsibility as posing a further question and as embodying questioning. Art is thinking by the invention of forms in such a way that sometimes "the possibility is concretized that the world could be other than it is" (Adorno 1997, 138). Poetry is seen here as a theorizing practice, a practice of thinking, and as a commitment to the thought that emerges in the subtle concreteness of segmented, saturated language. Poetry is not argument or image exclusively but an approach to knowing that dissolves into a variety of sensations or touches multiple scales of feeling. Sometimes poetry is a practice inside ideology that can be positioned as a commentary on (or a scrambling of) some of ideology's effects; thus Adorno's 1957 essay "On Lyric Poetry and Society" serves as ground bass of this book (Adorno 1991). This sense of an elsewhere and an otherhow in some poetic texts seems to be Maurice Blanchot's point when he says, "Philosophy, which puts everything into question, is tripped up by poetry, which is the question that eludes it" (Blanchot 1986, 63). Most of the poets I have chosen to discuss here rest on a cusp between materialist practices and a horizon that one used to call ideal. But it is more appropriate, if ineffable, to say that they manifest to philosophy "the question that eludes it." These poets at one and the same time honor the liberatory hopes implicit in being a historical subject and register the delights and pressures that come from a unique and exacerbated sense of linguistic nuance.

A number of people have spoken about the hypersaturated means of poetry to convey sociolinguistic intricacy and connection—for instance, Louis Zukofsky in *A Test of Poetry.* Poetry is not, nor should it be, a mode of propaganda, but it is part of ideological and discursive practices, and it offers information, conviction, knowledge. And these particularly in form and texture. Zukofsky worked with and through this knife-edge balancing act around the social meanings of the poetic act and the forms of a poetic text, making a helix of aesthetic and social conviction. One learns about a poet's opinions and the cultural forces at play in poems in a variety of ways deep inside the texture of the poem, not only from the statements the poem overtly makes. Subtlety, intricacy, and pleasures of language are ways of constructing poetic information, including about the social.

What is any poetry of negativity? And who are those poets? These poets use language but are wary of its effects. They each trouble "normal poetry"—its themes, its conventions, its uplift. They manifest an intense intelligence within language. They create syntactic, vocabularistic, modal trouble because they have looked into some political and ethical abyss. We can call this abyss "the long twentieth century." In response to all this, and the vast ethical and species questions it raises, we have the bits of justice and hope often compromised, the struggles for social fairness and just distribution. However, poets like George Oppen do not write directly in a rousing, inspirational fashion about social claims; rather they sidle and dart, so that one has conscience and consciousness startled by their indirection, as if in a vast afterimage raised by their poetry. This is a peculiar argument about indirection and implication perhaps, and it is related to an attitude about ego or subjectivity. A strange sense of anonymity, of disappearing into the necessity for *poesis* attends these poets, and it is a more desperate and intransigent stance than that of a Dante, or Eliot, whose impersonality is backed up by ideologies of redemption. Some of the poets discussed here are agnostic about redemption. Or any redemptive-ness. This poetry of negativity seems the poetry demanded by our conditions of existence. Poetry of negativity has the effect of doing away with what we thought of as scales or orders of value. Thus it is ideology critique. Further, with "Negative Capability"—Keats's enormously useful idea (in a letter of December 1817)—the poets of negativity can see, feel, internalize, and articulate both sides of a dialectic at once, without "reaching after" transcendence or synthesis (Keats 2002, 60). But they are most rich in suspicion, skepticism, investigation of the taken-for-granted, a resistance to category.

In *The Constructivist Moment: From Material Text to Cultural Poetics,* Barrett Watten reassesses and repositions the utopian agency (social building, future vision) of avant-garde movements, particularly putting in play "Soviet constructivists" rather than currently more familiar avant-garde sectors—Italian futurists, French surrealists, German dadaists—as privileged bearers of a link between radical form and political insurgency. In "Negative Examples: Theories of Negativity in the Avant-Garde," Watten locates moments when rupture, refusal, or resistance gives rise to a "horizon of possibility" (Watten 2003, xx, xxi, 192). This sense of negativity helps frame what *Blue Studios* puts forth. *Blue Studios* wants to make a claim for poetry as a rhetorical form intricately tied up with such a horizon. Ethical yearning. And ethical urgency. That is, poetry as a practice, as a choice (I am not talking about career) is a version of Adorno's "only responsible course" when he remarks that "the only responsible course is to deny oneself the ideological misuse of one's own existence" (Adorno 1974, 27).

However, if poetry and the poetic are going to help provide a "horizon of possibility," then one central feature of poetry and the poetic must be brought up to scrutiny and (fundamentally) altered. I mean the general gender narratives of poetry. These are not separable, contingent, or derisory but have been vital to the historical practices of poetry. This is a curiosity to me, and *Blue Studios* plays out my bafflement in a number of ways. Furthermore, the term *poetic* has often been privileged, as if it automatically meant high-mindedness and superiority, as well as automatic critiques of various kinds. From my perspective, however, the sheer claim of "the poetic" does not necessarily generate any critique of anything, certainly not of gender and sexual assumptions that have long been part of the social and formal aspects of poetry as an institution.

How have poetry and some of its institutions gotten so linked to gender commonplaces, and how can one unlink them? Certain gender materials are hardly a necessary part of a mode of writing that might be described as based simply in segmentivity, the practice of writing in lines and gaps, and in hypersaturations of verbal plenitude, signaled by Keats's curious "'load every rift' of your subject with ore" (Keats 2002, 464). I do not mean to be disingenuous about poetry and its continuing topoi, nor am I the police, but *Blue Studios* wants to help re-envision the "poetic" as something genuinely critical and rejecting of gender reductiveness. This is accomplished not to moot certain works but to bring their mechanisms up to scrutiny, to investigate deep apparatuses of poesis.

Looking at art history in *Differencing the Canon,* Griselda Pollock articulates her motivation as "feminist desire": "not only to do history differently but to tell tales in such a way as to make a difference in the totality of the spaces we call knowledge" (Pollock 1999, xvi). For *Blue Studios* there is no way to be "postfeminist." Indeed, Denise Riley argues that such a position is simply impossible: "For as long as the sexes are socially distinguished, 'women' will be nominated in their apartness, so that sexual division will always be liable to conflation with some fundamental ontological sexual difference. So feminism, the reaction to this state of affairs, cannot be merely transitional, and a true post-feminism can never arrive" (Riley 1988, 111). What perpetual investigative feminism might mean is taken up in several of the essays.

This book is divided into four parts. In Attitudes and Practices two intertwined questions are raised: what a feminist, or gender-inflected, reading of cultural texts involves, and how this feminist curiosity emerged in one poet critic—for "I" is cast as a character in this text.[4] To postulate the psychosocial importance of a feminist attitude to poetry—in its thought, its subject positions, and its practices—offers some perspective on the cultural tasks that have been begun in one recent century, to be continued in the next. This is not an insistence on feminist production (and especially not a demand for political and administrative tests for artworks) but a desire to sustain feminist reception.

To challenge commonplaces of gender, feminism has postulated at least one new social subject entering culture and the necessity for a new realm of critical practices. Often this new social subject has to probe the contested and vulnerable realm of the feminine, possibly to reclaim it, to reinterpret it, to debate it and extend it into heterodoxy or feminist realignments. A somewhat suspicious negotiation with and translation of the feminine is visible in a number of these essays. A claim of a new symbolic order of heterogeneity is Luce Irigaray's proposition, given her critique of oedipality, gender binaries, and the power asymmetries implied in a theory of phallic Logos. She proposes a heterodox subjectivity and writing practices whose elliptical, seductive, riddling and riddled inventiveness speak from that subjectivity (Irigaray [1974] 1985, 133–46). This hybrid, critical, and politicized subject desires amphibious modes of writing that no longer formulate in authoritarian, universalistic fashion but modes that investigate and return to complications, that enact provisionality, slippage, skepticism, and the randonné. By raising the question of the essay and its interesting poetics, this section expresses a desire for emotionally adequate forms, rhetorics, or, really, cultural practices and subjectivities that embody ethical attitudes deep within writing.

The first three essays are followed by a section called Marble Paper, elaborating for poetry Pollock's project of entering the canonical differently, an exploration of "feminist desire in the writing of [poetry's] histories" (Pollock 1999, xviii). Poetry often depends on the projection, dressing, and consumption of female figures. Thus I am interested in examination and destabilization of long-lasting mythoi of gender. Gender structures of feeling exist on a very deep level. This is why neither formal/aesthetic nor only thematic/imagistic rupture is enough—the rupture must reach into the places where ideology is stored (content and form helixed together) and to institutions of reception, including reader pleasure. This section offers some reading activities (methods, even) scrutinizing influential works in poetics as well as two well-known poems by Wordsworth and Pound. Marble Paper is a section about the work of cultural production and reproduction, the work undertaken within the apparatus of poesis. The institutions of poetry (poem construction, dissemination, reception, self-production within career, making of poetics) all demand work. And gender intersects with this work; gender is one of the studios in which poetry is made.

All the poets discussed in the third section of the book, Urrealism, would probably make the bridge between matters thought aesthetic and matters thought social that George Oppen summarized in a late aphorism:

> Poetry is related to
> music and cadence and therefore to the
> force of events.
>
> (Oppen 2003, 189)

It might also be written under the sign of Bertolt Brecht's question. Acknowledging that it is rather more straightforward to engage in socially inflected readings of novels, he asks, "But what about realism in lyric poetry?"—or perhaps "what's with the realism of lyric poetry"—this Yiddish inflection challenges poetry, as the other inflection challenged critics to consider poetry in a materialist theory (Bloch et al. 1977, 70; see also Kaufman 2002, 60–61; Ross 1988, 11). Despite what the word *realism* has meant for fiction, despite the mannered and melodramatic turns of realism, its sometimes stultifying conventions and tics, its ideologically controlled endings, so discerningly criticized by Joan Retallack as "unnatural realisms," I would think in its "ur" or primary form, a deeply realist sensibility emerges in these poets, though of course differently in each (Retallack 2003, 42).[5] This insistence on realism draws on Lyn Hejinian's extended metonymic argument linking the terms *ontology, introspection, description, scrutiny,* and *strangeness:* "When the term *realism* is applied to poetry, it is apt to upset our sense of reality" (Hejinian 2000, 158). The writers on whom I have focused, then, claim to be, in one way or another, realists inside poetry; all interpret that commitment critically, and all thereby "upset our sense of reality": Guest's "fair realism" answers "surrealism"; H.D.'s "spiritual realism" answers conventional materialist realism. Niedecker worked toward a fusion of "consciousness" and "actualness," a poetics of fusion based on interior and exterior realism (Oppen 1990, 290). Material mystery needs again to be evoked in Oppen's somewhat ironic "simple realism" (Oppen 1990, 410). His poetry is compounded of a sense of "Being" (or "the marvel of the real"), a "materialist ethics" of sincerity and "encounter," a meditative practice at once gnomic and lucid built of "assertions and negations," in a restlessly dialectical rhetoric of negativity and anti-instrumentalism (Oppen 1990, 410, 254; Woods 2002, 233; Weinberger, in Oppen 2002, x; Nicholls, in DuPlessis and Quartermain 1999, 251, 244). These writers might be joined by a sense of the "thereness" of the world and a mix of awe, pleasure and starkness that I associate with Adorno's evocative "Images say: 'Behold'"—a crystalline deictic formulation that stirs our attention even given its difficulties for poetry and for thought ("Thereness" from Hejinian 2000, 158; Adorno 1997, 168).

In discussing these poets I mix rubrics both formal and social: sound, the line, genre, and structure mingle with ethics, subjectivity, and social location. To speak of feeling and its range is also part of the real. One "essaying" principle under which these essays were constructed is the sign of "affective reading" (McCaffery 2001, 42). This practice does not aim to be unsystematic or inaccurate, of course, but offers interpretations "where one is carried along or set down, put in motion or at rest, shaken or calmed, according to the velocity of this or that part [of a text]" (McCaffery 2001, 42; citing Deleuze on Spinoza).

I chose these poets because there is something mysterious and unresolvable about their practices. These poets work in the studio of "austere hermetic readable urgency," a notion that seems to me crucial for a twenty-first-century poetics (DuPlessis 2004, 156). The awe that this hermetic urgency creates is the surplus, remainder, mode of proceeding assimilable neither to meaning as sheer paraphrase nor to agency as resolvable intention. These poets work the "between"—between vision and the real, between a spiritual dimension and a material(ist) one—a between that one might imagine as unstable, constantly under construction, difficult to sustain. To hedge my choices of poets (not really to defend them), Maurice Blanchot's aphorism about René Char is suggestive. Blanchot writes, "R. C. is so much a poet that after him poetry shines like a fact, but he is such a poet that after this fact of poetry all facts become questions and even poetic questions" (Blanchot 1986, 63). This could be said of the poets whom I discuss.

Art should "provide consciousness with a critical example" (O'Connor, in Adorno 2000, 281). But this means something very particular and careful about art. In his essay "Commitment" Adorno proposes that an artist should not produce straightforward political art, or art of commitment, but understand, rather, that the political has "migrated into" all art and work with those facts and their implications (Adorno 1992, 93). At this world moment (for many years, but acutely after the "legal" coup of 2000 in the United States and the fictive "mandate" of 2004), I feel precisely "migrated into." The fourth section of this book, Migrated Into, takes up *Drafts,* the project in the long poem on which I have been engaged for just about twenty years.

Part of the cultural work of a poet-critic is, precisely, writing poetry—a poetry thinking about the real; to cite Ron Silliman: "It is the moment at which the real generates new forms that the real itself becomes visible" (Silliman 1985, 34). Any extensive project demands to have its pulse taken, so these essays map versions of this project's purposes sometimes in relation to two of its precursors—H.D. and Pound. The three essays examine, from an author's point of view, what I had gotten, and continue to get, enmeshed in. Or—what has entered me and come through me. *Drafts* is influenced by objectivist arguments and propositions about reality. The image is encountered, not found (as Oppen said). *The* and *a* are words worth investigating, as suggestive and as staggering in their implications as myth (a proposition vital for Zukofsky). Materiality is nonetheless filled with sparks of our awe (which recalls Niedecker and Charles Reznikoff).

Indeed, by critique, suspicion, skepticism, and "cura"—significant care for language and choices—poetry can exemplify what it is we really want. Among other things, we want historical depth; critique of convention; scrupulous, moving, and invested language; poems saturated with a generous understanding of other practitioners. We want work and genres from the past treated at one and the same time with respect and with effervescent inspection. We want a sense of our social and aesthetic space—and the vertiginous astonishment of being here. Poetry can help tell us what we want and what we know: we want to know our own complexity and our own possibility. It can tell us what we might mourn and how we need to continue to examine systems and shards.

In this situation, as in so many others, I remember with attentiveness the poetry and example of George Oppen. His passion to confront circumstances and historical travail with scrupulous innovation and intransigent understanding offers one model of a struggle with language and time. He wanted to look, to see what was out there and to evaluate its damage and contradictions, saying in a pared-down, intense language not what was easy or right or neat or consoling but what he felt and thought when all the platitudes and banalities were stripped away. It is the residue of vision, the residue of hope when all due skepticisms and judgments have occurred. He called it the real, "the real that we confront" (Oppen 2002, 202).

I
Attitudes and Practices

1

Reader, I married me

Becoming a Feminist Critic

Doing This in the First Place

No innocence in the autobiographical. What with its questions of saying "I" and the issue "what I" and how that "I" negotiates with various "selves"; and the question how much (a lot) is unsaid or repressed. With resistance to the cheerful myths of disclosure; with suspicion of narrative in the first place, and no self-justifying memories to legitimate "me" rather than anyone else. If I cull my journals from the eager, pressured past, that self with its "experiences" is postulated as the authentic one, and this one as the processor of that truth. Which is not true. Finally, don't much like to take some, or any, "me" as exemplary, which is, after all, one of the necessary casts of an autobiographical essay.

Yet it remains true that feminist criticism exists. That it came from the women's movement and is in a continual constructive dialogue with both that movement and others for social justice. That academic fields were thereby overturned, remade (though not, of course, exclusively by feminism); that a maenadic pleasure sometimes accompanied; that professional careers were on the line, and—that some "we" accomplished this. We invented and sustained a major intellectual renaissance—possibly even a "paradigm shift"—in the past twenty-odd [now thirty-odd] years.[1] It would be irresponsible never to speak about this. Indeed, I hope many more people do. This is a historical exercise, not a confessional one.

The "I" implicated here is very precise yet more than half unspeakable. Its descriptors are not mere political trading chips. They are vectors, interlocked with energy, joy, imbalance, determination, depression, themselves not free-floating emotions but situated and socially formed. "I" can be said to be an off-white feminist, resisting even "enlightenment" Judaism, a radical but middle-class U.S. inhabitant in a professional job category. A person mainly gendered female, who maintains an imaginary bisexuality and a polygynous curiosity about the feminisms I and others have traversed. Who benefits from many world-economic interests that I abhor. I am a nonbiological real mother. Am a heterosexual married property owner. Poet, critic, and essayist. My writing space is still saffron orange. My iBook—is allegorically amusing. If I had not become a feminist, I probably would not have been able to write much or to think anything especially interesting in any original way. I would not have been able to create the works that came through me and go under my name. My title torques the ethical-romantic climax of *Jane Eyre* ("Reader, I married him") not to deny biographical marriage but to signal a polygynous entitlement.

Chronology is time depicted as traveling (more or less) in a (more or less) forward direction. Yet one can hardly write a single sentence straight; it all rebounds. Even its most innocent first words—*A, The, I, She, It*—teem with heteroglossias. And remember: there is always more to remember. If you choose to believe that this is memory; once it is words it's also fabrication. Some files are too far back in closets, in basements. Some things, some names are lost. Narration becomes judgment: it's hard to resist. To put things in an order is to lose some connections, gain others. To "develop" (express, expound) is to distort says I, at my most antiexpository, but what of minimalist aphorisms of obliqueness that others tax as unreadable? The texture of everything is reduced to nothing by the erosion of time, then boldfaced, barefaced, is recreated. Sentences structure. Cause mainly precedes effect, but effect effectuates selections of cause. Cause and effect affect. Can be affectation, a knowingness. My tone is turning arch. Also compressed. I am already leaving things out. Plus a memoir is already seduction, not the least is self-seduction. I am both pleased and uncomfortable to be telling you all this.

Way Before, or, Up to 1967: Inscribed Female (As Well as Other Things)

"Gee—I am living in a patriarchal family!" True. Favored daughter therein. But no dialectics, no dialogue, no interchange. Just a narrowly defined set of achievements: reading and writing: a little person of the book. It was the 1950s, and certain things seared me, although my parents were a middle kind of liberal (justice for some vague all) with a fervor around secular humanism (aware of First Amendment issues, giving much to the Ethical-

Humanist movement). Terrifying to me were the Rosenberg trial and executions. The McCarthy assault on civil liberties. And the silent seepage of the knowledge of the Holocaust. What is the pattern there? the knowledge of the potential criminality of state power. Confirmed during the civil rights, Vietnam War, and Watergate eras. And now.

Where had I come from; where did I stand? A little atheist, a reader, whose difference—in the contexts in which I grew up—was intellectualism (that was the religion), was secular humanism (as the positive vanguard). The universalism of ethics, the promise of assimilation of all differences (seen as unseemly disequilibriums), made any particularity theoretically unmarked, although all were covertly active—class, race, religious culture, gender. I had no temple, no Hebrew, no Jewish holidays, none of the mandated joys or commonplaces of a traditional spirituality. To be a Jew was too normal. My family narrative claimed its own further difference.

Class narratives saturated both sides of the family. My maternal grandmother identified with the Hapsburg Empire; three of her four daughters became Christian, though not my mother (Eleanor Weslock, 1914–90). My paternal grandfather, the rabbi (Joel Blau, 1878–1927), an elegant Hungarian, quipped, when a woman's necklace broke, clattering in the synagogue, that he'd thought he had been "the only one casting pearls." A man of such arrogant wit would not have lasted long at any one congregation; he did not, and died at age forty-nine, having wandered among congregations in New York City, Trenton, Rochester, and London. He was absolutely disdainful of Yiddishkeit for its class connotations, as was my British-Jewish grandmother, Rachel Woolf (1876–1932), who referred to the Yiddish-speaking Eastern European immigrants to London in the 1890s as "those foreigners." But in general the family ethos was based on a transcendent sense of moral and intellectual superiority tied precisely to the overlooking of prejudice, taken as a sign of other people's disdained inferiority.

Still, about a hundred Yiddish words floated through my childhood on my mother's lips, including phrases in which I now hear shadowy comments on the Holocaust—gunnish helfin (gornisht helfin—can't do anything about it); chaserei and tsuris (filth and trouble), gefeyrlach (dangerous, terrible), and mishigas (madness, craziness). But Yiddishkeit was not the hegemonic family mode. My father (Joseph, 1909–86) was a scholar of American philosophy and religion who read Hebrew and also wrote on Jewish history and religion. He had weaned himself from traditional and even reformed Judaism for a complex of reasons—in part a lack of conviction about religious rituals and practices but to a large measure from a principled intellectual commitment to transcendent liberalism. Claims of Jewish identity were only a burden from the past: he was a utopian, a Deweyan; he wanted new social practices (though they probably would remain patriarchal ones). He wanted to be one of the Chosen People, but differently.

Hence I was brought up as an explicit secular humanist in the Ethical Culture Movement. With my father's encouragement I acted, in principled struggle, against the aggressive (right-wing Christian) religiosity that afflicted the 1950s. My ten- and eleven-year-old child-self refused to say mandated grace in school, refused, chin up, the required in-school prayers when little heads were bowing right and left around me. "Under God" was added to the Pledge of Allegiance in that sanctimonious time, but this, I knew, was forbidden by the First Amendment, which rejected the establishment of any state religion, any theism, any gestures related to faith however apparently innocuous and blandly cozy. Yet as a secular humanist I was a daughter of the Jewish Enlightenment, and I had a stake in certain values: Learning, Aestheticization, and Self-realization (Harshav 1990, 122). And the female self was fraught territory, filled with active contradictions.

College, Barnard, luckily had an ideological commitment to neutralize (if not undermine) feminine conditioning: "You can have it all, girls! have a career, have a family!" Bless our robust cheerleader, President Millicent Carey McIntosh, with her familial link to the feminism of Bryn Mawr in the early twentieth century. If we laughed then, we were hardly to laugh last. And McIntosh (1898–2001) lived more than one hundred years, an allegorical fact. A major contradiction lay between the culture's incessant (and our internalized) demand for instantly ratifying engagement and marriage and any sense of independence, self-definition, autonomy, social commitment. Our rebellions could only be enacted in often damaging affiliations with various "scenes": Beatnik/bohemian. Theatrical male homosexual (as a female hanger-on; lesbianism was a bogey woman my friends and I scared each other with).[2] Poetry: as a muse-figure "trying" to write. In fact, I later learned you don't "try" to write; you write. And doing sex—this decision for autonomy, independence, and pleasure still hooked us into simulacra of the marital loop. In those days (pre-*Griswald v. Connecticut,* 1965) no one got legal birth control without being married. So there were all sorts of furtive forays—to find a gynecologist who would prescribe the diaphragm, for example. Or to find an abortion that wouldn't kill you. Why anyone thinks nostalgically (or "morally") of those days is beyond comprehension. Such nostalgia is a menace. As always, the contradictions between what we wanted and what we couldn't get, between what we had an inchoate, ill-defined "right" to (sexual choices) and what we were prevented from having, began a process of political arousal.

A minor contradiction for me lay between my being poetically awakened by the Donald Allen (ed.) *New American Poetry* (with Allen Ginsberg, Robert Duncan, Robert Creeley, Charles Olson) versus the Georgian poetic craft that passed for the only contemporary in the academy. I remember a "creative writing" class for its staging of narcissistic hypocrisy in which two men, a guest—in fact, Anatole Broyard, with (as it turned out) his own complex racial narrative of passing, and the teacher, Robert Pack—insisted, circa 1960, that "women can't (really) write." They affirmed this because women did not experience blood and guts, which they took to mean war (evincing a miraculous amnesia about menstruation, abortion, childbirth), and had no drunken bouts at 3 a.m. (QED). In short, the girls had no male life experience. This was a perfect example of vacuum-sealed exclusion by gender; we certainly were not male, a simple fact, and the argument was doing its level best to deny our potential via intricate snarls of assertion masquerading as fact. This thinking tried to cut the ground from under us.

The Golden Notebook and *A Room of One's Own,* books I read in 1964 when I was roiling around as an out-of-water female fish in early graduate school (so too *The Feminine Mystique,* later), named something extremely precise and, like diagnostic beams, honed in on some disease one hardly knew one had, so self-denying were the symptoms/sufferings (Lessing [1962] 1971; Woolf [1929] 1957; Friedan 1963).[3] It is clear that my narration right here and now of this "before" has placed a premium on a kind of parcivalian innocence; I am implying that I wandered, with a baffled charm, into many structured ritual sites but unerringly neglected to ask any questions. But this is not true. All the time I was asking deflected and depressed questions of the gender and sexual systems, something like the educative "what's going on here?" without always noting the wounded (but powerful) King at the center. For I was deeply discontented with the feminine, with most females, with womanhood, with women's roles, with my gender-future (however tidy and rosy and controlled I had once tried to make it), and this discontent had something to do with sex—by which we meant sexuality and gender all mushed together. In fact, in our sometimes considerable sexual acting-out we were probably uttering the "word" gender before we knew it. It was pre-feminist somaticizing.

I also kept on asking which was I, the woman or the artist, with a relentless and lacerating binarism. It was the greatest pain and grief—the sense that I had to choose, that one precluded the other, and that I was a bad woman for wanting an artistic career, a bad artist because I was a woman and couldn't work out the terms of any art. This ideological and psychological stalemate was perfectly ridiculous, now arcane sounding. Yet at the time it presented a powerful invisible barrier. It was as if I had been cast in a *Bildung* vs. romance nineteenth-century novel by my contemporaries, my men and boys, my mentors, such as they were, and my colleagues. Plus by patriarchal me. Self-repression and cultural censorship of females were in interlock. Adrienne Rich's "Snapshots of a Daughter-in-Law" captures the sense of desperation, loneliness, and near-paralysis women felt when faced with what seemed like a billion years of cultural and social despising. And any person trying overtly and loudly to exit from this gender system was rigidly, pointedly policed. My resistance came destructively, in not writing, in long silences around writing, in baffled and punishing blockage. This went on for years. I even said (I was proud to articulate this then, but it was, in fact, a nadir) that "I did not want to have my psyche female." I learned gradually, including in dream and in vision, that my muse was indeed (a) woman. An actual figure appeared—silent, smiling. This was a turning point. While I would now have difficulty with the word *muse,* and with its gender materials, there was no doubt about the seriousness of this vision.

True to Essentials Documentary of a Real Dialogue. Place: Columbia University, Butler Library, card catalogue room. Date: 1964 or 1965. Characters: prissy good girl RB and ET, Professor of English, female, noble scholar of the old school.

> ET: how are you doing in graduate school?
>
> RB: I love it it's wonderful.
>
> ET: you know, sometimes women don't have an easy time of it as professionals, getting a PhD is hard, things happen, there is prejudice, I wonder if you have run into any of that.
>
> RB: I don't know what you are talking about.

So much for false consciousness and rejection of insightful help. In 1966–67, after taking my [PhD] "orals" and thereupon having a breakdown characterized by a tidal wave of insomnia and a thick lump in my throat "imaginarily" impeding my speech and breath (imagine!), I was appointed as a preceptor in the Columbia College English Department. Apparently the decision to appoint women was highly contested and debated, very rancorous. These prejudices were accepted as if they were part of the weather. Prof. X won't allow women in his seminar, a person might note wryly, as if saying Sea Gulls nest in those Rocks over there. That was the way it was. Although, or because I was one of the first three women ever to be honored by this preceptorial appointment, my suspicion cut deep. Happily, I did not believe for even one second that we were the first or only three women PhD candidates ever to evince the requisite credentials, that no other females before us could have been called to serve in That Department of That College.[4] (Of course, token women are often asked to reject their peers, often seduced into thinking proud, heavily structured thoughts about the inabilities of other women.) My suspicion of the conditions of this appointment was deeply radicalizing, beyond tokenism. But being there, on the job, contributed to a token mentality, bemused, anxious at the pressure to "prove" something (unknown) to someone (unknown). We three were taken with that astonishing jocular mix of "seriously" and "not seriously" that was so destabilizing. For "them" I was perhaps some odd pawn; for me I was the whole chess set, though still lying around in a box.

The radical movements were in increasing ferment, and I identified deeply with civil rights and with anti–Vietnam War activism. The Columbia University campus was a most vigorously fermented site, with the issues of the increasing complicity of the universities in the military-industrial complex, issues of class and race and privilege, questions of the (mis)use of state power, the legitimating and sorting functions of education, especially given the Vietnam War, when losing student deferral could mean draft into the army and potential death. We constantly exploded level upon level of liberal contradictions, sometimes hour by hour. And during the Columbia Strike (spring 1968) I was, true to my liminal form, not inside the buildings with the strikers but just outside, attending the watchdog "Ad Hoc Faculty Group," which held an open forum throughout, a committee of the whole, which, if self-important and even relatively powerless, still provided more political education than I had ever had. And just outside, on the night of the police bust (a punitive police riot, in fact), I was, for one terrifying moment, cowering together with soon-to-be-dean Carl Hovde, encircled by mounted policemen on rearing horses.

First Feminism, 1968–73: Consciousness Raising and the Personal/Professional Project

In *The Emergence of Social Space: Rimbaud and the Paris Commune* Kristin Ross describes the feeling of working at a moment of great political empowerment, a "peculiar temporality" made "of events passing by quickly, too quickly, and of each hour and minute being entirely lived or made use of: saturated time" (Ross 1988, 42). What had happened—what was the time frame in that "saturated" spring that seemed to go on forever and mean everything? At one point (I think—in semester terms—fall 1968, but possibly spring 1969) feminism simply came to campus—Kate Millett (a PhD candidate and NOW activist writing her thesis—the remarkable, influential *Sexual Politics*) and Harriet Zellner (an economics student) brought it to Columbia from a mysterious "downtown" (Millett 1970). I thought—in a jealous fascinated tone of which it is impossible to give the palimpsests and nuances—"O the Blacks have organized, now it's the women. The *women* are going to organize?!" But I recognized even in the first dubious, snide, and suspicious glance that politics had, finally, come to where I was, to my contradictions. And woman/women was what, or where, I was.

I still do not understand, given my overt slapdash rejection, how in the world I ever got to that first meeting. Actually, a great, funny, and not ironic fact, I credit my rather supportive husband for suggesting it. But once I was there, it was the "Great [Political] Awakening" (Gilbert, cited in Showalter 1987, 35).[5] A giant room filled up with women—many of whom were prepared to testify: brilliant, angry, articulate witnesses to overt prejudice, sexist remarks, invidious discouragement, hostile intellectual atmosphere, sexual suggestiveness, instructions to "go home to your children," charges of "lacking seriousness," prejudice in the awarding of financial aid or TA's—the whole gamut of sexual and gender discrimination and second-class citizenship "despite" shining Alma Mater's light. It was a conversion experience; the scales fell from my eyes; my glance fell upon things and saw them new. An alternative to this inflection of metaphor would be to notice that we were at one and the same time inside and outside an institution, in a contradictory position that gave us, suddenly, analytic suspicion, observational leverage, and demanding questions that brought many political and ideological practices into question. The experience was powerful, energizing, defining, the birth of commitment and conviction. I became a feminist.[6]

And became one of the activists in Columbia Women's Liberation. The every detail of which was a passionate engagement for justice and equality for women, and the redefining of ourselves as productive, not sidelined or blocked by gender. "Woman" was a political, an economic, category. With Ann Sutherland Harris I counted up and sorted the percentages of female faculty at Columbia, adducing institutional prejudices. We made one of the first such reports in the country, and our dismal statistics made the *New York Times* (article by Linda Greenhouse, Jan. 11, 1970, sec. 1, 35).[7] We seemed to be constructing a mixture of radical and liberal feminism: equality of access was a primary and stated goal—getting "in" to our profession of choice, to the rewards as structured. But in the same breath, that "in" was called into question. We were newly in love with women, with ourselves, with each other, with our possibility for changing everything: marriage, beauty, writing, media, law, opportunity, education, stereotypes, art, history, child care, sex, divisions of labor. We thought all women were us, and we were all women. Of course we knew better than false universalism even then, but we wanted, I think, to share with all women the power of our effervescent politicization at this "saturated time" (Ross 1988). I remember prochoice marches; Lucinda Cisler's pathbreaking bibliography about women that revealed there was "a" field there; the odd sit-in (March 1969) at the *Ladies Home Journal;* the Second Congress to Unite Women (May 1970) and the "issue" of lesbianism; a sign "remember our brothers at Kent State" when women, too, had been killed there.[8]

So the ferment of the 1960s exploding in spring 1968 and beyond was a combustible politicization that made me both "68er" and feminist.[9] It also confronted me with several ideas, each to have great impact on my intellectual work. First, the idea that culture itself functioned as a political instrument and a social institution; that not only subject matter but also structural and formal choices were part of ideology; that language, hegemony, discourse, form, canon, rightness and wrongness, allowable and not allowable were historical, relativized, and interested concepts.[10] This insight was always mixed with a strong aesthetic sense of form and language.

The second idea was directly indebted to my reading of *Sexual Politics.* For in 1970 I received my doctorate, and went off, following my spouse's doctoral research, for two (isolating) years to teach in France (Université de Lille III), where my colleagues told me that they had already had feminism in France a long time ago, and didn't need any more, merci. I began tracking Millett's reading and branching out—beginning with the Brontës, Elizabeth Gaskell, George Eliot, Woolf's *A Room of One's Own* (in those years it was impossible to read it too often), Stowe's *Uncle Tom's Cabin,* Lessing's *Four-Gated City.* In a kind of electric intellectual shock, I began to see the feminist cultural project. No more and no less than the re-seeing of every text, every author (male and female), every canonical work, everything written, every worldview, every discourse, every image, every structure from a gender perspective.[11]

In 1972–73 I was teaching four courses per semester at Trenton State College, now College of New Jersey.[12] Toward the end of the year I was told by the chairman that I would not be reappointed "because you are a woman, and we do not know what your husband will be doing next year." Despite my letter of appointment reading otherwise, I had been moved, without my knowledge, to a one-year terminal contract. All so kind, and meant kindly, the evocation of husband and all, and of course, actionable. The denial of my right even to "compete on an equal basis." Their denial compounded mine. After mulling over how much he, the chairman, didn't mean it, and how dumb it was of him to say that, and how really, really nice he really was, how bad I'd make him feel, how much I didn't want to be there, and how uncomfortable I was with all of this, I brought a sex discrimination suit before the New Jersey State Commission on Civil Rights. When they took the case, their findings revealed that I was being paid a couple of thousand dollars less per year than my exact contemporaries, two young male professors, on paper precisely comparable to me. This difference was a small fortune in 1973. I won the case, the difference in pay, and a permanent injunction against the college directing nondiscrimination.

Second Feminism, 1973–79: The Cultural Project Reading Women Writers; Writing Out of/into Women

Suddenly, the feminist critical project extended to my creative work. Suddenly, on January 2, 1973, I awoke to my own poetry: "Idea: to retell myths involving women as radical reinterpretations of them." I began with Orpheus and Eurydice—he the figure of the poet, she a dead nothing. Where had that come from? Where, indeed. Experiences of anger. The sense of being culturally marginal. Entombed. At a career dead end. Couldn't write, no success with poetry, none with critical book, none with jobs. A couple of miscarriages already under my belt; there would be eight. The dream life of the cave. My poem says it is not Orpheus who turns back to Eurydice but rather she who turns away from him, because she wants to go deeper into the underground cave.

It was my Douglass College student Valerie Napawanetz who, after reading the poem, gave me a gift from the mythology course she was taking.[13] It was a copy of H.D.'s "Eurydice," a poem I had not known, although I was in an intertextual relation with it. And the facts of this encounter are astonishing. Since my own poem (altering and tampering with the hegemonic myth) had changed what was culturally legible to me, I could read and identify H.D.'s project. Working on my own poem, I gained intellectual tread, formulated the thesis of the revisionary relationship to hegemonic culture that fueled some of my critical work.[14] Writing a (feminist) poem allowed me to write (feminist) criticism; "Eurydice" led to *Writing Beyond the Ending.*

I had been trying to write about Pound and Williams, to "rewrite" my dissertation: a dead task. Dead and commanding. Dead and authoritative. Dead and obligatory. Having read Robert Duncan's illuminating essays on H.D. contextualized in a feminized and heterodox modernism (published in *Caterpillar* in 1967 and 1968), I had never accepted the mandated ignorance of H.D.'s work but did not bother to examine her power, for I had internalized the priorities and hierarchies of study and excellence: *Cantos,* worthy; *Helen in Egypt,* unread. But in 1975, after reading Susan Stanford Friedman's "H.D.: Who Was She?" in the context of my developing work on women poets, I was finally propelled to begin serious study of H.D.[15] I needed a woman, a poet, and a modernist, and I needed her badly.

Despite the fact that one of my first ideas of feminist criticism was the rereading of every cultural artifact (and, indeed, I have maintained, through the years, a feminist fascination with humanities courses and with male authors), I tilted with my whole generation toward the startling discoveries of women writers, female "voices," precisely because they had been culturally buried. This project was revendicatory: we were recovering something; we were claiming it. This began as "equal rights" criticism—female writers could be shown to "compete on an equal basis"; yet "women" did not necessarily live in social and cultural equality, and the position quickly modulated into the discovery of particularities in women's writing precisely based on various readings of female social and psychological specificities and differences (from males, and sometimes, later, from other women). Of course there was an immediate investment in unifying or totalizing the idea of "woman." As a real intellectual and cultural idea, it had just been won from a morass of prejudice, contempt, and misogyny, and it needed self-solidarity, which slid (often too easily) into the notion of affirmation and unity.

What else did the early feminist criticism of women writers feel like? If we found textual marks of wholeness, it was because we sought personal and social wholeness, in a spiritual sense, yes, but also as legal redress—to be made whole. If we sought heroes in both the women writers and in their personae and characters, it was because we had few with whom to identify. The affective imperative to "identify" with the objects of study I would later resist, but then it was crucial. This first hermeneutic circle was driven by deep necessity; one must now read it contextually, with empathetic understanding. However, I always distrusted victim-to-apotheosis narratives or even pure victimhood narratives in early feminist criticism.[16] Writing itself was a complex claim to agency, and, reflecting on the transformative energies of women writers, I called their processes of biographical and literary selection and transposition "the career of that struggle." I suspected the notion of authenticity—finding "the" woman's voice, as if it had—or could have been!—preserved in Atlantis-like perfection through the ages. This yearning for originary or organic moments of wholeness could be an enabling myth toward writing, but it was not useful for the critical analysis of writing. So I was constantly and skeptically skirting what has been called "cultural feminism." For me the significant moments of feminist criticism were psychosocial, culturalist analyses of literary production; "gynocriticism" was always a subset of that approach, in my view. Writing was a complex species of ideological negotiation, the constructive and formal transposition of cultural materials in a social matrix: that idea persists in all my critical work.

I got a tenure-track job (at Temple University in 1974), taught undergraduate "Women in Literature" and composition courses, and began writing about Rich, Rukeyser, and Levertov, an article scrutinized by Ann Calderwood's demanding editorial eye for *Feminist Studies.* When Calderwood no longer wanted to edit the journal she had begun as a pioneer, Judith Walkowitz, a historian, myself, and some others—convinced that *Feminist Studies* was a vital feminist institution—helped initiate a major transition (meetings upon meetings) to a collaborative and collective board, with Claire Moses as managing editor, the journal housed at the University of Maryland, College Park. I was an active member of the central editorial board for about fourteen years, from 1974 to 1987.[17] With someone—was it Judith Stacey, was it Rayna Rapp?—I wrote the statement of purpose, with its deliberate echo of Marx's "Theses on Feuerbach": "The feminist movement has demonstrated that the study of women is more than a compensatory project. Instead, feminism has the potential fundamentally to reshape the way we view the world. We wish not just to interpret women's experiences but to change women's condition. For us, feminist thought represents a transformation of consciousness, social forms, and modes of action." I'm citing it, of course, because I still think it is true.

Modulations of Second Feminism, 1979–84; Essays and Trials; Getting Some Work Done

In 1976–77, pursued by some happy daemons of voice, pressure, intensity, anger, and desire, I put aside everything I should have been doing, and everything I knew (though barely) about the academic reward system, and wrote my first essay, "Psyche, or Wholeness," a response to Erich Neumann's *Amor and Psyche,* an attempt to reread a myth about female development in ways beyond even what the sympathetic Jungian analyst proposed (DuPlessis 1979a). Because in the Jungian worldview, females played out powerful psychic dramas backed by noble, mythic types, Jungian thinking was often a portal to feminism in the 1950s and thereafter. I then wrote two other curious works, more and more committed to their disclosures, pace, discursive variety, and praxis of bricolage. "For the Etruscans" was followed by a double homage to Duncan and H.D.—"an essay on H.D. and the muse of the woman writer." The essay form permitted me to say what I wanted, and how, to link and to leap. Reader, I married me.

"For the Etruscans" wasn't prewritten—it was a negotiation with materials arrayed. After I had given a seminar at a Barnard College Conference on Women and Society on the question (not the certainty) of "a" female aesthetic—a burning issue in 1979—I was asked to write it up. So I did. Although I was committed to collaging other people's voices with my own as only one among many, in actuality it did not quite work out that way. Authorship is not dissolved by fiat. But that is why the "author" of that essay is myself and "Workshop 9"—the presence of interlocutors was crucial. The presence of a feminist movement was even more crucial.

Rhetorically "For the Etruscans" mingles manifesto, analysis, intercuts of material from that workshop, letters to friends, the fluid form of talking, and a sense of audience—the enormously excited and participatory group of women for whom, to whom, from whom I was speaking. The essay, with its commitment to multiple citation and to recording participants in that seminar, was writing into that fervent and palpable and aroused and debating female space (see Kaplan 1996). Thinking was a real situation and had real stakes. A rhetoric and an analysis have a social matrix; its ethics is created in responsibility to that matrix. Utopic love roused art for rethinking, re-seeing.

I did not want hierarchy or claims of controlling authority over a set of materials; thus I chose "collage" and "the field" as modes or methods of thought, quite aware of using modernist "devices" for feminist purposes. The two tactics were invested in the creation of a site in which things happen and are juxtaposed. Ludic things: Rhythms of apprehension. Stress shifting. Change-ups. Carnivalizing yet analytic discourses. Mongrel, hybrid sounds. Placing the reader, as well as the writer, in a variety of subject places. Faceting. Dissolving the author into the sounds of the text. Making chaos, diversity, mélange. Constructing a porous openness of thought. In this essay a particular female person makes analyses, has dreams, outcries, offers doubled-voiced montages, mats of citation, experiences longing, grief, and curiosity in and out of the situation of acute feminist attention. Its (apparent) inclusiveness and its fragmentation, its heteroglossic glissades are consciously oppositional and critical.

"For the Etruscans" has had a career of its own. It has been taken as an example of what it set out to study—of "the" female aesthetic. However, what it actually says is that women, like other members of "(ambiguously) non-hegemonic" social groups, are driven to use structural, rhetorical, and epistemological tactics that run counter to normative ones (DuPlessis [1990] 2006, 14). I did not try to falsify or distort what I thought: that "feminine" writing tactics were the tactics that can be chosen by any nondominant group. The rhetorics and strategies are situational, not essentialist. This was not a popular finding then, when we were, in general, in the full bloom of a dynamic, rather absolute and resolute, sense of female difference. Yet insofar as I was acting oppositionally—refusing patriarchal culture as a choice—I also chose to use the very rhetorics I discuss. The essay makes no special claim for *a* or *the* female aesthetic (or even solely *female* aesthetic), but its rhetoric can arouse hope for change of consciousness and ideology, can move the reader (at least temporarily) into a utopian space of gender hope. Doing that kind of work offered an artistic *ekstasis* that also proposed some serious principles about the polyvocal, the multigeneric, the interested, the nonobjective.

It seemed that one needed, as a feminist, to invent an endless number of forms, structures, and linguistic ruptures that would cut way beyond language-business-as-usual and narrative-business-as-usual, which always seemed to end up with "the same" kind of binary, "patriarchal" normalcy. Experimental writing of all sorts had always been crucial to the feminist project of cultural change: of revolution, not revision. It seems to me that feminism (with other socially based cultural movements) is a necessary completion of modernism. (Of modernisms, both "high" and "post-.") Writing cannot make these changes alone; but writing exerts a continuous destabilizing pressure and, in both analytic and formal ways, creates an arousal of desire for difference, for hope. If consciousness must change, if social forms must be reimagined, then language and textual structures must help cause and support, propel and discover these changes. So the essay aims at the decolonization of mind by the analysis of the deepest of embedded structures: gender.

When I first began to justify my essays, I called the mode "free-fall open prose writing which has speculative, critical, autobiographical material all together."[18] The word *free-fall* is a datum of early naming; risk, pleasure, and dreams of flying intermingled in the first feel of doing this work. But from the very beginning I knew I was making principles of art integrate with principles of analysis in ways that aroused readers to feeling, understanding, and response. These essays are sensuous theorizing. If I choose to create desire, attention, loose ends, and an endless intersubjectivity between others as equals (undoing "the" binary), then I am putting a little bit of utopian change into writing. The essay is antipatriarchal writing as a method of investigation and an instrument for change. The essay expresses the need to make something that gives pleasure. That is, aesthetic pleasure motivates political pleasure—toward transformation.

By shifting among stances and genres (from the citation of interrupting shouts to the telling of dreams to speculations about texts), there is a play among the subjectivities contained in my "I." The genres, with their own histories, tones, codes, social meanings, subjects of study, create the plurality of "I," dissolve "I" back into them. This is much more than the matter of "assuming a personal voice," which is not ever what I have said I was doing. I backed into an understanding of some of the poststructuralist theory behind this practice: multiple, even contradictory, subject positions; interrogations of the One, the Center, the Same; rejections of master narratives; issues about the dialectical loop between semiotic and symbolic arenas of language; social dialects and genres in relation. For me the texts began as gestures of emancipation and interrogation; they were not contained or incited by theoretical postulates.[19]

I sometimes now hear about *The Pink Guitar* or "For the Etruscans" as texts of desire. Critical writing in an experimental style became talismans for others. This makes me pleased and wary at once. What I am about to say is—it's not just a style. It's a method. Who gave me permission? How did I "do" it? Desire, need, and the political-cultural moment. Even reckless, but determined (or stubborn), I was willing to play and fail. I knew this writing was risky—indeed the title essay "The Pink Guitar" discusses some of the negative reactions to this essay writing from some thoroughly contemptuous, and momentarily powerful, people. Some critics are going to think you are self-indulgent or narcissistic (etc.) for choosing essay modes. Thus the risk of this kind of expression—the joy of it—must overcome and swamp prudence or narrow conceptions of what writing is, what a career is. It is a subtle and situational decision. There is no simple answer that the past can give the present on this issue. But the fact that joyous impudence, career imprudence, and aesthetic cunning have together made some feminist contribution is forever heartening.

The same astonishing work sheets from the summer of 1979 that produced "Etruscans" also produced the thesis, the set of working terms, and chapter sites for *Writing Beyond the Ending: Narrative Strategies of Twentieth-Century Women Writers* (1985), a moment of gynocritical consolidation with a materialist twist. One major project of twentieth-century women writers is the critique of the (heterosexual) romance plot and of the classic relation of romance and quest, by the invention of narrative strategies that erode and replace the heterosexual couple as adequate fictional ending.[20] The book argues that the narrative critique by women writers of the romance and quest plots signals their dissent from the conventional sex-gender system. This book was written from a fecund cross between feminist humanism and the neo-Marxist analysis of Raymond Williams and—a special debt—Virginia Woolf. Some of its hidden aims for myself were to create rich mixes and readings of writers who had not yet been spoken about in the same breath (Dorothy Richardson! Olive Schreiner! Zora Neale Hurston!); to offer analyses that were precise, synthetic, and illuminating; and to create a taxonomy of strategies beyond the conventional ending. I worked by specific studies of women authors, "female traditions," the identification of special relations of women to dominant traditions, the discovery or new legibility of "lost" works; the identification of concerns, allusions, cultural and linguistic stances read via gender. But I worried about the totalizing of the thesis—the argument that black and white; lesbian and heterosexual; British, U.S. American, and Canadian authors all saw the necessity of this critique of narrative—yet the use of a plurality of examples from different groups was a principle of the book for me. There was an unspoken tension in my thinking about these manifestations of sameness in different groups, yet this thesis and argument seem at the same time to be one of the achievements of the book.

Indeed, there has been a crucial interactive pattern to the production of my feminist work. My poetry propelled my criticism, criticism propelled poetry, and essays were originally born in a spurt between them. Essays then further incited my first critical book and even my next one, on H.D. The three genres I use offer (at least) three different and related subject positions, answerable to different social expectations and writing forums. But they were not separate tracks, and *Blue Studios* makes that fact visible: it is cooler than, but as passionate as, *The Pink Guitar.* Discoveries made in one mode led the way to work in another. I cannot say it strongly enough: writing long poems ("Eurydice" and "Medusa") opened my career as a critic, opened it intellectually, for the ideas in *Writing Beyond the Ending* on kinds of mythopoetic practices—ideas of "breaking the sentence and breaking the sequence," displacement, and delegitimation—were underwritten and enabled by my poetic practice. My turn to the essay form, an eccentric detour and divagation if ever there was one, allowed me to find a thesis for my first critical book. The point is—poetry is intellectual work, criticism is poetic work, and if these do not come as a necessity—a personal and cultural necessity—what good are they? My poetry (a somewhat hidden thing, a somewhat unrewarded thing, a slowly written thing), my essays (a dangerous, satisfying, sometimes misinterpreted thing) made me a feminist critic. Were part of my feminist cultural work.

What I found galvanic, beyond immediate female bonding felt intensely, were the political and cultural ideas of feminism and the idea of gender as a critical and compelling element of culture. From the earliest moment that second-wave feminism emerged from the analytic and political scrutiny of institutions of power and hegemony, I established my interest in a feminism of critique. From 1968 to 1970 to today, I have felt that feminist re-vision would necessitate the multiple, forceful, and polyvocal invention of a completely new culture and the critical destabilizing, indeed the replacement, of the old.

In 1980 I went through that peculiar hazing process of numerous feminist members of my generation: I was denied tenure at Temple University. While the signals were mixed, one of the then-powerful voices ran an exasperating condemnation of all feminist work in which my "appropriation of H.D." and the fact of my essays loomed large. (As with all tenure decisions, these words could have been a ventriloquized pretext, but one was obliged to take them literally.) Of course, it is true that the essays were intemperate and maenadic, though not that they were poorish art or unanalytic intellectual documents. This tenure battle was, of course, no joke. I worked with intransigence and strategy to reverse the decision and gained thereby yet a little more political education. My "risks" were patent: I wrote both creative and critical writing in a new field; I worked with other women to build a new feminist journal; the field was "political"—that whole story. But the cultural necessity of feminist work gave me the drive and the justification. It was just me; this is what I was doing. So there we were. But I was also more than simply myself—I had a small, but still symbolic, position, as standing for something, a politicized-aesthetic kind of gender-inflected cultural work in poetry and criticism.

Split subjectivity? wholeness? who knew?

1984 to "Now": Polyvocal Poems and the Pluralist Feminism-Plus of Cultural Studies

When I first wrote this essay in 1990, I was speaking "now" about an arc from 1984 to 1990, but now, when I rewrite this in 2004, what am I speaking about? We are not in the same emotional, professional, or political time. Not to mention what any "now" is when and why you are reading. I am not sure I can handle the tenses and the tensions of this, the deictic, yet inadequate pointing into different moments, so "now" I will simply make some sketchy remarks about the kinds of feminist criticism I tried to propose.

My whole career has been challenging the politically quietist sheer-formalist and challenging the formally stolid, narrowly construed political. Working the between. This "poethics"—a wonderful coinage of Joan Retallack's—involves investigation, examination, critique, resistance. To see, at least, where I'd been, as my feminist "poethics" debated modernist experiment, I collected ten years of my essays (mainly published by small press journals from 1979 on) in *The Pink Guitar: Writing as Feminist Practice* (DuPlessis [1990] 2006). Since a number of the essays concerned Pound, Williams, and Eliot, as well as Duchamp, at least I managed finally to "rewrite" my dissertation. This critical position went along with a mobile investigative strategy in writing poetry highly indebted to objectivist practice: investigation of "the real world, the real, real world," as Carl Rakosi once remarked in conversation. For some of the poetics and some of the intransigence, I was indebted to the work of the objectivist poet George Oppen, many of whose writings in poetics occurred in his self-chosen form: personal letters. With a perspective on archival work about neglected or marginal figures that I had developed from work on H.D., I engaged from 1980 to 1990 on a large-scale editorial and textual project: *The Selected Letters of George Oppen,* which presents materials important (in my view) to contemporary poetry and poetics (Oppen 1990). My interest in the critique and dissolution of the canon (note the working contradiction) is not focused solely on women writers.

Following the logic of feminist critique, I saw that reading gender needs to be further elaborated by analytic interplays among studies of race, class, sexualities, religious culture, and other psychosocial forces and locations and by studies of the manifestations of these markers in culture and text. Feminist cultural studies would be based on establishing a plural, dynamic relationship among social markers as constructed in and as text. None of these markers is static and already understood, but each is created in political, cultural, social, and historical interactions whose activities, contradictions, and textual manifestations need critical scrutiny.[21] I wanted to discuss all this for the poetic text. In doing this work I argued that modern poetry drew on, helped to create, and responded to several new entitlements for social subjects in modernity: New Woman, New Negro, New Jew. These subject positions brought other issues and subjectivities in their wake, including the discourses of maleness/manhood/masculinity, of whiteness, of mongrelization, and of hegemonic Christianity. But it was not simply the statements and themes of poetic texts that interested me; I rejected extractive readings for a study of the helix of poetic form and ideological positions. My book about modern poetry brings together my interest in the intense aesthetic substance of the poem and in sociocultural readings. *Genders,*

Races, and Religious Cultures in Modern American Poetry, 1908–1934 offers a postformalist reading strategy that looks at the deep mechanisms of literary texts with a kind of "New Critical" care yet, at the same time, links formal material to the issues that purist New Criticism rejected: social substance, biographical traces, constructions of subjectivity, historical debates, ideological strata (DuPlessis 2001). Thus the book foregrounds a practice of "social philology": the interdependent mesh of a text's social and aesthetic aspects, mediating between what is said *in* poetry and what is said *as* poetry.

I have never thought there was one way women did or should or could write: style, form, structure, language, rhetoric are all tools consciously and unconsciously used in the deep agency of writing. As Woolf said in *A Room of One's Own*—certain material differences between men and women are still constructed and perpetuated in our society, and it is the job of feminism to resist these, to try to dismantle these, and, as well, to understand their impact, which can be considerable in the case of artists. This is the importance of feminist reception and writing inspired in the general matrix of ongoing feminist critique.

July 1990 and July 1991
July 2003 and November 2004

2
f-words

An Essay on the Essay

In 1969 the Belgian artist Marcel Broodthaers prepared several tampered versions of *Un coup de dés jamais n'abolira le hasard.* On the cover Broodthaers's name was given as author.[1] My own quandary, in the spirit of that voracity, would be whether to offer "The Essay as Form" or *A Room of One's Own* by Rachel Blau DuPlessis. In Broodthaers's Mallarmé, a version called "Image," each of the lines is found blackened over, creating design across the fold but effacing all the words within a constructivist geometry. These black Montessori sticks of varying lengths and widths—indicating line segments but as an array of unreadable cul-de-sacs—are only temporarily charming. The analytically motivated *foutisme* of conceptual art makes the words into an unreadable visual "image" and icon by imprinting over the barely interpretable "images" of Mallarmé's own hermetic obscurity. For its charm—its play with erasure and dark design, with transforming writing into a visual text—does depend on the continued availability of that poem from other sources. To the degree that the version alludes to official gestures of effacement, like censored documents from an FBI file, these blacked-out lines evoke the problematic politics of censorship. Thereupon one yearns for even the dark opacity of Mallarmé's words because they validate the valuable privilege of reading and writing *what we will.* (*f*-words to date: *foutisme, effacement, FBI,* that last to stand, perhaps awkwardly, for the possibilities of state-fortified censorship and other political repressions of texts and writers.)

Another gesture of beginning would be Woolf's in the diary of 1899; her age is seventeen. Taking a book by Isaac Watts with the suggestive title of *Logick, or, the right use of Reason, with a variety of rules to guard against error in the affairs of religion and human life as well as in the sciences,* Woolf cuts pages from her own diary to fit his binding, and then glues them not only to Watts, inside his book, but uses Watts's pages, also glued together, to hide the existence of her own. She does so precisely to write *what she will.* And the hiding of her work is a poignant, discerning gesture and can be read within her mid-adolescent writing life as raising questions of autonomy, property, claims to privacy, and selfhood (DeSalvo 1989, 248–50). This book was, apparently, bought for its binding, not for the title and its ironic allegories. But the Watts title still makes a statement about turning method against itself. Woolf uses the book physically; its curious Logick of open-and-shut rules protect her from those guards and guardians of intellectual and moral method who, as she said thirty years later, "save us so much thinking" by propounding such axioms as "Cats do not go to heaven. Women cannot write the plays of Shakespeare" (Woolf [1929] 1957, 48).

Both Woolf and Broodthaers claim the book by saying it is a space in which one wants to make or leave one's mark as freely as possible. The book is just one institution of cultural accumulation; he also claimed the museum, she disclaimed the university. One gesture makes a book keep the secret of her writing; it is deftly marginal, deftly concealed. Her visual text calls us to register fear, cunning, and the hope of uncensored writing annealed to and sandwiched invisibly into treatises on propriety. His visual text frets replacement and effacement, fingering those strings, and firmly, *fortissimo.* Each is differently motivated, but both are methodological critiques of method. Her gesture places Watts's words—indeed whole pages—"over" hers; his gesture paints inked-out blocks over words, deposing Mallarmé's text. The gender issues of access and authority are rather stark in these examples, but taking the two together, one can say that writing on the side, through the interstices, between the pages, on top of the writing, constructing gestures of suspicion, writing what one will (what one wills), writing over the top, writing a reading, writing an untransparent text, writing into the book—all these practices and more frame the essay.

This is an essay (my essay) about the essay. Essay is always opposite. Well, often opposite. Oppositional. How does the essay function? What is it taxonomically?[2] The adjective *autobiographical,* often used for this manner of work, flails and gasps—it is an inadequate descriptor, even though some people may take the stance denominated "I." These are works of "reading"—for essays are acts of writing-as-reading. Acts of trying out, as the French root *essayer* says. It seems as if the essay mode, in our generation, was impelled by the social and cultural force of "1968"—and its motivations—as these forces and events coalesced and influenced "reading."[3] There was a particular flash point of interpretation among women, who began, as "68ers" (in Meredith Tax's phrase), to decode all the multifarious and dispersed signs by which gender had been inscribed. The questions of interpretation, of reading the signs by which one had been read, had similarly, and prior to 1968, become central to a number of cultural practices based in historical idioms (e.g., "race"; the colonized and the colonizer) and ethical ones (e.g., questions of becoming and of justice). It is clear that this desire to descry the ideologies and powers at work in one's own sociocultural formation is one strong source for the contemporary essay.

The practice of "reading" became a vital and earth-shattering act within one's investigative and imaginative life, quite charged with questions of access, consumption, positioning, pleasure, scrutiny, ingestion, interpretation, agenda setting. Reading the signs; crossings, as cross-signs, sighs inside signs, reading as cosigning, as if one also owned, had signed for, cultural materials and was not simply their object, or their dutiful consumer.[4] It was worth your life to "get" a specific book or text or document or event, to undertake it, to ingest it, to deturn it, even to detox it—a reading beyond reading, an impelled and propulsive reading. The word *analysis* should be able to stand for this, but it doesn't get the lift and loft of feeling-thinking about ideology and event. The word *deconstruction,* so often suggestive, did not uniformly offer a justification to seek political meaning with a defined ethical stake within the world. This kind of "reading" aroused serious personal emotions of pain and pleasure, grief and joy via cultural participation. These paradigm-changing moments on a mass or collective scale—a political conversion leading to serious growth in interpretive nuance; the notion that cultural acts play on our fibers . . . —all this was expressed within the essay.

But if contemporary essays are works of sociopersonal "reading," they are also works of "wrought," a thinking that occurs by the physical elaboration of language, a work and a working in language, not only a working through something intellectually or emotionally. Not language for a summary of findings, but language as the inventor of findings. *Wrought* is the past participle of *work;* but I thought (wrongly, but willfully) that *wreaking* was a related word. *Reading* and *wreaking* make a euphonious pair. However *wreaking* is at the far end of essay in its real meaning—its wrath, its venting, its drive. If "wreaking" could be altered somewhat—its propulsions made positive instead of vengeful, one would have the sense of the essay's energy, its wayward reach into utopic desires. Jed Rasula's *This Compost,* an ethnopoetic book of wisdom-essays, also offers a neologism for the activity of making and seeking: writing and reading fused together is "wreading"—a need-filled kneading of texts (Rasula 2002, 11–12). And wreaking and wreading are what interesting essays get to, one way or another, offering knowledge in passionate and cunning intersections of material, in ways excessive, unsummarizable, and (oddly, gloriously) comforting by virtue of their intransigent embeddedness and their desire, waywardly, to riffle and roam.

The word *poetic* for this kind of writing serves as a marker of untransparent textuality, in the realm of wreaking/wrought. The poetic study, the study as poem, poetic criticism, prose-poem expositions, criticism as fancy fictive acts that awoke to find them true—all these possibilities come to pool in the essay because of its enactment of a praxis. It is the genre showing how *poesis* itself turns back and forth between the discursive statement and the medium itself. The essay does a thinking that is of language in all its rhetorical density and snarls, its emotional evocations, associations, burrs, leaps, expostulations, and fleshliness. Sociality and textuality meet in the essay. It is not aesthetic only, not political only, but aesthetico-political.

The contemporary essay can offer a particular kind of social autobiography: "coming out" stories, "social reading," or community stories. These are readings offered by, and of, writers from formerly semisilenced, disparaged social locations—from woman, black, gay, Latino/a, Asian, lesbian—all claiming "voice." Particularism, the local, the nuance of place and idiom—our essay, one mode, has become travel writing into our past, our communities, an ethnography by citizens. At best, the unrolling narratives of pressure, prejudice, conversion, engagement, the precise articulation of speech and writing out of repression, assimilation, and marginalization are dramas well suited to the essay. The essay will serve for the bricolage of tools and packs, the space or continent to be trekked, the stamina and passions of both investigation and findings, the affirmations and their compromises. Given that the essay is all margin, marginalia, and interstitial writing, it rearranges, compounds, enfolds, and erodes the notion of center in textually and socially fruitful ways. Claiming a palpable liberation and a permanent engagement with one's social space, even with one's personal history, is one keynote of the essay in our time. Sometimes this freedom is enlivening, and sometimes it is enervating, its happy truths a religious structure of feeling to which some may be agnostic. It is an efflorescence of difference, now perhaps, and with no little irony, reaping hegemonic fruits.

Another essay mode offers an account of a main character, a character launched much like heroines of novels, in which self-fashioning and accounts of exemplary moments are central. As the concern for individual subjectivity is exploded in literary criticism, as the word *self* became, so curiously, taboo in certain contemporary theorizing practices, "selfhood" and "quest" and "growth" and "narrative coherence" reemerge in this writing.[5]

If one kind of identity writing is ethnography, if the work of poet-critics from modernism on suggests an epistolary mattedness, the post office, the blog and listserv, flying and flyting in all directions, this set of essays offers the classic realist novel of *Bildung*. Indeed, Woolf has called the self "the essayist's most proper but most dangerous and delicate tool" (Woolf [1925] 1962, 274). Woolf accomplished an effacement of self: her final work is done under the suggestive rubric of "anon." The essay's *f* is like the definite integral sign in mathematics, and self-integration is sometimes the watchword of this material, but *f* is also the sign of effacement, of a function between. For both what one knows and what one doesn't fully know can provoke writing. Hence for me "identity" is hardly the thing speaking; what speaks is something more fugitive. It is vulnerability fissioning within being.

Faced with all that, one might tend to say—essay? it's short but personable writing in prose, and it speaks from the heart (wherever that is). Essays tend to call the genre into question, which theory about genre does anyway, so it sometimes seems as if the essay is lots of modes, not one mode, a set of intersections of intention. Some, but not all, are "autobiographical"; some, but not all, are discursive; some, but not all, are heteroglossic; some, but not all, are theoretical; and on and on. Indeed, Réda Bensmaïa argues that the essay is not a genre, nor even several and mixed genres, but becoming itself: "a moment of writing before the genre, before genericness—or as the matrix of generic possibilities" (Bensmaïa 1987, 92). This offers a symptomatic aura of specialness to the essay, as if it were the universe one second before its big bang dispersion. It's not that the essay is unsusceptible to genre "definition"; it's rather that the nature of the essay asks one to resist categories, and it starts with itself.

There is some frank arousal within essay function, essay being the genre of spiritual arousal, of social mourning, of political fury as a kind of melody and the sense of a new day dawning. While this time may be (quite implausibly) redeemed, the essayist, skeptical and dubious (even of her-/himself, not to speak of the time), is acting to sift, against hegemonic narratives that would efface them, the debris and the wasted shards, the details that tell us why we are so. This is the "task to brush history against the grain" with penetrating bits of trouble, of the troubled, of the troubling (Benjamin 1969, 257). This nexus of arousal, fury, passion, and hope, along with cunning scrutiny of social and cultural texts learned, in necessity, through the scrutiny of official lies, should tell us again why this essay function was reborn out of (loosely) the long reverberations of the 1960s in U.S. thought. It's not so much before genre as under history.

The essay is restless. It is like a kind of travel writing, a voyaging, partial and never satisfied, always a little too hungry or full . . . a little too thirsty, or in the precarious condition of having drunk some strange new kind of water, wine, coffee, or *eau de vie* . . . the view you came five thousand miles for shrouded in clouds, or too sunny, too hot, giving you a headache . . . a particular mix, in short, of satisfied and un-.

Is it possible to synthesize these vectors—to offer any centers around which this writing clusters?[6] What joins tendencies in the essay is probably a renewed attentiveness to materiality, to the material world, including the matter of language. While this attention can also sometimes split into two emphases on either textual materiality or biographical/historical/topographical materiality, the real interest comes when these are fused: when textuality and social practices both compel attention to materiality. The essay is a way of representing struggle, crossings, and creolized exploration. Essays can be tested by the degree and tension of the struggles and passions with which they reverberate.

So while there are probably always essays, it only feels like a moment for The Essay when there is some materialist coagulation of meaning in the formal choice, when critique joins with passion inside language that materializes that passion as rhetoric; when interested and situated knowledge is exposed in its vibrancy; when people have undergone changes that resonate in all felt areas—ethical, intellectual, emotional, visceral, political. For "subject position" is "language position." Notice the tones in which you are fluent; then add the tones in which you stutter. You're beginning to get it. When a situated practice of knowing made up by the untransparent situated subject—as if figuring out on the ground, virtually in the time of writing—explores (explodes) its material in unabashed textual untransparency, conglomerated genre, ambidextrous, switch-hitting style, that's it: *f*-words.The essay.

What is taken (by some) as rhetoric or style or manner (these offered, damningly, as if they were detachable technologies of writing) is in the essay a way of knowing. A path. In some old woods, in the middle of something. The path of rhetoric *is* the path of knowledge. The digression is the subject. The polyvocal collage, the unmatted plurality, the tonal glissades, the upstart mischief, undecorous, suspicious, the probing, the backtracking, the outbursts, the resistances *are* a large measure of the essay's findings.

Essay is the play of speculation. The test of the essay is whether it opens a space for the reader, rather than closing one. The essay is interested and agnostic, situational and material, presentational, investigative, and heuristic. Writing an essay comes from curiosity and need—the need to examine opinions and contradictions and to interrogate cultural materials, especially those taken for granted. The essay has an ethos of porous, lambent, intense examination, an antiauthoritarian play of perpetual dialectics.

It is a text whose ideal state (that's a paradox), as articulated by Woolf, Adorno, and Benjamin (and by the critics Bensmaïa and Good speaking of Barthes and of Montaigne), contests any notion that writing or thinking leads to unity, system, abstraction, mastery. Indeed, "its structure negates system" (Adorno 1991, 17). The essay, as Adorno argues, protests against all of the "rules" of method (codified by Descartes)—claims of totality and continuity, claims of universality, claims that any concept emerges from a tabula rasa and independent of language, independent of its materiality. Essays can emerge from continuous free association, like Freud's "dream work," a way of reading the rebus of signs thrown into the conscious mind or found in the real, a tactic of inventive discovery proposed by H.D. in *Tribute to Freud* and other of her essays.

Driven, the essay is also relaxed, casual, humane. Humane, it is also angry, resistant, unrelaxed—passionate and driven. What has caused this double gesture? A political provocation and spiritual intuition both lead to the ethos of the essay. Writing an essay does not imply a proper (meaning objective) distance from something but a significant proximity to it, an implication. A being implicated. In fact, a being consumed. Even when the essay crackles with authority, it is not authoritarian.[7] Even when it's partial, it is never particularist. The essay, without ever claiming to be the messiah is messianic; it engineers rhythms of conversion; it raises and rouses readers, changes the little auricular feathers at its readers' ears.

The ethics of essay is most stringent: it involves the rejection of mastery. Adorno argues that the essay "abjures the ideal" of its own certainties as it moves into the force field created by its insights (Adorno 1991, 161). And yet the essay is also a response made in a smallness and minority so exacting it can be almost arrogant. A fine line. The essay can seem to be a genre of sensibility, expressing the fetishized individual, in various postures of apparent self-revelation. "Personal" may be an easy way of summarizing the upstart quality, the gestures of emancipation and interrogation that fuel the essay with situated, nonobjective thought. But it is not the most thorough way.

I am or was once writing this as a reluctant child prepared a written report on "the liver." Her tears, in fact, had stained my wooden desk, and she had labeled them "Koré's tears" with a little note taped next to the stains, now gone. In an earlier essay, "For the Etruscans," another child's shout up through the strained passages of the house, raising the question of "fig newtons," or a riff on "ricotta" seemed to evoke, for some people, the perpetual interruptibility, including self-interruptibility, of women trying to do cultural work.

So I have, so to speak, a personal stake in this question. Why are the *Pink Guitar* essays taken as personal? Is it because women's words must be (ipso facto) personal? Is it because the risk of the heterogeneric, of the tonal swoops may seem like a personal boldness? Is it because people reading any pronoun like "I" forget that what they are reading is not life but "biographemes"—selected, made—a work of art. The very danger of the personal is memorialized in this heavy word, a clinical term clearly designed to ward off any charge of unmediated spill (Miller 1991, 9, 19). So what, then, does the word *personal* mean applied to *The Pink Guitar,* whose autobiographical moments number barely twenty? Are these too many moments? Does the word mean no more than "situated thinking": the challenge "to the sustaining fiction of objectivity, distance, and neutrality in critical studies"? (DuPlessis [1990] 2006, viii). Does the word *autobiographical* get used sentimentally, to suggest "unmediated" and authentic? Or does it suggest a constructed, selected "fiction of memory" (in Sidonie Smith's phrase) (Smith 1987, 45)?[8] But though rare enough if one were to catalogue or number them—the glimpses of parts of "life" lived at one address or another, 317, 211, now 413, are finally only glimpses. I have told you relatively nothing.

However, that work spotlighted sudden, abrupt moments, intransigent, brimful of contradictions—a dream, an encounter: insoluble. It seems the suddenness and the amorality of the transition and the intransigence of the contradiction are arresting. Further, these essays (I mean mine, others' as well) evoke from the reader a set of emotions and responses allowably more varied and juiced-up, more open-ended, than what is asked by the general/normal material one reads. They ask for affective reading, to use the term Steve McCaffery highlights from Deleuze (McCaffery 2001, 42). Because readers have been moved, moved inside *their* lives, they think *I* have been more autobiographical than I generally have been. The readerly arousal to pleasure created by the essay generates the aura of autobiography. For who has not wanted to get some boards and nails after reading *Walden*?

Yet an essay is arguably a very un-narcissistic mode, for it maintains a notion of service, of the exemplary use of the ego or its testing dissolution within a cultural project. To illustrate, the person who speaks as "bell hooks"—a remarkable nom de plume given what she wants—says that the essay writes at and "about the points where the public and the private meet, to connect the two" (hooks 1989, 2). Precisely. What people mean when they claim "the personal" is often the reverberation of collectivity. The essay is (to borrow from Nancy Miller) "positional"; positionality, not personality is central.[9] The essay expresses community, even when apparently singular, and hence allows us to apprehend communitarian yearnings via what seems to be a private play of thought.[10] Far from being exercises in narcissism, in gaining a personal voice, essays are practices in multiplicity, in polyvocality, in other opinions intercutting, in heterogeneous, faceted perspectives. In short, essays are not a way of "gaining a voice" but of losing one in the largeness of something else.

My argument is abrupt, unregenerate, somewhat willful and overstated: the essay is transpersonal, collective, based not on *I* but on *we* and *it* (and other pronouns too). Indeed, the pronominals are so unimaginably interrelated that perhaps only invented pronouns (as Hélène Cixous invents *hesheit*) can intimate the social meaning of the essay. Transpersonal; even if apparently autobiographical, essay is more fundamentally collective, the sound of a *we*—an *I* dissolving back and forth into a listening, and sometimes speaking, other.[11] The voice of the essay at base makes a collective, not a personal speculation.

The collective upsurge behind the apparently individual subject in the essay is most visible at stress points of political desire and anxiety. In "Sorties," talking a psychoanalytic language of universal gender conditions, Cixous suddenly bursts out with this collective "song": "there is no *invention* possible, whether it be philosophical or poetic, without there being in the inventing subject an abundance of the other, of variety: separate-people, thought-/people, whole populations issuing from the unconscious, and in each suddenly animated desert, the springing up of selves one didn't know—our women, our monsters, our jackals, our Arabs, our aliases, our frights" (Cixous 1986, 84). The purely psychoanalytic subject splits like a fig, and out come the multiple seeds of social dynamics evoking a variety of rich allusions and narratives; these are a collectivity inside an individual, with some notable ethnic anxieties. In this polysocial collectivity, this "peopling," the individual has turned itself inside out, becoming social (Cixous 1986, 86).

Given the rejection of mastery, the arrogant minority, the glimpses of intimate moments, the tracking of a wayward mind thinking, one can also see why the essay has been summed up by the term *feminine*. Extravagance—said Thoreau—wanders around, eccentric, excessive, overdoing it in the strangest ways—why, it's a description at one and the same time of The Essay and The Female of the Species. *Feminine* is a difficult and untrustworthy word—but it makes an exciting gesture, points to a major alteration of thought, a certain wayward turning of practice. And all the negatives of the feminine, the overdone, the exaggerated, the brazen, the wrongheaded, the prone to error, the needing correction, the lack of *mesura,* the overspill, the loss of boundaries: all these become positive rhetorics. The essay embodies, and can claim, a feminized space: of interruption, of beginning again and again, of fragmentation, of discontinuities. But most in its distrust of system, its playful skepticism about generalization. And interest in the small, the odd, the quirky, the by-the-side, the thing changeable, the viewer changeable too. Skepticism even about one's own self-interested positions.

Yet I resist the term *feminine* or regard it with a wary suspicion. Given a 1950s adolescence, *feminine* means some pretty repressive things with burdensome social implications. I can't shake off these things even with repeated exposures to poststructuralist theory, in which "feminine" indicates an untheorizable, excessive writing practice, an untrammeled space beyond symbolic/logocentric order, a practice of immoderation, insubordination, and transgression to which women have a privileged relation. I don't think women as a group are (forever and ever) any more or less in process, indeterminate, fluid, beyond the cultural compact, that is, any more "feminine" than any particular men might be. It is a powerful enabling myth to think so, and it has led to compelling work of resistance and critique, but it is a faith claim. And try as one might to recuperate it, binarist meanings of *feminine* confuse me as a common reader whenever the term *feminine* is used to praise antipatriarchal urgencies or some zone imagined beyond the symbolic order. Indeed, there seem to be two completely opposite uses of this term in contemporary thinking: as affirming infinite free-play and as reaffirming the rigid manacles of gender binarism.

I think style and form are strategies of acquiescence and resistance, and the important question is how these rhetorics are used by writers (with what ideology and agency motivating the rhetorics) and how they are perceived by critics (with what ideology and situated reading practices). Hence one may choose, with authorial agency and wary senses of risk, those rhetorics that are (for whatever reason) currently called "feminine." I have said this since "For the Etruscans" (1979). But I said it in a certain tricky way, playing with that choice of "feminine" rhetoric—that is with collage, suture, association, tonal glissades, evocation of the quotidian and unsolemn, interruption, jump-cuts. Hence "For the Etruscans" was widely taken to defend "feminine" language. However, what I actually said is that all rhetorical choice was situational and that nonhegemonic rhetorical strategies are often grasped by groups (women as "ambiguously non-hegemonic") in need of oppositional statement.[12]

Still, it's important to consider the descriptor *feminine* to see what it has offered to significant theorists and polemicists who have used it. "The Laugh of the Medusa," by Hélène Cixous, is one of the great twentieth-century manifestoes (Cixous 1980). Like many manifestoes, it exhorts the creation of something that is rhetorically palpable, so the new time that is urged as coming in history is already present in its own prose. The insurgent force of the prose catapults us into the future perfect, with its fecund confusions of present and future tense. It is a work millennial, apocalyptic, and filled with that interplay between political and spiritual energies often found in feminist essays. In this work, exchanges among pronouns claim a new community—a border crossing among third person, second person, and first person, both singulars and plurals. The desire for a "feminine writing" occurs to undermine the central Freudian tenet of gender asymmetry: castration or lack. All logos-centered writing is interpreted as "writing the [male; universalized] body"; her response is that the body of the woman must also write itself (a much misunderstood point). She insists that the snakes on the Medusa head offer a fecund plurality of generative elements. Hence that scare head, in some theories symbolizing castration, is viewed by her as an affirmative copia of penile and orgasmic/clitoral abundance. With the knowledge of the multisexual female (the new bisexual in Cixous's terms), the phallic period in world history is ended (Cixous 1980, 252). Woman's insurgent laughter around a "vatic [i.e., liberatory] bisexuality," "which doesn't annul differences but stirs them up, pursues them," will break up the deep ideological laws of castration and female repression (Cixous 1980, 254). So the operable term in this essay should really be *écriture bisexuelle* or *polysexuelle;* her *f*-word *feminine* is a polemical gamble.

Similarly, Luce Irigaray proposes that the main concepts of psychoanalysis have taken no account of female presence or desire, so the system is not even so much binary as monistic. It is a model of one, in which women are seen by "hom(m)ology" to men and are thus mis-seen. This "economy of the same" should be refused. Her proposal of the term *feminine,* then, makes a collection point or site for all the excluded materials: maternal pleasure, clitoral presence, the formation of the daughter, a new rhetoric—a whole countersymbolic order of real interplay between two sexes that depends on asserting the powers of the female sex (Irigaray [1977] 1985).[13] The countersymbolic order (heterogeneity) has not been construed as a phallic order, and it does not depend on the postulate of loss in the formation of the sexes. She sees as in a vision not one vs. the Other but a play of "bothness." Irigaray thus hypothesizes a true heterosexual (which means a person whose sexuality is heterogeneous; at other times a self-stimulating woman independent of the heterosexuality we know) for a new economy of representation, a practice of "heterogeneity." The unleashed female imaginary, valued and active, is a necessary precondition for the establishment of true heterogeneity and involves a triangulation among sexuality, rhetoric, desire. So the heterogeneous involves a multidirectional, whimsical, passionate language, and it involves desires that seem to transpire at once in rhetorical need, social urgency, and sexual organs. Heterogeneity slides into the term *feminine* in Irigaray when the *precondition* for the establishment of a new symbolic order (assuming value to all aspects of femaleness) is taken *as* that symbolic order. In both Cixous and Irigaray, although without total exactness, the term *feminine* is a synonym for heterogeneity, multiplicity, and polysexual affirmation.

To call nonlinear structures, cross-generic experiment, collage, nonnarrative play with subjectivity, temporality, and syntax by the name of *feminine* follows the French feminism of Cixous and Irigaray. One could nod approvingly, as does Joan Retallack in *The Poethical Wager,* accepting the word—mainly but not totally: "it is the women among them [experimental poets] who—for the first time in large numbers—are using feminine formal processes and are thus presenting us with our strongest, most challenging models of literary feminisms" (Retallack 2003, 144). This is actually an argument that demands, rightfully, that the poetry of "established feminist circles" not be considered the only feminism in poetry, which must include works of "the experimental feminine" (that is, works by women using experimental rhetorics). Yet in *feminine* Retallack chooses a term that reinvokes the very rigidity it wanted to criticize, a term that has specific social connotations and nonliberatory uses (Retallack 2003, 141).

The female use of the "feminine" is especially striking for Retallack; she calls it the poethical—a radical changing of rhetorics, genres, and modes of writing that challenges thought, perception, and subjectivity. Her more absolutist heteronym, the equally provocative Genre Tallique, says, "Feminist writing occurs only when female writers use feminine forms"; that *only* creates difficulties (Retallack 2003, 127). I only wish I could be so certain. For instance, this means that no man could ever write a feminist work, even in feminine forms; further, this is a polemical argument taking feminism away from more rhetorically stolid women, so it is quite exclusionary. Also, it depoliticizes, or appropriates, the term *feminism* and makes it the property of specific rhetorical, modal, and genre choices. Certainly a rhetorical choice has historical and situational meaning—it is precisely a wager in Retallack's terms, not an absolute. But more than that, a rhetoric is only part of a politics—necessary but not sufficient.

Then in other of her essays Retallack is not so certain that *feminine* is the best term for what she wants: "Our best possibilities lie in texts/altertexts where the so-called feminine and masculine take migratory, paradoxical, and surprising swerves to the enrichment of both,/n/either, and all else that lies along fields of limitless nuance" (Retallack 2003, 113).[14] That *so-called* hints that the gender binarist terms are only a stepping stone to something postbinarist and possibly postgender—"a culture of reciprocal alterity" of the genders and dynamic (social and literary) uses of the possibilities of masculine and feminine by anyone and everyone. Would it not be more useful, for such a dialectic, to leave the terms *feminine* and *masculine* in the category of the to-be-sublated?

The category "feminine writing" has been so evocative because *feminine* serves as collection site for a variety of rhetorical/ethical theories that open the utopian possibility of serious intellectual and social change in the realm of gender. The term valorizes the demeaned or minoritized. And then the word evokes a fundamental change of everything, everywhere. Yet saying that there already exists a space ("the feminine") for this change begs the question, or slides across the question, of political and social struggle that could bring about this level of change. It is under these aroused rubrics of a social transformation that one can understand such an unpromising and confusing term as *feminine.* But only as a cover word, an encoded word. Just as the term *personal* veils the plurality inside one subject, the gender-hybrid subject, and community, so the word *feminine* is a flat cover term that veils its real meanings. If one wants to say transgressive, hybrid, antihegemonic rhetorics, why not do so in these words? *Feminine* names a suggestive site of what is yearned for in these essay-manifestoes: female (as human) agency beyond oppressions, sexual plurality, political change, cultural struggle. Sometimes the *f*-word *feminine* is a stand-in for reaffirming situated materiality (an old idea of female bodies, as if men's bodies did not suffer materially, were not subject to buffetings). I should, in any event, want to substitute untranscendent, situated materiality of body and text as a source for thought and mainly forget about the word *feminine.* Or affirm that the loss of any mind-body split is an ideological goal. All thought being so situated, so invested (in-*f*-ested), the issue is finding and tracking materiality and interests, not denying them.

The reason it has been blinding to call a certain rhetoric "feminine" is that it seems to credit our gender (speaking as Herself) with a style disruptive of hegemony. Yet it is not impossible (and can be seen, for example, in some of Charles Olson's essays) that this radical, rousing style can be coupled with ancient, patriarchal gender tropes.[15] Thus any call for the "feminine" in discourse is only interesting when crossed with a feminist, or otherwise liberatory, critical project; rhetorical choices are only part of a politics. There are my *onlys*. And further—no matter what kind of writing, it is important to understand it by assiduously maintaining feminist (gender-oriented) reception for all writing—one of the richest achievements of this creative period.[16]

Thus collectivity, heterogeneity, positionality, and materiality (although veiled under the terms *personal, autobiographical,* and *feminine*) buoy the essay—give it the density of texture, the sense of implication, the illusion of completeness—in a form that embodies its own fragmentation. The essay is the mode in which material sociality speaks, in texts forever skeptical, forever alert, forever yearning.

—fugitive, fissured, finding, effrontery, factor, fragmented, "feminine," foutisme, if, effort, foxy, fate, fancy, far & farthest, fast, field, function, effervescent, factitious, findings, feelings, effusion, flounce, forage, farrago, furious, forte, forth, flame, fluid, fronts, freed, fibers, riff, "force field," freely, fold.

3
Blue Studio

Gender Arcades

Dear Rachel: *from Barbara Cole, 1997:* "I have written to you before of my discomfort/concern/uneasiness with how I hear women—intelligent women, writing women, politically-aware women—discussing feminism and gender issues . . . [with] the same old [negative] arguments simply recirculated/regenerated." *Cole, 2002:* "It seems I have had so many conversations as of late in which an older poet is avidly arguing *against* certain labels, in particular, making public 'I am not a feminist poet' statements" (Cole 2002, 35, 33).[1]

Dear Barbara: You make me want to condense everything I know about gender and poetry and poetics into one leathery medicine ball and throw it toward you and to your "generation" or "genderation"—Hey, CATCH! The terms of your letters are various, and you constellate reactions from the enthusiastic to the suspicious re: feminism in culture. And what I'm going to write back should not imply that you will, or should, take up the same terms in the same ways that we did.

Do you remember Henri Matisse's *Red Studio* (1911, at MoMA)? The painting displays his work reproduced in miniature, in his studio, a passionate deep-but-flat red field. Iconic miniwomen are depicted—as a statue, on a plate, in a painting—these figures are artifacts of Art as an institution, made, contained, and set within his magisterial red world. To write in the spirit of friskiness, pensive loose ends, and rumination from a blue studio changes the direction of those female depictions to activated women, produced in and by, but also producing art.

Arcade 1. "Since 1953, Atlantic tropical storms have been named from lists originated by the National Hurricane Center. . . . The lists featured only women's names until 1979 when the World Meteorological Organization was persuaded to use male names and to name the storms in an alternating 'girl-boy-girl-boy' pattern" (Pamphlet, AMICA Insurance). Do you find this as amusing as I did? Amusing—and riling. That neutral "was persuaded" loses our political agency. The syntax allows turgid, lumbering institutions to re-figure themselves as originators of a helpful clarification by virtue of their benevolence. Official History: there it is. Another narrative?—Surly, intransigent, annoying questions, loud voices, and ironic contempt ("I mean they even name STORMS only after WOMEN"), anger about the deep cellular saturation of ideology in every detail ("storms after women—so destructive, so femme fatale-ish, like Men are never destructive!")—the whole raucous assemblage of rage, flair, critique, shoving, pushing, and analysis that was The Women's Movement did change culture. And still has the capacity fundamentally to call social and cultural arrangements into question. Here, Culture, in the form of the WMO, opens its wide gullet and swallows the critique whole. What critique? it says, licking its chops. Now think of the university. Feminist thinking has changed the grounds of fields, analyses, subjectivity, laws, customs. But will we be acknowledged? thanked? Not regularly. Are these gains permanent? Many, yes. These acts of erasure also make a backhanded (if problematic) tribute.

Arcade 2. In 1971 it washed over me (such was the force of One of the Great Books of the early cultural-social feminist movement—Kate Millett's *Sexual Politics*) that all of culture from the very beginning would have to be re-seen with feminist eyes. Everything would have to be remade—all cultural products, all fields—name them! In a minisecond, far beyond drowning in the enormous sea of this, I lifted up as on a gigantic blue-green-gray wave. Riding the "second wave"? A long march through texts and institutions is more like it. Everything! Remade! Ever since, I have been doing what I could. It's not euphoria or fashionableness. It's more like Conviction.

If "language is possible only because each speaker
sets himself up as a
subject
by referring to himself as *I*
in his discourse" (Benveniste 1966, 225),
one might be bemused
by all that "he" "his" and "himself," or, perhaps,
not
(it's not emphasized, not in italics).
Saying "language is possible only because each speaker

sets *herself* up as a subject, referring to *herself*
as *I* in *her* discourse" is not wrong
but it's not the form that *our* Generalizations
generally take.
Hence
it sounds more particular, less authoritative, less applicable to All.
Who are *we*? Are women completely human yet?
O there is a third (remember *The Waste Land*?)
travelling ahead of us or beside us (fascinating, Eliot's ambiguity)
looks like (Antarctic hallucination? ghost from the deep reaches
of ideology?) looks like
it's gender!

Arcade 3. Let's say a word about "woman" as a work site constructed and reconstructed in the crosswinds of political and ideological storms. The site *woman* has had a historically and temporally variable content and has pointed to a variety of meanings necessary at various times to embrace and deplore, to worm out of and to process, to affirm and to deny, to feel as central to oneself, and to feel as unimportant. A long-standing dialectical debate between female sameness with and difference from males has created a rich, contentious terrain with practical, legal, and policy implications—and implications for artistic practice and reception. Faced with this insoluble debate, some writers might find the debate itself annoying, articulating a position curiously similar (in a different context) to that taken by high-minded, pioneering women of the 1950s—one's gender does not (i.e., should not) matter at all. Another parallel working space occurs in the negotiation of similarities and differences among women—inside the group called "woman." These differences could be class or ethnicity or sexuality or other social and geopolitical elements of subjectivity. Under the rubric of queerness people might take a pluralizing position—so many gender identities to combine and proffer in creative performance. Or one might use gender and gender ambiguities to probe the political-ethical norms and assumptions about the human/personhood, recognizability, the real (Butler 2004, 58). Further, gender is not the only element of being; identities are "contradictory, fluid, multiplex," worked and reworked in historical time (Friedman 1998, 10).

Arcade 4. What is feminism? To me it means struggles for gender justice in the context of social justice. We do not have gender justice consistently in the United States, nor do people have it consistently in the world at large (vast understatements), although some people, mainly in the global north, might do better than U.S. women in particular legal and social rights (around child care, for example; around mandated gender balance in candidates for the legislature in various countries; around equal rights for sexual minorities). One needs gender justice in the context of social justice, so women do not benefit in their freedoms and rights from the exploitation of other people, male and female. Since in some places in the world, far from gender justice, the systems of gender and sexual enforcement, and multiple exploitations are intense, "feminism" is a viable position to claim. At least until another comes along that can offer solutions, analyses, precisions, and hopes for gender justice in the context of social justice.

Arcade 5. What has happened throughout modernity is that women are becoming not only coequal to but coeval with men. We can inhabit the same time, can define that time with our acts, agency, struggles, errors, leaps. Women want to be taken seriously, as humans, in all realms, to exist with rights, privileges, appropriate protections in those realms. Yet as Virginia Woolf said in *A Room of One's Own,* certain material and ideological distinctions (overcompensations and inequalities) between men and women are constructed and perpetuated in our societies. It is the task of feminist politics to resist these, to try to dismantle them, and it is the task of feminist-inspired gender critique in the cultural field to understand the impact of these material differences and inequalities on the production, dissemination, reception, and continuance of artists and their texts.

Arcade 6. Writing is not a gender-neutral site. To call for, to notice, to gloss, to comment on the productive presence of women artists and writers in this era and the eras long past is to be indebted to feminist cultural criticism and related modes of cultural poetics. To call for, to notice, to gloss, to comment on the productive, generative presence of gender ideas of all sorts—from the destructive and the lurid to the utopian—in male and female writers is to be indebted to feminist cultural criticism and related modes of cultural poetics. I could go on. But I would like simply and openly to declare our *collective* debt to feminism, no matter that some people might reject, balk, wonder, resist, demur, take themselves away or out of that, see it as a trap. Feminism, gender curiosity, and related investigations of social location have changed the terrain of the possible.

Once this general intellectual debt is fully acknowledged, I don't personally care who calls themselves/herselves/himselves "a feminist." I am agnostic whether another *individual* must accept that term. Agnostic, as in the dictionary—absolute truths are unattainable; one may know phenomena but not ultimates. Agnostic—more idiomatically, an intellectual position is not a church, a God, nor a creed demanding belief but rather a way of thinking through materials. Nonetheless, to live in modernity is to move collectively toward being gender-coequal and coeval. This is the inexorable direction, and it means the implicit or explicit investigation of gender; it means gender struggles, even discontinuous ones. Thus people will eventually engage—will be confronted with, indeed, have already confronted—the necessity of feminist investigations and critique.[2]

A refusal of feminist thought, to be most effective, should not be simply reactive, "against" something. Reactive, as: "I reject the term because the (now) powerful and annoying women of the generation before me embraced it, and I need to distinguish myself from them." Or: "The positions taken by feminism are outdated; we don't need them any more." Or: "They oversimplified somewhat; therefore I reject all of it." Or: "We need to get on to other issues." Debating with feminism, or going beyond it, should be creative, coming from another liberatory and oppositional space. But in my view such a position must have a dialectical relationship with feminism—precisely sublating and transcending it. Indeed, this is not refusal or a simple negative but dialectical negativity.

Arcade 7. You began your letter with a comment on production: a woman poet "producing" her own biography, rubrics, archive.[3] Simultaneously commenting on the reception of women, you use the shorthand phrase "canonized or forgotten" (Cole 2002, 33). Some of your remarks suggest there might actually be conflict and contradiction between cultural production and reception. The person saying "I am not a feminist poet" might nonetheless be struck that her (more rarely, his) reception is occurring because of feminist criticism. Indeed, because feminist critics have engaged a good deal with women writers' reception, if a woman is a writer, a poet, she might find it currently strategic to be friendly enough to feminist criticism. This certainly does not make that person a "feminist poet." Although these terms loop together, I'm going to separate "feminist production"—or more colloquially "I am/am not a feminist poet" from "feminist reception."

Arcade 8. Women have had a lot of different ideologies to help them take voice and vocation as writers and certainly a passel of ideologies and practices impeding that claim to voice and vocation. Writers might gain power for themselves or possibly cultural power by separating from the "group" Woman and/or from any "label" attachable to that group, from "feminine" to "feminist." This might be seen (judgmentally) as a form of denial or, more neutrally, as a circumstantial strategy. A person might find connection, inspiration, and intellectual bite in small groups of artistic women but not with Women or feminism in general. However, also strategically, a person—writer or critic—might not want to affiliate with all the positions ever taken under the rubric *feminism*. Of course! The whole point is disaggregating the blanket term, making it precise and situational. This seems obvious but worth repeating. *Feminism* is a capacious, historically mobile term filled with its own intellectual and political debates, filled with the tugs and pulls of other social-subject locations (class, for example, as well as sexualities, ethnicities, racial ideologies, religious cultures, national interests). Various manifestations (of the concept "feminism") have features that would be plausible, necessary, even crucial to criticize, in general or by other feminists. Indeed, any political position could be subject to criticism. So the questions: what feminism, where, facing what, defined by what, responsive to what, blind to what, hostile to what, benefiting whom, used by whom. That is—the questions must be the usual, normal, always new analytic questions.

If a person queries the term *feminist* applied to that person's apparently feminist positions, s/he is perhaps concerned that such a rubric brings in its wake lockstep allegiances and inflexible—as well as unsubtle—analyses. This may be true of any political or politicized position. Surely one cannot use feminism as a convenient "whipping girl" for all that! The hidden agenda may be rejection of, or claim of superiority to, "the political."[4] Hence the following rule: never let theory eviscerate matter. To claim unmarked or universal "identity," to claim that superior people don't bother with these mired and specific social locations but rather transcend them, to claim, in our field, that the aesthetic is a neutral site of excellence, to assert you have (immature) prejudices, biases, localisms, parti pris, but I speak from an untainted (mature) overview, are all policing strategies favoring hegemony and its interests.

Why should feminism be reduced to its own sentimentalities? Did it not have more to offer even to those who are invested enough in its meanings to attack it?

We said
feminist

Arcade 9. Whether any of the notably serious, committed, and inquisitive practitioners from your generation cited in this arcade would claim an explicit "feminism," all are working in the "blue studio" of gender horizons, making an oppositional helix of social and aesthetic concerns. Rachel Levitsky published this enabling statement for her chapbook series: "Belladonna is a reading series at Bluestockings Women's Bookstore that promotes the work of women writers who are adventurous, experimental, politically involved, multi-form, multi-cultural, multi-gendered, impossible to define, delicious to talk about, unpredictable, dangerous with language" (Levitsky 2000, n.p.). The desire for "polygynous poetry" ("married" to many women) continues; all those *multis* make this a very attractive statement. But it's more the notion of poetry as engaged with thought and language, with politics and poetics at the same time, that attracts me. Because Levitsky writes in the form of a list, the exact relationship of these elements to each other need not be elaborated. That's lucky, for it allows for a generative fluidity of potential linkages.

A rumination from 2002 by Juliana Spahr reenacts the inception of *Chain*, founded by Spahr and Jena Osman in 1994. Their goal was changing cultural competitiveness into a chain of challenges within a community, resisting what seemed unselfconsciously male-affirmative heroic ideals yet building female authority, and challenging unexamined assumptions about radical poetics in order to build a "new, wider heritage" for reading (Spahr 2002).[5] In the course of the Steinian rumination, Spahr notes that gender perennially becomes women's problem because males are not marked as such. "They [fellow students] talked not reflectively about male poets as MALE poets, but just compulsively about male poets as if they were not even noticing that they just talked about male poets." *Chain* does not publish women exclusively, but its first issue featured an eclectic forum by a variety of women editors, responding to queries *whether* and *how* their editorial practices were gender-/woman-related. This self-consciousness and self-scrutiny had interesting consequences. Once you declare curiosity about women, you are never, apparently, released from the charge of the narrow. By calling attention to certain issues, you became bizarrely taxed with these issues and only these issues. To translate: women are women's problems. Men's attitudes about gender materials are women's problems. Women are the repository of everyone's "gender problems," and they are the synecdochic marker for such problems. Men, apparently, do not have gender problems; they are neither responsible for such problems, nor do they have any agency in facing them. Are you calling general cultural attention to gender problems? Expect to be called "prejudiced" or "partisan."

Yedda Morrison and David Buuck's statement in *Tripwire* 3 (1999) reads as follows:

> The following pages contain a selection of writers and artists actively grappling with the complexities of gender as it pertains to daily life and social practice. Various tendencies seem to color these works: the continued influence of feminist theoreticians on current aesthetic,

> formal, and political practice; a recognition and inclusion of daily (domestic) life in both content and form; the desire for a simultaneous celebration and eradication of the traditions of one's gender; a deconstruction of male-female binarisms, towards a critique of gender itself as a rigid and socially dictated location which limits and delineates its citizens; and the recognition that any move beyond the confines of gender-based identity and sex-based roles cannot manifest itself by mere proclamation or aesthetic liberty, but must navigate the deeply embedded material and historical relations of patriarchy. (Morrison and Buuck 1999, 1)

This statement shows the conscious interplay between ideological and material understanding, between the end of gender and its continuing presence, between existing feminist thought and assessment of that thought in practice, between queer thinking and gender inscriptions. It is a notably dialectic statement.

When I read these and other manifestations of gender-inflected, oppositional thinking, I am not depressed (not blue that way), for it appears as if the cultural struggles in which gender debates play a central role do continue. The major reconsiderations of gender arrangements, and their implications for thought, daily life, politics, and art seem notably, even thrillingly, alert in these statements.

Arcade 10. To say "I am not a feminist poet" claims individualistic/individualized performance, beyond "group." One sees the temptation—to be taken as a pure individual without allegiances (as if poetry were not a social world?). "I'm not a feminist poet; I'm just a poet." Or perhaps—"I'm not a woman poet; I'm just a poet." These remarks, however apparently resistant, are working exactly in the cultural terrain opened by gender-inflected thought—that is, by feminism. Some cultural ironies result. Poets who insisted fervently that they were just poets, not women, have benefited from the existence of a feminist criticism born out of the women's movement; have had their work valorized as part of the group "women" even if they just wanted, desperately and even damagingly, to be poets, just ungendered poets. Other poets, who declared fast that they were feminists, experimenting with poetry and politics, have their solid, principled positions, their solid poetry found an annoyance, inadequate. Yet gender analysis surely must not mean that female authorship becomes a tight, airless, ideologically snug box where only certain allegories for authorship are approved.[6]

How about a female person's saying, "I am a human being, not a 'woman' "? Right, mate. There have been any number of feminist critiques of Woman as a concept, feeling it so riddled with bad ideology as to render it useless, even suggesting that we need another politically declarative name for that female person. The rejection of "woman" is a time-honored position within feminism, not outside it. The person saying "I am a person, not a woman" has perceived, even dimly and reluctantly, some economic, social, political tax and hampering attached to the enactments and meanings of "Woman"—and would love to declare herself exempt. Such a person is struggling within feminism, not against it. Try Denise Riley with her situational strategies of mobility, foxiness: "So feminism must be agile enough to say, 'Now we will be "women"—but now we will be persons, not these "women"' " (Riley 1988, 113). It is right to want to be human; we should underline that *feminism* is not the political force preventing women from being taken as fully human in the eyes of the world.

There have been reactions going in the other direction—the implicit—I am a woman not just a human being/man—because women are better, sweeter, nicer, kinder, more fluid, less linear, more accepting, etc. (This is a "girl scout" position, so to speak; here there is a gap to notice between ideology and practice.) Any idealization of one's group is an inspiring cultural myth for production—but not an inspired one for reception. Women are certainly very nice, and I for one like us very, very much, but this is not a tenable position, precisely because women are more or less human and subject to the vices as well as virtues of that fact. Any New Woman is a touching, rousing utopian concept; however, it is most practically useful when accompanied by enacted New Men, many other New Women, and a New Gender Politics.

Feminism began, and usually begins again, precisely with personhood in mind—the refusal of the ideological burdens of being lumped with all those droopy "women," a person's sense of specialness, the horror—and shame, too—of being so mired, the very definition of "woman" as "mire." Look at the ambivalences of Simone de Beauvoir. But this painful disidentification may turn to find what gets analytically dumped on women—and may become angry in the name of some women, or even all (perhaps that was overidentification, but it was functional and inspiring). Then there is the facing of the material conditions of everyone; why are only women considered "the body"? And finally there is female pride—women are not droopy at all, one might suddenly say. So optimistically, I see moments of painful, self-conscious disidentification of the kind that you have observed ("I am not a woman like those other women") ("I am not a feminist, but") as the seedbed for new efflorescence of gender-progressive thought.

Who wants to be a woman, who thinks she is a woman, a woman only, a woman all the time, a woman in every fiber? If I am going to hallucinate "gender" in my cold trek through culture, let me at least have freedom of visualization. Who is the third, fourth, fifth, and sixth who walks there beside you? Who doesn't now want female masculinity, males' girlishness, feminine and effeminate texts and acts by males as well as females, androgyny (hey there—lookin' *good,* again); poets embodying "malehood"; queer performativity; butch straight girls; male lesbians; matrisexual people; cross-gender folks; persons-gender-unimportant? Who doesn't want an array of subjectivities in their studios, all engaging in what they imagine is "*self*-fashioning"? How, under these plural conditions of social subjectivity, could we not want "women-as-just-persons" among them? Are these possibilities not, generally, a result of feminism? Taken, that is, as "a set of positions, not an essence; a critical practice not a doxa; a dynamic and self-critical response and intervention, not a platform"? (Pollock 1993, 100).

Arcade 11. Any woman is self-different, split and fractured, with a set of memories, ideas, histories, and self-debates. Susan Stanford Friedman has noted that feminist histories can only exist "in the plural," in "many localized narratives," not as one totalized narrative (Friedman 1998, 226). Feminism is not one thing; it is filled with contestation, not only among women but even inside individuals. This self-difference and historical situatedness emerge, for one example, from a textual and bibliographic examination of Adrienne Rich's galvanic "When We Dead Awaken: Writing as Re-Vision." Rich provided a manifesto for and a benchmark of the intense debate with cultural traditions and ideologies in which women writers have long been engaged. The inflected term *re-vision* meant rewriting, revising, recasting, demystifying certain (destructive) stories and ideas about women. Culture seemed rife with inadequate "stories" constructing female experience (the word *story* meant both "narrative" and "ideology"), which women writers were empowered to seize, rip up, critique, and transform in re-visionary poetries of dissent and re-creation. So re-vision involved rereading women's "experiences" and reframing these in representations, and as well interpreting the cultural mythologies in which female figures were actors or were acted upon.

This essay was itself revised, published at two different dates with quite different endings. The original ending (written in 1971) spoke positively about the births of new consciousness in women and men but also acknowledged what is "negative, regressive, Sisyphean" about women (Rich 1975a, 98). This version goes on eagerly to query the "future of masculine consciousness," suggesting that both genders will have to struggle against the damage inflicted by male power and patriarchy. The second version of this ending (written in 1976) has removed the curiosity about male consciousness changing and removed the criticism of women (Rich 1979). The essay insists on a "new space" (Mary Daly's phrase) into which women move, something right on the boundary of patriarchy, as if patriarchy were not internalized in ideology. Women-to-women relations are vital, and women as agents will bring patriarchy down. In the version written in 1971 (1975a), men and women were austerely curious about each other; in the version written in 1976 (Rich 1979), cross-gender contact and mutual interest are deemed unlikely, by virtue of the "fatalistic pessimism" of males combined with the "phallocratic sadism" of certain of their representative art products (Rich 1979, 49).[7]

For Rosi Braidotti, "The question for the feminist subject is how to intervene upon Woman in this historical context, so as to create new conditions for the becoming-subject of women here and now" (Braidotti 1994, 168).[8] This is not such an easy process, to intervene between the icon Woman and one's actual self. In an interview with Ed Foster, Anne Waldman precisely illustrates the messiness of strategic shifts around gender position, including evidence of self-division (and revision). Within the space of a half page she says the following things—taking up different emphases and different temporalities within the "feminist poet"/"woman poet"/"not" set of variables (Waldman 1994–95, 76; cf. Waldman 2001, 226). First, she notes "the information I'm providing in this roundtable discussion is not bound by gender." That is, she wants to be listened to. She has some sense that sometimes men, sometimes all people, don't listen to women, perhaps especially when they speak about gender as a topic. In this caveat Waldman indeed acknowledges the force of assumptions about gender power and authority.

Then Waldman tells an origin fable about Osman's and Spahr's journal *Chain,* whose first issue had just been published: "Well, this is a group of very strong [2001 substitutes: *diligent*] women who feel that there are stories [2001 adds: *and descriptions of poetics*] that need to be told and possibly wouldn't get told unless there was a specific forum [2001 adds: *for*] foregrounding women and their [2001 adds: *creative*] experience." A good deal of that is exactly and precisely what another person would have said about twenty years earlier about *Chrysalis* or *Calyx* or *Heresies,* notable, pioneering absolutely feminist magazines, often, though not always, with a "women's culture" position. That is, they thought there were "stories" untold that needed articulation. Even the term *stories* is parallel. But there are at least two strong demurrals needed here, aside from the fact that the telling of particular stories was not *Chain*'s goal but rather the establishing of a culturally active collectivity. First, "experience" is never recorded in writing—it's constructed (selected, rendered, transposed, invented, extended, appropriated) by writing. Does using the word *women* make us forget this basic fact? Is the word *woman* a synonym for "naive theories of representation"? The second demurral is that only issue number 1 of *Chain* was focused on woman; at the inception of their journal the editors simply investigated how other women had deployed their editorial authority.[9] And by publishing "chains" of writing by women, they were self-consciously textually and visually manifesting their interests in networks and dialogues in the process of creating work, jump-starting community.

Third, Waldman acknowledges *Chain*'s difference from earlier journals in a backhanded compliment: "If it were just a magazine of women writing about being women, it would be like other soapbox feminist magazines and, by definition, limited. They're trying to do something else." This remark rejects "women's poetry movement" work in poetry while paradoxically using the "untold stories" argument that was perfected by those interested in feminist cultural critique. *Soapbox* is a curious word for Waldman to have used, since she accepts and champions an energetic politicized chant-rant poetry; indeed, she herself has produced enormous jeremiads—even sometimes on gender—and "soapbox" declamatory poems. So is it simply that declamation on any topic except gender is acceptable?

Fourth, Waldman says: "Poetry doesn't have a gender, but I think you naturally write out of your gender at times. It's one of the energy sources." Naturally, indeed. What could "natural" now mean in this problematized setting of conflicting analyses, and does one write out of gender only "naturally" and not politically, socially, by cultural choice? Her closing remark, "I think bisexuality is the [2001 substitutes: *everyone's*] actual mental condition," is a fine version of the "androgynous thought" that made Woolf's *A Room of One's Own* so inspiring in the early moments of second-wave feminism; another remark insists that poetry is "transformative, transgendered" (Waldman 1994–95, 78, 76; Waldman 2001, 228, 226). A woman can certainly be a site for conflictual versions of being a woman.

Arcade 12. But oh, to be judged and appreciated as a person, not a woman, with all the assumptions that might entail. Wouldn't that be lovely? Maybe. Since men and women have different social and cultural positions, whose viewpoints will we be using when we discuss the female of the species as persons?[10] What is "universal" in this instance? Whose criteria? Who controls them? (This is a statement from "difference" feminism.) To want simple equality! To want simply to be judged as a person! Wasn't that all Mary Wollstonecraft asked for, too? Well, nothing comes only from yearning; gain involves cultural and political alertness and struggle.

Plus, there will always be a woman writing poetry who may right this minute be wishing there were *no such thing* as gender. No such thing as gender. Seems unrealistic, but who can blame her? (Could there be a male poet so passionate on this topic? What man has recently said—let's do away with gender? There definitely are some, but it is not a large, urgent movement. Think of how these investments differ.) Besides—it's not doing away with gender, whatever that means, but not having gender be figured as unequal social power in every sphere—economic, political, cultural, geopolitical—and on every scale from small to large. That would be a change, a bit of blue.

Arcade 13. You ask, at the end of your piece, "what now?" and one answer lies in reception: gender studies, more-more-more. Studies of women writers who have no feminist affiliation, and who have no overt thematic "female" evidence in their texts, looking for the traces and fissures of the female literary career as "the career of that struggle." Gender studies of male figures, masculinity, male privilege, the varieties of male formation as marked by locations of various kinds, including gender. Historicizing forms of manhood, ideologies of masculinity.[11] No longer should "men" function as the unchanging flat backboard against which feminist balls get lobbed. And gender studies of the networks of writing persons, with gender issues and others foregrounded—how do men and women, people of different sexualities, people from different backgrounds, from different environments interact to create their artistic production and reception? This work on cohorts is "feminist" in its sources and implications; it is politically and intellectually crucial work. As Myra Jehlen has remarked: "In proposing gender as a basic problem and an essential category in cultural and historical analysis, feminists have recast the issue of women's relative identity as equally an issue for men, who, upon ceasing to be mankind, become, precisely, men. Thus gender has emerged as a problem that is always implicit in any work" (Jehlen 1990, 265).

Another answer is to try to entangle social locations, to track the interface among the subjectivities one embodies, in all its modes. Susan Stanford Friedman has proposed that "feminism has moved to a concern with location—the geopolitics of identity within differing communal spaces of being and becoming" (Friedman 1998, 3). To accomplish this for literary products, to look at how gender links to a regional upbringing, a religious culture, a class position in an author is useful; it is most useful when those insights about ideological position are made in order to help probe the aesthetic nature of the artwork (formal, structural, textual, generic, narrative choices, and poetic segmentivities), as well as the social reasons for its themes, motifs, power. And one can try to analyze the gender conflicts in individual writers, the motives and outcomes for the self-differences one feels around gender.

Arcade 14. In the cultural sphere, to say, right now, "I am not a feminist poet" can mean (and imply) various things. It might be a protest about mainstream poetic style. It might resist feminism as a movement; it might resist the presentation of any political ideas directly in poetry. (How many times can I cite Adorno! In the context of a subtle argument about how the social appears in form, how form is a "magnet" for the empirical world including its contradictions, he says simply: "Among the mediations of art and society, the open or covert treatment of social matters, is the most superficial and deceptive" [Adorno 1997, 226, 229].) Yet work in poetry has been done by people who might well accede to feminism as a political and social demand for gender justice but who might *not* particularly engage with the "women's poetry movement," as Alicia Ostriker names it in *Stealing the Language* (Ostriker 1986, 13).[12] One might like the social, political, and economic benefits of feminist struggles and not like every single poem in *Rising Tides* or *No More Masks!*, poems that have been editorially *chosen* (not necessarily *written*) to show a feminism of production around themes, subjectivities, conclusions.

In the pedagogy of contemporary poetry, people may use movements or connections in poetics, groupings, manifestoes through which to read texts. This may be a simple tool (where should we put certain people—New York School? Beat poetries? Language poetries?), but it is educationally appropriate to show poets' working assumptions, and the various senses of poetry, a poem, a poet, a poetics that emerge. Of course, organizing reception by relation to some grouping is quite hard on outrider poets. What then to do with women poets when only some of the poets of this era found a home in "the women's poetry movement." Adrienne Rich, Audré Lorde, feminists certainly, but what of other people whose work this course should read: Sylvia Plath? Lyn Hejinian? Kathleen Fraser? Leslie Scalapino? Should they be inside nongendered (gender "neutral") categories like Language poetry—if they fit? And if not? And if their work, their careers are precisely not gender neutral? Should "feminist poet" be limited to people explicit about their connection with the women's movement? And what is the possible content of a category like "feminist poet" (some thematic or formal positions? some ideology?) or "woman poet" (physical gender?)? What does one do with the modern and contemporary burst of formally innovative women writers?

This is the pertinence of your set of questions, especially pertinent if one did not want "woman poet" to be represented only by a body of work that changed thematic content in challenging ways but did not change the form, tone, or diction of poetries. Hence: is *feminist* poet the best rubric for the work of various women? Perhaps the person you quoted who declined that category is right.

What, at any rate, could that rubric mean? Is there a well-understood entity denominated "feminist poet"? Brainstorming this possibility gets us a list of possible definitions, some quite contradictory:

- Feminist poet = one who talks a lot about gender and sexuality in her/his work. No, wait—that would be lots of poets—Olson, Williams. So try—a poet who marks the constructedness of gender and sexuality in her/his work, takes gender as an ideology about maleness and femaleness and wants to investigate, to critique, not simply to benefit.
- Feminist poet = woman poet, assuming that to be female is to be automatically feminist. What feminist where and when would of course still be a question.
- Feminist poet = [woman] poet who has certain themes in her work, themes (tautologically?) agreed upon as feminist. These themes—Alicia Ostriker names a number: self-division, anger, investigation of myth, assertion of the female body—are very palpable, valuable ways of organizing poetic texts but have the flaws of their virtues: of being reductive or focusing on only one dimension of the poem.
- Feminist poet = [woman] poet who writes poems about the liberation of women. Is Mina Loy then a feminist poet?
- Feminist poet = [woman] poet who resists stereotypes of women—in her life? in her work? both?
- Feminist poet = [woman] poet who resists stereotypes of women and men—again—where? life? work? Note how different these may be.
- Feminist poet = [woman] poet who comments on gender issues in her critical work, who thinks about gender in the cultural field.
- Feminist poet = [woman] poet who takes certain themes of "difference" involving women's experiences—menarche, menstruation, childbirth, kid life, sexisms experienced, rape, incest—as central subject matter (some of these topics are not exclusive to women).
- Feminist poet = [woman] poet who tells the truth about her experiences as a woman. And with that verbal emphasis on truth and the unmediated communication of experience, one also might want to investigate the word *tells* or representation. Further "experience" is not

some court of last resort, a primary essence—it itself needs to be analyzed as a made thing, a product of language, conventions, ideologies.

- Feminist poet = [woman] poet who used to be called a poetess.
- Feminist poet = [woman] poet in a certain anthology (like *No More Masks!*). (What then does one do with writers cut from the second edition of *No More Masks!* or with those never included?)
- Feminist poet = poet who destabilizes the normative terms of gender/sexuality and makes some kind of critique of those issues in her/his poems. This is closing in on the word *queer* as synonym for *feminist.*
- Feminist poet = [woman] poet who refuses (self-censors) certain themes or solutions, certain images or insights because they do not explore or lead, in her view, to the liberation of women.
- Feminist poet = [woman] poet who calls explicit attention to the relative powerlessness of women and the relative power of men—or who exaggerates this positionality into female powerlessness, male power in all cases.
- Feminist poet = [woman] poet historically coming to her production in some relation to the liberation of women, and to the cultural critique of female exclusions made by feminism in general.
- Feminist poet = [woman] poet writing something "politically involved . . . multi-gendered, . . . delicious to talk about, unpredictable" (the *Belladonna* formulation by Rachel Levitsky).
- Feminist poet = [woman] poet affronting the complexities of sexuality, eroticism, desire, odi et amo, frank and startling, decorum breaking (like Dodie Bellamy or Leslie Scalapino).
- Feminist poet = [woman] poet who investigates language, narrative, genre, and representation in its ways of constructing gender and gender roles. This is Kathleen Fraser's argument: "I recognized a structural order of fragmentation and linguistic resistance" that was antipatriarchal; she argues the crucial intervention of formally innovative and investigative poetry into a feminist field (Fraser 2000, 32).
- Feminist poet = a person who is a feminist, and who also writes poetry, any kind of poetry.
- Feminist poet = angry woman, writing poetry.
- Feminist poet = [woman] poet who is "disobedient" (Alice Notley's term for herself); transgressive (like Carla Harryman); "resistant" (my term about myself); imbuing knowing with its investigative situatedness (like Lyn Hejinian's "La Faustienne") in full knowledge of gender normativities (Notley 2001; Harryman 1995; Hejinian 2000).
- Feminist poet = poet making antipatriarchal analyses of culture

when much of culture is patriarchal; that is, a poet throwing herself/himself into the abyss.

- Feminist poet = a poet who knows what she thinks about gender ideas and arrangements in a culture and does not particularly change her mind.
- Feminist poet = a poet who sometimes shows herself/himself to be ironic and skeptical about gender and sexual arrangements, but other times is not, or not overtly.
- Feminist poet = a woman protesting the place of woman in culture and society (in her poetry? not in her poetry? I didn't say).
- Feminist poet = one who finds herself and himself "mounting an enormous struggle" within culture, including poetry, because of its deeply constitutive gender ideas.
- Feminist poet = male feminist who tries to do gender provocation better than all those women.
- Feminist poet = woman poet whose work is selectively seen, certain materials heavily valorized because of the existence of feminist criticism and its paradigms. This is like selecting the poems by Countee Cullen that comment on blackness as the ones most interesting to read now. Note that there is nothing intrinsic about the category—it depends on critical and readerly reception.
- Feminist poet = woman poet consumed (studied, read, appreciated) under the regime of or in the economy of feminist perspectives, whether or not she is a feminist.

From that contradictory, jubilant, and annoying list there's sure a lot to choose (and you might want to suggest still more options). Feminism in poetry is absolutely not one position. Indeed, one might say that feminism will circulate among, or manifest itself as, a number of somewhat alternative positions. Further—remember—these might be inflected with: Difference (women are really different from men; have their own life-themes) (Some women are really different from each other). Androgyny/mental bisexuality (best person is fused genders in some way). Rights/sameness (equality of access, of laws, of treatment, generally). Transcendence (have gender but transcend it—it does not play in the realm where writing is made). Queering (breaking the binarist gender norm; resisting any social and aesthetic forms that depend on binarist hierarchies). More than all this, we have uncovered a large area of terminological ambiguity that has to be raised but might be impossible to resolve.

Arcade 15. A lot of the above list is implicitly about production. That is—

to define feminism in poetry, many people have settled on a feminism of production: having the poem "come forth" as a "statement" that shows certain "ideas" or "themes" or "identities" or "images." But all of this is why I do not want a "feminism of production" to be taken as the central cultural act performed by feminists and their intellectual kin. Instead, I want to say a very positive word for the feminism of reception. What does this mean? To maintain feminist (that is, gender-alert) *reception* is crucial, not to insist that certain forms, styles, strategies, subjectivities, themes are more female, feminine, male, masculine, gay, straight, queer on the level of *production.* The feminism of *reception* means a high level of analysis making legible gender materials and the materials of other social matrices, and showing a subtle alertness to the play of gender (and other social mechanisms) and its deep structures, in culture, everywhere. Gender-alert, materialist-inflected *reception* is interested in the discussion of social location not only of artists but of genres, discourses, images, textualities, ideologies, communities, and of critics. Feminist reception demands that everything that has been written needs ample, multiple modes of gender analysis. And feminist reception can solve the problem of grouping women poets together for whatever reasons—for this is an act of reception.

Arcade 16. Feminist cultural poetics has, to date, primarily engaged itself with *female* subjectivity and *female* agency, but with the tools developed from this phase of feminist thinking, one can begin to talk about male subjectivities and agency. Thinking about gendered subjectivities, performative genderings, styles of femaleness or maleness, sexualities as represented in artworks, thinking about ideological attitudes to gender of any individual author are all modal moves within the feminism of reception.[13]

One little attitudinal (and therefore methodological) practice that one might learn from the practice of feminist criticism—whether or not one likes, admires, cathects to, or loves any individual woman writer—is the necessity to offer at least as much empathetic understanding to the products of women as to those of men. This is linked to the historical responsibility to examine what women did and are doing and why: motives, constraints, their own reigning ideologies as they entered the world to speak. These reigning ideologies need not be attractive; they can involve self-disparaging *moues,* resistance to other women, contempt for the female, brilliant rage, saccharine charm, performative minority, and so on. This insistence on being willing critically to examine female work comes from my historical experience of the notable erasure, disparaging, and undervaluing of women's cultural products and testaments. This point must not be misunderstood as being uncritical of or sentimental about women. No more empathetic understanding than one offers the work of men—just approximately the "same" calibration, interest, and allowances. This statement comes from a feminism of "equality/sameness," not one of "difference." At the same time, because the literary products and careers of women have been generally a bit rarer than those of men, and because sometimes misogynist punditry has been exercised on them, one might offer a tiny dollop of identification, walking some paces into an extra mile. This statement comes from a feminism of "difference," not one of "equality/sameness." Watch out—I just somewhat contradicted myself. Look at that oscillation, the dialogic shimmer, the wobbling, the wavering, the fluidity, the tacking between semicontradictory positions! Having A and not-A coexist—both/and thinking (as I said in "For the Etruscans"). Or speaking, as Anne Waldman does in *Iovis* I, of "both/both," deconstructing even the tinge of unevenness in the phrase "both/and" (Waldman 1993, 1, 3). There's the blue studio of my feminism. It is "negativity"—oppositional and intricately modifying at once.

Arcade 17. Since "feminism" changed the cultural landscape, willy-nilly, there are plenty of female poets associated with the avant-garde who are indifferent to "feminism" and disinterested in "women" per se, but who can be considered, as you obliquely suggest, a nexus, not a feminist but a female nexus.[14] This framing from *The Objectivist Nexus* offers many advantages, although the terminological solution is not perfect. "Thinking about writers in a nexus allows one to appreciate difference and disparity among them, to pinpoint perhaps radical disagreements, to attend to rupture as well as continuity. The term 'nexus' is useful because it describes a relationship among writers based on their shared meditations, but not necessarily shared conclusions or even practices, about the particulars of their writing life and their historical positions" (DuPlessis and Quartermain 1999, 22). The participants in a nexus didn't have to agree; they didn't have to like each other or be a school or sign a manifesto—but they had to be engaged with each others' work or engaged with comparable issues for a central part of their writing life.[15] They can fiercely debate each others' gender investments—but nonetheless they choose precisely these issues to debate.

If there is a "Female Nexus," what is it? Of what does this Nexus consist? Of the "polygynous" (postpatriarchal?) innovative poetries within the years of, just after, and in some cases parallel to the women's poetry movement and the feminist political movement. Some female writers of this era had their work magnetized by the fact that certain rubrics ("feminism"/"the [political] women's movement") were set in motion, even if their work in poetry preceded it or paralleled it. This may be temporally peculiar, but their work got, innocently or decidedly, involved with certain historical responsibilities—in this case the pressure from feminist thought and action, even when they dissented, claimed to look away, said they were not affected, said they had begun before the women's movement and didn't care about it (and so on). Some of the most fruitful moments of women poets' exchanges on these issues came during the twenty-plus years from the 1980s to the present under the rubric of "innovative"—when at least multiple sets of women writers were engaged, at least sporadically, in utopian projects, in their own Blue Studios—to examine what the regime of gender-marking gave to culture and to see what the economy of gender-investments gave. A number of fruitful cross-fertilizations among women have emerged in the past three decades of experimental writing—everyone going into the Tunnel of Love and coming out with different people's lipstick smudged on them, and smudging in return. This has indeed been a very merry and lively moment. There have also been annoyance and ambivalence, rage and suspicion. Sometimes, forget lipstick, blood has been drawn. But being in a nexus does not demand assent (see Oppen vs. Zukofsky); it simply demands attentiveness, fixation, sureness that these poets must be read.

The Female Nexus came into being as a "nexus" in linkages among coterie formations—St. Mark's; early Language; *HOW(ever)*—but also in relation to the "women's poetry movement" and interventions in feminist theory, particularly from France. That is, there were propulsions from a materialist political/cultural movement called second-wave feminism, from the cultural artifact called theory, and from "the women's poetry movement" as spurs to the reception, if not the production of women's innovative poetries. This "nexus" thinking is of great significance to the consolidation of innovative women's writing as a practice. So instead of asking whether people are or are not "feminist poets," why not see their work as part of a "Female Nexus" and ask how, why, and when they could be interpreted under the general arc of feminist reception?

The writers in the "Female Nexus" kept reading each other, kept poking at each others' ideas, engaged, even if annoyed at the turn some took in relation to each other and in relation to the women's poetry movement. The other part of the constitution of a Female Nexus is the interests of certain critics, themselves brought up with gender analysis, to try to study the work of women poets. Their groupings of material help constitute, support, and reaffirm this Nexus all at once.[16]

Have we given this avant-garde nexus the appropriate name? Gender Nexus suggests (yet again!) that men have no gender. If the term Female

Nexus seems rather ghettoizing in an era when the on-off, one-two binarism of gender has come under increasing scrutiny, what other solutions are there? Feminist Nexus suggests the feminism of reception of course but, as I've already said, does not necessarily sum up particular authors' politics. This nexus emerges in a site triangulated by the terms *female, feminine* (defined as a space beyond patriarchy), and *feminist*, but "3F" Nexus is like code. The Antipatriarchal Nexus might work. Or Postpatriarchal. But are we?[17]

Arcade 18. A moment of silence. For the women who jumped from windows, away from the blue.

Arcade 19. If you are impatient with other women for having to go over that ground again and again ("the same old arguments simply recirculated/regenerated or, even worse, left to stagnate") and then, if you say that you didn't "fully understand [at one point in your own life] that my own thinking might be considered 'feminist,'" take a look at what you've said! (Cole 2002, 35, 36). These two statements construct a great generative contradiction (saying two opposite things, A and not-A), from which you might make a number of surmises and dialectical resolutions. One might be patience with the positions of others. Though I know it is hard to be that which is called, and calls itself, feminist. You can become a lightning rod for many a free-floating electric strike. But if you were once "not" (not quite) willing to say the word *feminist* about yourself, you might see others the same way. Perhaps they will become your allies in a little more time. And/or you might also allow that you could change.

Arcade 20. Can one be a political feminist—committed to gender justice, to resisting (as possible) hierarchies and inequalities based on gender, privileges, and constrictions in the social and economic realm *and* also be a cultural agnostic, demanding the interest of complexity? Can one admire certain poetic projects and works and resist, while discussing, their gender politics? Can one be rigorous and empathetic? Antisimplistic, but with clean lines? Can one illustrate opacity and confirm clarity at one and the same time? You'd better believe it.

Tell her "she"
Tell her "him"
Tell her "her"
Tell her "us"
tell her what
I can
Time for the wake-up call—

"Rise up paginal" says Anne Waldman (*Iovis* I, 187)
vaginal page, erect
page in service apprenticed to culture
to hope

in the Blue Studio

Begun April 21, 2001, completed May 21, 2001
Revised 2003 and 2004

II
Marble Paper

4
Manifests

O great classic cadences of English poetry
We blush to hear thee lie
Above thy deep and dreamless.
—Denise Riley, *Mop Mop Georgette*

Those tall white pasture clumps called cow parsnip, Queen Anne's lace magnified, are, in Latin, *umbellifers,* flat-topped or rounded flower clusters. But sometimes people call them "umbrella flowers." This work is closer to umbrella flowers than to umbellifers, down there on the ground with bricolaged theorizing practices, folk etymologies, and intransigent details. Those metaphors pay tribute to Good's sense of the essay as woodsy ramble (see Good 1988, xii and x).

And to the essay as personal—a way of marking and mocking the professional codes and impersonal solemnities of the representation of thought. If saying "I" like a heroine will adequately undermine unsituated false universals, I'll say "I" yes I will. "I" will report that in 1967 or so I could only write gnomic statements, absolute, but *culs de sac.* The kind of development they needed was not rhetorical but historical.

I, Lady, you are my true love's lady.
You stand in the middle of the room,
Sunlight streaming around you.
Sunlight takes hold of the seeds in you
And wets them.
I want to hold myself to you,
But you are myself. Can I?

This fragment issues directly from, and is a preternatural reminder of, a passionate problematic—questions of gender, in relation to an engagement with poetry, poetry figured as a set of psychosocial and intellectual conventions imbuing a practice of writing in lines. This fragment knew political and cultural contradiction about the construction of authorship and the poetic career before their maker could see them precisely as such. The fragment was a cognitive act, not just in autobiography. It probed a situation then almost invisible and always underacknowledged; to have understood it then, one would have needed the cultural apparatus invented (though not elaborated) by a social movement—second-wave feminism, an invention that had not yet occurred.

Despite mirroring each other with Lady as hinge ("I, Lady, you"), the female "I" is separated by the very concept "Lady" from her addressee, that traditional addressee of poems, the female "you." "Lady" is both hinge and barrier; she belongs to "my true love"—a charming and smug ballad turn. Yet the "I" wants to hold this "you" figure to herself, actualizing in female-to-female attraction the Petrarchan structure of feeling. Now that gesture could be interpreted as desire (in a lesbian, matrisexual, or "preoedipal" plot), or as self-aggrandizing egoism. Is the desired embrace regressive? immature? narcissistic? self-serving? greedy? masturbatory? (All these as bad attitudes with a bad press—one might now wonder.) Fueled by an ambisexual or polysexual suggestiveness, the poem makes a wobbly declaration of vocation in its desire to embrace woman herself, yourself, myself.

The fragment stops, startled, where the cultural problem begins. The "can I" is not simply a personal questioning of my own powers but queries contingencies of gender and female authorship. Am "I" forbidden to poetry by one—but one key—law of poetry—the cult of the idealized female? How to poke at a Petrarchanism that seems utterly belated, and not, after all, the whole content of poetry? Should "Lady" be ditched totally? or examined? both? For any number of writers do take "Lady" for granted. Many male writers get to say Lady early and often (as often as they'd like, or not); this thought of Lady mediates their access to themselves, to their imaginations, and helps create readable poems—in romantic works, in surrealist works, in modern works, etc. My relationship to poetic tradition is more wary and suspicious. I want, but can I? And if this is what poetry is, should I?

My desire to embrace the Lady parallels terms later elaborated in the 1970s for matrifocal, woman-woman relations, as if one could heal the wounds of the female cultural position by assertive female bonding of all kinds; to some degree this is true, and there is great justice in it (see Godard 1994). But Lady is two-faced—desire and blockage is that Lady. Can she withhold her blessing? Is she ambivalent to the female seeker? Am I withholding my own blessing on myself, and how did that get engineered? And how in the world did these characters get in my head, locked there, the way, as Dante says, a fossil is embedded in limestone? Are they only in poems? Are they in psychological structures? Are they formed in our relationship with language? For it has been forcefully suggested that access to language is gendered in particular ways that put all speakers in a feminized position in relation to a Logos (called, to complicate matters in an almost unseemly fashion, the Phallus). Does imagining a beneficent muse neutralize the feminized position of a man confronting Ultimate Logos? One can also be skeptical about universalized ideas of Logos and still discover (as Woolf argued in *A Room of One's Own*) that social institutions offer plenty of conditions that passively or actively discourage and destabilize the speech of female cultural actors—in production, reception, and sense of pertinence.[1]

1972. Dream, the Three Graces, perceived as alienated labor.

Muse figures, a subject position in ideology and biography, are often, but not exclusively, female—for they can be racialized figures or figures offering class narrative. Muses are vibrant, but mainly silent, or gnomic; unsophisticated yet unconsciously creative or ethical; desirable yet appropriated; givers but not owners. As a psychosocial institution supporting poetic production, muses clearly have a demanding role to fulfill inside poems and outside.[2] They are projected inventions of the imagination inside poems and have historical status as cultural tropes; they can involve actual historical persons attempting to fill these support roles. There is a two-way exchange between the projection and the actuality.[3] Are such characters perpetually unrolled cultural mummies on which male writers are only ironically dependent, as Wallace Stevens's poem "The Worms at Heaven's Gate" suggests? (Stevens 1957, 49–50). Is this figure obsolete, or is it still found in many contemporary poems? Are these female characters direct images of, or snailish residues of, social relations of gender? Are they reversed images of gender power? Do they have to do with maternal figures and the social practices of exclusively female child rearing (as Dorothy Dinnerstein might argue)? Are these invented characters—"ghosts of cultural metaphors of femininity" in Svetlana Boym's terms—fixed in their repeating narrative? (Boym 1991, 200). Will social change in gender relations alter these characters, or will social change make "them" (or the agents who continuously write them) more stubbornly attached to these stories as a refuge from the social demands of historical women? Is poetry, then, a gender-conservative institution? Will poems written in any changed relation to this figure look precisely raw, crude, tendentious, and culturally excrescent? If this Lady story had not been felt as hegemonic, would there be other more muted stories available through which "I" (the female poet) would more speedily pass to answer the question, "Can

I?" But aren't the old stories, the old images just more satisfying, more poetically mature, having stood the test of time? How can any writing woman invent her capacity for mastery—with or without the Lady?

What happens when you are an actual-historical woman, whom the poetic ideas of Woman have molded, entranced, partially colonized, partially rewarded, provoked, and annoyed. Lyric poetries certainly build on female inspiration, those invertebrate muses, love objects, wraithes, haunting figures with armes long and small. Armes of the woman I sing. Satiric poetries build on suspicious objects, the Juvenalian deceits celebrated in certain works of Swift, T. S. Eliot, and Coleridge. The muse/beloved or antimuse/cautioned and reviled is a central (though not exclusive) discourse of poetry and art-making based on the structures of difference organizing persons asymmetrically by gender. What happens when you are a female poet wandering in the museums of, the mausoleums of, poetry—given that the most poetical subject was said—albeit by Poe—to be the death of a beautiful woman (Poe [1846] 1984, 19). Do you turn away? Does turn away mean stop writing? or just become unreadable, become hysterical (I think of Marcia Nardi, that marvelous girl)? Is "hysterical" a powerful rhetoric and diction; can one live with the fact that in women writers that tumbling pulse is heavily unrewarded?[4] Is turning away an option if you are saturated with that residual feminine ideology and its privileges and charming escapes?[5] Do you confront—gender this and gender that—what a bore? Do you risk thereby being single-minded, not broad-minded? Do you try to write "otherhow"? Then how can you make products readable by cultured eyes when you want to leverage out of this long-standing proposition of culture, and maybe others, besides? How to read the products of critique or muted debate that do exist? How come poetry—which is just selected words arranged by segmentation on various scales—is so invested in female figures? And, not incidentally, shouldn't these oldest griefs of ours be bearing more fruit already? Or, as Rilke said, Nu?

Adorno has argued that lyric poetry refracts and sublates social materials, projecting utopian yearning and protesting an untransformed world (Adorno 1991). Gender is one of these social conditions, even in poetry (Homans 1985). Poetry as an institution constructs female figures crucial to poetry and offers interpretations of female/feminine, male/masculine. One might even argue that the female "ghosts" haunting poetry do powerful cultural work to block, screen, and obscure the social materiality of the genre; the female/feminine matter of [lyric] poetry, figured as the need for beauty and as ahistorical transcendence, helps readers to ignore the materiality of poetry as a practice, including the labor of females in support positions, both inside and outside the poem. At least the lyric/odic mode (I would add the satiric) has certainly been wedded (somewhat monotonously, or monogynously) to very few ideas about Woman, as it proceeds, in Susan Stewart's words, to distribute and administer pronouns and to help "determine the positions of subjects, the frames of desire, and the possibilities for recognition and apprehension of and by others" (Stewart 1993, 15).

When one holds anything like these views and tries to analyze poetry as a social practice impelled by gender ideologies (with codicils proposing that parallel materials about class narratives and race/ethnicity would be fruitful terrain to examine), it is interesting to observe the coagulation of psychoanalytic theory, religious thinking, and interested citation from ancient myth and the classics that get arrayed in opposition. Whether from dominant or alternative practices, these universalizing metanarratives reveal the deep sedimentations of gender conventions that form poetry both as an institution and as a praxis. Allen Grossman, an inspiring academic and theorist of poetics, and Charles Olson, a charismatic theorist of poetics and leader of men into poetry, did much thinking about gender in poetry, thinking whose emergent potential calcifies into familiar, even archetypal, binaries. Then there is something more: the "Ladies" themselves. Where is the manifesto of the muse? What does a woman say as she becomes iconic, her presence invisible? Is there evidence from any particular historical woman who became muse-ified? Where are her outbursts and her desires? Frances Boldereff's writings, given to Olson, offer a third set of materials in gender poetics to examine.

To scrutinize gender narratives underpinning and motivating poetry and its institutional culture, to read the subtextual circulation of social ideologies, I will apply Leo Spitzer's method of close reading, looking even at "futile" details of language, for these may reveal and exemplify the "interrelated and intertwined aspects of human affairs" (Spitzer 1948, 24). In his remarkable "Summa Lyrica" Allen Grossman announces the force of poetics as ideology, for he describes the purpose of this meditative and speculative work as "stating—aphoristically—some of the commonplaces by means of which poetry and poetic purposes are accounted for in the West . . . [offering] assertions which are possible to be made (and generally are made) in the presence of poems" (Grossman 1992, 207).

Allen Grossman's study of poetry works such double-edged, revealing "commonplaces" as the following:

1. "Unlike the father tongue which is primarily word, the mother tongue is the source of silence." (Grossman 1992, 362)

2. "The immortality of the father and the immortality of the mother are not the same immortality." (Grossman 1992, 363)
3. "Hence, we find the mother slain in the poetic; we see Orestean murder as the normal rite of passage into the cultural estate." (Grossman 1992, 357)
4. "The speaker in the [i.e., in any] poem is the man who has usurped the right of the first night in which he was conceived." (Grossman 1992, 278)

In citing even snippets of Allen Grossman's propositions in "Summa Lyrica" one is treading the vatic waters of an oedipal narrative, tempting, resonant, and powerfully interpretive, displacing other ways of reading the access to words and the vocation it discusses. One lives in these mottoes (selected from a brilliant array formulated, as if provisionally, as a notebook) within an electrifying gender binary. Two limit concepts, silence and immortality, divide the male from the female as if they were different species. Cora Kaplan has observed that silence is always social (Kaplan 1986, 79–80); we certainly know that immortality is. Grossman has two attitudes: he isolates his materials as ideological commonplaces of Western Cultural Understanding (for which he has been the medium), and he invests in them as oracular truths.

Grossman interprets the entrance into culture as the self-election of an individual hero undertaking sexual-linguistic quests. One is said to give up one's rights in a crucial woman, the mother, to gain, culturally speaking, rights in all women. Grossman accepts the second part but not the first; the fascination of his claim is his refusal to take up with acquiescent temper the son's position in the oedipal narrative; instead, he will enter the bed of the mother as if he were already the father but a father committing incest. Male authorship thus takes shape in a Protean claim to exist at all male points within the oedipal compact. The one position he does not want to take up is "Lady." Can one imagine a poem by the female Allen Grossman?[6]

I was closer than ever to the lunge of living.
Power stood up; it was myself.
I cleared the water back.
I was the maker.
Thereupon molten rock at the deepest level
rose forth tidal and ceaseless
horrible juice infusing and freezing me.
Interdicted, without stamina or power,

I became stark borne at my own limit.
Thus was I marked, manufactured of
hard muck left behind. Another maker
at this muddied stone made solemn vow
"o my mother, o my weeping weakness,
"o my sleeping trundled other
"I am not you." His luck.
For what I am is mummified, hidden.
Speechless pain of power forbidden.

At issue is the silence of the mother, and therefore of any female.[7]

Of course, to test out these propositions, one could try the liberal substitution of "woman/she" in the place of "man/he," correcting Grossman by evenhandedness.[8] The kinds of aphorisms one then invents out of Grossman's are derisory reminders not of absolute difference but of social inequalities. One rephrased aphorism would become "the speaker in the poem is the woman who has usurped the right of the first night in which she was conceived." Words like *usurped* and the rhyming "right of the first night" bespeak aristocratic or political fantasies of defloration, a kind of porno-frisson around the issue of power over other men by rights in women. One might credit this substituted aphorism by saying that the first sexual experience of the woman might be lesbian (a woman next to another woman, who is/is not her mother), but the usurpation differs dramatically from what Grossman intends. The revised aphorism puts heterosexual hegemony in question by the displacement of the father; this is not a "commonplace" any more. Yet even in this revision the questions of agency and power resonating from the original Grossman sentence still constitute "the mother" as terrain. For even a counterfactual version of Grossman manifests the agencyless, choiceless position of the mother.

One might say that a woman poet must fantasize herself as the inseminating figure and "take the phallus." This is a hard issue, the performing of what one considers maleness, and although it may offer some plausible strategies or at least metaphors for being powerful, gender asymmetry can also rebound and boomerang; those performances may hit punitive social limits. In Gayatri Spivak's words, "Even if one knows how to undo identities, one does not necessarily escape the historical determinations of sexism" (Spivak 1987, 144). One could also argue, based on a different reading of Freud, that polymorphous multigendered sexuality (called bisexuality) could persist (rather than being organized and smashed by oedipality). This buried plurality, resurgent, could nullify the theory of binary and unequal gender, and this could erode distinctions between male and female, poet and mother, and that, if history and economics and politics could just follow, being female or male might become about as important as having particular ear shapes. At that point the "right of the first night" would be simply quaint.

In any event we see that Grossman's idea about poetry rests on the transfer of semen into the unprotesting mother; the power to speak as a poet is the power to conceive oneself—*literally*, a most intimate event of pure oedipal fantasy. One therefore imagines a little poem by the female Robert Creeley:

So I am the Other; well, fuck
you, so I am, for
you.
Fuck.
Wherever I fuck,
I fucks.
Je est une foutre.

Is the inseminating fantasy adequate as a theory even for the formation of male poets? One might question why someone wants to be in on or know the *first* sexual experience of his mother as a question of defloration, or rights? Wouldn't it be friendlier to think, in general, of her pleasure? One might agree with Luce Irigaray that the pleasure of the mother, maternal orgasm, the libido, and desire of women have not yet been acknowledged and represented, though they are fundamental to any theory of subjectivity and gender (Irigaray [1974] 1985, 42–44, 62). And agree with Gayatri Spivak that "the clitoris escapes reproductive framing"; that the Tiresias figure who informs the world of the power of female orgasm unlinked to reproduction is the "master of ceremonies at the Oedipal scene" (Spivak 1987, 151).

Given this symptomatic reading, harrying the vatic with what it excludes, it becomes clear that even to write poetry with a gender critique in mind, one must attempt to withdraw from these universal narratives. Resist the transhistorical. Reject special spiritual access ascribed to one group. Suspect exclusively oedipal theories or family narratives of poetic power. Disclaim any theory that ascribes full subjectivity to one gender (etc.) only. As a key mark of that skepticism, it is necessary to refuse seduction by *any* theory of poetry that postulates the mysterious, beneficent, blessed, angelic, uncurious, static, or downright dumb *Silence* of others. Of capital-*O* Others, as one says. Especially that silence as an enabling condition of "your" poetry. And to refuse any theory of an asocial textuality with a nonsecular sheen.

Insofar as we have been discussing oedipality almost exclusively, some comments need to be made. Such theories can only be galvanic; they cannot be disproved. We are following Grossman, unfortunately, as treating psychoanalysis as a near mythic system of explanation, not as a field in its own right with internal debates, modified findings, new practices. Oedipus has become a set of foundational premises to poetry offering apparently explanatory narratives about the formation of gender and consciousness. Oedipal theories have taken on exclusive relevance to the formation of poets because both oedipality and (often) poetry construct fixed genders and positions in sexuality. But because we postulate that the Oedipus complex happens to each individual baby one by one in an isolated asocial family, oedipality is never seen as a social theory of interaction, with social rewards, related to other practices of differentiation. We never ask what the parallel "complex" is for race, for the formation of white persons' "whiteliness" (Marilyn Frye's term), for the taking up of one's "raced" position in hierarchies of value (Frye 1992, 147–69). We don't inquire about material practices and social learning generally supporting literariness—these become "biography," not deep theory. Why not a theory of educational access, or a theory of elaborate playfulness in small groups, or a theory of interactive and conflictual communities, or a theory about agency through mastery of narrative and song, or a theory of resistance to colonization through deformation of linguistic markers—I am gesturing to social explanations of poetic production.

Meantime the/your father seduces [you] by proposing the inadequacy of the/your mother as an essential condition of her existence (and of his). Power seduces by propositions of the inadequacy of the despised; Grossman's oedipal model is really a political statement. Grossman is "right"—poetry as the socially mystified institution that we know seems to demand, or at least to encourage, the silence of women and representatives of other social groups, but he sees this situation as a transhistorical given of the mystical or essential nature of poetry. Instead one must read these so-called silences as culturally variable, historically situated, irregularly practiced, and even, if one looks carefully, not always as silent as they seem at first glance down the millennia.

We could, for instance, disaggregate and analyze silence. Silence can be a condition of utter (but not asocial) voicelessness. This voicelessness can be imposed or assumed; it may even be assumed in protest. Silence can be the condition of speech unrecorded but alluded to. Silence can be what you hear if you are not listening or have untrained ears (like walking in the woods and hearing birdsongs and leaf breeze as "silence"). Silence can be attentive listening. Silence can be the condition of speech virtually erased, disappeared with hardly a trace, or totally. (Which does not mean that there was no speech.) Forced silence can attempt to provide its evidence and its stories by constructing other signals (as the Prochne/Philomela story tells). What Grossman takes as pure (mystical) silence may not exist, though it is an enabling myth of tabula rasa. Silence is probably more often a version of the other social situations.[9]

As an indicator, look at Exodus 15:1–23, my interested citation of a hieratic classic text. After a wind shift on the Red Sea drowned the pursuers of the ancient Hebrews in exodus, Moses, it is said, sang a song of praise. This song, as if cited, takes up sections 2–19, or eighteen verses in the sacred book of Judeo-Christian culture. Then the Bible records: "Miriam the prophetess, the sister of Aaron [and Moses], took a timbrel in her hand, and all the women went out after her with timbrels and with dances. And Miriam answered them 'Sing ye to the Lord' "—but the biblical account stops after just one verse paragraph, containing the topos of the song, which repeats what Moses's first verse paragraph had said. Miriam's song, the women's song, is not recorded, eighteen verses are not devoted to it, yet serious care has been taken to present the fact of its existence. These women were not artistically or prophetically silent, but their poetry is not recorded in our document.[10] One can therefore postulate a good number of undocumented poetic texts, materials, and practices of which we have traces only.

Let us reinvent a bit of Grossman. Interestingly, it won't sound vatic anymore; in fact, it will sound like Raymond Williams, with his tendril-like uncurling modifiers tracking social processes. "Unlike the father tongue, which is often, though not always, recorded, the tongue of the mother, often, though not always, *un*recorded, may fool some people into speaking of women's silence." Therefore, it may indeed follow that "the immortality of the mother and the father differs socially, as do immortalities of any other groups and sites that exist in power differentials. This is a situation that could be rectified, but for many reasons, rectification may continue to involve loss. It is even more generative, however, to recognize power (and to attempt some rectification) than to mystify the existence of power with metanarrative."

Metanarrative gets motivated, in part, by somewhat belligerent, somewhat embarrassed, somewhat mournful and apologetic responses to situations that involve female occlusion. And sometimes one can see structures of erasure or disparaging peeking around the universalizing comments on female "disability" or "absence" or "silence" or even "special privileges." To illustrate this kind of situation, one might simply adduce Pindar's pique; when he lost to Corinna in one of the ode contests held in the fifth century BCE Pindar did not concede that Corinna was a better poet/writer in general, nor that she had written a better poem in this particular case, but said that Corinna won only because she was beautiful and the judges were taken in by her attractiveness. He also complained that she wrote a nonhegemonic dialect Greek, which the judges did not fully understand and/or which they thought was cute (Campbell 1992, 21–23).[11]

If one begins thinking of the history of poetry as involving active female and underclassed, underhegemonic producers of art (rather than silent female Icons), one can postulate the existence of poetic activity of many kinds, some that is missing and unavailable (Miriam's Song), and some that can never be credited in a fair fight (Corinna's Ode) but must be disparaged. There are other situations, too—a woman's poem used to prove her unfittedness for the poetic calling. Thus Praxilla's Silliness: derision at Praxilla's poem eulogizing the beauty of cucumbers, apples and pears, the sun and the moon, shockingly, without hierarchy, put together. This scandal is, ironically, quite appealing to the aesthetic taste of today (Edmunds 1922, 73, 75). Or what one might call Nessuna's Babble: hearing any woman's words as senseless gibberish or gossip; she is thereby "nobody" talking about nothing. Through these counterhegemonic historical allegories the mythologized figure of the [male] master poet can be disturbed. One can also postulate missing communities of many producers of poetic materials, especially in the classic eras of our culture. These communities of absence are a terrific responsibility and motivation: to offer, as lucidly as possible, witness to the absent in ways that do them justice.

This might be taken as a motivation to claim a female practice of language. This is the purpose of Luce Irigaray's manifesto in *Speculum of the Other Woman,* when, after intense critical deconstruction of Freud's essay "Femininity," she breaks into maenadic overdrive, calling precisely for an energized, world-upside-down rhetoric that will nullify any theory that calls any "her" silent, lacking. The female writer must "rack everything with radical convulsions," open up all silences and blanks to "divergencies," break down the "logical grid" of statement, "overthrow syntax" by the rupture of teleological sentences and order, have otherness irrupt so that there is no more univocity of discourse (Irigaray [1974] 1985, 142). Irigaray is not calling for women to draw on the presymbolic but is precisely insisting that this "heterogeneity" of radical linguistic effervescence is inside the symbolic system and not outside of it. Women have logos; their logos is heterogeneous, polyvocal, critical.

The manifesto by a poet-critic that has had, arguably, the most decisive impact on contemporary U.S. poetry is Charles Olson's inspiring "Projective Verse" (1950) (Olson 1997). Emblematical words open Olson's essay and metonymically modify its title, "Projective Verse." The spaced title represents an inseminating event, in its Aristotelian interpretation—via the reader's eye movement, the active word *projective* crosses into the waiting *verse.* The further emblematic words are *(projectile, (percussive,* and *(prospective,* set in anticlosural, slingshot parentheses. Not only thrusting outward, a plan for an anticipated course of action, and the unconscious attribution of one's feelings to others, "projective" is also an image produced by mapping three dimensions onto two (and Olson is momentously inventive in page space). "Percussive" is a struck sound made by beating, and the act of detonating a firearm. A "projectile" is a missile like a bullet. Standing, as they do, at the beginning of a postwar essay in poetics, and just at the beginnings of a number of postwar wars, these words (re)claim poetry for masculine discourse, making poetry safe for men to enter, making poetry a serious discourse of aroused, exploratory manhood.

In a comment on these remarks, Don Byrd usefully contextualized Olson's essay as emerging from that project of becoming a poet that Olson, at age 40, had barely begun.[12] The heightened tones and rousing desires have a strong biographical function as a prod. Byrd is absolutely right. It is interesting, however, that to constitute oneself as a poet with a poet's attendant vulnerabilities and doubts, Olson invented a homosocial and gender-exclusionary subtext.[13] Fascinatingly, many women were inspired by this Olson essay.[14] They could read through the homosocial narrative and block or transpose it while appreciating the hopes that this manifesto of poetic energy performed. Olson's manifesto aroused. The gendered social limits it simultaneously set in motion are, however, hard to overlook. Here is an unfinished fragment by the female Charles Olson:

In the underworld, she will
be like the dead. But never dead, never un-shining.
She combs through the domed dimple of darkness
for the exit key. The birth of birth! where is it?
Cunning vulval valley with its abyssal
waterfall, her power's cryptic
claim, revealing and enveloping the snake
indwelling THERE

in strange room of the world where
silence IS and all incipience, all. . . .

Manifestoes have many agendas; one is newly to assemble literary history. A poetics of "rapidity of movement" offering an "anthology of transit" or "a pleasure that can be held firm only by moving rapidly from one thing to the next" (like Olson's "high energy-construct" and "MOVE, INSTANTER, ON ANOTHER!" [Olson 1997, 240]), and other vital rhetorics for contemporary writing—open form, quick metonymies "despising connectives," nonexpository development, dynamic visual text, and composition by field—"the intersection of loci: from all angles lines converging and crossing establish points," *all* were credited in 1925 by William Carlos Williams as having had their origin in the work of Marianne Moore (Williams 1954, 124, 122). In Williams's 1925 essay on Moore these rhetorics are, for the most part, gender neutral or have a charming balanced androgyny of traits: "there is a multiplication, a quickening, a burrowing through, a blasting aside, a dynamization, a flight over" (Williams 1954, 121). Twenty-five years later, by Olson, these same rhetorics are gendered male. If nothing else, this illustrates the nonessentialist, historically contingent positioning of gender materials. If in one genealogical history, Williams (and thus Olson) is born from the rib (so to speak) of Moore, in another, Williams is being born from the head of Olson, for Williams cites the manifesto approvingly in his *Autobiography.*

Olson's term *projective* has reigned, implicitly and explicitly in alternative American poetries, to suggest a world-vast space to claim and enter, with a liberatory orgasmic, or orgonic (Reichean) model of energy collection and then "energy-discharge" as the model for the poem (Olson 1997, 240). Of course, orgasms can be high energy without being projective. The notion that the poem is, "at all points, an energy-discharge" opens the way to a nonprojective model of energy-discharge, which is immediately swallowed up as if it had not been said. This is a loss to his theory. A little rule of thumb: all orgasmic models for artistic production should be checked for tolerance to nonprojective and nonpenile pleasures.

Orgasmic models are incidentally also common in contemporary narrative theory explaining the Aristotelian trajectory of plot as arousal, then dilatoriness and elaboration, then discharge of tension; these are more gender-neutral terms.[15] Olson's view of the dilatory middle is peculiarly fraught and vulnerable, because he wants to change it into the projective end as fast as possible. He seems to see an instantaneous move from arousal to discharge in the exhortation: "USE USE USE" and "in any given poem always, always one perception must must must MOVE, INSTANTER, ON ANOTHER" (Olson 1997, 240). The emphatic tripling of *must,* as well as the doubling of *always* in this sentence, and other repetitions undercut the temporality of the unrolling text by drilling into one spot. And yet, in a swift, asyntactic alternation of verbs, nouns, pronouns, he styles a metonymic exhortation about motion that is all middle: "get on with it, keep moving, keep in, speed, the nerves, their speed, the perceptions, theirs, the acts, the split second acts, the whole business, keep it moving as fast as you can, citizen" (Olson 1997, 240). Does a middle of perpetual discharge create satisfaction or frustration? I am writing shorthand binary either/or questions, mainly because there is both excitement and frustration in my response, as if I were being exhorted and excluded at once.[16]

The Olson manifesto also rings with its own homosocial enthusiasms. "There it is, brothers, sitting there, for USE" (Olson 1997, 240). Here, too, poetry and poetics are gendered male. As a condition of the employment called poetry, male pretenders to poetry who are inadequate are, to say it short, not-men. *Men* is, as it often is, a cross between a gender category and an ethical category. So while Olson's essay is critical of religious hegemonies of assent (alias *The Four Quartets*), the subtextual gender narratives are complicit with parallel exhortations to assent: "go by it, boys"—a coach to his team, a prophet to his as-yet-proleptic followers, inspiring, firing, tapping, extending, projecting, pushing, and tracking, as though these human activities of *poesis* belonged to one gender only. Although made as dissent, and effective as a terrific blast against academic poetries of the "New Critical" period and their contemporary inheritors, Olson's is not a poetics that undermines the poetic compact of male mastery. Those positioned as "not-men" are dismissed, and the speaking female is missing.

The only exception to these absolutely gendered exhortations is the word *citizen:* "keep it moving as fast as you can, citizen" (Olson 1997, 240). Citizenship in an alternative nation of poetry was certainly attractive to women "getting" this manifesto as joyous inspiration to their performance. They ignored the gender exclusivity as if it were accidental, a peccadillo of no import, or rhetorical only ("men" is a universalizing convention; it means everyone). One can also understand why a tempting response to this kind of poetics and construction of social institutions of poetry has been the corresponding exhortation—"go to it, sisters"—in the same grammatical form constituting a group but beginning with a different relation to power and practice.

Olson makes a physiology of poetic matter, culminating in this famous mantra-formulation about making poetry:

the HEAD, by way of the EAR, to the SYLLABLE
the HEART, by way of the BREATH, to the LINE
(Olson 1997, 242)

Head and heart together are an androgynous bundling, challenging mind-body splits. But the syllable is the "king" and rules over men: "the choice, if a man is in there [i.e., in that poetic practice], will be, spontaneously, the obedience of his ear to the syllables" (Olson 1997, 242, 241). The loyal fealty of a man to his king makes a homosocial and (strangely) feudal political subtext. Then suddenly, the statement fissions into another metaphor: of brother, sister, and incest.

For one lone female item does appear in this statement of poetics, not a functioning poet or artist but an appendage, a "sister," a helpmeet, already bound to the economy of the male since she lives on the poet's body. She is an ear, the birth passage between head and syllable. The ear is a perpetually open orifice that cannot close itself; it must take in, but need not always register, all sounds. Mind and ear, brother and sister-helper, create syllable from what Olson calls "the incest of verse," a taboo, but fascinating heterosexual union of the consanguineous, hereby proposing a rupture with meter and postulating a new, influential, way of building the line (Olson 1997, 242). This sister ear is a muted, intimate, and formerly invisible portrait of Frances Boldereff.

Boldereff was an independent scholar, writer, and book designer, Olson's powerful friend, active in his life (mainly 1947–50) just before the deep and inspiring bond with Robert Creeley formed (Clark 1991; Maud and Thesen 1999; Mossin 2005).[17] At the time Olson was driven to write "Projective Verse," he was engaged in a vivid and explosive sexual, intellectual, and poetic relationship with Boldereff, a relationship whose dimensions were certainly absorbed into his work and directly inspired some of it. The paper trail of their passionate bond comes in letters between Boldereff and Olson, in Boldereff's own writing, and in Olson's poems refracting her. Through the first two, we can examine the gendered ideologies about artistic production and their bond that each brings to this relationship. All the sister and ear imagery of "Projective Verse" encodes Boldereff—and further, Boldereff claimed that "the main points" of that essay "have points lying behind them which are all Motz [i.e., her] points" (Thesen, in Maud and Thesen 1999, xv, cf. 172). This is more than plausible. Olson was the mouth speaking poetry out and the metabolic furnace taking in her suggestions and processing them; he was cooking, transforming her gifts of bibliographic materials, passionate hopes, and intellectual verve into poetics and poetry. She was that through which Olson became himself. Her contributions of Sumerian materials to his imaginary (from the translations of Samuel Noah Kramer), the concepts of the postmodern, posthumanism, and of the poem as energy field are some elements showing her influence (Thesen, in Maud and Thesen 1999, xv). In the terms offered by the essay "Projective Verse," Frances Boldereff was one vital place "where the poet got it." The encounter was decisive for Olson's poetic career, but Boldereff was as if erased by him, when he turned to another explosive, generative poetic bond—with Robert Creeley. It is only through the biography by Tom Clark and the recent editorial work of Sharon Thesen and Ralph Maud that we have some version of Boldereff, Olson's "muse, sibling, and sibyl," to set into literary history (Thesen, in Maud and Thesen 1999, xii).[18]

But if her erasure can be read as Olsonic cunning (constructing his career narrative to ignore her influence), or shame (at their affair while he was also in a common-law marriage), or a reassertion of the pleasures of homosocial bonding after a period as the recipient of the outpouring of ideas by a woman, or queasiness about his vulnerability (given his augmented indebtedness to her), or bad faith about her role, or the pragmatic construction of an optimum situation for his writing—keeping the sexually demanding Boldereff at a textual distance (as Thesen argues, xiv)—it is also true, and striking, that the erasure of Boldereff was eloquently set forth in a script that she proposed, based on her own gendered theory of female agency. Both Boldereff's tremendous usefulness to Olson and her effacement emerge from a specific gender ideology, one allowing her the option of pouring her intense hopes over and into him, as the great soul she selected, as the male destined to be sparked by her ideas, as the one who could make those ideas active in and credible to the world.[19] To be plowed under, even anonymously, to give her intelligence and energies to animate a male genius was her overt goal in that relationship. That is, Boldereff accepted and enthusiastically claimed the role of female muse, inspiration for a male poet-genius. Freedom for women comes in hyperfeminine muse behavior—to plumb to the depths that role of giving: "devotion—generosity—warmth—passion and above all—joyicity" (Maud and Thesen 1999, 14). While she also claimed coequality in their behind-the-scenes relations, Olson did not respond to her work with the same passion and joyicity with which she responds to his. It appears that his response was inadequate to what she had hoped or needed (this probably inevitable, under the circumstances). In her writing, then, we hear the agony of ambivalence, along with a tragic acceptance of what she takes to be her tragic flaw—female gender.

Frances Boldereff was a person of passionate desires and insights, a condition that caused her extraordinary pain and anguish. Like a number of creative women from the 1930s to the 1950s (or even early 1960s), her relationship to her own powers was charged with her deeply held opinion of the impossibility or compromise of female achievement. At that time intelligent women felt highly exceptional. They hyperidentified with male triumphs, often feeling separate from women or dragged down by contact with women.[20] They felt like traitors to their gender roles, not-women, or escapees; one response was the intensity of their conviction that female gender roles were their tragic fate. They often experienced outright economic discrimination. These are women whose ideological conditions of employment and self-divisions around achievement, not to speak of discouragement from the outside world, left them so battered that they visibly stagger in the ring, using up their power throwing wild punches (sometimes even at themselves), or go down for the count forever. Outside this, looking into all that historical poignancy and damage, one begs them to get up. But not all could or did.

Struggles around gender are visible in several texts that pass from Boldereff to Olson. The first received by Olson is a manifesto-like document, an electric set of notes about gender, femaleness, creativity and women called "A Primer of Morals for Medea," based on photos of sculptures by Michelangelo. Boldereff wrote this essay in 1948 (before meeting Olson) and self-published it in 1949.[21] This white paper shows Boldereff in an agony of renunciation, for the piece was written "scalding hot" in, as she writes to Olson, "young woman terror" (Maud and Thesen 1999, 16). "You are a slave," she addressed the exemplary woman, curiously named Medea (Maud and Thesen 1999, 13). The female is a slave to "nature," which means biological "motherhood" and the immanent physicality of women. "Nature" cannot be escaped; hence it is fruitless to fight against the fate of women—such "combat" will only "destroy yourself" (Maud and Thesen 1999, 14).[22] Instead women should accept their role as givers to others, in devotion and joy; the name *Medea* offers to this advice a lurid, melodramatic counterpoint of destructive female agency that suggests what forces are sublimated.

This manifesto for selfless giving to others calls for an intellectual risk and existential generosity that are both brave and attractive. But what this muse role actually means is set out in the final propositions. The female's relationship to things is forever "indirect." When she talks about this, Boldereff modulates from addressing Medea as "you" to addressing her with the more intimate, and more biblical, "thee." "For thee will everything take place but thy name will be everywhere unknown except to him alone in whose heart it burns. The direct tasks belong to a man. Thine are the indirect" (Maud and Thesen 1999, 15). This credo of the muse, the joy of being transposed into a man's art, was also made explicit in a letter to Olson—metaphorically cast as Christ the Messiah to her John the Baptist: "I am not the one to *write* it—I am the one to live it—it states that there is a man—a writer—who will come after—you can judge yourself if it is you—certainly if it is not you, it is no one else" (Maud and Thesen 1999, 16). There are many such supportive, bolstering, even exaggerated statements; once in 1950 she compares Olson to Michelangelo (Maud and Thesen 1999, 105). Olson owed her his "genius," and he paid up well. We could name this the agon of the gender martyr: the woman ideologically (and socially) convinced that passivity and giving were her exemplary, naturally mandated, position but nonetheless continuing to pulsate with agency and intellectual, creative powers. Gender martyrdom was a definite, if pathos-laden, subject position for women in this era; the pathos for us lies in the clash of power, desire, and prospective agency with internalized limits and intricate justifications for those limits. Boldereff made herself the "muse" and, despite this generosity, was always in uproar, agony, and revolt.

> *Dream (October 1973). Dream of what toys to give a girl child. Buy her "electra dolls." Little dolls with nasty faces, dressed in black, hair, black done up in snaky braids standing up like a headdress. Suggested game: possible to act out the story of Medea killing her children with these dolls.*

A second site of the Olson-Boldereff interaction around gender occurs in April 1949. The text was a notebook from May 1936 that Boldereff had lent him, a Weiningerian spiritual autobiography of her ideas about gender and sexuality, based on her personal crisis in 1923. In sharing this journal with Olson, Boldereff opens a whole world of female anguish to him: "let a woman admit . . . I am a lesser creature, from me no great thing will ever proceed"; she cannot be free, and she lives in "profound inequality" (Maud and Thesen 1999, 27, 28). This is, again, a remarkable document, detailing the "shame," "sorrow," and "disgrace" of feeling, simultaneously that woman as a creature is only a "tool" "whereby man destroys or saves his own soul" and feeling herself selected by the universe itself to show at least one single "life wherein God set one woman free" (Maud and Thesen 1999, 22, 27).

Talented women, like Frances Boldereff, struggled to accept the notion that woman as a gender does not use her talent because she feels no "necessity"; her satisfaction in childbirth is "complete satisfaction," although her desire for coitus puts her in considerable discomfort because of the double standard (Maud and Thesen 1999, 27, 28). Men, on the contrary, cannot create anything from their bodies to give them that satisfaction—so they have the terrific, but culturally productive, anguish of trying again and again to make art: "Out of that pain comes his intense mastery, his freedom, his glory and his bitterness. For life he never will be able to grasp. Now a woman cannot grasp life either, but she is it—she partakes" (Maud and Thesen 1999, 27). Boldereff agrees totally with the claim that a woman is satisfied because she is "an actual or potential mother," but a man is always frustrated by his lack and is always frustrated by the art he makes and is thereby driven to make more. Her "pity" for men seems a displacement of her mourning for herself.

She confronts, with other women of her generation, a central question about the "terrifying burden" of womanhood:

> Did woman make herself bound, or was she born bound—does she not belong all days, in all moods, to the earth—and is this not the cause of her great sadness, her slavery, her pettiness, her vengeance, her intense pursuit and glory in a man's soul betrayal, her triumph in a child, her never ending convergence on her own tangent? Let him who has a great soul weigh this in silence—*who* is responsible for the profound inequality of a man and a woman—for the absolute impossibility of her escape from earth. Who? (Maud and Thesen 1999, 27–28)

Boldereff sees this injustice as "inherent"—structural. But her protest brings down the skies. She cries out in a kind of agony about gender injustice, "the profound inequality of a man and a woman" since a woman cannot ever escape "the earth" or her body (Maud and Thesen 1999, 28, 29), and the only path (sexual repression, rejecting sexual intercourse) is impossible for herself. This analysis of a woman being mired in immanence while man "can be free from his body, can possess his own soul in strength" is like Beauvoir's *Second Sex*, but the solution Boldereff proposes is not Beauvoir's exceptionalism (the leap of individual woman from immanence to transcendence) but instead an existential renunciation of the desire for autonomous power and creativity (Maud and Thesen 1999, 30).

When Boldereff writes (in 1936) "What I say is,—let a woman admit in her soul her burden—let her say to herself—I am a lesser creature, from me no great thing will ever proceed," Olson's comment (1949) is exact, pinpointing her ambivalence to this renunciation: "((THIS IS THE RUB, for FB,))." At another moment when she speaks of women's "essential inequality" (something that she must postulate, though it "burns a deep hole in me"), Olson's response seems to be the terse rejection of that inequality: "((SHIT))"

(Maud and Thesen 1999, 22, 28). The woman renounces coequality, manufacturing herself in pain and reflected glory as a stunning muse figure, a maneuver, in her terms, as the result of "essential inequality" between the sexes, to which the man has a terse, obscene response, but nonetheless a response that does not challenge this ceding of her powers to him or support her coequality.

There is no doubt that, however awkwardly, Boldereff and Olson were discussing, enacting, and struggling with gender and poetics, with sexuality (and its deferral) and social/spiritual renewal. Olson enthused, for example, about "the absolute dynamiting of, the PATRIARCHY," although the contexts for this remark suggest it concerned an evocation of "archaic," "mythopoetic," even "matriarchal" formations that, as sketched by Olson, left quasi-archetypal roles for women to fill. Further comments show the degree to which Olson, like Boldereff, was invested in woman's absolute "difference" even though they were spiritual "siblings" (Maud and Thesen 1999, 413, 412, 417, 422, 468). All these volatile struggles, and more, lie behind the sister-incest-ear motif in Olson's manifesto.

In the contrast between an oedipal sensibility and a revolutionary "deterritorialization," Deleuze and Guattari contrast two incests. These two models may be said to correspond to the Grossman story and the Olson story of poetic practice. The incest with the mother affirms the familial and conjugal triangle; in contrast, "schizo-incest" with sisters, maids, whores is said to offer a line of escape from the family and its version of gender reproduction. Escape? for whom? This delightful story is being told through the eyes of the male baby. For where does one think sisters, maids, and whores come from? Sisters certainly come from the economy of the family, while the two categories of working women (maids and whores) have fantasy roles based on social class in the sexual and even the familial economy and hardly escape from fringe service positions near the family. (Further, they do not even represent the possibility of incest but rather normative sexual access to the vulnerable or to the professional sex worker.) Can a male figure escape via a figure who cannot escape? An ethical question. Here, too, the female figure has no material and historical existence; she is a function through which the male world may experience revolutionary shift. As Dana Polan notes, the Sister has been "reterritorialized" and reified into Femininity.[23] It seems harder to get rid of these ahistorical binary gender narratives than it at first appears. It is hard also to lose the notion of a service function for female gender, however embedded in revolutionary proposals.

In a work called "Sorties" Hélène Cixous confronts the vacuousness of the gender binary by suggesting that specially gifted "poetic persons" slide between genders and sexualities (Cixous 1986, 83). She is clearly proposing gender hybridity, even a kind of queer performativity, as a way out; what is amusing, given the struggles I have just detailed among historical poets and creative persons, is her honoring of this idea with the term *poetic.* For we have seen how this term, without being contested, will not lead for a minute to a critique of gender, given that hyperactive gender binaries seem to be one major ideology of the institution called "poetry."

Recall Olson: "the choice, if a man is in there, will be, spontaneously, the obedience . . . " Once this attitude is formulated, obedience to what may not matter (he is speaking about syllable sound)—the attitude of spontaneous obedience is more notable, that mix of authoritarian and upswelling fealty that verifies manhood, a deturning of contemporaneous political dictatorships to the more benign field of poetry. The brotherhood or new citizenship of poetry is formed by those who can understand and "obey" a wonderful new "principle" or "law" ("FORM IS NEVER MORE THAN AN EXTENSION OF CONTENT"), a law that has its own kinetics (keep it moving, tracking one's own line of thought), making a major critique of formalist claims to poetic excellence (Olson 1997, 240). The several capitalized statements are called, in a fond but pleased self-mockery, "the dogma" (Olson 1997, 240). Does the push of these influential statements depend on their format of expostulations and scout's oaths? Can one—ironic question—separate the ideology of presentation and style from the propositions in content? It seems that Olson does—stylistic freedom vs. aesthetic dogma. Curiously, given this notion of "dogma," the announced poetics involves humility and opposition to abstraction and mastery. Olson's announced (and influential) poetics, also enunciated in his essay, is about the loss of ("getting rid of") ego, subjectivity, soul, and standing like an object among the other objects of nature (Olson 1997, 247). Informed by a mystical participation and a tender listening appendage, a man takes the imprint of natural laws. Thereby his projective acts are organically valid. Thus, as is well known, Olson proposes a posthumanist and post-Graeco-Roman examination of the world. Yet he also does so by primitivist investments in the Noble Mayan and by masculinist investments in helpmeet ears.[24]

Is there any use to this? (It does say, attention, humility, location, contact.) (But it says aggression and humility. It bullies but provides alternatives; it bullies to tell you to stop bullying reality.)[25] What taints what? Does the exhorting rhetoric of gender (and, in "Human Universe," the sentimentalities around ethnicity) undercut the attraction of structures of kinesis? Are the contradictions in function between attentive obedience in the male poet (as he stands in reality among objects) and in the female ear (as she perches on the male mind of the male poet) too much for the female poet to bear? Is the contradiction between the critique of anthrocentrism and the assertion of projectile manhood too damaging?

In short, "[Poetic] representation needs to be [acknowledged as] the site of [gender] struggle, [since it clearly is]" (DuPlessis [1990] 2006, 145). The stories commonly told by radical or influential thinkers like Grossman or Olson, or underknown thinkers like Boldereff, about access to language, the formation of the poet, the possibilities and reception of poetic practices, the motives and causes of cultural action have made use of gender and sexual (and—certainly—ethnic and class) narratives that depend on, or are indebted to, rigid categories of behavior and limit for females. When the "silent" one speaks, in works circulated privately, she is in agony, yet she accedes to these gender arrangements. That model for poetics cannot function in a condition of auditory pluralism, of chosen (not imposed) listening, and the necessary assumption of silence as vital for every aspect of poetic form and text. Such a model imputes silence (or its corollary—gibberish), or passive reception of semen or sound, to a specific social group. At worst, these models seem to be constitutive of poetry itself as an institution, which makes "poetry"—or at least many of its tropes, climaxes, productions of authorship, and sustaining fantasies—seem a closed shop, damningly conservative (offering advantages, such as transcendence, to few, by accumulating the energies and powers of others). Yet "poetry" as a formal medium does not depend on anything like these stories and may be agnostic to them. Could the formal aspects and the ideological aspects of the mode "poetry" be at odds?

What is to be done? Socially and culturally speaking male/female polarization as a human trait is a mythos—a psychology myth, a religious myth inserted in, and working through, conditions of gender creolization. Citing Kristeva: "the very dichotomy man/woman as an opposition between two rival entities may be understood as belonging to *metaphysics*" (Kristeva 1981, 33). However, given that it is a metaphysics with historical results, one's attack must always be double pronged—on a metaphysical level by cultural critique of these binaries and on a historical level by specific political and economic interventions, possibly in the name of the very category "woman" that one is attempting to lose (Riley 1988, 113). One must work at undoing the gender dichotomy (and rejecting its binary) with one hand, while with the other work on undoing its social and political results (and thus perhaps strategizing via that binary). This would be the both/and paradox of feminism. However, critique may need to occur in the name of other materials, for Judith Butler has proposed that continuously evoking "woman" reinstantiates the very binary and sets of norms, including normative heterosexuality, that one desires and needs to criticize (Butler 2004, 48). That direction of argument refuses so-called postfeminism; however, it will predicate thinking, at least, "post-woman" and "post-man." That sounds dreadful only for a moment; in many ways it is cheering. But the embodiment and sedimentations of already-existing gender modes cannot disappear without political, ethical, and cultural struggle, and most people will not yet think of themselves as postgender but as inside a changing gender matrix, considering materialized concepts like "man" and "woman" as locations for critical intervention.

What is to be done with the persistent gender narrative of poetry? Can its recurrence, its solemnities, its central location, its serious claims be put "in the past"? Considering most of the users of this narrative, this question is not up to me; insofar as it is a construct supporting male authorship and female muse-ship, it is ultimately up to others, in their own time, to act out the level of critique they feel they can sustain—or not to. Their project might be framed as "undoing masculinity in and of poetry" rather than the normative poetic project of "praising femininity," which already has, to say it dryly, an adequate number of texts.

Sometimes I have said that this is the reason I don't write "poetry," taking "poetry" polemically to mean the gender fantasy structure we've just seen, still pretty toxic, even with its loopholes. This is my claim to write "otherhow"—"Not 'otherness' in a binary system, but 'otherhow' as the multiple possibilities of a praxis" (DuPlessis [1990] 2006, 154). This claim of "otherhow" can also be imagined as a determined walk away from the claustrophobia of some gender narratives, carrying talismans of these debates as urgent reminders but traveling, perhaps, into another space.

5
Marble Paper

Toward a Feminist "History of Poetry"

> . . . in production not only things are produced. Social relations are reproduced and this means the production of ideas about these relations.
>
> —Patrick Joyce, *The Historical Meanings of Work*

> Caution: Muse at Work.
> Road Sign on the way to Here.

Preface. Marble paper. Endpapers of old, beautiful books. Shadows edging their pages. Drops of color, a specific mix of water and oil, pigment thrown down, a gelatin "size," rich color stirred, disturbed, swirled, combed, patterned, or random. Curious—sometimes water paint, on oil, sometimes oil paint on water, in precise interplays beyond domination and resistance. A bliss in pattern, intensive, sometimes irregular. So gorgeous, so sensuous, so "oily with color, who could want to pick it apart?" (DuPlessis [1990] 2006, 140). To pick apart beauty, poetry—churlish. Ungrateful. Resistant—for what? To separate the elements in marble paper—like analyzing the sheen of a butterfly wing. And so on. But the main ingredient for marbling is ox-gall, the bile of an ox. "Each new colour. . . . forces the earlier colours into veins, but needs extra strength—i.e. more gall—to do this" (Chambers 1986, 61). I want a feminist marbling of the paper, with its own curiosity and gall. Time to refigure work within the "work" of art. Claims of the "loss of the magic" exist only to protect the tropes. For when work is taken up, the monologue of "lyric" cracks open, revealing occluded dialogues.

Suggestively, the word *marble* evokes the "not marble" topos of Shakespeare and others (and Horace's more enduring than brass), the brave claim that poetry stands beyond time's depredations. By extension standing beyond history. This too needs modifying. Behind *marble paper* lies the term *white paper*—"a paper published by a government to justify a position in some matter of international interest" *(American Heritage Dictionary)*. Swirling color and pattern propose a critique of the government of poetry. For all these reasons marble paper is the physical sign of the temptation and critique that motivate this essay. A sign of pleasure, intense issues/colors afloat on gel, bile to gain the color swirl, alum to make it fix. This allegorical essay concerns one part of the apparatus of *poesis:* the beloved female muse and her work. It is a sociopoetical intervention, sometimes a little willful. The labor concealed in poetry is not only the labor of the poet (marked everywhere in a text) but also the labor and social situation of the muse.

Chapter 1. Adorno/Erato. In which is examined his useful claim that lyric poems have social meaning and show historical tendencies. His interpreting of "love"—epiphanic luminosity and erotic yearning—to indicate desire for community and utopic change. His bypassing of heterosexual love and the male-to-female gaze as an analytic curiosity or gap in his depiction of lyric.

What does poetry represent beside the fact that it is poetry? *crystal over ideology.* While many critics of poetry have resisted any analysis of poetry's political and ideological representations, Theodor Adorno has not. "On Lyric Poetry and Society" (1957) argues "that the lyric work is always the subjective expression of a social antagonism" (Adorno 1991, 45). Adorno responds strategically to all formalist claims about the ultimate transcendence of society by the poetic text, for he identifies not direct representations of social issues inside a given poem but antithetical, folded, trace, or negative relationships between issue and statement, mediated by subjectivity. "The poetic subject, which always stands for a far more general collective subject," he says with allegorical finesse, has a relationship to "the social reality that is its antithesis" (Adorno 1991, 46). For Adorno, social reality is marked indirectly, in reverse, on a lyric poem's speaking subject. This relationship between "I" and "society" is not thematized, or not interestingly so, but "in every lyric poem the historical relationship of the subject to objectivity, of the individual to society, must have found its precipitate in the medium of a subjective spirit thrown back upon itself" (Adorno 1991, 42).

By taking up the issue of the lyric, Adorno wants to adjust and rectify a central claim of romantic thinking: that lyric poetry has no historicity or conceals its specific temporal moment (Adorno 1991, 52). How, then, can one historicize such poems? how bring them into the realm of materialist critique? Adorno accomplishes this by a neat dialectical twist of reversal and sublation. Any lyric, he argues, *is* otherworldly. Yet the degree to which a lyric seems out of the world is the degree to which it is marked by a social yearning for a better world. The apparent distance from materiality and contingency in the themes of a lyric poem evokes pure spirit—the spirit of utopian longing itself. This masterful Hegelian turn has at least one problematic dimension. In this essay Adorno does not particularly comment on the materiality of the poetic text itself—its words on the page as a sign (a Bakhtinian sign) of articulated social discourses, its genres, its formal modes (rhyme, diction, and so on). A lyric poem is found to be a utopian site, reacting to reification and commodification by embedding protest against the world as it is and foreshadowing a changed world. Such poems overtly refuse apparent relationship with the social, refuse "contingency," but encode a deep desire for general social liberation (Adorno 1991, 52).

Adorno follows his oblique, suggestive insights with readings of two German lyric poems. These poems present a general yearning via specific muses: the poems desire a "free humankind," something visible in the idealized Self-Other relations in such works (Adorno 1991, 53). In one poem the lyric diction of intimate heightening restores a sense of spiritual joy; in another the poem is highly selected and condensed, an "ascetic omission of whatever might diminish its distance from a language sullied by commerce" (Adorno 1991, 52). Indeed, Adorno's investment in the lines of Stefan George occurs because the poem has "lines that sound as though they were not written by him but had been there from the beginning of time and would remain as they were forever" (Adorno 1991, 53). Poets most definitely manipulate linguistic layers of temporally evocative discourses and syntactic placement along the line to produce an "eternal" or "always already" sound. In our own tradition, John Keats, Wallace Stevens, H.D., and T. S. Eliot work this way, and so, though in odder ways, do Algernon Swinburne and Charles Bernstein. Note Adorno's argument that in the very language and music of a poem, historicity is eroded. The poem is deindividualized—it gives the impression that no particular "person" wrote it—but rather it speaks from *poesis* itself—from poetic assumptions and conventions. The poem is also detemporalized—it sounds as if it were not written inside a given time. This is logically unnerving, for this idea either cuts against the historicity that Adorno elsewhere proposes, or it suggests that the lyric poem's language—drawing as it does on deep wells of syntax and diction, and on the material relations of syntax, diction, sound, and segmentivity that we call "music" in poetry—conflicts with other more temporally located elements of the poem—subjectivity, references, tropes, conventions, images, allusions, "plot" structures. Perhaps "lyric" is the mode that embodies a contradiction between poetic language as a quasi-eternal music and the poem's subjectivity and tropes as temporally fixed. The present essay examines some gender materials thrown up by this contradiction.

Because neither poem that Adorno isolates in "On Lyric Poetry and Society" is dated, nor are the poets' dates given, he marks his greater interest in trends of *longue durée* than in specific historicist readings. Eduard Mörike (a late-romantic writer, 1804–75) is presented in a poem that speaks of a little town and its streets, blossoms, and breezes, suggesting "the paradox of lyric poetry in the ascending industrial age" (Adorno 1991, 50). Mörike's poem concerns those spiritual, numinous, or attentive moments when everything seems to scintillate, when travel, shift of place, and a touch of estrangement at the heart of anticipatory consciousness bring the intense pleasures of meaning and rightness. The lyric rises to epiphanic flashes of comfort and pleasure that restore (via that cozy town and domesticated, accessible nature) a sense of psychic equilibrium and hope to an individual despite the unspoken changes to both nature and town caused by industrial society. Adorno finds the poem compensatory for losses it does not declare. At base, this poem talks about a love for the world experienced transcendently: "Oh, how bright the world is here!" (Adorno 1991, 47). The poem finishes, "Oh muse, you have touched my heart, / With a breath of love!" (Adorno 1991, 48). This turn startles the reader; nothing before had indicated that a muse was at stake. The word *muse* seems to have been held in reserve so that the poem's various materials (including the town and a voice glancingly heard) can be focused at the conclusion by this poetic convention.

The second lyric, by Stefan George (1868–1933), is a work of idealized yearning. George's lines concern the non-(hetero-)normative love object, a male youth named Maximin:

> From a moist night
> A gleam ignites—
> . . . .
> Now I must
> For your eyes and hair
> Every day
> Live in yearning.
> (Adorno 1991, 53)

Michael Davidson identifies this "George-Kreis" as a "homosexual cult devoted to art and beauty" that also influenced the San Francisco Renaissance (Davidson 1989, 40). In George's poem the erotic other, the yearned-for boy, is given no lines, no speech, despite Adorno's notion that the poem shows "the voice of human beings between whom the barriers have fallen" (Adorno 1991, 54). In this sense the lyric situation is triumphantly, if unconsciously, colonizing—lyric speaks for both characters. Difference, discussion, the push-me/pull-you of distinct needs and agendas even in identificatory "love" are unrepresented. No barrier exists between the speaking subject and the yearned-for object because only one of them is depicted with a voice. There is no sense that there might be politically and culturally meaningful "social antagonism" between the speaking subject and the silent, beloved other.

In this poem Adorno sees two trends central to modernity. The first is the Mallarméan dream of "language's chimerical yearning for the impossible," expressed in the "insatiable erotic yearning" of the speaker, which "finds relief from the self in the other" (Adorno 1991, 53). This "other" is set as the terminus or focus for otherwise overwhelming or engulfing feelings (this is definitely muse service). The service that the beloved "other" performs can be seen as rather more suspect than Adorno suggests. Like the service of the African American in Toni Morrison's and similar analyses, the literary depiction of a silent "othered" figure buffers the speaking subject from being overwhelmed by feelings too powerful to confront. Such an othered figure also saves the speaker from listening to, or (really) the writer from finding out by imagining, what such a figure might say in dialogue. The speaker is given the sociopoetical privilege of taking both roles in a staged "dialogue" that is, in truth, monologic.[1]

Second, Adorno argues that lyric language, with its burden of erotic longing for the other, "represents the idea of a free humankind," a yearning central to modernity (Adorno 1991, 53). This idea demands feminist critique. This utopian dream—let us fill in the details: the desire for social and political and economic compacts that would offer all more justice, health, and fairness; that would reduce or outlaw criminal gaps of income; that would support adequate education regardless of class, gender, or ethnicity; that would prevent heavy poisoning of the environment, chemical dumps and despoilings, fifty cents a day in prison-factories of virtual enslavement, children at labor, and forced mono-crops (I see I am moving into a staggering and uncontrollable list and will stop)—all this is summed up allegorically as erotic yearning and practically as poetic diction. Can specific political urgency really get suggested by the genre "lyric"? Do personal love or muse materials have no social meaning unless they offer an allegory of community? Is poetry only socially suggestive when it is *not* about the social relations directly depicted in it?

Making episodes of erotic yearning indicate such a vast political area suggests that "love" and "muse" in poems are simply cover stories for social democracy and economic justice (granted these are noble and important goals) and have no political or social meaning of their own. The *Oh muse,* the *breath of love* in one poem, the *live in yearning* of the other lead to and provoke social interpretation for Adorno, but they are not seen by him as what needs to be interpreted. Has Adorno taken these gendered elements of poetry as not-social so he can look through them to what he assumes are the real social forms and practices—community and utopia? Further, by choosing these particular poems (in which town is muse, then luminous voice is muse, and in which boy is muse), Adorno avoids or sidesteps the situation of yearning most common to the lyric as a genre: the fact that the adored object is a female figure or that the muse is female. The gaze on the beloved, the heterosexual object of yearning, the scrutiny of the female figure, the inspiration females provide—all parts of the "foundational cluster" of the lyric, all central to the lyric, are not taken up as the lyric by Adorno.

Thus a close reading of Adorno's essay on lyric poetry, especially of its lacunae, demands a study of gender in poetry that approaches (at least as a first move) some conventions surrounding female figures. One might, like Adorno, take up key—even canonical—lyrics and examine poems of modernity, that is, works from the years when the social materials of gender were in deep shift—of both long and short *durée.* What are the relationships among historical women, the female figure addressed in any given poem, and the apparatus of poesis that might guarantee the place of that figure?

the concept of human desire
petrified in (or by) poetry
evaporates leaving sweet encry/ust residuals
candy house in the wide forest
I didn't feel that I should be coming back
to the same place I left from.

Chapter 2. In which it is argued that a feminist "History of Poetry" (drawing on Adorno, but investigating the gender relations that he occludes) is an intervention contra the eternalizing of poetry as a mode. Such a rereading of poems and of the apparatus of poesis precisely temporalizes poetry, making it subject to and expressive within its time. Two features that this Marble Paper resists: the notion of poetry as ahistorical, transcendent, and the notion of female figures depicted in poems as ahistorical, transcendent. These are related resistances; in their turn they involve the traces of labor in poems.

I am the ghost of the future; under the rubric "feminist" all culture and all cultural products would have to be reconceptualized. In particular, it is time for a totally different History of Poetry talking about "woman/women," "man/men," femininity, masculinity, sexuality, effeminacy, female masculinity, and queerness, torquing and resisting binaries. Poetic traditions, genres of poems, poetic authority as textually manifested, representations of subjectivity and social location, discussions of relationships including romance, love, desire, inspiration, and repulsion—all elements deeply constitutive of poetic texts—can reveal gender assumptions that open the "field" of poetry to new ways of envisioning its purposes, problems of representation, and meanings. Looking at art history, Griselda Pollock articulates her motivation as "feminist desire": "not only to do history differently but to tell tales in such a way as to make a difference in the totality of the spaces we call knowledge" (Pollock 1999, xvi). She wants to engage in what Teresa de Lauretis, treating film, fiction, and theory, calls a "view from 'elsewhere' " (De Lauretis 1987, 25). This approach now needs to encompass poetry. Further, De Lauretis suggests:

> we can perhaps develop a *feminist theory of textual production* which is neither a *theory of women's writing* nor just a theory of textuality. In other words, it is not a matter of finding common elements among the texts written or produced by women and defining them in terms of a presumed femaleness or femininity, which, to my mind, is highly suspect of sexual metaphysics; rather, it is our task to envision a feminist theory of the process of textual production and consumption, which is of course inseparable from a theory of culture. (De Lauretis 1987, 92)

Here the project of writing an "otherhow," an "elsewhere," a "feminist desire in the writing of [poetry's] histories" will identify, seize, and work through points of contradiction whose gender drama is inscribed in the poetic text, deep inside poetry as such, and in clues about historical figures suggested by the text (Pollock 1999, xviii).

Chapter 3: In which is made a little productive addition to Antony Easthope. Why resist authorship, agency, intention so famously? Of course, they don't explain everything! Discourse may write, but my fingers are on the keyboard. Kitten on the keys.

Think of the poem as having an inside and an outside. The inside, any figures, pronouns, speakers, characters, or personages in the diegesis are the "subjectivity of the enounced," while the "enounced" itself is the narrative or narrated event(s) inside the poem. What, then, is the outside of the poem? It is the whole thing on the page as a work or text within language—what one might call the material and extradiegetic text. Following Antony Easthope and Roman Jakobson, call this the enunciation (Easthope 1983, 42–

47; Jakobson 1971, 133–35). This may be anything about the poem's textual presence aside from its interior action; it might be a stanza break, or a pun, or a revision; it might be "the text's bibliographical codes" in Jerome McGann's terms (McGann 1991, 16).

There is also a "participant of the speech event . . . whether addresser or addressee" (Jakobson 1971, 133); this is odd and peculiar. It historicizes the situation of writing to a fault, insists on the specificity of any given performance of a work inside this time. You are listening to this poem now. You bring your "issues" and degrees of attentiveness, your social formations (and so on) into this reading; you are trained in our various schools to know what reading strategies are allowable and to reject insights that are by current definition "silly" and "irrelevant." The semi-imaginary subject articulating the total statement as object is called the subjectivity of the enunciation—the fabrication, the production, the dramatic construction of voicing made in any individual poem at any one time. Here, too, the careful multiple temporalities of reading or performing are given loving attention, and the poem might well be dissolved as an object, heard one way at one time, another at another.

But Now what about the Poet? Oh, the poet! Some of her, in or for any given poem, is the subjectivity of the enunciation. However, there is something left over, left out. This (unspoken by Easthope) involves another relationship half textual and half in "biography" (that is, in history, in temporality) between the subjectivity of any poem's enunciation and the historically existing writer (however variously one imagines this writer—as constructed by herself and as constructed by the critic). This euphonic terminological parade might be assisted by designating the poem's authorial agency by the term the *announced.* The announced is the public notice of something—here of the structuring of agencies in, around, and by the author that led him or her to make this poem. For a variety of reasons Easthope wants to bury or obscure such issues of subjective agency. It no longer seems productive to do so.

In many poems there is a confluence between the subjectivity of the enounced and that of the enunciation, as the poem's speaker (inside the diegesis) seems to be the depicted poet making the words of the enunciation. This is the famous "I" of most of our poems—and it has been famously analyzed by Easthope. This mechanism generates the humanist illusion of totality and presence. Easthope sees this confluence of the speakers of enunciation and enounced, the "I" of our lyric tradition, as creating the humanist illusion of personable presence—a (represented) poet really speaking to us directly. Hence while these four-square terms (enunciation, enounced, and the subjectivities of each) may seem distasteful, antiseptic, confusing, and unnecessary, they offer a way to refuse to be taken in by the illusion of sincerity, authenticity, and expressive presence that poems often create. They help readers recognize that poetic subjectivities (the "I" adequate to speak poems and the "I" speaking inside poems) are created as ideological formations: of gender, of class, of social location by an "announced" who also has these social and political markings, and other tasks, too—for example, the task of sustaining a poetic career by writing more poems. For the figures depicted inside the enounced (inside the action of the poem), I will always use the term *female figures, male figures.* This will prevent our thinking of them as women or men, for they are not "real" people—they are made of ink, representation, and ideology. Think of them as paper dolls played with by the speaker of the enunciation, who is a warm puppet created by the personage of the "announced."[2]

Chapter 4: In which the question of the "male gaze" gets lightly discussed. In poems there is a focusing eye, of course, diffused inside language itself. But there is also the "ear of power"/"voice of power." Poetic subjectivity, the subjectivity of the enunciation means never having to let "anyone else" speak in your poem.

I do/I don't want to talk about "the male gaze" (Mulvey [1975] 2000; Kaplan 2000). Early feminist film theory talked of the "male gaze"—a hypostasized disciplinary Male Eyeball that does not "really" exist as one focusing apparatus, while, conversely female and male filmmakers, as well as audiences, have various gazes, that engage, respond to, register any film. Yet the "male gaze" is suggestive for this discussion of the depiction of "muse figures" in poems. This theory attempts to state why hegemonic culture will sometimes limit the full range of female agency in its depictions, or stylize the depictions in certain conventional ways, even if actual women, historical women have had a considerable amount of agency, and, like any other human beings, are always in negotiation with power, needs, blockages, abilities, limits, their own fetishization, and repositionings that address their agency. That "gaze" was a way of noticing the contradiction between the female figure in artworks (her limits within the conventions of representation) and historical women, both as actors represented in artworks and as readers of artworks. Thus thinking about the "gaze" (whose, how deployed, with what tacit demands) would also be a way of bringing "female spectatorship" and its oscillations, sincerities, masquerades, and productions of critical distance—its essaying—to bear on the apparatus of *poesis* (Doane 1982, 80, 87; see also Kaplan 2000).

Even with its conceptual inadequacy, the male gaze still haunts us, for it partly describes and partly explains humanist subjectivity with its overview, controlling, and scoping out, its taking nature as a privileged site for education and understanding, its taking female figures as sites of education and pleasure, transcendence, conversion. Such a female figure might flee (as in a Wyatt sonnet or like Keats's nightingale), but she never could get too far. Given the gender of most poetic makers, given the lens of lyric, the idea of a male gaze may remain more useful to discussions of poetry than of film.

Poems, especially the humanist poems that bulk large in the Norton or any teaching anthology, are built (to follow Easthope) of relations between enunciation and enounced that generally do not leave room for two speakers in the enounced: the issue is not so much "gaze" as "voice." Remember, this was the situation that Adorno mystified, loosely suggesting two speakers in dialogue in the George poem, when the poem shows only a smile from the loved object. His mystification is a terrific clue to an issue for the feminist history of poetry. The situated silence of the gazed-at figure is not uncommon in poems. Indeed, to fault poems for this would be to change the whole nature of poetry, would be to demand the dissolution of the humanist lyric into something else, to write poems "otherhow" or to find, and anthologize, the poems that were written with some indication of dialogue between the speaking subject and the other. This would involve an investigation of one of the two main tropes of lyric, as Jonathan Culler proposes, "apostrophe (the address to something that is not an empirical listener [like 'O Wild West Wind']) and prosopopoeia (the giving of face and voice to and thus the animation of what would not otherwise be a living interlocutor)" (Culler 1995, 44; see also Culler 1981, 135–54).

The workings of prosopopoeia would need fullest examination, since a poem may animate and give a face to its "you" in the "I-you relations . . . characteristic of the dramas projected by lyric," but it is much rarer to find poems giving voice to the "you" (Culler 1995, 44). The subjectivity of the enunciation has the words—and his mirror in the subjectivity of the enounced does also; in the enounced "you" is rarely found speaking. Could a speaking subjectivity "give" the opportunity for words to anyone else? Could a poem be built to allow the words of the normally silent? The answer seems to be No, not usually, not by the convention of the poems we know as constituting the lyric tradition. We're not talking "drama" here. But perhaps we don't know or cannot yet find the terms to acknowledge the whole tradition of poems written as short works. Perhaps the humanist critical emphasis on interiority and subjective expression has made a grid that obscures, makes unimportant, or refuses to foreground another lyric experience in which there is true prosopopoeia (the giving of voice to all characters in the enounced).

But one might question this mechanism of voice, dialogue, dialogic monologue, missing interlocutors, and how these are handled by the subjectivity of the enunciation inside poems whenever one writes a "marble paper."

As an exemplary instance of avoiding "her" words even when the play-by-play description seems to demand them, one might note how, in John Donne's "The Flea," there is one female action between stanzas 2 and 3 (she kills the flea), and then she "say'st" something in the third stanza. But that something is not recorded in "her"/his-her words but rather is immediately surrounded and elaborated by the argument in overdrive against chastity and for sexuality. There is no doubt that putting his arguments in her mouth creates some of the comic brilliance of this poem. The subjectivity of the enounced is in monologic dialogue—dialogue is asserted and claimed but not enacted. This is also the intractable nature of humanist subjectivity—that "I" of the enunciation, who is also an "I" in the enounced, what one might call, in this marble paper concerning a feminist history of poetry, the subjectivity of "powetry" (a neologism indicating unquestioned poetry and unquestioned power relations). This doubled subjectivity corresponds to the construction of a silent, often female, figure in the enounced.

The issue of acknowledging speaking others inside the enunciation as well as in the enounced occurs in Langston Hughes's "The Weary Blues." By its citation of two different songs sung by the performer, and by incorporating choral outcries ("O Blues! Sweet Blues!") arguably from a collective called-out response, this poem constructs a doubled or even tripled speaker of the enunciation—poet and blues singer (and perhaps even speaking listeners). This citation strategy is particularly marked because the two cited stanzas have an entirely opposite meaning: in one the singer proposes to "put ma troubles on the shelf," but the other is totally foreclosed: "I ain't happy no mo' / And I wish that I had died." Hughes has made a lyric whose prosopopoeia does animate other voices.

Want poems talking back to seductive humanist subjectivity? Late-medieval pastourelles are avatars of a poetic critique of (humanist) poetry. These joking, class-unequal, and fully comic poems feature, in the enounced, a fresh, sharp-tongued female shepherdess resisting her threatened seduction by a knight, both voices constructed by the subjectivity of the enunciation. Another such poem is Wordsworth's "Resolution and Independence." Although the leech gatherer is not depicted as saying much, the poem makes his words both direct and allegorical in their simplicity, and his repeated intervention (moving from indirect to direct address) tends to cut through a frothy hysterical tone in the speaker. Foregrounding poems that challenge "powetry"—the power relations of gender and class between the figures in the enounced, and between enunciation and enounced deep in the ideology of poetry—helps construct a feminist history of poetry.

Talking about the possibility of speaking others in lyric poems, as the evocation of Hughes and balladlike poems suggests, raises the issue of the apostrophe as a central rhetorical marker of the lyric. For the condition of the apostrophe—as Culler and Barbara Johnson have argued so dynamically—is that it is a speech act without an answer. Apostrophe is an act of calling into an evocative space: whether to the oceanic "O Lady" of Samuel Taylor Coleridge or to the ghostly aborted fetuses of Gwendolyn Brooks's narrator whose absent presence and evocative tautologies are traced by Johnson.[3] The apostrophe is a trope so powerful that the reader does not feel the lack of the speech of the addressee. Yet one might wonder whether there are other kinds of lyric rhetoric in which both "I" and "you" have voice. What other rhetoric or rhetorical positions might one find in lyric-length works that would leave the speaking subject calling to something that might speak or whose voiced presence was textually palpable?

Chapter 5. In which a poem by Wordsworth, a famous muse poem oft anthologized, oft taught, and oft thought, is examined under the sociopoetical regime of Marble Paper. These readings will be deliberately slow, myopic, and perhaps contradictory.

Wordsworth's "The Solitary Reaper," a thirty-two-line poem in four stanzas, concerns the sight of a female figure in Scotland, reaping grain (possibly oats or barley) and singing a mysterious song. The ability of this female muse figure to work in two autonomous ways—to reap and to sing—is crucial to my sense of the poem.[4] The poem reveals how the singing of that balladeer or cultural worker inspires the *echt* poet, the poet of the literary and not oral tradition. The general poetic conventions discouraging dual speakers are reinforced in this particular enounced by differences of language, class, gender, and national status. Hence we readers cannot hear the Reaper's song. We hear the speaker's admiring, yearning words about this situation—those words constitute the poem. But Wordsworth (for a variety of reasons) also cannot fully hear the Reaper. His incomplete understanding acts like a tear in the fabric of desire that animates this poem. The issue of (uncited) sung ballad versus (palpable) poetic text is further complicated by Wordsworth's having invented the lyrical ballad, a major innovation that realized his radical desire to reconfigure the field between popular and literary poetries. The poem seems like an allusion to his own achievement—

both his own accomplishment, the singer's confirmation of the importance of his ambition, and the perpetual sense of inadequacy that comes with great cultural desire.

Formal mechanisms being one way that poets think with their poems, here there are specific structural and thematic relations among the stanzas that construct an architectonic web of thought. Each eight-line stanza is divided by rhyme into two quatrains: the first is either a modified (abab) or a real (abcb) ballad stanza, whereas the second is made up of double couplets (ddee). The first quatrain of the first stanza and the first quatrain of the final stanza are real ballad stanzas (rhyming abcb, though the meter is not really common meter), which lets the first and third lines swing free and unrhymed on the key thematic words *field* and *herself, sang* and *work.* In another thematic structure the first and final stanzas concern both work and song together, while the middle two stanzas imagine the nature of the Reaper's song. Not only the isolation of the figure, but her lack of coupledness, is underscored in the first stanza (*single, solitary, by herself,* and *alone* are the four descriptors used). The fact that couplets rather than a second ballad quatrain complete each stanza provides some kind of answer, inside the form, to her singing singleness, her autonomy.[5] The poem tries to double her, to shadow her.

The plot of the poem is simple: the speaker of the enunciation addresses himself to us: "Behold her," he says, pointing into the enounced. (My pronoun *he* is overdetermined, by the male writer who provides Wordsworth's source, by the male signature of the poet in the "announced," and by the muse relationship claimed.) With this "Behold," we all look, as through a window, at a memory borrowed from another tourist. We are also told to "Stop" (or, to go quietly along so as not to disturb her) and "O listen!" These are all weak imperatives; power seems to lie elsewhere than in the subjectivity speaking these words, although the imperatives do arrest the situation temporally so the real poem can happen.

One can only "hear" the Reaper through the poet's narration of the impact of her song. He does not quote her words, for they are not in his language but in a form of Gaelic spoken in the Scottish Highlands whence the Reaper comes. (Wordsworth's source calls the language Erse.) Hence no matter how closely the speaker approaches her, he will never comprehend the words, only the melody. The poem's speaker, a perfect humanist subject, is in two places at once—he is in the enounced, listening to the Reaper's song and taking it to himself ("the music in my heart I bore / Long after it was heard no more") as inspiration. And he is in the enunciation, instructing us to behold and then to listen, querying the nature of the song (birdsong, ballad about the past, ballad about the present). As if marking this doubled subjectivity of "powetry," the tenses of the poem shift in alternate stanzas from present to past.

The amazing line that joins the two temporalities—the time inside the poem when the female figure is seen singing and the time of the poem presenting the impact of this incident—is the outcry in the enunciation, "Will no one tell me what she sings?" that opens stanza 3. This is a crucial line about need, desire, lack, nonaccess, response, a line destabilizing power in the otherwise calm muse-poet poem. To whom is this line addressed? It's over our heads, even though (to follow the theorizing I have outlined) we are the readers and hence the subjectivities of enunciation internalizing the words. Yet "we" cannot know the answer to this outright appeal—"Will no one tell me?"—and can only accede to the speaker's frustration. And there's no one else there in the situation of the enounced; the Reaper is too far away in place and time, not an English singer, hard at work, too autonomous (or too vulnerable in gender terms) to be approached inside the narration of the incident to answer the question. Blockage is built in, even as frustration is expressed. I therefore take Wordsworth's line as being addressed to something way beyond the concentric subject positions of the poem (enounced, enunciation, announced) into the very gendered and sociopoetical situation of the genre, into the apparatus of *poesis.* It is an example of prosopopoeia calling to poetry itself. This exposed moment is part of the value of this poem.

The line "Will no one tell me what she sings?" concerns the frustration of being excluded, rebuffed in understanding, the song not accessible to the speaker, in a different language, at a distance, and having mysterious meaning within the opaque life of another. The line acknowledges the unreachability of this figure, her autonomous cultural work, even as it tries to absorb this figure into the poet's own system and need, despite coming from another's tourist experience.[6] Yet the poet wants to claim this figure as muse, which means an idealized inspiration to a real artist: a figure accessible—even if iconic, understandable—even if mysterious, useable—even if pristine. Is this poem, then, a miniaturized version of the thesis of rape and appropriation—"the way Wordsworth precariously represses the Other," in Anne K. Mellor's reprise of her own and other proposals—"for Wordsworth's sublime self-assurance is rendered possible, as many critics have observed, only by the arduous repression of the Other in all its forms: of the mother, of Dorothy, of other people, of history, of nature, of 'unknown modes of being.'"? (Mellor 1995, 140, 125). Is the poem, as Nancy Jones argues, an appropriation undergirded by a metaphor of rape and the genre of pastourelle in which a knight addresses, flirts with, tries to seduce and is often, but not always, resisted in his goal by a witty shepherdess? (Jones 1991: 263–77).[7] Of course, here the characters do not speak, nor do they engage in badinage about seduction, but this is a suggestive observation, given the class of the characters in the enounced and given elements of the final stanza—the interplay between her "bending" and his mounting up a hill to walk away.

My reading will not find that degree of repression, although these are strong readings; what is striking to me is that this repression of the Other cannot be negotiated. Perhaps in the context of Wordsworth studies this poem may be viewed as another one in a series of repressions of the Other, but in the context of muse poems of modernity, in the building of a feminist history of poetry, the poem can be parsed differently. I want to unconceal the "labor" that went into this poem in a slightly different sense than Adorno means in *In Search of Wagner,* where he argues that "a contradiction of all autonomous art is the concealment of the labour that went into it" (Adorno 1981a, 83).[8] The work, the work in poetry, and the autonomy of this figure are maintained in a conflictual relation with the absorption of this figure into Wordsworth's muse system and its concomitant historical vagueness about social location. In my reading, this muse figure is the site of intense contradiction between appropriation and creative and historical autonomy. This is because the Reaper, by every historical evidence, can be, even must be, acknowledged as an autonomous poet, someone who has constructed her sung words and possibly her melody.[9]

First off, at least two historical people are working for Wordsworth within this brief poem: the Reaper and Thomas Wilkinson. For the situation described here has been borrowed—Wordsworth never heard or saw it directly. The fact that he made a poem of it (although certainly associating it with other materials that he did hear and see on his 1803 trip to Scotland) is a testimony to a pulsating sensitivity on issues of inspiration, appropriation, muse, femininity, and female autonomy, an interest so powerful that the incident leaped out of someone else's descriptive memoir as precisely his kind of material. For Wordsworth did not have to write a poem that expressed this level of ambivalent frustration about female work and his muse desire. The material on which the poem is based enters in the last line, an almost verbatim citation from Wilkinson's *Tours to the British Mountains,* circulating in manuscript before its publication in 1824. The generative sentence is "Passed by a Female who was reaping alone, she sung in Erse as she bended over her sickle, the sweetest human voice I ever heard. Her strains were tenderly melancholy, and felt delicious long after they were heard no more." In the poem Wordsworth uses *strain, melancholy, alone, reaping, bending, sickle, voice*—and, as we will see, *sweet.*[10] In the struggle for cultural materials that this poem documents, the fact that the last line is an almost direct quotation from his male friend must be set against his frustrating inability to identify what the Reaper sings, except to think it sad and foreign.[11] A baseline interpretation of this poem by Stephen Gill sees the Reaper as a straightforward self-mirror of Wordsworth's difficult life in poetry: "What particularly moves him is the image of someone with few material comforts, toiling arduously, but joyously self-sufficient in her own power of song" (Gill 1989, 246). However biographically evocative this is, class, nation, and gender have unselfconsciously disappeared in this reading; for Gill the poem represents equality between two singers.

In contrast there is a good deal to say about power and social location beyond the power of song. But what is said about gender depends on which text we have read. For this poem occurs in at least two main versions: the 1807 version and the 1827/1836 version. In brief, the former is "sweeter" and also more explicitly sexualized than the latter. This poem's textual variation illustrates a truism not the less true for all that: how a poem's argument may shift according to apparently minor changes of words in different versions. In this case the variations lead to different gender ideas.[12]

Is the situation "No sweeter voice was ever heard" (1807) or "A voice so thrilling ne'er was heard" (1836) (or even "Such thrilling voice was never heard" an interim in 1827, but rather direct, without the poeticism "ne'er" that softens "never")? The sweetness is an echo of Wilkinson's original observation—a citation from him but also from a general gendered notion about what female song should be. Sweet goes with grace and a kind of unchallenging niceness. If the singer's voice is thrilling, a different implication, a double arousal, and something more abrasive, more alert, takes the place of feminine adjectives. It's subtle excitement, shudder, tremor, throbbing, and someone affected or moved with a sudden wave of emotion. This has a higher degree of feeling and a more sexual allowance for the feeling in her—since it is her voice (and not his response) that is, at least in the overt syntax, at issue. The 1827 (Norton) version gives a less feminine and more aggressive agency to the female figure. Then does she "chaunt / So sweetly to reposing bands / Of travellers" (1807) or "chaunt / More welcome notes to weary bands / Of travelers" (1827)? These options seem similar in their gender implications. Still, in the earlier version, a reiteration of sweetness evokes compliant feminine ideology, while the listeners, mirroring that passivity, are reposing; in the later version her song actively intervenes with a "welcome" (maternalized?) sound.

Finally, what is the difference between "I listened till I had my fill" (1807) and "I listened, motionless and still" (1827/1836)? This difference is large. The first implies for the male listener a satiation (sexual or oral in implication, though through the ear). It even suggests an outright taking of her song ("I had my fill of it"). It therefore further supports the motif of masculine excitement and sexual appropriation that emerges as an interpretive possibility for the final three lines (as in Jones's reading). Having one's fill is a crediting of the need of the speaker of the enounced/enunciation, the doubled subjectivity of "powetry." But "motionless and still" in the later version suggests a wariness in the speaker inside the enounced, who depicts himself as more attuned to the autonomy of the singer. This line slows down or even blocks the sense of appropriation of her song into his poetic equipment. It is also a feminine response in a male speaking subject. It is even possible that the doubling of the text exemplifies a split emotional pull in Wordsworth between a masculine excitement ("a voice so thrilling") and a feminine attentiveness ("motionless and still"). Indeed, if the "voice so thrilling" line (1827) had appeared in the same version as the "had my fill" line (1807), the "rape" motif lurking in this poem would have been more incontrovertible. But it is not so. The later version (in the Norton) credits the autonomous artistry of the Reaper and the quiet passivity of the inspired listener.

Thus I do/do not want to argue for the male speaker's appropriation of this female muse's song. About appropriation, one could simply say what Maeera Y. Shreiber does: "the poet-speaker appropriates the uncomprehended song of a distant singer (she sings in Erse) as the source of his own utterance. . . . The history of the poet's discourse may thus be glossed as an effort to colonize the space of her song" (Shreiber 1998, 274).[13] Somehow, in the Shreiber, the insult is even more patent because the poet does not understand the words; this is the force of "colonize." So I do want to make this argument, because of the touristic visitor's smugness and the poetic patness of the last two or three lines of this poem even if Wordsworth did not, in fact, hear this singer. Thereupon the tone of the key line "Will no one tell me what she sings?" would be read as blocked entitlement. His possession is frustratingly incomplete, despite its force, but the emphasis falls on his entitlement; the speaker wants to take possession or use her song exclusively for himself, without permission, to make her song his own even though he cannot record it and does not claim to reconstruct it. Indeed, it is only Wilkinson who heard it. In some moods I want to agree perfectly with Shreiber on appropriation and with Jones on the "rape" undertone, the interplay between her bending (over the sickle) and his mounting (up the hill) at the end, as if he rises above her on the bend her body makes.

But now I don't want to make this argument, since to argue for appropriation, I would have to ignore the complex, polyvalent force of the line "Will no one tell me what she sings?" This line marks (within the enunciation) the resistance of her words and her song to his ear in the enounced. It is a temporary split in the humanist fusion of the "I" of the enunciation and the "I" of the enounced, a tear in this thick fabric of poetic ideology woven (and warped) by desire. As the poet with a high-art status, Wordsworth carries her song forward; the singing enters "in my heart" and functions both there and in the poem we are reading "long after it was heard no more." But the song is also her autonomous artistic production, from a real Gaelic singer, not a silent muse, and he is frustrated in having no idea what the song is saying. Hence I take the outcry "Will no one tell me what she sings?" as a sign of the unpossessability of the female figure as autonomous working artist despite Wordsworth's repeated argument that she is a muse figure.

"Will no one tell me what she sings?"—is no one able, is there no one sufficiently informed? is one translation of this line. A first reading of the line might simply express Wordsworth's annoyance with his source text—why didn't Wilkinson find out what the song was about when he could have! But the force of the line exceeds this possibility. The sense of lacking information acknowledges the traditions of popular poetry-song in Scotland, but the line evokes a strong cultural difference.[14] Does no one want to tell me? is another translation. This reading acknowledges some guilt and disease of the interloper in nation, gender, and class. A third meaning is: after all the work I've done with ballad, and my claims on the folk, how come I am still excluded? Despite all I have done, I still imagine myself unable to understand her song—is a paraphrase with some bitterness and resentment in the undertone. The poet is isolated in relative ignorance, dramatizing himself as excluded from the traditions, the language, and the artistic production that animate the female figure even as he admires her artistry (conflictually) as a natural outpouring—*natural* meaning that she does not have to work at it. The line that indicates his own lack ("Will no one tell me") depicts him as rebuffed by the object of his own appropriation: a female figure at work in agriculture and in song.

To elaborate these claims, we must put some version of history back into a poem that alludes pleasantly enough to the past but does so vaguely. That is, we must examine the historical woman behind the female figure in this poem. This is far more difficult to do here than with the Pound poem "Portrait d'une Femme" or with the Charles Olson–Frances Boldereff connection, because in this case I can't identify and analyze "the" specific historical woman, understand her workings in his career, or read her writings but must synthesize some "woman" as representative of a certain gendered condition at a particular place and time. However, my interpretive process will put a female figure found in a poem back into some version of real time. A second, related move is to allow criticism to enter into the "announced"—that is, biographical and historical investments made by the poet, the writing agent, to see what might be at stake (in any way, but let's say in a gendered way) in the poet's use of his materials.

The realness of this source-person is an amalgam or overlay from Wordsworth's own Highland tour and the isolated, impoverished, striking, and hardworking figures he saw there, and Wilkinson's *Tours to the British Mountains*—which could have memorialized a Highland woman working in the Lowlands. The "real" reaper, as reconstructed via social history, existed at a time of increasing economic polarization in rural society (Whyte 1997, 47). She was an agrarian worker, plausibly a seasonal worker from the Gaelic-speaking Highlands who worked at harvest time in Scottish-speaking areas farther south (Houston 1989, 126; Smout 1969, 321; Whyte 1997, 46–47). This would explain the sense of loneliness that pervades the poem, with the figure wrapped in her "foreign" song. If not this, the reaper was possibly a member of a tenant family, helping to work its holdings as part of family labor or possibly a hired servant of one of the tenancies (Whyte 1997, 39). She would own neither her land nor her product; she may indeed have gotten no wages for her work, since agricultural labor was sometimes paid in kind (Smout 306), but if, as is likely, she did get paid, female labor was remunerated "pathetically" (Whyte 1997, 42)—"48 per cent of the male wage in 1791 and 33 per cent in 1797" (Houston 1989, 123). Despite this picture of grinding poverty, being in farm service (husbandry) had, according to Bridget Hill, certain advantages for women: they shared tasks with young men (with a rough-and-ready sense of equality based on skill, not role); they left the family home and gained in "independence and self-reliance" (Hill 1989, 84).[15] Hill postulates shared agricultural labor in the late eighteenth century as a relatively golden time for female equality, in which there is less sexual division of labor than in the incipient industrial age (Hill 1989, 84). Soon, as the heavier scythe replaced the sickle she used for harvesting, such a woman would be excluded from this branch of agricultural work. During both collective and individual work—rowing, waulking (fulling), and reaping—intense, rhythmic songs could be sung or even extemporaneously composed.[16] Although the Reaper is singing alone, still this collective idea haunts her song as it haunts Wordsworth's third stanza. The poem is both peopled, in a shadowy way, and quite lonely—this is also part of its power. Given the postulated conditions of the singer's employment and the nature of her labor, the Reaper really controlled only the production of her song and its fruitfulness; her labor power was perhaps constrained by tenancy or family relations, or perhaps it was "freely" negotiated but poorly paid.

There are several ways that Wordsworth considers or suggests her song's content in the middle two stanzas; these suggestions can be set within the traditions of Gaelic song as we, nonspeakers, can access it. Roderick Watson's anthology *The Poetry of Scotland* contains the anonymous ballads in English and Scottish that constitute our sense of that genre (like Sir Patrick Spens, Mary Hamilton, The Twa Corbies, and Tam Lin) (see Watson 1995). Despite some barriers to their recognition, by the mid-eighteenth century there was a strong tradition of women ballad singers. Indeed, Deborah A. Symonds proposes the development of an "arrogant, powerful, canny, and Scottish" "ballad heroine" as a cultural figure inside these female-authored songs (Symonds 1997, 10); there was also some modulation of the topics of ballads so that the gender of the singer or inventor was not entirely predictive of the topics discussed in the song, although topic and gender seem often to coincide.[17] The Watson anthology also presents, in both Gaelic and English translation, composed ballads that do have named authorship, all from the period whose terminal date is 1805 (the composition of the Wordsworth poem) and whose beginning date might be postulated as circa 1700. This was "Gaelic's most fruitful period," and there were "several remarkable women poets" at this period (Watson 1995, 230–31). Although it is not necessary for us to imagine that the Reaper is singing the work of a woman if she is simply a singer of songs of others, there were some gender divisions in topic within the songs that made it likely that she is singing a "woman's song." But it is even more powerful to the Wordsworth poem, and to the argument here, for me to conjecture that she has invented her own work and is singing it. Nothing in the Gaelic—Highland—tradition would make this a historically inaccurate assumption. She could be seen as a Màiri Nighean Alasdair Ruaidh/Mary MacLeod (1615?–1706?), a Sìleas na Ceapaich/Cicely MacDonald (1660?–1729?), or an Ann Campbell (fl. 1773), all of whom composed elegant, narrative sung poetry in Gaelic.[18] Scottish Highland women were often "monoglots" in Gaelic, which might have "enhanced" their "status as transmitters of traditional oral culture."[19] There are also a number of actual women poets who composed and sang in Scots (a dialect of English, something that would not need translation but intense gloss), who also could be imagined as the Reaper's analogue: for example, Jean Elliot (1727–1805), who composed "The Flowers of the Forest" as an elegy for Scots soldiers fallen at the decisive battle of Flodden (1513).

What are some of the topics of Gaelic songs in this period? The song of a rejected lover "exiled by passion," who proudly announces her pride that she was not sexually dishonored despite her passion, and her judgmental sense that her suitor rejected her because she was not wealthy enough (Anonymous, "Thig trì nithean gun iarraidh," in Watson 1995, 204–7). A male-authored ballad lamenting the loss of clan comrades and sorrow that he has outlived them (Donnchadh MacRaoiridh/Duncan MacRyrie, "Fada ata mise an deidh chaich," in Watson 1995, 212–15). Male-authored work with political resonance, including a recounting of The Battle of Inverlochy, which Royalist forces won against overwhelming odds and weather conditions, and a song against the Union of Parliaments, naming with contempt and flyting nastiness those who acceded to the Union with England (Iain Lom/John MacDonald, "Song against the Union" ["Oran an Aghaidh an Aonaidh"], in Watson 1995, 224–29). Female-authored lamentation at being far from home (Màiri Nighean Alasdair Ruaidh/Mary MacLeod, "Tuireadh," in Watson 1995, 230–33) and a lamentation of sexual jealousy ("An T-Eudach," in Watson 1995, 232–35). A female-authored political poem of lament for a clan chief inflected (the editor tells us) by the personal loss of the author's own husband and child (Sìleas na Ceapaich/Cicely MacDonald, "Alasdair á Gleanna Garadh," in Watson 1995, 244–49; here the editor enforces a sense that women's song must be personal even if it is also political). A male-authored blessing on the foxes who kill the sheep whose introduction was forcing smallholding tenants off the land they had worked for generations—an economic analysis in song of the breaking of a whole tenant class by the Clearances (Donnchadh Bàn Mac an T-Saoir/Duncan Ban Macintyre, "Oran nam Balgairean," in Watson 1995, 330–33).

How does Wordsworth imagine the Reaper's song? To answer that question is to enter the poem's middle two stanzas, the first essentially with metaphors of birds and exotic geography, the second with its particular imagination of history. The narrative of these interior stanzas starts at a crescendo of exoticism that is modified and tempered ethically by the end of the third stanza. In the second stanza two birds are linked to two sites. "Arabian sands" with a "Nightingale" joins together two very poetic, imaginatively provoking terms for a fantasy of travel and even a natural artlessness but two things that could not exist together (as nightingales were foliage birds)—the consideration of art as a product of tradition, conception, and even thought is reduced in any bird metaphor, and song becomes outpouring without control. The second bird, the cuckoo, is set in the wild islands northwest of the Scottish Highlands. The Reaper's song has a world-ranging scope; it can stand up against the best [bird] song in two far-flung lands. This metaphor of natural outpouring is ambivalent to her work in song.

The next stanza offers a set of hypothetical song topics in chiastic form. The song could concern history, which is, unsurprisingly, "old" and "long ago," or it could concern the eternal problems of being human: "Some natural sorrow, loss, or pain / That has been, and may be again." While this stanza tempers the exoticizing of the other one, it also produces subtle ideological proposals. The argument that history is "old" and "long ago" obfuscates the crises of quite recent Scottish history in the eighteenth century, with its deeply felt losses of cultural and political autonomy: 1707, the date of the Act of Union, which dissolved the Scottish Parliament and united Scotland with England; 1715 (a Jacobite rebellion); or 1745–46—(another Jacobite rebellion)—the '45—with the 1746 defeat of the Highland rebels by English and Lowland Scots at Culloden, which was, inter alia, the beginning of the outlawing of distinctive forms of Scottish culture: tartans, kilts, and bagpipes (Whyte 1997, 95). This history is foregrounded in quite a number of Gaelic songs. Further, in the Highlands there were interclan battles, filled with fallen heroes, strong leaders, internal tribal hatreds, and externally manipulated betrayals that were also the subject of much song. Wordsworth seems to be able to acknowledge the striking individuality of such Scottish figures in their landscape (the Reaper and so on) but cannot get a poetry moved beyond the mists of time and acknowledging the particular material and historical conditions within contemporary post-Culloden memory in which this individuality is forged.

The second topic Wordsworth suggests, "natural sorrow, loss, or pain"—such sorrows as lost love, murder, jealousy, rivalry, infanticide, widowhood, loss of employment, while apparently "natural" or eternal, may also be politically inflected with specific twists. Symonds's study of Scottish ballads of infanticide tracks how the capitalist transformation of the agrarian economy and the impact of improving and enclosing movements impacted agricultural workers seeking to marry; under such new economic difficulty, "courtship became a tougher, meaner negotiation" (Symonds 1997, 5).[20] One poignant outcome might be infanticide (Symonds 1997, 9). In two ways this more sympathetic, less exotic stanza by Wordsworth still erodes the lived historical experience of the "real" people on whom this female figure is based. In one part the ideological motive has to do with nation—that is, nonnation: Scotland absorbed into England, its autonomy dissolved. In the other part the ideological motive has to do with eternalizing issues of social class, and perhaps gender, that are historically and territorially specific. Both workers and women are interpreted as existing in an eternal cycle of "has been, and may be again"; from both workers and women emerge songs that are "humble" based on griefs that are "natural." So specificity is bleached by the ideological evocation of "nature" to soften the blows of particular historical conjunctures.

Dehistoricizing a Gaelic female poet is a good way to negotiate resistance to historical crises of nation. Similarly, the muse is a user-friendly, ideologically conventional, and poetically traditional site at which to negotiate resistance to acknowledging the work of historical women. It is also plausible to consider this poem as John Powell Ward does briefly, focusing on the key line ("Will no one tell me") as expressing Wordsworth's anxiety about women poets and their poetry, part of his "tangled" attitudes to women (need, condescension, sensitivity, appropriation of sensibility) (Ward 1997, 612). The poem can be seen to contain the marks of Wordsworth's occlusion of his own influence by such women writers as Joanna Baillie, Charlotte Smith, and Helen Maria Williams.[21] Wordsworth made an effort similar to that of Pound later, and equally inconsistent, to downplay, erode, erase, or even hide outright the influence on him of the work of contemporaneous and older women authors.[22] So instead of being writers, singers, authors, agents, or people with literary careers, historical women, turned into female figures in a poem, become inspirational conduits for a male poet's sense of his poetic agency and entitlement. It is in this sense that we can return to the word *appropriation.* Rather than use it to deplore what is every poet's right—taking cultural materials and refashioning them by any means necessary and also signaling power relations at ease in claiming the cultural "right" to do so—we can make the word announce a finding about gender in the apparatus of poesis. There is a clear poetic mechanism—the muse—available to help change a historical woman into a female figure. That ideological move, however, shows strain in modernity. By conducting a reading by sociopoesis—the close reading of text for what form, allusion, and diction tell us, and the examination of some version of the historical record to understand the woman behind the figure—we can begin a feminist analysis of poetry.

In the period of modernity, certain muse poems actually concern female work but are constructed to occlude and downplay both the economic and the autonomous cultural work of the female figure depicted in it and possibly the work of the "real" or historical woman standing behind that figure. But this female work breaks through (as in the Wordsworth outcry). Within the present "marble paper" sociopoetical analysis, the discovery of the historical woman shadowing a poem's female figure can be deployed analytically to puncture the poem's denials of female agency and autonomy. In modernity there is an emerging contradiction between the growing autonomy of historical women as workers and the poetic convention of the muse.

To appropriate a pun from Mary Ann Doane: in this poem we have "a Lass but not a Lack" (Doane 1982, 77). First, there is a kind of reverse pregnancy that shifts gender materials cross-stereotype. The male speaker is fecundated by the Reaper's song and is bearing that song in his heart. He becomes a version of a female, while she with her sickle offers a kind of pointed strength that we read as male but historically is simply the strength of a working woman. Perhaps more important, the Reaper is imagistically depicted as an orgasmic, productive female. She can "reap" and cull; she has a double fruitfulness (of song and grain), an "overflowing . . . sound" that fills the vulval Vale in which she stands with an endless generativity ("as if her song could have no ending"). The description of her song and voice uses adjectives as various as *melancholy, welcome, thrilling, plaintive, unhappy,* and *humble.* Such terms, while signaling sadness ("some natural sorrow, loss, or pain"), do indeed outnumber words like "overflowing" or "thrilling," yet the pleasure of female power in production (to echo Johanna Drucker's words) needs to be acknowledged as part of what the poem depicts.

Drucker was speaking about the pleasure of production for contemporary women visual artists, but we can transpose her words into the pleasure of production that Wordsworth captures for this Gaelic female poet. "That women engage in this pleasure [of artistic production], are involved in it, unbounded and bounded in it, find subjective identification, formation, expression and articulation through the [aural], visual and material pleasure of such production would seem to be obvious" (Drucker 1992, 8). The poem sees autonomous female pleasure, and female work within a community of difference, in class and language, and it registers the shock. The gaze is nothing to the Reaper (it is significant that we do not know how far away she is), and "Will no one tell me what she sings?" becomes a remark processing the shock of her autonomy, as well as of Highland difference. At least Wordsworth offers a self-qualifying sense that he knows he is missing something. So another way of seeing this poem is as a figuration of female pleasure in singleness and as the depiction of a female figure having pleasure in her own song and productivity without any intervention by the male figure, without even being (depicted as) interrupted or bothered in any way by the "male gaze" and male "ear" so patently exercised upon her. This is a figuration of the orgasmic female whose pleasure escapes the gaze. The poem depicts female autonomy. What happens to the song within the poet is a postlude to her own pleasure.

What are the social processes and contradictions here represented? There is a struggle in the poem between taking her song and acknowledging it, between her as an autonomous, autotelic figure joining nature and culture inside work and him as a listener getting her goods. The poem is not only about her as a muse for him; it is also about her work in song. The tension around female work and autonomy is clear in this poem of yearning within romantic modernity. The strangeness of that particular poetic apparatus—muse—has become visible.

We begin to see a reconfigured dynamic of gender in the poets of modernity. "Muse" relations—the construction of a female figure artistically (and erotically and intellectually) charged for the male writer—can still occur, but the poems that celebrate the figure nonetheless also reveal a contested area. A conventional muse can be written in such a way as to ignore the poet, who can still construct of the female figure a situation of iconicity and longing in his depiction. But when the muse figure is also another poet or artist? when the muse figure is a double worker—in art and in economic labor? when the muse materials even as written and contained in an enunciation controlled by a male poet reveal some tear or strain in the enounced, the enunciation, or the announced? We are then in another historical epoch in poetry. Looking forward to Pound's "Portrait d'une Femme," the muse figure has to be carefully described to obscure her artistic production. And when one arrives at the relationship of Marcia Nardi and William Carlos Williams, of Frances Boldereff and Charles Olson, historical figures—women who do cultural work—passionately contest and analyze the exposed appropriation of their materials.[23] These later examples show a tremendous abrasion in the construction of male subjectivity in the modern period.

In Wordsworth the sense that something has escaped him over which he had almost assumed he would have an overview makes for a quick anguish of failed possession that breaks through the tone of the poem. By emphasizing the moment of abrasion between the subjectivity mainly evinced in his poem, and the outcry and the textual changes that suggest that possession is no longer assured, that inspiring use is not guaranteed, I have argued that the "muse contract" has been breached in part by class and national identity, in part by a particular performance of gender in the subjectivity of the poem. To echo one of my epigraphs—Patrick Joyce's own echo of Marx's *Theses on Feuerbach:* in artistic production not only artworks are produced. Many kinds of social relations are reproduced and forwarded in form, in structure, and in the general ideology in which that artwork participates, and to which, by not contesting, it adheres. One captures, in this artwork, a moment when Wordsworth tries simply to reproduce social relations of gender and nation, but a new formation is emerging. An artwork—even a poem—can express contradictions about social relations, can negotiate its own queries, and can leave traces of those contradictions and queries for those willing to engage them.

6
Propounding Modernist Maleness

How Pound Managed a Muse

Critical cliché says that analyses of the ways social debates and meanings are inscribed in poetry cannot be aesthetically nuanced. But this is not so. Culturalist readings need not lose formal specificity nor overlook the saturated, pleasurable textiness of poetic texts. We need reading strategies to help mediate between what is said *in* poetry and what is said *as* poetry. Without attention to the interdependent helix of a text's social and aesthetic aspects, a poetic text has to be viewed reductively as a bizarre choice of message-delivery system for ideas and themes—a choice inexplicably quirky and rather less effective than writing polemic or sending an email. Yet paraphrasable meaning is hardly all a reader seeks, and authorial claims of what is intended cannot illuminate all a text's territory or its effects.[1] A postformalist reading strategy—a "social philology," or sociopoesis—must look at the deep formal mechanisms of literary texts with New Critical care yet link formal moves to the issues that purist New Criticism rejected: social substance, biographical traces, constructions of subjectivity, historical debates, and ideological strata (DuPlessis 2001, 9–12).

As part of its "repoliticization of the aesthetic sphere," gender studies, or feminist criticism, needs to commit to the examination of gendered materials in the apparatus of *poesis,* as well as in narrative and performance (Felski 1989, 175). Such criticism may look at institutions around poetry (patronage, publication, reception, canonizing trends, coterie groups, poetic careers) and analyze cultural conventions and institutionalized topoi inside poetry that have a gendered torque. This project enacts, for poetry, what Teresa de Lauretis proposes for other genres: "a *feminist theory of textual production* which is neither a *theory of women's writing* nor just a theory of textuality" (De Lauretis 1987, 92).

One part of the apparatus of *poesis* is the relation of gendered muse to poet. This is a particularly fraught site because it involves cultural convention, biographical materials, literary representation, and their reinvention in any particular situated case. That is, subject positions such as "muse" or "inspired by a muse" appear variously in poetic tradition as figures and in real life as biographical choices and activities ideologically and culturally available to people situating themselves inside careers.[2] Other gendered materials in the apparatus of *poesis* are the subject positions of poet, poetess, and genius, what is played out in each, and how these interactive postures emerge both inside texts and in personal life at historically determinate times. That such subject positions are culturally institutionalized and personally, if unevenly, internalized is shown in Svetlana Boym's work on the tropes of femininity in "the death of the poetess," which examines her character as a mix of excess and lack, and in Barbara Johnson's work on "male [poets'] privilege as the right to play femininity" (Boym 1991, 192–200; Johnson 1998, 127). These positions can emerge in texts as recurrent, but variable, motifs, topoi that are necessarily susceptible to some kind of situational reading because of the mix of social, ideological, and even historical materials condensed in them.

A glance at one-frame cartoons, whether in the *New Yorker* or elsewhere, will convince anyone of the ideological persistence of muse motifs (often figured in relation to visual artists): at its most banal, a beneficent, lovely, noble, and saintly female figure inspires a male artist, yet she may capriciously, inexplicably, or pedagogically withhold favors, thereby causing artistic blockage or further growth. Parodic and satiric uses of muse motifs depend on our sense of the convention. The interplay between passivity and activity, initiator and recipient seems to run counter to gender stereotype, raising the issue that—in a kind of Dinnersteinian historical psychology—the muse has her psychological origin in the imprint of the powerful mother on the needy baby (Dinnerstein 1976). Considering the muse in his 1994 "Gendering the Muse," Jed Rasula has proposed the figure as embodying the hope of surpassing one's own limits, thus acknowledging the creative self as hybrid—a gender hybrid. He builds a mythopoetic argument that what we call the muse is the site of a poet's own internalized otherness. Poetry takes shape in an "underwriting" or "underwritten" guarantee of "male poetic authority" by a "differently gendered" voice "pre-articulated inside" a poet (Rasula 1994, 161). But once the "muse" is thus interpreted as a metaphor for an interior projection of power that allows one to hybridize oneself, there is no particular reason for it to manifest any gender narrative at all. Rasula speculates why it would. For male poets the sense of having another growth inside is a male imitation of the feelings women have if and when they are successfully pregnant, since the fact "that men don't give birth is one of the more thoroughly repressed of cultural traumas" (Rasula 1994, 160). Rasula presents the primal scene of *poesis* not as maternal nourishment, sublimated sexual intercourse, or eroticized chastity but as imitative pregnancy: a couvade of a semiautonomous otherness that speaks from the inside. This formulation does not straightforwardly transfer to women poets, but it certainly foregrounds gender conventions in the apparatus of *poesis* and might suggest that looking for "repressed gender traumas" of women would be a place in which to speculate (trans-)historically about muse figures for females.

Even granting some of this suggestive synoptic generalization, I propose being a little less archetypal and more situational. Any muse figures used in a particular poem or active in life draw on specific gender relations that are sustained, remixed, and activated in historical time by individuals seeking to establish their creative agency. Thus I want to undergeneralize, even myopically, and offer a close reading of a well-known poem in order to discuss how one female figure is represented by one male writer, reading both his investment in this figure and her own qualities.

A study of Ezra Pound's "Portrait d'une Femme" (1912) is undertaken here because this often-anthologized work models gendered ideology concerning creativity, elaborating that part of the apparatus of *poesis* called "the muse." Tracing the actual addressee of this poem and contrasting her achievements with those that Pound has selected to depict reveals how his "propounded" forms of modern maleness and, more loosely, of poetic genius depend, as subject positions, on proposing and maintaining a dehistoricized, despecified female figure. That the negation of her agency as the "real woman" passes into her figured representation as muse is not simply Pound's, or any artist's, choice of what and how to represent. This critique does not debate his right to write the poem he wants or needs to write, but rather it examines the contents of that need and points to the ways this poem reaffirms conservatizing gender narratives.

Attention to the poetic subjects inside and outside this poem provides an understanding of the gendered "micropolitics of literary culture" (Watten 1998, 107). This "portrait" alludes to visual art even in the French of the title and, of course, both to James's novel of passion, entrapment, renunciation, and collections and to Pound's admiration of James's ethical realism as a model for poetry. Pound proceeds by deeply interested interpretations—indeed, repressions—of the historically attested work of a particular creative woman. But *Une* is unspecific, not *La Femme;* with no name given, this "femme" is discussed as a limited muse, a semiadequate inspiration for a functioning artist, someone whom the speaker must treat elegiacally, regretfully, from a position of farewell (Pound 1926, 61). He represents his female figure within the text as virtual lack, inadvertent creativity, and compromised ability.

The female in "Portrait d'une Femme" is, in Pound's depiction, a semi-bourgeoise protobohemian, having rejected marital loyalty to "one dull man, dulling and uxorious." She is an older *salonnière* who holds court but whose materials are so piled up, impacted, "dimmed," and "tarnished" that they seem virtually useless. Yet the figure surprises the speaker by what she can give to others and by her "patience" at collecting or letting material pool around her. The muse motif is strongly, if secularly, articulated:

> . . . now you pay one. Yes, you richly pay.
> You are a person of some interest, one comes to you
> And takes strange gain away.
>
> (Pound 1926, 61)

Although the metaphors here are Jamesian, the speaker of the poem sits in some judgment of the figure being portrayed; there is no particular hint of bachelor impotence in the speaker's voice but rather a kind of elegant, summary, appreciative condescension. The Jamesian images of paying and double-edged interest and the sense of possession still conclude in "nothing":

> . . . In the whole and all,
> Nothing that's quite your own.
> Yet this is you.
>
> (ibid.)

Having the final line be a two-beat hemistich (after a passage of iambic pentameter) dramatizes this inadequacy. Being an unpossessive conduit is a precise description of the "conditions of employment" for a muse figure.

Pound brings the whole tradition of Shakespearean blank verse—the articulate packing of the line, the mobile caesura, the personable, meditative tone, the Renaissance diction with its "mandrakes" and "ambergris"—to bear witness both to this female figure's inspiration and to her passivity. The female figure is the site at which such bisexually fertile images as "pregnant with mandrakes" (giving birth to phallic materials) and "ambergris" (an excretion of sperm whales, used for perfume) can emerge, be articulated and taken as the "gain" of the male speaker. The female object can manifest or exude these goods but cannot claim or use them. Thus the poem presents the homosocial bonding of Shakespeare and Pound (in the enunciation) over the body of the female figure in the enounced, one who inspires genius but cannot herself create.[3] The diction is highly motivated: the supplement of Shakespearean tonality supports Pound's own genius subject position. By its diction the poem is taken out of time; it has created a magic world where no modern markers intrude, no technology, no motor horns, no signs of modernity in the language. The only time marker alludes to the figure's age. The line "London has swept about you this score years" reduces the figure's agency as it notes her long-lasting presence.

Thoroughly static, and like a stall and trap for ships (the Sargasso Sea), the female figure of the enounced is a spot at which a terrific amount of detritus and rich materials passively collect and jumble. The figure lacks center and teleological energies; she is only a dump or midden, "naturally" accumulating debris: something indicated in the long, syntactically flexible list in the second half of the poem. Yet although she is taxed for unoriginality, she is (appropriately, in 1912) inventing collage: accumulating fragments, juxtaposing these, resisting representational design, foregrounding the detail, combining the old and new ("strange woods half sodden, and new brighter stuff"). Thus the speaker describes the figure as proposing, semiconsciously, a major strategy of modernist presentation but in a retro "Victorian bric-à-brac" mode (Feldman 2001, 453). The poem becomes a muted, backhanded tribute. In the strain of the thrice-repeated word *strange*, the speaker acknowledges this artistic mode while disparaging its source.

"Great minds have sought you—lacking someone else. / You have been second always." These ferocious lines in this otherwise temperate statement depict her as an apparent stop-gap in a narrative of inspiration or romance. All these issues can be elaborated when the poem's historical addressee is identified. Florence Farr is the original of the "portrait d'une femme," and the poem is a Poundian redaction of this New Woman of striking cultural force from a generation before his (Pound and Litz 1984, 130–33; see also Johnson 1975).[4] A. Walton Litz calls Farr an embodiment of an Ibsen type of " 'transitional' woman" but certainly more than "Shaw's 'lover' and chosen mouthpiece, Yeats's musical muse, Pound's passive sitter for his twentieth-century version of a Jamesian portrait" (Litz 1996, 86). Beyond the interest of this historical woman, I am methodologically interested in the tone, mechanisms, and materiality of the poem as artifact and will not import "facts" about the identification of Farr as if these "facts" could prove or disprove the poem's force. Indeed, the gap, contradiction, and interplay between the depiction of the female figure and Farr's work give the most information to this reading.

Florence Farr [Emery] (1860–1917) was an actress, a socialist, a theosophist, a feminist, and (in her final years) an educator in Sri Lanka. Farr was friend of and coauthor with Olivia Shakespear (Pound's future mother-in-law), friend and inspiration of George Bernard Shaw (his *Arms and the Man* was written for her), singer for and inspiration of W. B. Yeats, an actress, novelist, and polemicist—and taken, in her time, as a quintessential New Woman. Farr played the character Rebecca West in the 1891 London premiere of Ibsen's *Rosmersholm* and, in 1907, published a series of six essays treating Ibsen's heroines as if they were real female types with contemporary problems, doing striking character analyses of their motivations and passions. As she moved from the Shaw orbit into the Yeats orbit—a serious shift—Farr produced one Yeats play in 1894 and acted in others (in 1899 and 1905) (Laity 1985a). She was active with Yeats in Golden Dawn occult and mystical performances and was the recipient of his letters from 1895 through 1906.

While she emphatically "inspired," she also emphatically possessed and deployed considerable artistic and critical agency. Farr is an emergent New Woman with emancipatory flair, one of those "heroines of modernity" in Rita Felski's terms, who gives the lie to implicit claims of many theories of modernity "that women were situated outside processes of history and social change." Hence this poem allows us considerable purchase on the problem of reading "the modern in relation to gender politics" (Felski 1995, 16, 18). As a woman who played the muse but also mused the play, she situated herself on both sides of the muse-agent compact. Perhaps her passionate inspiring of these men was a useful cover for her active agency, or perhaps, more likely, for females entering modernity, artistic agency and erotically charged inspiring with free love bravura are mixed together and give tremendous professional power and satisfaction in ways that the pure stereotyped form of "muse" wisdom-in-passivity-and-sublimation cannot articulate. In the 1890s Farr's intellectual or cultural allegiances were split between spiritualist, theosophical practices of esoteric "religious" forms and socialist critiques of bourgeois life; that is, she made herself the container of debate between these two rival worldviews. In biographical terms this debate is enacted between Yeats and Shaw, who each regretted the influence of the other on Farr (Jayawardena 1995, 138). Yet because the theosophical was also very feminist in implication, with its priestesses and goddesses, offering women adepts paths of spiritual power and cultic status, and because the antibourgeois socialist asked a number of telling questions about women's status, one might see Farr's position as synthesizing elements concerning female power and critique from these two rival worldviews.[5] When Litz summarizes her *New Age* articles and publishes her Ibsen character portraits, he argues for her as primal embodiment of Ibsen's ideas on women's passionate striving—sexually, intellectually, socially, in the world and in the family.

It is the Yeats aspect of Farr's life—her sexual, productive, and professional life—that interested Pound; he met Farr in 1909 at the Poets' Club as he was hoping to enter Yeats's orbit himself (Longenbach 1988, 11–14). Farr, a noted performer, had been known for chanting Yeats's poems to an instrument "half-lyre, half-psaltery" (made for her by Arnold Dolmetsch), an activity that the two took very seriously from about 1901 to 1905 (Pound and Litz 1984, 128, 343; Yeats 1955, 274, 353–54, 373–74, 384, 394). She wrote music that Yeats was very eager to see included in an edition of his plays; some of which appears in Yeats's essay "Speaking to the Psaltery," from 1907, which also contains a section by Farr (Yeats 1955, 491–94). Yeats defended their music-of-poetry practice in letters to both Robert Bridges (1901) and Arthur Symons (1902). Yeats and Farr gave lecture-demonstrations in a number of cities to showcase her "extraordinarily impressive and poetical" method of *sprechstimme;* in 1907 she toured America giving lectures on music and poetry (Yeats 1955, 384; see also Ellmann 1961, 133; Litz 1996, 87). Mark Morrisson has commented on how Farr's artistic elocution helped to focus modernist poetics on "the impersonal performance of the pure voice" (Morrisson 1996, 40–41). Farr's book *The Music of Speech* (1909) solidified her position as an expert in both the theory and practice of the relation of poetry and music; notably, this book was dedicated to both Yeats and Arnold Dolmetsch. Pound also researched the relation of music and poetry, possibly impelled by, inspired by, or catching up to this Yeats-Farr-Dolmetsch cluster of activity. Pound's essays-in-tribute to Dolmetsch date from 1918 (Pound 1954, 431–40). Through the years from about 1909 to 1910, Pound seems to have had a sense of rivalry with Farr, an interest in focusing Yeats's attention on himself in an area in which Farr had significant professional expertise.

While seeming like a romance/muse plot in the poem, the speaker's line to "Farr" as "femme," "Great minds have sought you—lacking someone else," can be re-seen as an articulation of Pound's rivalry with Farr, a statement signaling Pound's desire to displace Farr's analysis of the musical performance of poetry with Pound's (the "someone else"), in the sight of Yeats, the great mind.[6] The speaker of Pound's poem seems to allude to Pound's own desire to catch up with these influential music-and-poetry ideas, the poem itself offering the sub rosa claim that the Farr-based figure (and, covertly, her work) had, by 1912, become collective property, belonging to us. This is suggested in the pun propelled by an emphatic, odd line break: "I have seen you sit / Hours," encrypting, "I have seen you sit[,] / [ours]." This line also alludes to Pound's construction of a homosocial bond between Yeats and himself via Farr, instead of an oedipal Pound looking at the intense couple Farr and Yeats, a couple professionally and at times sexually active. Indeed, the plethora of art-objects in the poem, the wash of furniture and stuff, might be thought of as being precisely *not* about music, a deflection from the medium in which Pound's actual rivalry with Farr was expressed. On displacing Farr, Pound may have been celebrating some real-life satisfaction in this poem: Yeats wrote to Lady Gregory in December 1910 that "this queer creature Ezra Pound, who has become really a great authority on the troubadours, has, I think, got closer to the right sort of music for poetry than Mrs. Emery [Farr]."[7] Although Pound "can't sing" and sounds like a "very bad phonograph," Yeats nonetheless accepts him as a belated, amusing, but sincere collaborator (Yeats 1955, 543).[8] No matter the biographical facts of Farr's agency, originality, and influence on music-poetry thinking, no matter her spurring of Pound's interest, the poem constructs "femme" as having become inadequate, displaceable.

At the beginning of his "Treatise on Metre," in 1934, several decades after Farr's death, Pound has another last word. Pound positions himself as having performed a great service—a troubadour-like service—in this music/poetry nexus: "I heard a fair lady sigh, 'I wish someone would write a good treatise on prosody.' As she had been a famous actress of Ibsen, this was not simple dilettantism" (Pound 1960a, 197). This is again a portrait, by Pound, of the unnamed Farr as female figure. In this comment he honors Farr, yet his honoring has two conflicting dimensions. He mentions her fame and her work (which nonetheless exist faraway in the past perfect—"had been"), but focuses on her "fair lady" needs, whose desirous "sighs" (a metaphor from romance) he is about to satisfy with his knowledge of prosody. The phrase "not *simple* dilettantism" (my emphasis) raises the damaging specter of *complex* dilettantism, certainly a possible reading of Farr's life and one reading of all the floating stuff in the poem as the remains of dilettantism. But Pound's raising the specter of the dilettante at all, rather than the fact of Farr's professional expertise, is reductive and a striking choice in 1934, when the wench, so to speak, is dead. Farr's expertise is thus something that Pound had at once imitated in his criticism and carefully, jealously reduced both in the portrait and twenty-two years after, in his remarks prefacing "Treatise on Metre."[9]

The particular mechanism in Pound's poem has to do with the repositioning of female work. The word *work* appears in the poem as a noun: the female figure is not depicted as working but as someone who sits in the vicinity of "the loom of days" and whose visitors find around her "tarnished, gaudy, wonderful old work," an accomplishment without agency, for which she is not visibly responsible. The poem itself is a mechanism that separates Farr from her work (in acting, in writing, in theorizing song and performance), while it claims as collective property anything found, pooled, or caught near this female "Sargasso" figure; the poem is as if under admiralty law, with the speaker claiming the right of salvage to whatever is washed up. Some form of "possession" of Farr and her work—parallel to her work with Shaw and then Yeats—marked a male artist as possessing status; Pound's tactic is to take this work and to insist on the passivity of the muse rather than the push-pull activity of male and female cultural workers.

Pound produces his work—this poem—by the thematic occlusion inside it of the work of the woman on whom the poem is based. Farr at fifty-two years in 1912 was still a token of enough importance or suggestiveness that in the poem one might discuss or produce her marginalization. This is visible in Pound's allusive word-layering: the speaker of the poem shows ambivalence toward the female figure's power in the minor phallicism of the phrase "strange spars of knowledge," from the "bright ships"—by adducing her lack, in the word *sparse,* but also acknowledging how the figure "spurs" the speaker on. *Spars* may also be a noun meaning the act of sparring, disputing, boxing, or contending with words. This shadow of possible debate or sparring and the eloquence of the figure—or of Farr as model—is also very suggestive, given her own passionate analyses of female passions, sex and gender struggles, and women's "burning will and striving intellect"—a Keatsian/Yeatsian phrase she uses to describe the character of Rebecca West, in the "Ibsen's Women" series (Farr [1907–8] 1996, 94).

The poem's mechanisms propose a solution not only to Farr's talents on the music-poetry scene but also to her "problematic" feminist opinions. Farr's other 1907–8 articles were full of feminism: the feminism of women active and independent for the (eugenic) good of the race, the pleasures and dangers of sexual expression, and the outrage of the "economic bargain" women must make in marriage (Farr [1907–8] 1996, 88, 89). In her essays on Ibsen the one word that recurs is *passion,* and she is exact about what Ibsen came to represent in the way of radical, tragic striving of women whose passions and social spaces did not coincide. Farr speaks of women "bored by marriage," with "dim yearnings for an intellectual comradeship with men"; whose lives are bounded by "Suburbia"; who struggle against "social convention"; and who have a particular resistance to the insincere "general atmosphere of mutual flattery" that characterizes the bourgeois "home as an institution" (Farr [1907–8] 1996, 92, 98). Farr argues for open relationships, "social units constantly subject to change," wherein men and women can attain "a more vivid existence" through rejecting the "little stagnant pools" of their mandated ties (Farr [1907–8] 1996, 98). This rejection of stagnation is precisely opposite to that stasis with which, in the "Sargasso" metaphor, Pound taxes Farr.

The "Sargasso Sea muddle" also appears in Dorothy Shakespear's remarks on Florence Farr's 1912 novel, *The Solemnization of Jacklin: Some Adventures on the Search for Reality.* Dorothy Shakespear's comments of July 1912 may have given Pound his image or may simply echo the Sargasso Sea image already in the poem.[10] Engaged to be married to Pound (they were to marry in April 1914), Dorothy is clearly provoked by Farr's essayistic fulminations on marriage and the market value of women. In Pound's poem Farr's principled suspicion of marriage emerges, weakened, as the figure's choice to avoid boring middle class "uxoriousness." *The Solemnization of Jacklin* is rather more a watered-down Meredithean study of a female's search for experience than an antimarriage novel. Still Farr's work does contain studied passages that offer stiff and radical New Woman critiques of marriage for its "commercial aspect" and of women for their degraded complacency in economic slavery, their offering sexual services for money outside marriage—or even inside it. "Why was it, she asked herself, that it was impossible for women to make money as easily as men did; why was it always slavery or marriage for them? . . . She suddenly realised that she belonged to a race of creatures maintained for the pleasure they could give their masters—their paymasters" is one such heartfelt and bitter chunk, linking prostitution and marriage as parts of the same sex-gender system (Farr 1912, 73). Of these revelations and others Farr's narrator remarks: "Poor Jacklin [the heroine] woke to this situation in the year 1904, long before the women's movement had any driving power behind it" (Farr 1912, 74). This date is not meant to be comically ironic, although it sounds that way to us; during the years Pound knew her (1909–12), Farr was rather cheered by feminism's driving power for social and political change.

Her novel is dedicated "To the Man Who Shall Be," suggesting that a subject position like New Man should follow on the New Woman. But the novel also sits in judgment of the reckless female main character for her disparate variety of yearnings—Fabian, independent, decadent, woman as "the slave of emotion" (Farr 1912, 241). The novel ends with the remarriage of the original couple after various overheated flings. A child from one of those flings sits with them while "husband and wife looked at each other with eyes full of mutual charity" (Farr 1912, 248). Thus Farr's Ibsenish opinions were rather tempered by a narrative compromise around the marriage plot engineered by the author—hardly a totally radical solution.

It is probably irrelevant to discuss Farr's *Modern Woman: Her Intentions* (1910) at any length because the sheer fact of a fervent, public feminist book stating "This is to be the Woman's Century" only two years before Pound wrote his poem may be all we need to appreciate his work of interpretive erasure in the making of the poem (Farr 1910, 7). We can take the poem as indicating, in encoded metaphors, his view of Farr's declamations on marriage, prostitution, the vote, economic independence, love, divorce, and chosen motherhood as just passéist trappings, possibly what is referred to as "strange spars of knowledge . . . some curious suggestion . . . fact that leads nowhere." At the very least her book touches, topically, on many of the political, social, personal, and moral issues of this central period of feminist struggle. Farr's book is an enthusiastic polemic on many topics but especially on how the fight against the "prisons" that keep women trapped is larger than the vote and how such struggles will transform social life within modernity (Farr 1910, 93).

Nonetheless, a glance at her introduction offers some sense of Farr's particular politics. It is spoken from a patrician, aristocratic, explicitly "white" feminism and is tied to the medieval courtliness of white men, who have had their historical day in the sun as knights and troubadours. They are imagined by her as fighting inspired by "their ladies' colours"—as if all of medieval life were a defense of Western women or done in their name—a peculiar position at best (Farr 1910, 12). "White men have fought in the past [against what is not said, although to honor women is strongly implied], and it remains for white women to fight now, and at last rid their sex all over the world of the ignominy of this false doctrine." This "false doctrine" refers to Semitic patriarchal institutions, since the enemy of women's freedom is the "Semites" (Jews and "Mohammedans"—i.e., Muslims) whose patriarchal control of women was inexplicably re-expressed in Christianity (Farr 1910, 12). Farr claims that the world-historical problem at the root of women's oppression is that "the white races adopted the Assyrian Semite's Scriptures" (Farr 1910, 8). This snarl of scapegoating, Semiticized representations, patrician racism, overgeneralized history, and feminism is worth far more than the cursory glance I give it here, but her general position is clear. Feminism offers a powerful "alchemy" to ignite the modern world, transmuting its institutions and revaluing its values, but, alas, the world doesn't yet credit this "fire that is to burn it" (Farr 1910, 7). If this book is any indication, at age fifty, Farr's outspoken, intellectually wayward fire was still ablaze.

Pound's poem shows a fascinated ambivalence toward the creative power and political bite of Farr, both as a New Woman and as a serious, respected contributor to a Yeats-centered poetry scene, as well as, before that, to a Shaw- and Ibsen-centered theater scene generally encoded as "feminist." The real figure has been transformed from a critical, powerful, influential, outspoken, and original historical woman to a textual "femme"—one form of a muse of modernism—an inadequate, anonymous and displaceable female figure. Hardly static or a dilettante, though a woman of many interests, Florence Farr—artist, actress, thinker, and performer—has been rather startlingly recast by Pound. His poem portrays Farr as empty and "second always," instead of as a formidable cultural activist, her fervent female striving interpreted as a seaweedy trap, or "slow float," and her energetic social criticism a useless backwater.[11] All in all, Pound's poem is a mechanism in the service of one kind of male subjectivity by the active creation of a shallow but provocative female muse for the containment of historical New Woman effervescence and achievement. This is an important transposition in the relationship of modernism to modernity. By representing a female figure in this way, Pound has contained, grounded, or stalled consideration of the impact-laden presence and agency of the "real person" on whom the poem was based, making the figure an Old Woman with useful muse properties, an exemplum of old stuff that still somehow inspires. Poetic representation masters this female figure, using poetic institutions like "muse" in order to deflect attention away from the historical achievements of Farr, the hidden subject.

What else could be at stake here? To answer, I must assume that the "over-elaborate post-Browning 'Imagiste' affair"—a poem that Pound sent to Harriet Monroe in August 1912—is "Portrait d'une Femme" (Pound 1950, 10). This poem thus marks a curious conflictual transition in his poetry—for how could something be at once "over-elaborate" and " 'Imagiste' " given those "few rules" of imagism, a movement invented circa December 1912 and elaborated in now well-known dicta early in 1913. "Portrait d'une Femme" is arguably the precise opposite of imagist work: it is an *indirect* treatment of "the thing," saturated with adjective and repetition far beyond condensed efficiencies of "the presentation," and composed not in forward-looking, musical free verse but using a pentameter "metronome" (Pound 1954, 3). Given this symptomatic conflict between statement and poem, given Pound's resistance to his possible appearance in *The Oxford Book of*

Victorian Verse, one might imagine how he registered the pressure from futurist polemicist Filippo Marinetti (Pound 1950, 12).[12] Marinetti's work was available in London from 1910, when he presented his ideas at the Lyceum Club (Lyon 1999, 97), and in 1912, when his March lecture on futurism was given the same day that Pound delivered his second lecture on the troubadours, concerning Arnault Daniel (Litz and Rainey 2000, 68). In a "careerist" reading Litz and Lawrence Rainey propose that the enormous 1912 success of Marinetti's avant-garde proposals and affronts, in contrast to Pound's work in "literary culture" as "a restricted aristocracy of sensibility," directly motivated imagism's invention (Litz and Rainey 2000, 68).[13] To make his cultural mark, they argue, Pound felt he had to construct some distinctive, audacious product, and not one that only embodied and represented the cultural heritage of the past. The poem expresses this debate.

The "femme" is surrounded in her pool of debris with all the cultural materials that kept Pound from being perfectly modern, in the audacious Marinetti sense: a lack of an "aggressive character," an attachment to beauty, a "pensive immobility," and stasis (rather than "speed"). A whole past of beautiful but waterlogged cultural goods swirls around this figure—goods by which Pound was insistently and overwhelmingly tempted but which were ultimately cast away in Marinetti's millennial futurist provocations: "we will destroy the museums, libraries . . . will fight moralism, feminism" (Marinetti 2001, 187). To rid himself of the "museum"-quality goods that make culture soggy, Pound attributes them to the "femme," finds them damaged although tempting, and then wards them off in the emphatic "No!" and "Nothing." To possess these materials is to be swamped by culture as it was, to have nothing that's "quite your own." The double move of identification with the materials and rejection of them is contradictory, of course; this contradiction is a coiled spring giving the poem its power. No matter that Farr's own personal culture (as a real individual) may have been as modern (in her feminism) as it was retro (in her medievalism). This was exactly the kind of synthesis Pound used to desire but now had to reject in order to position himself as adequately, truly modern from not quite modern enough.

Thus the poem is described proleptically as "post-Browning" although it is not at all beyond Browning—it is Browningesque, imitated after Browning, and "post-" only in that sense. The poem is described as "Imagiste" although it is not *imagiste* at all; it is rather rhetorically "overelaborate." Hence this lack of fit between his description and his poem is itself precise evidence of the tension between Pound's "Victorian modernism" (Feldman's phrase) and his desires for a diction-cleansing, culture-purging rupture in the modern mode. The inaccurate description of the poem exposes his inadequate modernism; the poem is an act of dislodging to rectify that inadequacy. To acknowledge the old muse, to establish his career power, to scapegoat her materials even as he is tempted, to cast her off in the last lines as unoriginal—these are vital accomplishments.

Furthermore, if it is possible—and it is not unlikely—that in hearing of Marinetti's ideas, Pound might have caught wind of the "disprezzo della donna," this program might have focused his attitude to his "femme." The part of Marinetti's program called "scorn for woman" is an "ideological double helix," in Janet Lyon's words (Lyon 1999, 101). If Marinetti meant "scorn" for the bourgeois, romantic ideology of Womanhood, with all the conservative, madonna-esque, or feminine manipulations that implies, his phrase could betoken feminist critique of the gender system. If he meant scorn for women as actual people standing in the way of the sleek automotive purgations by violence that his manifesto enacted, or meant scorn for the effeminate in men, then such scorn had ideological implications in the building of muscular modernist claims by strategic attacks on specific women, on women's activism, and on transgressive gender ideas. This poem, arguably registering Marinetti's interventions, although hardly as slashing, overstated, or absolute as Marinetti's claims, could be described as Pound's soft-core scorn. In "Portrait d'une Femme" Pound makes the past—his past—*passéiste* by putting it into a female site of entrapment, by revealing the enormous temptation of this site, and finally by rejecting that past.

Pound's particular modernism—soon to be under war pressure, as well as being already under New Woman pressure and pressure from alternative, transgressive sexualities—is gradually coming to affirm noneffeminate maleness. Despite the enormous contemporaneous critical thinking on this issue, one kind of masculine sensibility—"the real sperm of them"—triumphs within his thought ([1917], Pound 1991, 97). Propounding this particular version of maleness is central to Pound's notable achievement during this period; it is probably one of his most culturally influential acts within the reception of modernism, as well as its production.[14] One part of Pound's constructed maleness is sustained, though not without unevenness, by various short- and long-term strategies working against the acknowledgment of women as coequal and cotemporal producers of artistic and critical works, yet he evinces a good deal of conflict in relation to any specific woman. As we have seen at length, in this poem the trace of the female figure as coequal and cotemporal is reduced, something rather startling when the nature and opinions of the "real woman," Florence Farr, are considered.

The poem is the mechanism for the imaginative, and possibly real, consolidation of a male poetic subjectivity as modern by the mellow "reluctant" disparaging of a female cultural producer, whom Pound perceives as a rival and as a backwater—in two different, conflicting narratives involved with fellow male artists: the "Yeats" (and "Shaw") narrative and the "Marinetti" narrative. Making a coequal historical woman into a poetic muse thins her, controls her agency and impact, evokes the past of poetry as an institution obscuring her, voids her critical Ibsen-inspired interventions into issues of gender, avoids her accomplishments as a performer and musician, and reduces her own modernity to a retro backwater. Indeed, as a cultural institution of poetry used by a modernist, the muse is a mechanism that takes a modern subject—a New Woman—and changes her into an encumbered, static, nonmodern subject. The poem moves Farr backward, setting her "scores" of years behind her own historical time and achievements, creating female belatedness from a woman pioneer in order to consolidate a male pioneer from a man's sense of his own belatedness. The resistance to acknowledging females as modern subjects (a denial of historicity noted by Rita Felski) may be said to begin, in Anglo-American modernism, with poems such as this one.

Pound wittily and carefully uses the poetic conventions of the lyric—the muse figure inside the apparatus of *poesis*—to construct a passive muse, a female figure from an active, provocative influence in historical time. Pound uses poetic convention to protect himself from historical shifts around gender. One can see that his poetic career is forged from intricate cross- and intragendered power interactions that include among them friendship, mentoring, misogyny, sex-radical thinking, male potency, sexual hopes and fantasies, and male panic, all of which play against and are inflected by poetic subject positions such as muse. The ultimate purpose of this feminist and historical examination of a poetic text is to change the terms and understandings of poetry definitively, placing issues of gender, the apparatus of *poesis*, and power-oriented production and reception centrally in play. Asking gendered questions of the ideologies and social situations of poetry as a mode of practice constitutes an opening into the deepest apparatus of *poesis*.

III
Urrealism

7
Lorine Niedecker, the Anonymous

Gender, Class, Genre, and Resistances

> A poem is a peculiar instance of language's uses,
> and goes well beyond the [person] writing—finally
> to the anonymity of any song.
>
> —Robert Creeley, "'Statement' for the Paterson Society"

> Anonymity was a great possession. . . .
> We can still become anonymous.
>
> —Virginia Woolf, "'Anon' and the Reader"

> Remember my little granite pail?
> The handle of it was blue.
> Think what's got away in my life—
> Was enough to carry me thru.
>
> —Lorine Niedecker, *Collected Works*

That's it. One quatrain. *Remember* and *think* guide the meditation, *remember* addressed to a listener, *think* addressed to the self. The poem is syntactically eerie, ambiguous in meaning, and split in impact. It speaks from an adult voice, but the first two lines emerge as if from a child. One might imagine the first line seemingly more open, not fraught, somewhat casual, or wondering. The second two—or three—lines "signify" on the first—in these lines the speaker shows a deeper evaluation but possibly only to herself. The movement between little or miniaturized subjectivity and far stickier, complex thought produces an interplay between surface and depth with special meaning for a female poet. Already the poem has put a lot in a small space: the famous Niedecker "condensery."

In this poem *granite* means graniteware, a grainy pattern of speckled enameling on tin utensils, but the word also leaps to the stone that connotes hardness, steadfastness, solidity, monumentality. These terms envelop that little pail, so there is a frisson between the words *little/pail* and *granite*, and the pail becomes a monument to that lost time and to other losses. Thus the conventional memorializing functions of the lyric drop down into and around that pail. Neither marble nor granite eventually withstand the ravages of time, but poetry, those succinct words, prevails through storm and destruction—at least that's what Horace and Shakespeare say about various hard materials. Sometimes this is believable. This poem functions like an epitaph, asking us to remember what is buried at its site. It is a lively rumination from the dead moment.

And that is only one of the poetry allusions in this quatrain. For the word *carry* contains poetic implication, given that the "carrying" literalizes the term *metaphor* itself. *Metaphor,* opened etymologically, indicates carrying over, carrying across—in metaphor meaning is transferred (though never totally) from a literal to a figurative site. So this poem simultaneously presents a literal pail, lost forever, and a symbolic pail-action based on metaphor itself: "carrying thru," by means of the poem and its language, everything that "got away" despite the loss of all the literal things. But a pail could not carry all of that! So loss and presence are simultaneous, undecidable. Remember my little poem—the handle of it was blue.

I remember that pail, too, on a Far Rockaway beach. And this literal blueness evokes a large horizon, a strained hope, a moodiness. Blueness is evocative—why? In part because of the inverted syntax. "It had a blue handle" is all it would take, but *handle* provides neither convenient nor straightforward rhyme. The rhyme word *blue* got wiggled into its necessary position by Niedecker's syntax. By means of that inversion blueness is highlighted as the intensity of childhood memory and adult desire. I take that blue handle to parallel Walter Benjamin's "*weak* Messianic power": the thin yet possible aura of a transformed reality within the difficult and unjust reality we know. "In other words, our image of happiness is indissolubly bound up with the image of redemption" that one might, borrowing from Benjaminian concepts, also say is bound up with a sense of any time being Now-time, a time of intensity and plenitude (Benjamin 1969, 254). Niedecker's and Oppen's uses of the fragment, of the incomplete, evoke Benjaminian "chips of Messianic time," startling us in our "heterogeneous, empty time" (Benjamin 1969, 263, 261).

The second two lines of this ballad stanza contain a marked ambiguity, poised on a mark of punctuation—the dash at the end of the third line that makes you pause (Niedecker 2002, 96). The toy pail was formative, or at least memorable and amusing, but it is now gone. All those little artifacts that one had, the line says, all the little ribbons and doll clothes, the tattered books and Teddy bears, become traces that generate fantasy and yearning.

What is the ambiguity? One interpretation of the last two lines tends to a sense of fullness, of adequacy. The pail, though it no longer exists, did carry the speaker, because it re-presents itself to her via poetry's memorializing functions. A paradoxical dyadic parent-child picture is painted, where the child carries the pail, but when the person grows up, the pail (maternally/paternally) carries the adult. One depicts a simple act of purposeful playing; the other shows a need for containment and palpable support. The poem's logic reveals that though the pail is no longer here, it was enough—adequate, sufficient. It "carried me thru."[1]

Yet the alternative and simultaneously emerging interpretation of the final two lines tends to a jaunty, devastating assessment of *in*adequacy. *If* I had all the things that got away, things summarized in the image of the pail, I would have made it; I'd have been carried through all the times bad and good. But the pail is lost, gone, a symbol of all the things I had but also lost. Things (not just physical things, but every thing) did "get away"; I didn't get carried; I was not supported in my need. The two readings hinge between the issues of deprivation/adequacy; of the missing/of the available; of being carried or not being carried.

Why is this a ballad stanza? Because ballads are implacable: they deal with what has happened, what simply is. Ballads say *It Is.* "The handle of it was blue." Niedecker's ballad joins the deictic pointing of the first two lines to the inferences about loss, adequacy, sufficiency, insufficiency, ambiguous in the second two lines. There are two kinds of pointing: one to a simple object, the other to a richly complicated double emotion. Was it enough? Was it not enough? The finger pointing emerges in (or as) the dash between the third and fourth lines. This *volta* pivots the poem in an otherwise grammatically unified statement. If the dash were not there, the sentence would not be abruptly interrupted. And a reader would not be forced to consider the two opposite perspectives on the granite pail: what I lost carried me thru despite its being lost; and what I lost did not carry me thru—I experienced deep loss.

There's a certain ice-blue Slant
of messianic light
that pressures. Here or absent?
Such words, really Any words,
incite Conceptual
affright.

The Blueness of her handled pail
arcs between Extremes.
Hope or burden, radiance or Stone?
Either? Could be

Neither fully holds or words
the Sum of all that Seems.

Lorine Niedecker, an American woman poet, born in 1903, lived most of her sixty-seven years in rural Wisconsin at the confluence of a lake and a river, in a small cabin like those that her father, then she, managed for vacationing fishermen. She was married twice—very briefly in her late twenties and in the last seven years of her life—but she was more deeply marked by her bonds to her parents and to Louis Zukofsky. She died in 1970. Her life was modest; her poems, mainly, short; her friendships among some literary folks—Zukofsky and Cid Corman—and some neighbors (Gail and Bonnie Roub) were few, but they nurtured her intent and elegant working mainly in the objectivist poetics within modernism. During her life her work was published only by small presses. She is barely anthologized.[2] She made no obvious literary career.

This could be told as a narrative of female pathos, victimization by literature or its representatives. What alters that story is a feminist emphasis on the agency of writers, on the choices (even among narrow options, even favoring self-erasure) that allow a person to construct an oeuvre. In her late and unfinished essay "Anon," Woolf argues that "Anonymity" was a great possession of the past, giving us ballads, songs, implacable attitudes, nonegoistic subjectivities, frankness, and abilities to articulate communal values. The notion of anonymity saturated Niedecker's attitude toward the poetic career. She worked to claim the non-elite, nonhegemonic literary career (anonymity, erasure, loss) as a cultural identity: she will return to the folk with whom she identified. This is a gesture emerging from her self-contained class location and her loosely Popular Front politics. Indeed, she embraced, worked toward, and improvised playfully on the condition of anonymity as a gesture of career building, maintaining the position of Anon. in several ways.[3]

Being female is not a transcultural absolute, though it is still a marked position. Femaleness always plays itself out in specific historical and social conditions and in relation to other social markers. For Niedecker one such marker was her social class or, more accurately, her multiple class facets—as a person from a formerly comfortable, property-owning family, as a poorish, semirural person holding mainly low-level jobs, as an intellectual poet responding to at least three very specific poetic traditions (folk, surrealist, and objectivist), and as a political radical making a left critique of American culture and society. She was visually disabled as well, and she had spent a good part of her life involved with her impaired mother (deaf, with her "big blind ears" [Niedecker 2002, 107, 174]). The resistances Niedecker makes in her poetry involve her critical discomfort with gender norms, class assumptions, and Americanist ideology as she lives out her intense marginality to a dominant culture of materialism, bellicosity, bigness/bestness, and fame developed in the postwar period. These resistances play themselves out not only thematically but in her choices of genre: Mother Goose rhymes, ballads, and haiku/renga. She may seem to seek a minority, a littleness, a miniature scale almost unthinkable, especially for a female writer who can be culturally coded as minor no matter what genre she chooses, but especially if she chooses tiny-looking and folk forms. Many of the assumptions in poetics made by Niedecker distance her poetry from the glut and fattiness of mainstream poetries. Because of the little magazines and presses in which she appeared, the nonhegemonic "objectivist" cohort with which she mainly affiliated, and the subtle smallness of the work, Niedecker has had no particular impact until quite recently, with work by Jenny Penberthy and others (Niedecker 2002, 1993; Penberthy 1996).

In addition, her loyal, marked friendship with Louis Zukofsky and his family was part of her formation that had been interpreted to tell a familiar master-disciple story. Zukofsky's son Paul (the well-known violinist) figures in Niedecker's imagination as a sibling artist, or even as an imaginary son, for the complexities of affiliation, some filial piety, some love longing carefully set aside, and continuous artistic camaraderie between Niedecker and Louis Zukofsky make one of the decisive stories of her formation and arguably his as well.[4] Her poetic development was interdependent with his colleagueship, but she also assumed the pose of loyal disciple as a strategy, using a demeanor of intentional modesty while articulating her own cultural attitudes and practices.[5]

A striking "Mother Goose" work—the first stanzas chanted like a jump-rope rhyme—is Niedecker's limpid feminist poem about female erasure and underknown foremothers, about a historical woman at the triple crossroads between anonymity, erasure, and renown:

> Who was Mary Shelley?
> What was her name
> before she married?
>
> She eloped with this Shelley
> she rode a donkey
> till the donkey had to be carried.
>
> (Niedecker 2002, 212)

Along with folk wit about the donkey where a woman just wore that animal out, this poem connects to a love motif ("Who is Sylvia?"), a familiar site for female figures in the lyric tradition. The love plot erases the character's life as it erases her future—the poem ends:

> She bore a child
>
> Who died
> and yet another child
> who died.
> (Niedecker 2002, 213)

The poem is deliberately terse, laconic, incomplete, filled with loose ends; it anatomizes the achievements and losses of a woman whom Niedecker saw as virtually missing to literature, despite her power, as the author of *Frankenstein* was in the 1940s to the 1970s, before feminist scholarship. This oblique allegory of female cultural power and virtual anonymity is motivic for Niedecker.

In a similar spirit of anonymity, Niedecker dealt with a young poet who cited an Al Millen story about mowing a carp while cutting very swampy grass. First, Niedecker made him take his dedication to them off his poem, feeling exposed that they have been mentioned, especially in a poem she felt was "indecent" and perhaps expressionistic and histrionic with its blood and guts. She would not lend her name to tones and poetic modes that she felt were melodramatic. But then she teased Corman: "Well, someday the world may hear someone say 'Here is where the husband of Lorine Niedecker mowed a carp'" (Niedecker 1986, 214–15). This comment shows a real investment in the possibility of her fame—but masked by concerning her husband's story (not one she told) and the erased poem of an unknown youth (not one of hers).

Anonymity for Niedecker may be construed in both gender and class terms. She always accepted herself as a populist, a member of the populace, the vox populi.

> The clothesline post is set
> yet no totem-carvings distinguish the Niedecker tribe
> from the rest; every seventh day they wash:
> worship sun; fear rain, their neighbors' eyes;
> raise their hands from ground to sky,
> and hang or fall by the whiteness of their all.
> (Niedecker 2002, 100)

It is a "minor" subject—women's work, and people's commonplaces, including cunning commentary on how primitive religion manifests today in social uniformity, in "white" tribes that worship conformity. ALL, an iconic washday detergent, is evoked, as if its racialized and commodified totalities could succor us (Niedecker 2002, 100).

Yet her relationship to the people is never without the judgment of an outsider: she is inside in social class yet outside by virtue of her artistic production. Niedecker proofread for *Hoard's Dairyman* (from 1944 to 1950), and when her eyes went bad, she became a cleaning woman from 1957 to 1963 at the Fort Atkinson Memorial Hospital. This doubled position, central to the social and cultural meaning of the writer as woman, is manifested in the following anecdote from 1958: when hired as a member of the hospital housekeeping staff, she concealed from her supervisors and fellow workers her copy of *Art News Annual:* "I think they know they have a cleaning woman who is a little different from the usual, but it wouldn't do the slightest good to show them how different" (Niedecker 1993, 244). They would not understand, and she says, all she would have been doing in her self-revelation is "getting uselessly involved just for the sake of a moment of less loneliness." Part of/Far from the working class, part of/far from the middle-class perspective on a domestic worker, she is also an intellectual, carefully choosing her audience, unwilling to indulge in needless rear-guard explanations and self-justifications that would involve the packaging of her personality. Her anonymity was principled; it was a choice. My argument echoes Adrienne Rich's essay on Dickinson—she chose her own terms, made her own psychic "economies" in order to do her work (Rich 1979, 160).

Although Niedecker may have been figuratively lonely, she was not literally isolated. I was astonished, in visiting Niedecker's one-and-a-half-room cabin outside of Fort Atkinson, Wisconsin, to discover that she lived year-round in a summer colony. The cabins are packed along the two sides of a road on the narrow peninsula, and she was unbelievably close, in a physical sense, to her neighbors' houses.

Her poverty, however, was a condition. Cold drafts through wall holes, old wash dresses, a rivered lake that floods and leaves stink and mess behind, a "soak-heavy rug" appear in her poems; they are not props. Subsistence. Eking: these are some of Niedecker's prime subjects. She does speak from "nature" as a pastoral trope (a literary space) but in nature as a material condition—that is, inside subsistence. Spending her life, she has chosen poetry; the recurrent floods have chosen her. In one of her fiercest poems, brilliantly depressed, she declares (merging with a maternal voice): "I've spent my life on nothing"—poetry and poverties, poverties of class and gender intermixed.

I'm pillowed and padded, pale and puffing
lifting household stuffing—
    carpets, dishes
    benches, fishes
I've spent my life in nothing.

(Niedecker 2002, 148)

"On nothing": on kinds of work that reduce to zero, poetry, and housework; and "in nothing"—in a place and situation (poor land, strained relationships) that reduce one's status to nothing. Even the furies that pursue her are "nothing": insects, mosquitoes, or mites. I take this poem as an indicator of the consciousness of her choice of small scale—because of the rage that choice can sometimes induce.

In both class and gender this is a poet for whom material cares were palpable. She, or her persona, makes barbed political observations about class and the construction of leisure:

We know him—Law and Order League—
fishing from our dock,
testified against the pickets
at the plant—owns stock.

There he sits and fishes
stiff as if a stork
brought him, never sprang from work——
a sport.

(Niedecker 2002, 99)

A piercing pun on *sport,* certainly. Niedecker understood work and its costs, sexuality and its; understood right-wing rigidities and the dangers of their apparently comic pretense.

Indeed "Poet's work," a poem framing her poetics, wittily uses the metaphor of laboring and working-class tragedy: the layoff.

Grandfather
  advised me:
    Learn a trade

I learned
  to sit at desk
    and condense

No layoff
  from this
    condensery
      (Niedecker 2002, 194)

When her grandfather says "learn a trade," her choice is a playful distortion of his intention to encourage her to master a marketable skill or craft. For instead of learning a trade, she makes a trade, trading his intention for hers—poetry. Then she produces a factory superior to his: "no layoff / from this / condensery." Niedecker's "condensery" poetics may well be a bilingual pun on Pound's influential injunction in *The ABC of Reading:* that "*Dichten = condensare,*" or, to write poetry is synonymous with the imperative infinitive to concentrate / compress / condense (Pound 1960, 36). Niedecker's "Poet's Work" or "trade" (that is, *Dichten,* with the further pun on "diction") is boiling down, paring down in the "condensery." To Corman, Niedecker wrote about the tension she felt between plenitude and compression: "You and Jonathan Williams have thrown off the shackles of the sentence and the wide melody. For me the sentence lies in wait—all those prepositions and connectives—like an early spring flood. A good thing my follow-up feeling has always been condense, condense" (Niedecker 1986, 33). This statement shows the temptations of excess and emphasizes the corrective discipline of the condensery. This is a further elucidation of her choice of scale: the haiku-lyric, the miniature may even offer its own barbed commentary on monstrous, overweening cultural ambitions. On the other hand, as with many women writers in modernism, the very humility is implosive. An overweening humility, we might call it.

Niedecker also made barbed comments about gender institutions. She resists beauty, construed as a trap for women, for females in general, for herself—the critique of beauty as a part of both general ideology and poetic ideology makes her refuse the romantic lyric and its rhetorics of transcendence. Her refusal is anatomized in a balladlike work of intense feminist critique:

I rose from marsh mud,
algae, equisetum, willows,
sweet green, noisy
birds and frogs

to see her wed in the rich
rich silence of the church,

the little white slave-girl
in her diamond fronds.

In aisle and arch
the satin secret collects.
United for life to serve
silver. Possessed.

(Niedecker 2002, 170)

This negative version of the happy ending of romance for both women and men critiques normative feminine commonplaces and female goals; the bride is "the little white slave-girl." The silver service (punningly, for Oneida was a silver company) is an appropriate bourgeois wedding present for the couple, but "United for life to serve / silver. Possessed" shows the newlyweds possessed by their possessions, in marital jail, enslaved by propriety and property.

In contrast, Niedecker, like a mummer or "green man," decks herself with the "noisy birds and frogs" and greenery of her swamp. The "rising" of stanza one makes a devastating intellectual pun on Darwinian evolution (mud to algae to flowerless seedless plants to more complex plants), where churchgoing civilization is shown ironically lower on the evolutionary scale. Its materialism makes meaningless and crude display, while natural materiality is integrative and generative. This poem is about the "ascent" of the active subject "I." She criticizes contemporary materialism in its impact on both genders and criticizes marriage as an institution, in which man possesses woman and both are possessed by the things they own. Niedecker's contemptuous pity for, and distance from, these values is very plain. A similar comment occurs in a blues poem in which the female-enforced culture of materialism is deplored by means of the catchy judgment "fads" rhyming with "woman and those 'buy! buy!' / technicolor ads" (Niedecker 2002, 165). Another poem reminds us that to be alone is "hard" but at least there is

. . . no (TV) gun
no more coats than one

no hair lightener
Sweetheart of the whiter

walls.

(Niedecker 2002, 229–30)

Niedecker's early "Wasted Energy" (1922) appeared in her high school yearbook (Niedecker 2002, 368). This piece of witty verse concerns language, gender, and class:

> When Tom, Dick and Phil are conversing,
> The effect is entirely unique,
> We can't quite make out what they're talking about
> But we gather it's Sheba or Sheik.
> . . . .
> It's amazingly queer, but from all sides we hear
> Of the "crooks" and "tough birds" in our town,
> Of "wild women," of "guys," many "I wonder why's,"
> "Juicy" tales and requests to "pipe down."
>
> (Niedecker 2002, 368)

This is a folklorist's collection of slang phrases in which the prancing poet seems to mock her own pretensions to verse. The title suggests that making rhymes is worthless because all one really needs to get along is to "hand people lines." Not, of course, lines of verse but the lines of formulaic slang responses, bromides and turns of phrase that blur distinctions and precisions. She tells "Tom of the quake that made Mexico shake"; his response is a standard line: "'Well, ain't that the berries?' quotes he."

But in that "line" that is popular, Niedecker conceals allusions to that "line" that is seductive. For slang seems to be a medium involved with stories of sexuality: Sheba or Sheik. So when Niedecker distances herself from yet collects this language, she is setting herself at a class and gender distance from her peers, unwilling to be absorbed into the same joshing easygoing formulas. She answers by encircling this language with her own "lines," a poetic practice of scrupulous segmentivity.

Her strategies grew more subtle, but the same verve, energy, and outrageous claims for and about "the people" appear in her cold war poem, "In the great snowfall before the bomb . . . " This important poem captures her difference from those among whom she lives as if in disguise ("I was Blondie"), yet tries to understand the energy that she admires in "the folk from whom all poetry flows / and dreadfully much else" (Niedecker 2002, 142–43). Niedecker proposes a distinct political critique of the easy efficacies of postwar culture, of the bellicose power of the bomb, of the banal commodities that we trust. Some of the "much else" may be glossed by another of Niedecker's piercing epigrams:

Beautiful girl—
pushes food onto her fork
with her fingers—
  will throw the switches
of deadly rockets?
(Niedecker 2002, 185)

The plethoras of plenty and the smug pride of gender are joined to unthinking political destructiveness. These poems propose a judgmental alienation from yet love for the People, with whom her fate—in the fact of the bomb—is inextricably intertwined in the post–Hiroshima-Nagasaki era. "In the great snowfall" depicts aggression, posturing, slavish relations to popular culture anatomized in a series of puns and homonyms ("rehashed radio barbs" to "barbarous"; "hirelings" to "higher-ups"). The people have uncritical but bitter relations to power, whether office politics or beyond. Insofar as their violence, political sleaziness, and banal language are also "folksy," one must come to terms with this dreadful "folk" who are, at the same time, threatened by international politics far beyond their control. Niedecker appropriates their language in a deliberate but contained moment, using the *em* of "right down among em," while judging her choice in the word *down.*

The double position of the word *poetry* in "In the great snowfall . . . " is one of its most striking features. "Poetry" comes from the people's vitality and their aggression, their snide, snappy, clichéd language, emerging from mass and folk cultures. "Poetry" conversely is made by the quiet, solitary Niedecker "sitting" for months on a few lines; Niedecker is the broody hen hatching the potential of a folk whose manner she finds both dreadful and admirable. Her resistance takes the shape of anonymity; she hides her vocation for its sake, and for hers, the better to observe and conserve. The question in the bemused last stanza is unanswerable:

What would they say if they knew
I sit for two months on six lines
of poetry?

The quiet rhyme of "knew" and "two" functions to isolate and make superfluous the latter lines of the poem—the reference to her own slow, considered poetic practice.

In another poem her late-in-life, second marriage is set eerily in two bleak contexts: for warmth and companionship "at the close" of an individual life and, simultaneously, to have "someone" "in the world's black night" during an era of political fear and despair—the cold war era, registered as the poise of potential, mutual destruction.[6] "I hid with him / from the long range guns" (Niedecker 2002, 228). The claustrophobic description, with its witty use of page space to define head and foot, "We lay leg / in the cupboard, head / in closet" is certainly about the (tragicomic) narrowness of a marriage, possibly about a compensatory snugness, but certainly about the prissy domesticities of shelters that one pretends are adequate in the face of geopolitical fears no less compelling for being distant and inchoate. "'Shelter'" is another such poem, which alludes to the American 1950s hysteria for bomb-"shelters"—note Niedecker's mocking quotation marks in the title (Niedecker 2002, 246). Pensively she alludes to the death of even the outlying regions of earth, "beyond / the main atrocities." True to her watery place, she imagines the destabilization of her piece of earth and makes an ironic commentary on "property" in apocalypse.

In her resistance to commonplace values, Niedecker asks again and again what our power and possessions really cost and struggles with her troubled ownership of "debts / and two small houses," and her larger ownership of her own poverty and poetry:

> Property is poverty——
> I've foreclosed.
> I own again
>
> these walls thin
> as the back
> of my writing tablet.
>
> (Niedecker 2002, 157–58, 194–95).

Her ethical adhesion to clarity of rendering is linked to an ethics of the subjectivity produced in the words. She worries that her new plumbing—a luxury, she insists—might disturb the old "plumbing," making her neglect the straight Thoreauvian (plumb) line of "principles." In her little poem—regretful, wry, Horatian—about the pump, plumbing for principles with the lead mark is a form of clarity. Niedecker nonetheless (eventually) succumbs to modernizing, giving up her outside pump (once visible by her cabin). And the poem consists mainly in a catalogue of plumberie:

. . . faucet   shower
heater   valve
ring seal   service

cost to my little
  humming
    water
      bird.

The stanza break combined with the line break makes one wonder whether the phrase is "service cost" or a more ambiguous "service [of plumbing apparatuses]" which come at a high "cost to my little / humming / water / bird"—the "sure pump," of "my pres-/sure pump" in the dedication, perhaps the spirit of her poetry (Niedecker 2002, 201).

Niedecker's resistance to plenty, while driven by necessity, also defines her aesthetic and her moral sensibilities. Two abstemious genres specially mark this: haiku and ballad/nursery rhyme. What does it mean for an insulated American woman, on a watery island, to assimilate the influence of the Japanese writer Bashō to the degree that she did? There are several allusions to him (Niedecker 2002, 225–26, 204, 270, in two poems) in which she admits "Bashō / on my mind," and it is clear that she knew of haiku from early in her career (Niedecker 2002, 226).[7] Even in the first years of her correspondence with Corman, she already had haiku on the bookshelf she dubbed her "immortal cupboard," and she appreciated Corman's (2003) exemplary translations of Bashō. As well as constructing many poems with the succinct obliqueness of the haiku, she titled a collection *In Exchange for Haiku.*

To choose a foreign marker for this contained, oblique mode (when there was already a long imagist tradition of Anglophone work) is in part to deny one's own belatedness, declaring Bashō her source, not Pound, Williams, or H. D. Niedecker finds comrades in an international style that transcends barriers of language and ethnicity, an international style that constructs a formal answer to Bigness. One can never, of course, perfectly mimic the force and the tradition of Japanese haiku in American poetries. But using that tradition marks certain desires. Niedecker plays renga—linked haiku—with herself, imaginatively creating a community; in Japanese practice the poems are written with others at a ritualized writing party. The form is quite austere, brief, subtle, working by indirection, inference, juxtaposition, and hint. In American poetries haikulike objects have been used to make emphatically antirhetorical claims. Ever since Pound's imagist poetics, the desire for the presentational, restrained, abstemious, anti-moralizing Image always bespeaks a desire to separate some essence of poetry from packaging, poeticisms, and ornamentation.

Haiku seems to have been Niedecker's means to a commentary so buried, so deeply concealed in apparently artless word choice, line break, and tone that one must tune in to a very subtle understatement. The facade of inability, artlessness, and the almost unspoken hint are very feminine strategies; her haiku furthermore work as gifts on a small personal scale. Haiku are part of a poetics of gift exchange that she constructed with both Zukofsky and Corman. Thus she made a familial economy of affiliation that rejects the feedback loop of impersonal publication, prizewinning poetry, and fame. She wrote to Charles Reznikoff, "Reading *Inscriptions: 1944–56* I often feel a kinship between us in the short poem. And if you are my brother-in-poetry then we have Chinese and Japanese brothers. But I have a great deal of practicing to do—of quiet insight—before I can enter such a good family."[8] The implosions of humility in this letter are as striking as its principled internationalism. In addition, from a class perspective the lack of high poetic language (in Anglophone haiku) infuses dailiness and life as it is lived with the possibility of poetry.

"My Life by Water" draws on the radical condensations of haiku; this work may be thought of as an elaboration of the "sound of water / water sound" of Bashō's great haiku about the frog jumping into the pond (Niedecker 2002, 237–38). And as "watersound," the word *by* in the title might mean "next to"—as Niedecker spent her life in the flood-prone spillway, "a section of low land on the Rock River where it empties into Lake Koshkonong" (Dent 1983, 36). But *by* might at the same time open much-debated questions of authorship and point of view. Could this really be the "life" of someone, her biography, whose author is water? The angry, hapless Keats epitaph, also a trope on anonymity and fame, reverberates: "Here lies one whose name was writ in water" (Keats 2002, xxxii). With *by* Niedecker claims the doubled position of water and author. Water surrounds her as amniotic medium and author of herself; she writes the "water borne" or water-related aspects of her life. The fluidity of boundary between self and setting is a theme: she sees boats "pointed toward / my shore" or may herself be the "one boat" that "two" (her parents) "pointed" there.

Nine intensely compressed three-line stanzas are framed by two dashes, so the whole poem is caught (dammed) between the words "My life / by water" and "Water." She catalogues animals: frog, muskrats, and rabbits, whose activities are in some continuum with human and other forms inhabiting the same terrain. Either a frog or a cold board makes a cracking noise. Muskrats create "wild green / arts and letters," a diploma of nature, from, or out of, the "doors" that separate us from the out-of-doors. The "lettuce" nibbled by the rabbits chimes pointedly with our phrase for the humanities as a discipline: letters/lettuce. Puns and line flow communicate intersubjectivity and webbed relations.

The little stanzas climax in a series of kenninglike combinations. The kennings *birdstart* or *wingdrip* remove the transparency and limpidity of nature; the compound neologisms construct linguistic possession without possessiveness, sound ebbing in the loosening of the hyphenated "weed-drift." She is mothered by, nourished by, the place. Niedecker need not search for anything beyond the "here" in which (and much is through the ear in her work) one can "hear." With the ear she tempers the domination of the "eye" and scopic practices. The poet sustains an attitude of wonder and readiness at the quirky holiness of the ordinary. The universe is nondualistic—both awkward and beautiful.

If this poem is (auto)biography, it also constitutes her poetics: a poetics of rumination, meditation, circling around, and "reflection." "The basis is direct and clear—what has been seen or heard—but," stated Niedecker, "something gets in, overlays all that to make a state of consciousness." There is an "awareness of everything influencing everything," with networks of linkages and not the "hard, clear image" only.[9] But this is a poem that also tracks a political attitude: how to have the environment as a source without imposing ownership. Possessions (as things, pots, clothes, appliances) and possession (as mediumship, shamanistic behaviors, poetic transcendence, vatic or bardic claims) are both resisted in Niedecker's work.

The title of her first collection *New Goose* (1946), with its main allusion to Mother Goose, makes statements worth hearing from a gender and class perspective. Mother Goose, child rhymes, and folk melodies are a series of palimpsests of different origins and different voices—some with political allusions—that have "somehow" gotten redacted together. The forceful, often trochaic, rhythms (Barber, barber, shave a pig), and proverbial solidity (Some like it hot; some like it cold), the highlighting of a few dialogic daily objects (curds and whey, fat and lean), the luminous melodic lines, yet undecipherable density of allusion, all together provide models for Niedecker, not only of stylistic choices but of the precise nature of her ambition. *New Goose,* as a first-book title, is a serious declaration of intent, suffused with a brisk, humbling wit ("silly goose") that comments on the apparent smallness but folk fullness of the scheme. Moreover, the title may conceal a serious critical project.

The dust jacket copy of the book contains four sentences, the first two of special interest for a critique. It is not clear whether Niedecker wrote these words, whether they were based on her statements to the publisher, or whether she approved of the statements, but they are a significant datum: "She speaks and sings against all that's predatory in 'Mother Goose.' Whatever in it is still to be touched or felt she recreates for people today to feel and touch in her—their—own way." *Predatory*—plundering, pillaging, victimizing, destroying others for one's own gain—all of these ideas suggest class and power relations in the "real" Mother Goose: the kings and queens, the taunted children. Indeed, *New Goose* proposes a number of different subjectivities; the poems are spoken by sharecropper, Stalingrad fighter, fishermen, a variety of country people (men and women), and cite approvingly Black Hawk who "held: In reason / land cannot be sold" (Niedecker 2002, 99). The poems are not all, or even mainly, written from the point of view of the artist or an observer of others. She puts the poems about writing amid the voices she has created for the people. In addition, the jacket statement says she does not prescribe a way ("her way") to assimilate this work but equalizes and fuses "her—their—own way."

Niedecker is the woman who "sings at the top of [her] voice when folky records are being played on the phonograph" and who "must have that blues book you speak of."[10] She wrote, joshingly (to Zukofsky), "Mebbe I shdn't ever have gone to NY to meet the real writer [i.e., Zukofsky] but shd. have stayed in my little country patch and written country ballads to be sung with a *gee*tar!" (Niedecker 2002, 408). *New Goose,* she states, "is based on the folk—and a desire to get down direct speech (Williams influence[)] and here was my mother, daughter of the rhyming, happy grandfather mentioned above, speaking whole chunks of down-to-earth (o very earthy) magic, descendent, for sure of Mother Goose (I her daughter, sits and floats, you know)" (Dent 1983, 36). She is a writer whose saturation in language was initiated by her maternal grandfather, "who somehow had got hold of nursery and folk rhymes to entrance me." If her mother is "a descendent for sure of Mother Goose," then no reason why the child of such a mother could not be a "new goose"—enfranchised by maternal earthiness and paternal charms. The sense of descent and parenting is one that, I have shown before, is an enabling feature of the female artist, who stands in a triangular plot of nurturance that repossesses and transforms oedipalization, transposing the undervalued arts of the parents into those channels wherein they can be culturally assimilated (DuPlessis 1985). In Niedecker, however, one loses any sentimentality with which this genealogical narrative could be invested because all three "parents" are depicted as resisting her vocation.

Many of Niedecker's poems have a nursery rhyme sound: the poem beginning "Missus Dorra / came to town" (Niedecker 2002, 88); "Petrou his name was sorrow" (Niedecker 2002, 89) or the insouciance and bitterness of

> Half past endive, quarter to beets,
> seven milks, ten cents cheese,
>   lost, our land, forever.
>
> (Niedecker 2002, 111).

Her political poem "1937" contrasts hope blooming in the Spanish republican struggle with a dim and depression-laden "Here":

> Here we last,
> lilacs, vacant lots,
> taxes, no work,
> debts, the wind widens
> the grass.
> In the old house
> the clocks are dead,
> past dead.
>
> (Niedecker 2002, 120, 164).

The diction is telegraphic Mother Goose; it criticizes the predatory. The folk origin is consciously articulated, knowing, witty: she teasingly says to Zukofsky—"time for BP [her mother] to write / me a poem" (Niedecker 1993, 159). Whether she assimilates the Goose of childhood rhymes, the native ballads, proverbs, or even the blues, Niedecker chose her literary means as a political stance. Echoes of, allusions to, appropriation of the sounds, rhythms, patterns of nursery rhymes abound in Niedecker's work, not to speak of other kinds of allusions, such as titling a poem "Nursery Rhyme" with the dedication "As I nurse my pump" (Niedecker 2002, 285).

Even more poems draw on the ballad.[11] Certain elements of the ballad might have had a particular intellectual and emotional appeal to Niedecker. For one, there is little of the personally expressive "I" in them, appealing to her coolness to conventional subjectivity. Her "I" is often an observer of her/his own fate in a subjectivity mixing first-person experience, third-person emotion. They often speak from an implied speaker who hasn't a lot of social power at the moment of the song—except the power *of* the song (like Mary Hamilton in the old ballad). Then there is an interesting stylistic relation between imagist/objectivist tactics of selection, condensation, and juxtaposition and ballad tactics of "leaping" and "lingering" (Gummere

1907, 91).[12] Leaping involves a springing forward, the omission of details, the overlooking of connective and explanatory materials, the lack of causality, the disregard of elaborate narratives of time and place. Like the antirhetorical poetics of imagism, the ballad works by the caveat against excessive words, by condensation and intentness of the framing of significant images, by a "terse narrativity" (Stewart 1990, 148). By means of the "leaping" and "lingering," ballads move with buried, compacted affect. They run on inference. Ballads leap between materials, do not back and fill, and they override the claims of ego.

Even more notable is the ideology of the ballad in relation to Niedecker's work. Traditional and literary ballads are good for expressing the implacability of things that happen, especially in personal relations involving grief, violent emotions, or tragic events that one could not prevent—perhaps because one was always already politically disenfranchised. Most ballads can be summed up as "something dreadful happened, something driven by a fatedness that cannot be stopped—or even explained. It just *is*." Sometimes this fatedness is actually very bad politics, like the politics of racism depicted in Gwendolyn Brooks's and Sterling Brown's ballads; fate there is driven by an often unnamed but deeply represented white racism, but it might as well be fate in its dreadful, unstoppable effects. Sometimes the fatedness involves gender assumptions (i.e., sexual politics), as in Keats's "La Belle Dame sans Merci." The ideology of the ballad form creates an ethical witness about political power, and the ballad can engineer a partial reversal of this situation, because by witness, by song, one reclaims cultural (inspirational and, in rarer cases, political) power. The tension between fate and politics gives a dialectical edge in the ballad.

Actions have little background or motivation; their political and social materials are absolutized, not analyzed. Ballads do not tell you why something happened in a cause-and-effect sense (why did Lord Randall's lover poison him? exactly why did Sir Patrick Spens get sent off when the king knew he would have to sail on a dangerous, winter ocean?). Rather, ballads offer images *that* it happened—eels in frying pan; courtly, fashionable shoes floating on salt water. One rarely hears answers to the question "Why?" But (in part as a deflected substitute, in part as a memorializing of the intensities of the event) one hears many answers to the question "How?" So ballads spotlight circumstantialities—names, places, times, colors of dresses—but leave motivation, psychology, and rationales totally in shadow. We get, in ballads, the facts and the effects, not the causes. This gives a sense of inevitability, implacability, an ajudgmental stance, or a judgment very oblique and almost affectless.

The ballad therefore has the possibility of a class figuration. It can be used by, or can sing of, the relatively powerless, those who, for reasons of positionality (woman to cruel man; man to vampish woman; commander to king; pregnant lady-in-waiting to court; laborer to exploitative boss; black person to white person) have a minimum of choice or agency, or those who for similar reasons wish to sing of that divestment of agency. Ballads condense and focus areas of emotion and social pain, yet they are rather uncomplaining. Ballads are sometimes like epitaphs and revenants at once—telling you what social forces are "buried" at a site and what ghosts have been created—the ballads of Sterling Brown are like this. The ballad's implacability is the freezing of divested social agency into fate. Yet given the tradition of the protest song that also evokes the ballad mode, this kind of poem can also be used to protest a sense of plunder and being ripped off; people want social agency; they want their politics to be heard and their understandings to matter. Thus the ballad can also express the heating up of a sense of disenfranchised social agency into political outrage.

Or the ballad can exercise a satisfaction at the ending of one particular political outrage.

> Laval, Pomeret, Pétain
> all three came to an end.
>
> Bourdet, Bonnet, Daladier
> so did they.
>
> They tried each other
> they sold out their brother
>
> the people of France.
> Let's practice your dance.
>
> (Niedecker 2002, 144)

We know that certain "nursery rhymes" were old political jingles of oppositional mockery and carnivalesque puncturing of authority. This is a new goose aspiring to the same social function in a satisfied antifascist statement.

A balladlike poem in which powerlessness claims a desperate hope to continue to impose is Niedecker's "Old Mother . . . " This poem cites her mother's uncanny last words, exhorting her daughter to compulsive female drudgery:

"It's a long day since last night.
Give me space. I need
floors. Wash the floors, Lorine!—
wash clothes! Weed!"
(Niedecker 2002, 149)

In this hallucinatory poem of final panic, final orders, Niedecker provides a subtle opposition between floor and earth; earth indicates the fear of death and burial; floors are domestic order and containment. The apposition of "Death from the heart, / a thimble in her purse" may be said simply to connect two details or, more suggestively, to make the second phrase provide metonymic comment on the first. Niedecker offers a picture of her mother's reductiveness and the almost empty bit of love.

Another notable ballad of the family living under the sign of "water" sums up her father's life and extracts a blessing from her father despite his unfulfilled desire that she improve her life and work in a bank. Three of the five stanzas of the poem spin past the life on water of her father: "out of flood"—like a kind of creation myth—

came his wood, dog,
woman, lost her, daughter—
prologue

to planting trees,

which he still fertilizes with carp (Niedecker 2002, 169–70). The latter two stanzas define her father's desire for her vocation:

To bankers on high land
he opened his wine tank.
He wished his only daughter
to work in the bank . . .
(Niedecker 2002, 170)

Again, as with the poems to grandfather and one of the poems to mother, their instructions for her vocation are definitive and in conflict with her real choice. In each instance each of these figures, without their knowing, offered her a truer gift, "a source," in a fascinating feminine rhyme at closure,

to sustain her—
a weedy speech,
a marshy retainer.
(Niedecker 2002, 170).

That last word is one of Niedecker's semantic images. This term offers a way of noticing how meaning is constructed from word choices that seem "artless," or virtually without metaphor, but that travel laterally across a dictionary definition, assimilating all definitions to the poem. *Retainer*—in apposition to "speech" or oral language—is a richly allusive word involving some thing or person she is able to keep or hold in her possession, keep in a particular place, keep in mind, or remember, or hire for a fee. The first three meanings of the language suggests the memorializing functions of poetry and the language's status as Niedecker's most precious (sustaining) possession, her source—which is, of course, water welling up, and buoying her up. The financial meanings of that word allude back to the narrative of deals and banks and the family's poverty and financial losses. Language that works as a financial allusion, as hireling, as retainer—a "trusted servant or companion"—but as well alludes to a relationship in which she is held or bound, evokes the material ground of poverty and failure, the actual cost of her father's life choices. Marshland is also notably unstable. Therefore it needs a "retaining wall" or retainer, someone who holds it, and by holding it—the whole life by water—holds and retains herself and her speech, no matter how wayward and weedy. The memorializing, storehouse functions of poetry are again subtly evoked. As muses, these parents are disgruntled, almost inadequate; the mixture of pride and disability is so deeply inwoven as to be inextricable. Niedecker puts these summary words in her mother's mouth:

I've wasted my whole life in water.
My man's got nothing but leaky boats.
My daughter, writer, sits and floats.
(Niedecker 2002, 107)

Here the whole family is washing away, unanchored, dependent on water and yet victimized by it. The *boats-floats* rhyme suggests the connection of daughter to father and their greater acceptance of cycles of water. Yet from the ungiving, deaf, and angry mother, Niedecker has fictionally extracted the word *writer* to allude to herself.

The intensity and seriousness with which she debated anonymity vs. fame can be measured by an early poem, appearing in *New Goose:*

She had tumult of the brain
and I had rats in the rain
and she and I and the furlined man
were out for gain.

(Niedecker 2002, 94)

What indeed can that startling poem mean, arranging its poets in a phalanx, even, as part of a strange robber gang, and including Niedecker among Dickinson and Zukofsky. "Out for gain"! What is the gain when in the same sequence a pendulum shine outshines her beauty; her coat is "thread-bare," and "our land" is "lost." It can only be fame—Fama—poetry, and the intense work of making a name for oneself—a name that is deeply, ethically committed to its own anonymity and disappearance: from the folk, into the folk.

Scuttle up the workshop,
settle down the dew,
I'll tell you what my name is
when we've made the world new.[13]

(Niedecker 2002, 87)

Her anonymity is, then, a utopian gamble; she will have a name when poetic changes (Pound's "make it new") and social and political changes—even unto revolution—begin to transform the class and gender materials that she spent a lifetime analyzing in pretended simplicity and principled anonymity.

8
The Gendered Marvelous

Barbara Guest, Surrealism, and Feminist Reception

Some constellations. In a discussion of Charles Baudelaire, Walter Benjamin states that the "conditions for a positive reception of lyric poetry" have become more problematic in modernity because of a "change in the structure of [people's] experience" (Benjamin 1969, 156). What has changed? The "replacement" of narrative by information and "of information by sensation" means that both "experience" and memory become more desiccated (Benjamin 1969, 159). Involuntary memory, the memory activated in poetry, has not been assisted but, in fact, prosthetically replaced by mass-market pictures, such as news photographs, that cathect an individual to a managed, commodified memory. This limits the emotional ground for the lyric, for, at its best (an important qualifier), the poem activates involuntary memory. At the same time, the stunned senses of exposure in urban crowds, the "defensive reaction to [the] attraction and allure" of the "masses" that Benjamin calls "shock" have increased (Benjamin 1969, 167). Thus the formulation: "The disintegration of the aura in the experience of shock" (Benjamin 1969, 194). That disintegration does not mean the disappearance of aura (particular emanations from an artwork that incite awestruck response) but its attenuation and splitting.

Shockingly enough, this shock is particularly located in the implacable gaze of certain females in modernity, underlining the impossibility of the saturated mutual gazes of lover to lover, or the gaze of yearning at an iconic female, as models for the look of "recognition" between viewer and artwork. Benjamin speaks of an ideal reciprocal gaze in which lyric poetry is received, a moment when all the "objects" in the poem seem to look back at the reader from a saturated distance.[1] He takes it as a problem for the lyric when this reverberating gaze back does not occur, for it is this imagined look that creates aura. Aura is "the aura of distance opened up with the look that awakens in an object perceived" (Benjamin 1999, 314; see also 447). But something strange has happened to the lyric; a closed up, resistant, implacable gaze has been found in it, a "gaze in which the magic of distance is extinguished" (Benjamin 1999, 314). Whose gaze is this? From a Baudelaire poem, words given much status in this argument, it comes from "satyresses or water sprites [nixies]" ("Satyresses ou des Nixes") in a gaze that resists the "plunging" glance of the [male] viewer.

Benjamin's commentary opens fascinating issues concerning the lyric and the female in modernity. If lyric aura occurs with the postulate of reciprocal gazing or yearning distance, then the blank "inhuman" stare of women on the street, in Baudelaire's world the stare of prostitutes, has helped to destroy aura, because aura draws on and resembles erotic desire, not commercialized sex (Benjamin 1969, 188). Perhaps it is the particular commodification of sex in modernity that stares back and challenges, given the fact that there have always been prostitutes; their existence as such is not a historical change. The smooth, nixielike, implacable stare of a female figure who is linked to commodities and public spaces, the challenging stares of sexual women somehow destabilize lyric poetry. Thus lyric poetry and female gender are again, as conventionally, intertwined.[2] This loss of aura, the cost of modernity in poetry, is attributable to females (Benjamin 1969, 194).

This gaze is supposed to "come back" from objects as if they were agents, yet the gaze of females at work and at large in city spaces is not credited with agency but is a symptom. This look does not respond, does not mirror, does not glow with the light from the eye of the viewer but is autonomous, cold, calculating: "the woman represents merchant and merchandise in one" (Benjamin 1999, 896). Do objects have more ethical autonomy than females in this formulation? I mean: is the autonomous alterity of objects honored, while the challenging sexual commodification of loose women is considered an insurmountable challenge to lyric culture? Why do prostitutes symbolically bear the full onus of commodification, given that capitalist businessmen also exist? One answer—they are women. If one wanted an example of commodified, unfree, resistant figures who might produce mean glances back to (bourgeois) flaneurs, one might as well have chosen male *lumpen* or working-class figures. Benjamin did not. Why do certain women in modernity imply the impossibility of lyric poetry? The implacable gaze of the female apparently has enormous, destructive cultural power.

Benjamin's argument is hard to parse; it loops from term to term; we don't know, for instance, whether the masculinization of modern women is simply discussed or deplored (Benjamin 1999, 318). But it is clear that the ferocious, sexualized women of modernity have destructive impact on lyric poetry. The question whether or how modern women, their particular commodification, and changes in gender relations have "ruined" the aura of the lyric is provocative and provoking in equal measure, and Benjamin seems to mourn and to be resigned to the change about equally. But can it be believable, in any sense, that unfeminine modern prostitutes, that women with an attitude, have ruined lyric aura, or offer the allegory of its ruination?

What to do now? Reject the theory (as "sexist") and proceed rudderless and uninformed? Accept that "Woman" (like "God") is a position in ideology believed in once upon a time, and just carry on with the theory as if this belief had no political effects? Say that this idea still has serious social-political consequences in the present, and call attention to its blind spot, thus becoming annoyingly ambivalent to the theory? Say it does not matter (it's just theory, it can't help itself); like formalism, it plays inconsequently with its own ideas and systems? Deconstruct it as hedging, protecting itself against that carefully constructed Other—but then what? Selectively bracket some ideas, but on what basis—which ideas are decorative and which constitutive? Once there are no genderless subjects of perception and of interpretation . . . there are consequences.

How many times, in typing, have you put femininine*—an indication of the endlessness of the formation* in *in it, nine times nine, you ninnie. Or* femininie *the little* ie *being a feminine ending. How many times?*

Another constellation. To be the guarantor of the site of current nostalgias for former nostalgias, Women were designated as the holding tank of the Eternal Feminine. To bring woman back to a fixed meaning, to bind her to the feminine, to reject any destabilizing of this residual formation, to be loudly horrified by any change in the "image" of woman is the cultural work of an art-world document from 1948, a portfolio of prints and writing called *Women.* The subtitle makes Women precisely "A Collaboration of Artists and Writers"; "Women" are not so much a gender as an occasion to affirm masculinism.[3]

Samuel Kootz describes how he commissioned, from both the artists associated with his gallery and some writers, a "special show to be devoted to 'Women'": "The idea for an exhibition of paintings of 'Women' came into being in February, 1947, with my acquisition from Picasso of his savage 'Woman in Green Costume.' I began to compare this picture with the painting of women done in the French tradition, which reached its sensuous culmination in the work of Renoir and Bonnard. And I thought of all the modern artists who have painted women: how different their points-of-view from the Renoir tradition, yet how inevitable their return to and concern with this same subject-matter"[4] (*Women* 1948).

In the essay he contributed to this portfolio, William Carlos Williams speaks in binarist cliché of man doing and woman being:

> There's really nothing much to man aside from what he does, what he knows, what he desires or makes. Take those things away and you have no man. But woman, that's something else again. . . . To a man the more loving and willing she is and the more she gives herself, the more remote she becomes to him. What is he to do? Impregnate her? Kill her? Avoid her? You see, it all amounts to the same thing: do what he will she remains in spite of his greatest doing or not doing the same thing, woman, woman in the abstract, something without a face, something beyond his power—something that (according to his nature) he can abstract, generalize upon, devise means for elucidating. (Williams 1978, 180–81)

The enormous difference between male and female subjectivity is striking; women and their remoteness, beyond male power, seem to frustrate imperium, to enrage. The double bind of women is alarming: if you give (the way you are supposed to—see Frances Boldereff), you are as wrong as if you don't. The ideology of difference, of total inhuman (nixielike) difference of women from men is a tenet of masculine culture. It enables men to make art.

In the same portfolio Barry Ulanov (once of Barnard College) made a richly symptomatic analysis of the desire to hold women in the gaze, to keep women out of historical time, to keep femininity functioning: "Twentieth century woman has been so ceaselessly subjected to psychoanalysis and socioanalysis, her rights have been so assiduously supported, her position in the economy so fanatically fought for and defended, that she has almost blanked out as a subject for painting. The first half of these hundred years should be long remembered as the time in which women manned trolley cars, mustered rifles, crossed legs before an infinite array of typewriters and became passionless creatures when confronted on an easel at the same time as they won their suffrage." In this analytic mush, social gains of women, their political passions, rights for women, and their struggles for redress are viewed sourly as an artistic loss. "Woman in the painting of our time has been a singularly empty creature."[5] To regain sumptuous art, male painters must deny claims for female social rights. I hope, as Virginia Woolf once said, you will make a note of it.

In modernism the contradiction between mythic and historical women takes acute and symptomatic shape in surrealism. Simone de Beauvoir summarized the dilemma presented by André Breton's idealized essence of the feminine and his idealized figure of the erotic femme-enfant: this female figure was not, despite her tremendous iconographic privilege, a female "human being" but rather an essence, an elemental force, a revelation for others. The figure is not for herself, not a subject with agency, but rather an object of erotic, exciting, odd, enigmatic sex-gender formulas (Beauvoir 1953, 222). These were some of the cultural coordinates when lyric poet and female poet Barbara Guest began her artistic career. These constellations of material make Barbara Guest's effervescent awakening via surrealism, her presence in the United States art world, her commitment to the lyric something to discuss, given that her achievements occurred on ground almost entirely cut away by these theories of the female. Yet there she is.

no w-
under cultures'
temple wander

seminal ambiguous
out of kilter;

know wonder-
kultur's tempter

kilted
crystal clepsydra——
Her.

To analyze the production of artists, their production of artworks, the tremors of dissemination, feminist reception is crucial. This reading strategy puts no limit on the nature of the work and is disinterested as to whether it conforms to particular rubrics for womanhood (but not disinterested in the nature of the rubrics). Nor does feminist reception care whether the writer be assimilated to available, contemporaneous, consistent, or currently popular feminist positions; analysis of those positions is, however, vital. Acts of feminist reception would notice, gloss, and reflect on the productive presence of female and male artists and writers wherever they are at work and discuss how their work expresses or exposes gender materials and contradictions.

Reception and dissemination are never neutral phenomena, and the familiar bumbling can always occur ("Gee, honey, I lost women's writing"). Barbara Guest was once scandalously excluded from a defining anthology of that New York School in which she had been a key participant, *An Anthology of New York Poets* (Padgett and Shapiro 1970).[6] These gestures of neglect, with their personal ties, mistakes, rejections, apologies, and counterturns offer many-sided stories. We can only wonder how the exclusion changed Guest, for example, and what debates, quarrels, or ennuis, if any, it marked. We don't know how such an exclusion functioned in the minds and the careers of those who initiated it, or whether it did particularly. There would be many dimensions to this issue, some quite superficial but curiously (especially given the lighthearted, gestural poetics of many of these writers) now engraved in stone. Here one can simply propose this as yet another "case" for feminist studies of reception. Kathleen Fraser observes that the exclusion of females at the consolidation of literary groups (never mind their participation at the inception of such groups) is a "common historic practice" (Fraser 1993, 57). It is part of the overlooking of the cultural labor of women. Guest is, so to speak, in excellent company. In *The H.D. Book* Robert Duncan turns to the reputation of H.D. in the late 1940s, precisely as *Trilogy* appeared. He reports, "when Karl Shapiro and Richard Wilbur, two of the younger members of the new poem-writing caste, came to edit Untermeyer's *Anthology of British and American Poetry,* H.D.'s work was eliminated from the canon" (Duncan 1979, 84–85).

In contrast, though not in compensation, Barbara Guest was central to a slightly earlier anthology edited by one of the art dealers and curators central to that conjunction of painters and writers, John Bernard Myers. *The Poets of the New York School* was published in 1969, though not, as the other anthology was, by a widely circulated trade house. In his introduction Myers positions surrealism as the historical, philosophical, and aesthetic precursor of the New York School of both painters and poets. Guest is accorded a strong accolade by Myers—she is of the "lineage" of André Breton for being "so directly concerned with this sense of 'le merveilleux'" (Myers 1969, 13, 25). The marvelous seemed to be an invitation to the liberation of the unconscious, to dream imagery, to spontaneity, to acknowledgment of the attractions of the fetish object. Putting Guest in the lineage of Breton, however, does not simplify the question of Guest's place or status, nor their gender narratives, once Myers expounds the centerpiece of Breton's thought: a sublime dependence on Woman and heterosexuality.

> The sexuality in which he was involved was rigorously against what he considered perversion. For example, he detested male homosexuality to the point where he once threatened to expel a member of the surrealist movement if he didn't get married. On the other hand, voyeurism and lesbianism disturbed him not at all: the Woman must at all times be in some way idealized. . . . [A]s a surrealist, Breton maintained that desire must be infinite. He conceived of desire as the energizer of the will: hence whatever militated against sexual desire must be regarded as destructive of ultimate fulfillment. (Myers 1969, 11–12)

Myers's discussion confirms that the female figure (or capital W, "Woman")—exoticized, sexual and idealized, desirable, suggestive, the provocatrice of male energies—had a special status in surrealist and neosurrealist work, not to speak of "Her" general status in the cultural milieu of the 1940s and beyond. Permission for pleasure and free-floating, even flaunted desire was part of the New York School ethos (a group that was, contra Breton, populated with gay as well as heterosexual men). But if desire is infinite, there is no reason it should not also be polymorphous. Linking desire only to female figures and only to heterosexuality curbs it. Defending women from the vagaries of the depiction of females is chivalry; idealizing them as a fixed act is hard to correlate with a mobile sense of "the marvelous."

The emancipatory goals of surrealism cut two ways—into a politics rich with the liberation of id and a sense of "human becoming" (Breton 1969, 232, 233) and into a psychological attitude about the fusion of all modes of reality (dream reality, consciousness, unconsciousness, association, pulsations, hypnagogic pleasures) into one "surreality" (Breton 1969, 14). The evidence presented in Whitney Chadwick's articulate study of the women artists associated with the first wave of surrealism is complex and double—the "abyss" opening between Breton's sublime "ideal of sexual and spiritual liberation" for all and his imperial "Romantic vision of perfect union with the loved one," for example, or the contradiction between the effervescent presence of the historical women artists and "surrealism's idealized vision of woman . . . like an albatross around the neck of the woman artist" (Chadwick 1985, 8, 66). Renée Riese Hubert's study of couples in surrealist partnership reminds us that the movement and its impact on women in its various pronouncements and networks were not static across time and, further, that one can construct a narrative of surrealist women's "liberation" not only their palpable "repression and victimization" (Hubert 1994, 371, 373).

To say that surrealism offers contradictions about gender issues is incontrovertible.[7] To say surrealism was generative is equally incontrovertible.[8] Like the women who first read Olson's "Projective Verse" and did not notice or mind all the exhortations to the "brothers," indeed, who saw themselves as "brothers," these artistic women may well have developed a thick-skinned take-it-back ethos and a transformative energy and agency when faced with their depiction and iconization. This energy, as the careers of surrealist women artists have shown, can use, even plunder, the attention given to Woman as muse, cultural icon, exotic object in order to liberate their own imaginations and erotic desires. If females, children, and "primitives" are particularly gifted in surrealism, one might, as a woman, take this odd privilege as license for loss of inhibition. If women are audaciously transformed, be-furred, bound with thongs, pasted together with machines and birds and beards, this audacity might be seen as radically deconventionalizing or energizingly metamorphic for females. If Breton refused "repopulation," then sexuality was for pleasure, and a woman might thereby be liberated from the family economy, even if then an exciting or bulbous fetish. Surrealist androgyny and experiments with recoding and cross-dressing valorize witty and metamorphic uses of one's ascribed gender; Marcel Duchamp's critiques of binarist gender might be better known, but Claude Cahun's are also striking. If Max Ernst made collages whose title punned (*La Femme 100 Têtes*), a woman might see that there were one hundred heads ascribed to her (cent têtes) and ignore, or shrug off, that she was also, simultaneously, headless (sans têtes). Selective appropriation offers a law of survival for women in unevenly misogynist art movements.[9] Women also might have ignored or overlooked their femaleness in favor of their humanness, another liberatory strategy. The sense of transhistorical, dynamic, and erotic power ascribed to them may have energized some women, so long as they also had access to, or could claim the very historical mechanisms of, an artistic career: publication, reception, dissemination.

Adorno has argued, counterintuitively, that far from proposing the "invariant, ahistorical images of the unconscious subject," as surrealism claims about itself, its interest as a movement is the creation of "images of a dialectic of subjective freedom in a situation of objective unfreedom" (Adorno 1991, 89, 88). This, in context alluding to European history, also sums up the position of a woman, such as Barbara Guest, inspired genuinely and fully by the long reverberations of surrealism within the New York School. For according to Guest, surrealism was absolutely liberating. "It meant freedom, especially for a woman," she said in a phone conversation (May 6, 1997). The "especially" is fascinating.[10] The word precipitates the contradiction between the poetics involving female figures (Woman), the responsibilities of being the recipient of "mad love," the (inspiring) necessity to be continuously "strange" on one hand, and, on the other, the creative effervescence of "poetic mobility" by virtue of an "associative art," the power of "breaking rules," and the intellectual and sensual liberation all this offered (Guest 2003a, 51, 53). Having a mandated role as somehow embodying the waywardness, vagaries, and charms of free imagination (that is, being a woman), might be "especially liberating," because you were given creative license both as an artist and as an artistic object.

For Guest surrealist practices annihilated "separation between the arts"; this led to its close analogue, "an escape from literature, or from 'the literary'" so that "one could never again look at poetry as a locked kingdom" (Guest 2003a, 51). Guest's escape from the literary led to a particular imaginative approach, a translation of modes of representation in painting to language. This technique liberated Guest from any allegiance to the expository, labored, all-too-well-made poetry of the 1950s and gave her permission to fuse images by association, not to have them lie "motionless within a linear structure" (Guest 2003a, 51). This was a methodological heritage of surrealism; Breton speaks of the "desired suddenness" of "random assemblage." The techniques that surrealism opened and its revolutionary élan, not its bombastic pronouncements, nor the headless, footless, handless, agencyless (and sometimes bootless) female figures it represented were what Guest and other women grasped (Breton 1969, 41; Caws 1991, 11–13). Surrealism encouraged Guest's particular mobile subjectivity and her complex negotiations of the lyric gaze. Guest's nuance of vision and wide story range also show her methodological debt to the associative, lateral *combinatoire* of surrealism. Surrealism also encouraged Guest to write poetry that was "like" producing a painting; sometimes these are ekphrastic works, as Sara Lundquist and Terence Diggory have shown.[11]

Guest can further be taken as a visionary flaneuse inside paintings; the power of her work is the through-the-looking-glass step she makes again and again, to construct something like the interior of a painting, or the distances created in a particular artwork as a site of the marvelous. Guest has cited Benjamin (his *Moscow Diary*) in her "Walter Benjamin in a Museum," insisting that the viewer does not enter the space of a painting; rather the space of the painting "thrusts itself forward," which is parallel to what Benjamin argues about reciprocal gazing as aura. With that thrust is the activation of memory; the viewer associates with the painting elements of "crucial experiences of the past" (Guest 2003a, 55). This passage, one might say, reclaims aura for the lyric poem; the materials are "gazing back over distances."[12] Guest has apparently considered Benjamin's theory of the aura and reconstituted it without the damaging gender argument on which it depends. Through a series of meditative practices, Guest creates the space of vision in which the painting "enter[s] my unconscious" and "begins to exist spiritually" (Guest 2003a, 53). For Guest, the surface methods of paintings and their sensual attractions are only part of the question: "I am alert [she says] to the task concealed within method" in which the sensuous is revealed to have compelling intellectual rationales or propositions (Guest 1986 ["in the shadow of Surrealism"], 3).[13] Thus her work fuses dazzling textures on the surface, diaphanous beauty, with the creation of imaginative pattern: a sense of the visionary behind physical or focused vision. "Vision is part of the poet's spiritual life of which the poem, itself, is a resumé" (Guest 2003a, 27). In these statements, Guest asserts her version of the visionary poetics bound to the real: the austere hermetic urgency of a "blue studio." She ends the essay with a citation from Breton in which the romantic poetics of surrealism sustains and frames the real: "'to imagine is to see'" (Guest 2003a, 32). This evocation of Vision may trump any potential misogyny of the gaze; it allows for a mutual project of looking. The question remains how gender resonates in her particular articulation of the marvelous.

In "The Poetess" Guest begins with "A dollop is dolloping," choosing first a silly, gleeful word and then inventing an even more gleeful word—the awesome *dolloping* (on the analogy of galloping)—for her activity (Guest 1995, 78). This noun turned verb—dollop means a large (or small) lump, helping, or portion and as well a slatternly woman, a trollop—bounces up as if to say—"I'm here to stay, like it or lump it." Dollop could be a descriptor of the shmoolike black blob in the Juan Miró painting that is the poem's "source."[14] With a large-spirited tact, and verbal excess, the poem accepts the minoritizing and quasi-insulting term *poetess* and mockingly debates women's speech or silence—"what natural c/o abnormal / loquaciousness" (Guest 1995, 78). The poem assures us it is good to be a poetess; such a figure evinces pleasure, excitement, glee, liveliness.

This brisk jeu d'esprit ends:

> . . . the
> Poetess riddled
> her asterisk
> genial!   as space.
>   (Guest 1995, 78)

That "asterisk," also from the Miró, suggests the footnotes and errata to which also-rans and poetesses used to be consigned, yet it can indicate something *omitted*—or something *added*. This is a nice turn. "Asterisk" also draws on the etymology for star. *Riddled* and *genial* are even more complicated words. Since *riddled* means to solve, speak in, or propound riddles, it is a word indicating a power—even the power of playfulness. Since the word also means pierced with holes, put through a sieve, and showing weakness, it indicates a vulnerability, or possibly simply a porousness in the Jamesian sense—open to experience. The palimpsest of this word reveals the debate between competencies and weaknesses that "riddles" the career of the female poet. It is the same dilemma as the place of the female figure in surrealism—one can see her as triumphant and crucial or as controlled by the imagination of the men who idealize her.

Genial also demands a vertical reading down through its definitions and etymologies. Apparently unassuming, even unprepossessing in its meanings of pleasant, cordial, friendly, festive, and entertaining, the word gains in discursive kick when it relates first to genius, and sub rosa engages a debate about the minority vs. the genius of *poetess*. It also relates to marriage festivals and engages with the productive, generative, and fecund and with spousal encounters.

Seeing a reproduction of Miró's "The Poetess" (on the poster for the Brown University conference and celebration of Guest held in April 1994) only doubles or triples the interpretive problem. It is possible to identify the characters in the poem ("Poetess," "vain ignots" [or unknowns], "a scoop," "mishaps of blackness," and so on) with specific elements in the painting as a portrait of events around a character called the poetess, but it is also plausible to suggest (in Gestalt terms) that the whole painting "is" the poetess with all her parts, conflicts, and projections. For example, the vain ignots fleeing may be running away from her, or may be unknown parts of her, running (in vain? in vanity?). The "dollop" could be different from the "Poetess," as well as the same. The poem contains many pulls among the various elements of the poetic character. This staging offers a very important clue to Guest's poetry of positionality, which does not so much celebrate personal identity as the spaces of the in-between and the investment in a variety of subject positions.

Guest's poems are supersaturated with travel, geography, landscape, atmospheres, shifts of light, and peculiar alienations of feeling. Guest's metaphysical vision of travel is inflected with symbolist poetics, projecting unknown or mysterious sites, landscapes in which one could live an emotionally subtle, visually lush, attentive life. Neither homeless nor exilic, she travels into the gendered marvelous. "Mysteriously Defining the Mysterious," subtitled "Byzantine Proposals of Poetry" (1986 and 2003a), offers considerable insight into Guest's poetics, for it narrates a primal scene of the construction of poetic meaning. Byzantium is at one and the same time a reality (an actual place seen on a real trip, offering real events to ponder) and a cultural metaphor—the Byzantine—or labyrinthine and intricate.

Disembarking from a ship, already in a state of political/poetical excitement from the proximity of Russia and the East, she and her party enter a bazaar. "Before us were laid golden, silken stuffs of such serious and sophisticated spinning and weaving only to be exhibited in the expensive shops of the West. Palatial silks, subtle in color and meaning" (Guest 2003a, 83). Access to a poetically invested subjectivity comes from the pleasures of exotic luxury, "listening to the silk," which in turn penetrates beyond culture to nature: for the listener thereby "hears the singing of birds" (Guest 2003a, 84). Guest has passed from an economic-social narrative involving class and desire, purchase/accumulation, the role of travel, translation of a thing into one's own world, imports, and appropriation, to an aesthetic narrative involving sensual pleasures, visual and aural bliss, texture, sight, "realms of gold," in Keats's phrase. In such argument aura, aural, and the aureate pulse together.

Buying some of the silk, the visitors "sailed on with a memory of simple grandeur, as unlikely a mixture as could be found anywhere except in poetry" (Guest 1986, 12). Poetry is, then, allied with and motivated by a special kind of riches, pure beauty, a bliss of physical vision and tactile desires satiated, which satisfaction leads to the opening of spiritual vision. This is hardly a poetics of deprivation or austerity but rather one of pleasure and extravagance, an opening to pleasure as an opening to the spirit. This parallels Guest's argument in "The Shadow of Surrealism" detailing the cross-fertilization of painters and poets and the envy that poets feel about the materiality of painters' work—the physicality of canvas, the gorgeousness of paint, the money that can be made, the "gratification of secret desires" that are both cause and effect. This open, pleasurable extravagance primes the painter, "prods his greatest possession, the imagination" (Guest 1986, 2). The combination of spiritual seriousness and depth with frivolity and pleasure is one that, in Guest's view, has greatly influenced poets. One can see, then, in her "Byzantium," that the silk, far from being judged as merely surface and gorgeousness, is being sought in Guest's allegory precisely because of its grand sumptousness and tactile/visual beauty.

But there is more. "The silk was turned into curtains and began to lead a domestic existence, its history asleep, much as a poem enters into an anthology" (Guest 2003a, 84).[15] This simple grandeur, with its aura of mystery, comes to exist inside a domestic space, which becomes suffused with its secret presence. This narrative of the passage of silk from an Asian bazaar to domestic possession is Guest's allegory of the feeling poetry offers. Once one has traveled in realms of gold, one finds the arresting possibility that poetry can be gently "domesticated" without losing its underside—its "secret life," that "'*inner sound, the noise of the imagination*'" (Guest 2003a, 85; the citation is from Kandinsky). All the negative connotations of domesticity are thereby evaded; such a space of privacy and freedom to possess gorgeousness is a bourgeois ideal. In this world of mystery, poems are the summary or essence or registered impact of "that which is convoluted, difficult to track down, complicated. Underneath its apparent surface there is the presence of 'something else'" (Guest 1986, 12; second sentence in Guest 2003a, 84). In the book publication of this essay, that climactic moment is rendered: "Imagination is the spirit inside the poem, a nostalgia for the infinite, louder than silk" (Guest 2003a, 85). Guest identifies Keats, Mallarmé, Blake, Shelley, Stevens, and Shakespeare as those capable of rendering this "aura" of the special sense of the world revealed by poetry.[16]

Guest speaks at once for the silk, for its transformative passage or conduit, and for the final ("domestic") product. The best poetry will be metamorphic—a silk that can be "respected" and that has "an ability to exchange its contour for a curtain without losing an identity imposed by the bartering of one idea for another" (Guest 1986, 13). It is a way of saying that domestication (curtain-making from that exotic silk) may complicate beauty but does not reduce it, certainly readable as an allegorical comment on the life of the female poet. "Silk" itself makes interested choices in Guest's narrative, for, taking on a personlike agency and consciousness, it accepts merchant-bazaar-market value-display in order to also have or reveal "a Byzantine preference" for "hidden noise" and "mysterious deep" (Guest 1986, 13); in the book form this part of the argument evokes the Mallarméan sense of the dimensions not of a thing but of an effect, a sense of disguise and hidden dimensions that can only be suggested, not stated (Guest 2003a, 84).[17] In this comment we are meant to see that poetry draws on psychic processes, fantasies, needs, and fulfillments in somewhat guarded, disguised, displaced ways. "In the cloak of Byzantine colors the poet spins a secret life" (Guest 1986, 13).

A variety of gender-laden materials are evoked by this set of arguments. This poetics of the carefully hidden inner depths of philosophical import and its attractive and scintillating surface draws on one definition of the feminine. The attraction of the silk as exotic and as domesticated alludes both to the female place in Western imaginations and to the gendered marvelous. But the whole narrative of the Byzantine is the story of the potency of the artist in her ability to transform and be transformed, to claim power and to metamorphose by asserting her aura and her capacity to create aura. It is possible to see this as an argument for female potency compounded of voyages, strangers, and Keatsian "golden, silken stuffs," French symbolist invitations to voyages—a whole panoply of suggestively gendered materials. It is possible to see this as an argument for beauty and lushness that embraces the feminine in the imagination of a female, a way of appropriating what is powerful and pleasurable about that ideology.

Guest's cultural task might then be said to be torquing surrealism in order to allow for the potent female artist, torquing modernity so that the aura of the lyric (pace Benjamin) can thrive in the hands of the female artist rather than being ruined by her approximate freedoms. In this task Guest is not alone, but she is uniquely positioned to address surrealism for its advantages, and she is capable of expanding those terms via an engaged and subtle critique. In her work, then, Guest produces the female-gendered marvelous. In the book with the title *Fair Realism* poetry occurs by an act of transformative translation, a meditating over "realism" (the word is redolent of novels, of narratives) until it becomes "fair."

That word, *fair*, begins by meaning beautiful, clear, and sunny. The word also re-evokes the "fair," or bazaar, of Guest's allegory of poetry in the purchase of silks in which the secret aura inside things is discovered by acknowledging desires for sumptuousness. And the word also denominates the "fair," that is, the fair sex, with their traditions of being looked at, a practice that organizes the gaze. I propose that "fair realism" is Guest's female translation of "surrealism," a way of acknowledging the powers and subjectivities of the female-gendered marvelous while holding its less comfortable effects at bay: loss of agency, exoticized bedecking, and the possibility of historical erasure.

"The Farewell Stairway," where the "fair" go down a deep "well," overtly concerns saying a long good-bye after a visit (Guest 1995, 117–22). This work of mythopoesis is premised on a "telling" of a painting by the Italian futurist Balla, who depicted the wide looping stairwells of European bourgeois apartment houses as a descent, to an unknown, unseen space, down a "vortex" (a Poundian word with modernist evocations). Three fashionably dressed women make the journey. Guest names two of them Ceres and Hecate; a third, unnamed, is clearly Koré or Persephone (and thus the three together make the triple goddess). According to Sara Lundquist, Guest chooses the version of the myth that speaks of a female initiation ritual, or a female mystery, a version disinterested in Hades, "'patriarchal violence,'" or the abductor (Lundquist 1997, 278–81).

Guest's observations on multiple speaking and viewing subject positions are summarized by her critical term *plasticity:* "The poem stretches, looking outwardly and inwardly, thus obtaining a plasticity that the flat, the basic words—what we call the language of a poem—demands and, further, depends upon" (Guest 2003a, 21–22). This poem proposes a multiple subjectivity quite characteristic of Guest's poetic production. First, the speaker of the poem takes the position of viewer—the person within the narrative at the top of the stairs, watching the women descend; second, she is one of the women descending, unwillingly, frightened, while "Hecate managed me" (Guest 1995, 120). This is joined by a third subjectivity—of omniscient viewer, like a novelist who sees the charming women on "a roman *scala.* / in the neighborhood of the *stazione*"—and even by a fourth, implied in the third and the first alike—a viewer called forth by the metaphysics of the scene, one who feels its "mythic potency" (Guest 1995, 120, 122). The gender of these subjectivities is more female than male; and the plural *she* (by virtue of the shifting subjectivity of the poem) both possesses the gaze and is scrutinized by it. Renegotiating the gaze in lyric seems to be an advantage claimed by the female poet.

The speaker/viewer who is both inside and outside the narrative looks at the scene variously: descriptively, dramatically, naturalistically, formally (speaking about folds and volumes), and, in a recurrent word: *futurally.* The image of the vortex and the descent into a dark point is the spot, postulated "futurally," at which the three women at three stages of the life cycle disappear into a vanishing point beyond any gaze. "I saw it futurally," says the woman left on top of the stairs, and later the departing women are said to be "futurally extended" (Guest 1995, 119, 121). It is certainly plausible to say that this word represents that seeing like a futurist, which, as Lundquist wittily notes, Balla was in the future to become. But seeing "futurally" is what will happen, something always becoming, not something always already constructed, not the icon.

The women and their descent are regarded over and over, for the poem's eleven sections are built on folds. The work is organized by "pleated moments" saying almost everything again, as the figures are imagined continuing to walk downward (Guest 1995, 117). Guest creates a slow-motion metamorphosis of her characters poised in the descent, whose narrative is both reasonably realistic (their serapes, their phrases in Italian) and mythic or antique (the "mythic potency" that the poem postulates).

One of the problems for the woman as writer, as I have repeatedly argued, is to face whole traditions of depiction of female figures and to get some tread on what to do with them. A characteristic of that cultural figure is her stasis as icon and her quality as a receiver of the gaze—a semifrozen, singular figure whose spiritual responsibility is often already to "be there" so that with great sweetness and intensity she can induce the male follower to "get there." (And possibly, as in the 1948 fulmination by Williams, to take some grief for her causeway status.) In contrast, the traveling women of "The Farewell Stairway" may "be there" (by virtue of their mythic names), but they are also only "getting there," slowly yet intrepidly in the descent. One of them is very reluctant even to go "there." This tension between being and becoming is uncharacteristic of the use of the iconic female in poetic tradition. Guest's projection of an (arguably) multiple *female* gaze looking at female figures splits the figures differently, not between self and other, for those terms no longer apply, but between interior vectors and the "reality of place": "a pull in both directions between" (Guest 2003a, 20).

The multiple positionality of a wayward creature sometimes named "I" is articulated quite directly by Guest in her essay "Shifting Persona": "The person inside a literary creation can be both viewer and insider" (Guest 2003a, 36). This is certainly the situation of the "persons" of "The Farewell Stairway." The business of a speaker being in at least two or three places at once, speaking from the vectors of a site, and not from one voice or any one identity is typical of Guest's poetry. Being at all points entails a creative splurge, an investment in multiplicities. It is as if, in onomastic duplicity, she were host and guest at once. Thus when Guest articulates issues of femaleness, maleness, gender, and sexuality, she stages a different kind of gender encounter than one might see in contemporaneous poetries from other women's communities. Guest's work multiplies "the gaze" so that she, as a female poet, can claim some power over the many dimensions of sight and seeing. In a sense, this power of envisioning could be what Guest's interest in painting is all about, not only ekphrastic (though it is indeed that), not only formal or allusive of a variety of painterly styles, but about vision—as in visionary—and sight—as in the powers, the vectors, and managements of the gaze.

It is this vision-inducing quality that Breton ascribed to the female figure, but Breton avers that she does not herself become illuminated by that power. In contrast, Guest argues that such a figure is herself illuminated. Whether this is an explicit response to surrealist poetics is not important; it constitutes such a response. Thus Guest ascribes vision-inducing qualities both to painting and to the female figure, but there is a special intensity when Guest chooses to write from a painting concerning female figures (as we have seen with both the Balla and the Miró). Perhaps, one could postulate, concentration on an individual painting contains, filters, buffers, or refines some of the more lurid claims about the surrealist Woman, and refocuses attention on core issues: pleasure and the "marvelous." In any event, in Guest's work painting is a privileged space in which issues about vision and gender emerge. Guest approaches these materials in the spirit of shifting personae, with multiple identifications at work: sited as painter and model, as Picasso and Dora Maar, and as the third term viewing them, identifying with both, and with their painful, generative symbiosis.

In Guest's poem "The Nude" a male painter regards a female model. She seems the very embodiment, to him, of "shadow"; she has strong therapeutic significance, of "holding" in object-relations terms:

> The narcissism of the artist escapes into a body
> that defines his emotions,
>
> An interior where his own contour is less misty.
>
> (Guest 1995, 143, 144)

Here the model is a boundary, or a limit term, for something otherwise infantile and chaotic. The nude model is judicious, forcefully linked to her own situatedness, her own "realism," despite the (again tenderly banal) depictions of traditional claptrap around models:

> A severe distance is established between her realism
> and his anxious attempt to define it.
>
> The painter desires the image he has selected
> to be clothed in the absolute silk of his touch,
>
> Lonely himself he has admired the glance
> of kimonos, mirrors, fans and bestowed them on her . . .
>
> (Guest 1995, 144–45)

And later: "He searches the world to find those spheres / that will confine the fluid nude" (Guest 1995, 145).

When the nude sees the painting, "she asks, where am I?" Finding that "he has not drawn her," she takes power over the moment (Guest 1995, 148):

She turns herself into a star
above the unattended foliage,

He views her as she glistens,
silver enters the picture.

(Guest 1995, 148–49).

The roles of model/painter linked by banal binary gender narratives to the terms *passive* and *active* can no longer be sustained as given. The model self-metamorphoses and takes agency.

The transformation narrated in Guest's poem is especially marked in relation to the artwork that accompanied it in the original publication. Warren Brandt's work plays with nudes from the history of art, for he offers his history of the depiction of the female nude as a metaphor for the history of art as a whole.[18] Thus he mimics, or alludes to, the *Olympia* by Manet, as well as to nudes by Gauguin, Picasso, Fragonard, Rodin, and many more. He also uses various media and techniques in this history of art, including watercolor, drypoint, charcoal sketch, pencil, pen, oil, photo, and thereby makes allusions to different media and modes of production of the nude woman (such as nineteenth-century pornography). As Guest says, "The artist borrows mannerisms and technique," and "each day there is a different voice" (Guest 1995, 146, 147). "He confides, / 'Each day I define myself' "—and he does so by virtue of drawing a female nude (Guest 1995, 149). When Guest's poem is put next to the artworks in the book to which she has contributed, the poem seems quietly critical of the power of the male gaze and offers the poetic work as a site in which the female writer's gaze trumps the male gaze and enfolds the whole situation. Guest tries to rectify the power balance, the eroticisms and agencies in the artworks Brandt has made with her own.

In Guest's poem the model's changes, including consciously willed changes, transform the painter's picture and his palette. She "leads" him. He interprets her. The relationship is symbiotic. And both figures are powerful. Despite the nude's own narcissism familiar from pictorial and literary tradition and re-presented by Brandt ("She was either admiring herself or bathing"), Guest's nude engages with aplomb the fearful, the unknown, and the threatening: "She reaches for ombre, noir / 'It is the narrowness of time' " (Guest 1995, 148, 149). The nude is not solely or only the object of a fixing gaze, although the poem knows that it would be naive and untrue to the history of art to posit that she is never so. Thus, she is at one and the same time the object of a fixing gaze and the subject meditating herself. Both positions are discussed within the poem. So, too, the painter inside the poem has at least a double position; he has the power of sight, of skill, of desire, of address. But sometimes he is blind or veiled in his understanding. Both, indeed, may be surpassed by another even more philosophically inclined party to the exchange—"the [not her] body" itself:

> He explains he is thinking of the body.
>
> Its behavior is strange, hiding behind leaves
> he can never trap or bribe it.
>
> So deep is the body's memory of self.
>
> Each day there is a different voice,
> today while wearing no clothes
>
> It spoke of the essentials of life which were evident,
> but the body took an invisible position . . .
>
> (Guest 1995, 147)

With an uncanny negative capability, Guest depicts shifts between both the male painter and the female nude, as well as among "the body" depicted in the artworks and "the viewer": "You are the viewer and without you / the picture cannot exist" (Guest 1995, 145). These bonds are (as in Wordsworth and Stevens) absolutely spousal. The viewed and viewer of art, the model and painter present a shifting but articulate symbiosis, one peculiarly formative and satisfying in their dialogue, perpetually knitted up and unraveled, between reality and the imagination. Most viewers outside the work of art (in other words, us) are usually asked by "art" to be inside the painter's eye. So the normal institutions of viewing or reading further frame and contain the nude. Guest's poem is critical because it gives us other places from which to see. Rather than seeing the nude only via the painter's eye, Guest's poem makes us see the space and symbiosis between painter and model, body and time, viewer and situation. She is working the negative spaces, the push and pull, the in-betweens. This dialogue and give-and-take, this unstable synthesis of the two players, is one interpretation of what Guest means by "fair realism." "Fair" means justice has been served: it is a "just" realism because it does justice to all parts of the relationship.

These gender materials also occur, with drama and pathos, in the poem "Dora Maar." Because Maar was a historical person, one of Picasso's many lovers, Guest raises the issue of appropriation and gender in the case when "her tears benefit his painting," and her zaniness and visions are actualized through his work (Guest 1995, 129). "Dora Maar" is a poem in six parts, an allusion to a series of six progressively more abstracting paintings of Maar by Picasso.[19] Maar, like so many of the women one now knows only as ancillae to male masters, had a serious career. She was a photographer and painter, described by one critic as a "bluestocking," always a term of fascinated resistance when referring to strong-minded women. She met Picasso in 1935 or 1936, apparently in a surrealist incident very like Guest's depiction: "In a cafe he watched her throw the knife / between the fingers of a gloved hand" (Guest 1995, 129). Commentators point to Maar's intelligence and autonomy as unique to Picasso's women—"Dora was a formidable muse" (Richardson 1982, 281)—but her fierce moods and mental instability link her to several other of Picasso's love-choices. Guest spoke of her as "a surrealist painter" who "escapes [limitations] because of surrealism" (conversation, May 6, 1997). This use of surrealism could be Guest's displaced self-descriptor, especially when we learn that Guest "deliberately did not read Surrealist literature or study the history of the movement, because I wanted to be sure to have my own Surrealism" (Guest 2004a, 31).[20]

Maar was thus important to Guest for her ties to surrealism and to the poet Eluard, and thereby to a more politicized modernism than had, to date, distinguished Picasso. John Richardson argues that with each new mistress, Picasso shifted painting style; Mary Mathews Gedo makes the corresponding argument that these shifts are linked not only to new women but to serious and productive male friends. The Maar-Eluard combination was especially potent. Maar's and Eluard's left politics buoyed Picasso's support of the Spanish Republic. A mural by Picasso had already been commissioned for the Republican Pavilion at the Paris International Exposition of Arts and Sciences; after the April 26, 1937, fascist bombardment of Guernica, with its then-scandalous (but not the first-ever) air assault on civilians as targets, he took the commission as an occasion for a major protest. Maar documented the remarkably quick evolution and realization of the mural *Guernica* in a series of photographs and, apparently, helped the quick realization by painting the side of the horse.

There are allusions by Guest to Maar's double position in relationship to the mural *Guernica:* first, as muse-inspiration—"*she was that woman holding a light,*" and "She was the woman who fell from the house / in the daylight bombing"; and second, as artist-photographer "*She photographed the hysterical success* / stage by stage with her alphabet of sighs" (Guest 1995, 129, 130).[21] Guest represents the muse figure positively yet ruefully, and so, too, the male artist, whose energy and drive have a magical quality.

The relationship of woman to male master is lucidly articulated: "her tears benefit his painting," Guest says.

> *He raids her hallucinatory bicycle for an object*
> *he calls "found" as the handles and bicycle seat*
> *are transformed—*
>
> (Guest 1995, 130)

But *found* is a term of erasure, by a randomizing of his access to the image; it denies indebtedness. This account in the poem is, in any event, quasi-factual; Guest depicts how Maar's imagination and her instabilities spur Picasso. Guest shows a painter whose imagination is sometimes banal and needs to be jump-started by the nervous energy and surreal vivacity of this woman (among many others in his career). Guest represents a symbiotic relationship in which the female seems to have imagination and vision to spare, yet the male artist has the career.

She shows that the male artist operates with a mythically sanctioned lèse-majesté:

> Eclectic and careless like Jove when changed
> into a bull he finds the classical
> screams of maidens exciting. . . .
>
> (Guest 1995, 130)

Guest depicts a male-female relation in which the painter is able to give back to the model-muse the gift of her own vision, which she describes as an enchanting experience for Maar:

> once he had drawn her torso with wings
> afterwards she saw the river
> with a translucent depth
> when her arm was a wing. . . .
>
> (Guest 1995, 130)

Or—shifting again—is it that Picasso has "raided" her vision and constructed works in which "her appearance is meddled with"? (Guest 1995, 130). Sometimes the female's emotions, dreams, and body are a kind of raw material, the straw that Picasso spins into gold. But sometimes the transformative powers of Maar are described as preceding Picasso's painting, as if she proffered a new reality, one that Picasso did not invent but belatedly records:

her noble forehead is a sand cap water deftly clears,
one of her eyes is red, the other blue like a portrait
of Marie-Thérèse though bolder.

(Guest 1995, 129)

(Marie-Thérèse is another mistress of Picasso.) Are the terms appropriation? metamorphosis? Are there other terms? Can we balance the conflicting gender claims that these terms suggest?

This female figure's waywardness and uncontainability are a trope for the unchained imagination. If the female figure exists in a kind of feminine space familiar in at least surrealist ideology, still, in Guest's depiction the agency and bite of this figure belie the culturally familiar "feminine" of Beauty, Mystery, and Exotic Otherness. In Guest this muse has been invested with a force, deliberateness, and will that undermine more familiar postulates of passivity, solipsism, and unconsciousness. Despite choosing gendered protagonists, and in the case of Maar and Picasso writing about a historically documented interaction, Guest works to neutralize either-or gender assumptions and moralized assessments by her both-and-but-and elaborations of the gendered marvelous. The [female] poet becomes the privileged site in which the gender materials of culture can be examined in their mystery and impact because such a poet can identify and elaborate all sides of the exchanges. Surrealism is realigned in this metamorphosis as Fair Realism, a version of surrealism that is fair (just) to the fair (women in culture) by offering a fair (bazaar) of mobile subject positions.

Of course, as with any work, Guest's poem diverges here from certain data and interprets the situation with certain materials selected, others undivulged or unavailable for consideration. In his memoir James Lord recounts saying to Maar that she'll never be forgotten because Picasso had painted her so often. Thereupon, according to Lord, she replied: "Do you think I care? Does Mme. Cézanne care? Does Saskia Rembrandt care? Remember that I, too, am an artist" (Lord 1993, 123). Maar's articulate, angry riposte comes to almost nothing without feminist reception; without it she is placed in the structural position of Cézanne's apples given Picasso's overwhelming position in modernism. Reception that dissolves, erases, and buries the work of female artists in modernism, good, bad, or indifferent, is culturally inadequate. Picasso himself contributed to this climate with such opinions as "No worse than any other woman painter" about the watercolors of Ferdnande Olivier, his first mistress (Richardson 1982, 278). Or when he grafted a dog's face onto Maar's, and stated, with Aristotelian flair, that he had thereby made a comment "on the animal nature of woman" (Richardson 1982, 283). In calling attention to the problematic of Maar, Guest does not attribute anger or resistance to Maar at the end of the poem but rather produces an elegiac, bucolic aftermath.[22] Guest's Maar lives in her farmhouse, a gift from Picasso. "Sweetness returns to her scorched tongue," and "Grief is banished from her coveted roost" (Guest 1995, 131).

Guest's poem masterfully evokes these issues by confronting us with the notable ambivalence of culture to productive female artists/muses, and to the richness of art—and its cost—in the marring of Maar. The way Guest depicts the model-painter and Maar-Picasso relationships interprets the allegory of a relationship heavily gendered throughout artistic tradition, moving the figures around and adding to them, elaborating multiple points of view, making in-betweens speak, all with the aim to equalize and complicate the positions. When there are two terms, Guest talks about a kind of spousal event, a symbiosis, a fittedness of one to the other. But her aim is to pluralize the terms, by adding "speakers" and by a strong lateral movement, the "plasticity" between the diegetic and the extradiegetic spaces in poems: "giving a view of the poem from both the interior and the exterior" (Guest 2003a, 20). The female poet—Guest herself—takes the responsibility, examining the gender materials of culture in their mystery and ethical ambiguity.

Art is, for Guest, a sublime and transcendent place, and the feminine/female figures (from silk to models) offer the privilege of access to the visionary and the contemplative. In more recent work, Guest has written a Mallarméan poem remaking Mallarmé, a poem eulogizing the clairvoyant presence of the beautiful female figure within culture as a whole. Unlike *Un coup de dés,* Guest's *Quill, Solitary APPARITION* is not a poem about absence, struggle, the void, shipwreck, and the intangible but about presence, pleasure, adequacy, buoyancy—and the intangible. In this suggestive work, in short, Guest seems to be engaged on a metastudy of poetic pleasure. What would be female pleasure in poetic production, analogous to the physical, tactile "pleasure of production . . . one of the most fundamental elements of most painters' work—[where] nothing quite beats the satisfaction of mushing pigment around on a surface in thick, loose impasto or veiling washes" (Drucker 1992, 7). This citation from Johanna Drucker's call for a theorizing of pleasure by feminists seems, at first, tonally provocative, not connected to the textual delicacy and limpidity of *Quill, Solitary APPARITION.* Yet one may recall Guest's witty expostulations about painters and how their desire for instant gratification conceals their problem-solving panache, or her appreciation of how Matisse, "this great sensualist," is, at the same time, "an intellectual manipulator of space" (Guest 2003a, 53). The merging of terrific pleasure and terrific intellectual force is of decided interest to Guest, under the rubric "imagination."

So one arrives, finally, at pleasure. Drucker calls for a "theory of female pleasure" that can emerge "from production" (Drucker 1992, 9). Similarly, Mira Schor calls for a "regendered version of visual pleasure" and a "feminist erotics of visuality" (Schor 1997, 168). This call has resonance in poetry. What would a poetry of imagistic, tonal, linguistic, and textual pleasure look like from a female subject claiming the marvelous, absolutely entering the space of meaning, of the symbolic, and exerting her right to vision, clairvoyance, and agency? It might well engage a transformation of surrealism to fair realism.

9
"Uncannily in the open"

In Light of Oppen

> What is socially decisive in artworks is the content that becomes eloquent through the work's formal structures.
>
> —Theodor Adorno, *Aesthetic Theory*

> The word in one's own mouth becomes strange as infinity—even strange as the finite, strange as things. Which means again that the prosody and the "philosophy" cannot be separated as of course you know.
>
> —George Oppen, "Statement on Poetics"

I have chosen this topic, yet it is difficult for me to speak about George Oppen, since in a certain light everything I write is set against his uncompromising sign.[1] When a person writing poems is frightened by George Oppen, she may have started (cf. *SL* 123–24). Oppen writes a poetry of negativity and commitment. Like Paul Celan, Walter Benjamin, and Theodor Adorno, Oppen asks in every word how to make art, what art is possible, what must be said given the pressures and demands of our position in history. In their anthology Jerome Rothenberg and Pierre Joris debate the aestheticized naming of an epoch: "not so much post*modern*—as it would come to be called—as it was post-bomb and post-holocaust" (Rothenberg and Joris 1998, 4). Work, mind, and understanding are inflected with political and social disasters, and with failures of a political and cultural dream of just societies that shadow these events. Charles Bernstein adds a dimension about social mourning to a sense of these popular-front hopes variously compromised when he proposes, similarly, that one project of contemporary American radical poetry mourns Auschwitz and Hiroshima; these disasters are encrypted and repressed information at the core of social identities and artistic practices (Bernstein 1992, 193–217).

Theodor Adorno's 1962 essay "Commitment" contains elaborate second thoughts, his own midrash, or exfoliating gloss, on his intransigent, enraged, doomed sententia (dating from 1949) that to write a poem after

Auschwitz is barbaric. To argue that such a poem would be an expression of the impulses that created Auschwitz in the first place is a massive accusation against culture, a massive extension of responsibility for Shoah to the whole of German culture, if not to all culture (Adorno 1981b, 34). That infamous original statement is motivated in multiple ways; one may see it, in part, as a desire to halt in one's own tracks by stopping a hapless part of cultural production (poetry) and thereby clearing the time to engage in mourning beyond mourning. Adorno is propelled to criticize one genre, poetry, in which mourning is conventionally undertaken (Adorno 1992, 87). The passage from "Commitment" is very intricate, as it would necessarily have to be.[2] At the end of his consideration, Adorno says something quite simple, but rich with the intricacy of his prior argument: that an artist should not produce straightforward political art, engagé art, an art of commitment, as this word is conventionally evoked in the postwar context by, say, Jean-Paul Sartre. An artist must understand, rather, that the political has "migrated into" all art and must work with this situation and its implications (Adorno 1992, 93).

Oppen's art is political in this way: commitment has migrated into form. Oppen exposes and explores the riven and fraught nature of subjectivity in a state of political and existential arousal that cannot (yet) be satisfied. His poetry traces the dialectical motion of that arousal. Oppen argues that light is as inadequate as darkness, pure reason as problematic as mysticism. Imagery in his work makes us see that fire or "blaze" exists in a narrow site between hyperrational, overly bright light and hyperirrational darkness, obscurity, and obscurantism. Thus tiny "temperate" images of rot, change, smallness, process, human scale ("cozy black iron work"—cozy! *NCP* 230) are so vital.

> We have gone
> As far as is possible
>
> Whose lives reflect light
> Like mirrors
>
> One had not thought
> To be afraid
>
> Not of shadow but of light
>
> Summon one's powers
>
> (*NCP* 233)

In "The Second War and Postmodern Memory" Charles Bernstein follows the implications of Adorno's critique of the Enlightenment values embodied in claims for European social and intellectual systems: the "war undermined, subliminally, more than consciously, the belief in virtually every basic value of the Enlightenment, insofar as these values are in any way Eurosupremacist or hierarchic" (Bernstein 1992, 198). At the same time he notes the simultaneous problem "of the vatic, the occult, the charismatic, the emotional solidarity of communion" such as one might see in fascism and elsewhere—in any mono-ocular, nonsecular, affirmative belief system (Bernstein 1992, 199). We live in a space (newly inflected by other failures of the West and the East) in which neither positivist enlightenment nor its opposite, positivist antisecularism, is adequate. In his time Oppen explicitly resisted the mystical irrationalisms prevalent and making revolutionary claims in the 1960s: drug culture, Jungian thinking, and surrealism. If neither the irrational nor the rational is adequate, this effectively ends many binarist oppositions in which we have believed, or at least that we have credited. Where can we stand? What can our writing say or make of this? These were dilemmas that Oppen faced, incited by the sickening political rupture of the 1963–68 assassinations of U.S. political leaders, including a president, and ignited by the corrosive Vietnam War, with its lies and manipulations in a frayed democratic context.

As close as one gets to "stopping" writing (something Oppen, of course, did, a silence generated and supported variously, a sociocultural act), that temptation and its complex overcoming "expresses negatively" (in Adorno's terms) "the impulse that animates committed literature."[3] But beyond that almost twenty-five years of not talking to the page (1934–58), Oppen's later poetry seems continuously to be stopping at virtually every line, at every porous white-space caesura, and then picking up the commitment again to go on. His "Adorno-esque" commitment is made precisely against Tendenz literature but precisely for engagement inside form, in, I will argue, the line itself. Understanding commitment as manifest in form, I want briefly to think through connections between Oppen and certain European thinkers and poets. I am doing so dependent on translations and despite the fact that I am not versed in philosophy as a tradition but only in poetry as tradition and practice.[4] Versed, in part, by Oppen. Hence I will begin in memoir, with some of the terms activated by that interchange.

I was a graduate student at Columbia University when I met Oppen in 1965; we were introduced by a fellow student, John Crawford, later the founding editor of the socially committed West End Press. I was fascinated with the work of Pound and Williams, alternative poetries uninteresting to my erstwhile graduate professors. I was beginning an unmentored dissertation (completed 1970) about *The Pisan Cantos* and *Paterson*—under the predictive rubric the "endless poem," investigating how imagist "intensity of seeing" modulated into, demanded, or necessitated such sprawling encyclopedic poems (Pound 1967, 102; *NCP* 167). Later I wrote a comparison of Oppen and Pound, trying to establish the different historically changing politics of the use of fragment in a poetics of sincerity and taking, as flash point, Oppen's late career poem about Pound (DuPlessis 1981). Pound's use of fragment and parataxis became a totalitarian and mystical way of carrying out objectivist poetics (*totalitarian*—meaning totalizing and authoritative—is Pound's uncanny term from Italian fascism); he used the fragment to headline affirmative ideas he wished to promulgate. Thus he was inadequately investigative or, rather, held he had already investigated and was declaring (establishing) permanent results. Oppen, in contrast, maintained a use of the fragment negatively, as moving among contradictions, and proposed that vectored movement as veridical—constructing situational truth.

My calling card to Oppen was work on *Paterson,* original at that time, regrettably never published. I was awarded a prize for this article, the Bunner Medal, but when I thanked the proper university authorities, I kept on typing "Bummer." Speak of ambivalence. In any event the paper evoked from George a striking letter about mythopoesis and the long poem, a subtle critique of Williams (*SL* 117–18). This was our first exchange. Issues of seriality, long poems, the alternative modernist tradition (mainly male modernists), experimentation, political stances, addressing one's society (or one's "peers," at any rate)—these issues and more were opened (*NCP* 158). I was a sympathetic and willing reader of the rhetorical austerities and the objectivist stances that Oppen exemplified.[5]

Given the ruling counterpoetics in New York City in the mid-1960s—Deep Image, the New York School, both generations, the fascination with French surrealist and absurdist models (in drama and poetry)—what Oppen said rejecting surrealism became annoyingly, provokingly important to me. He took surrealism as a poetic diction or rhetoric, not as a method or an ethos, considering it as yet another one of the "obvious" period styles that he challenged as being inadequate to epistemology: to "asking oneself what one does know and what one doesn't know" (*SL* 121, 120). I was living in a particular 100th Street poetry group within a backwash of surrealist strategies, and George took issue with my fascination in a very didactic way; he truly saw surrealism as a path that should not be pursued, and he mustered a good deal of wit and argument to that end.[6] His own poetic texture of abruptness and unexpected shifts of voice and mode were to become startling, but they were never done for what one might call stylistically avant-garde reasons. Any hint of "manner" was anathema to Oppen.

In his interesting position of old younger poet (his second book published in 1962 at age 54, his third in 1965, at 57), Oppen made sets of remarks that criticized various contemporary avant-gardes for their poetics—aleatory work in music such as John Cage's, happenings, the Judson dance scene, and Fluxus-inspired poetry such as Jackson Mac Low's (*SL* 67), "the new dadaisms or the new derangement of the senses"—the Rimbaudian term he hated.[7] Plus Allen Ginsberg, with a too-flip quip, "merely Howling" (*SL* 78), and finally "Deep Image-ists," whom he couldn't quite get a handle on, in part because they were all his friends, but whom he saw as not secular enough, too symbolist and mythic (*SL* 78).[8] Aside from showing the sometimes notorious "Oppen judgment" in the absolutism of these remarks, he was clearly trying to carve a place for himself among the active 1960s counterpoetics when he mostly disagreed with just about everything that was happening in alternative poetry.[9] The resistance to surrealist/dada is based on a principled critique of "irrationalism" as a source for knowledge. In that he was conservative, one might say, or classical (might be better), but he also was engaged in the functional strategic analysis possibly learned in Communist circles: these methods (dadaism, derangement) might be subjectively exciting and tempting, but they were objectively (as it were) counterproductive.

Oppen wrote me forthright corrective statements on surrealism, about how you can't just put an elephant into a poem for reasons of decoration, association, free play, neat juxtaposition, or charming willfulness. That is, "One cannot make a poem by sticking words into it, it is the poem which makes the words and contains their meaning. One cannot reach out for *roses* and *elephants* and *essences* and put them in the poem——the ground under the elephant, the air around him, one would have to know very precisely one's distance from the elephant or step deliberately too close, close enough to frighten oneself. When the man writing is frightened by a word, he may have started" (*SL* 123; see also 389n21). Thus if the word *elephant* gets there, you have to measure the force and meaning and contexts and solidity of the thing and what it was actually doing there, not as ornament or shocking pendent of your poem but as itself and as whatever brought it into your poem, compelling thought. Compelling a commitment. You had to think about what was true, not just whatever could be sutured or combined together. Oppen's later poem "West" begins:

> Elephant, say, scraping its dry sides
> In a narrow place as he passes says yes

This is true

So one knows?

(*NCP* 215)

I see these lines as Oppen's last word in that debate on the surrealist impulse. In this poem he calls for "The rare poetic / Of veracity"; he probably considered this the opposite of surrealist practice (*NCP* 215).

Oppen once said to me, "Why don't you put all of your intelligence in your poems." That is—make poems of thinking. Use poems to think with. They are a commitment to thinking.[10] One must gasp: that was a breathtaking thing to say to a struggling "girl" to whom poetry had been more or less forbidden as a career or vocation by her own formerly wayward, but now rather academic, father.[11] Oppen's invitation had a tremendous long-term impact on me. It was certainly a way of honoring the potential of a young woman, a not otherwise notable person, and certainly not a person doing much yet (in 1966 to about 1976) with her poetry. In writing to me, or imagining some "me" to write to, he said some pretty remarkable things, "Notes on Prosody?" for example, from which that elephant emerges. I am grateful for whatever it was in the "me" that elicited these remarks. Oppen was about equally attentive to women and men as poets, a very good, a very lucky, and somewhat rare thing to find in an older male person in c. 1965. This didn't mean he had no gender-laden demands or only positive ones. But he didn't seem to cut women any slack (rejecting, mostly, that buried chivalric condescension), and he was mostly angry when women tried to be too nice or too good (*SL* 392–93). That's what, in his view, ruined Denise Levertov's poetry (which he had at one point somewhat admired)—he was absolutely adamant about this. It was a cutting and admonitory remark. Oppen had no trouble, as I've said, with judgment.

Oppen also read my early struggling work in poetry. This he ruthlessly cut, rejecting large parts of it, teaching me thereby how to hear, read, and listen to a genuine statement that had some grit, some meaning, and how to remove, cut, toss out the rest. After the editing, what was left got linked—one simply linked the genuine material (possibly resequencing it). This was his method—making of every poem a "discrete series" and attenuating or cutting the "argument" or the "logic" or the "development" one might so laboriously, so banally, have constructed. Indeed, "discrete series," as we know from a good deal of commentary now, was an epistemological argument Oppen made about reality and knowledge, as well as an implied argument about the ethics of writing. The proposition was that startling and original logic or sequence would emerge from the editing out of the non-genuine, something quite far from the conventional—from the conventional *anything*. You would confront what you really thought in cutting what was inadequate, generic, or "poetic," and trying to comprehend the rest in whatever form it emerged, as traces, fragments, phrases, as constellations.[12] It was the opposite—but the reverse image—of a surrealist combinatoire; here it was excision, not association, that created startling juxtapositions. Oppen rejected both language as fill and the decorative, a clarity Poundian in origin, although without its political baggage. This, along with his suspicion of tidy, nice, good-for-you moves at closure, made people's poetry and their conclusions or endings a site for a good deal of correction. He enraged both Jane Cooper (who was polite) and Armand Schwerner (who was not) by his ability to dismiss notable sections of their hard-won words. If you sent him work, if you asked him—he told you. Then you had to live with what he said. Oppen was quite serious about the ethics of writing, and the tactic of such sincerity was uncompromising. He was also, given this austere picture I am limning, one of the wittiest people I have ever met.

About a poem I wrote in 1976, he even said "can't keep my hands off it" (*SL* 317). This was somewhat chilling and warming at the same time—a displaced Petrarchan freeze and burn. Or was that Pater-rach-an? Was this flattering? Sort of, but it was appropriative and manipulative, too. I wanted to make my mistakes on my own time. It's a wonder I learned anything. Did I know what to do with this remark? Yes, I knew. This comment demanded that I completely reject his interventions into this poem, no matter what, and it marked the last time he intervened thus. The fact that the poem under discussion was a work ("Voyaging") dedicated to Oppen himself, one even might say an elegy before the fact, makes for some intricacy in both the approach and the rejection (DuPlessis 1980). The fact that the exchange elicited from Oppen a remarkable statement about line break and "the vertical dimension" is something, however, from which I still do learn (*SL* 316–17). His ruthless editing was an immeasurable gift, but because it involved judgmental lucidity, it was not an easy gift to receive. Certainly, to say the least, such scrutiny did not encourage fluidity or ease of production. Internalizing such a scrupulous, intransigent standard is a permanent challenge to exclude unmotivated words.

"A good one line poem is not nothing" he once said to me. He meant some poems that were somewhat magical, image-y, and woman-oriented, tattered Sappho after the almost complete loss of her oeuvre. This grim "one-line" moment occurred when the combination of my own wayward, self-quarreling seriousness, my nothing career—a woman in a university was rather endangered then—, my desire for poetry so great that it stopped poetry, and my inchoate quarrel with gender narratives in the lyric, not to speak of the austere Oppen-standard that did nothing for fluency and exposition—all conspired to leave me with the tiniest seedlike works. One-line poems—it was the next worst thing to total erasure. The glass was almost totally empty! (I might mention I was writing my dissertation at that time.) However, from his poetics, Oppen could helpfully, if optimistically, view this attenuation as the proper beginning of a full glass, as material boiled down or taken down to the drop of the essential. *Wells* was published in 1980 by Eliot Weinberger of *Montemora* magazine and press. Or, to say this with another inflection, my first book of poetry was not published *until* 1980. I was then thirty-nine.

Oppen had a horror of the willed, of the forced, of the fake. The main criterion he taught was sincerity. The testing of the words, the emotion, the meanings, the feel of the work by a deep inner ethos and a stubborn inner ear. This was expressed as primary resistance, on the level of visceral stubbornness and intelligent suspicion, to all exaggeration and elocutionary rhetorics. His sincerity was also, simultaneously, a political sincerity. This involved an ethics about knowledge, accuracy, clarity of mind, a willingness to say what one wanted, for oneself, not speaking for others but joining others in demands or in speech. What it means to link poetic and political sincerity can be seen in Oppen's critique of Ginsberg: "There need be nothing ephemeral about the lyric poet who responds passionately and in his own way to his own vision, but if the poet begins to ask us to accept a system of opinions and attitudes he must manage the task of rigorous thought" (Oppen 1962, 329). I remember (1967, 1968 maybe) trying to write a New Year's poem, a poem of vocation called "Calling" in which I was unmaliciously but ignorantly talking about what people in New Jersey thought. ("New Jersey" is a New York topos; I was a New Yorker. I was also awkwardly bumbling after Oppen's commitment to speak of social class in his poetry.) And George called me on it. Calling, indeed! He said I didn't know what those particular people thought; I was faking.

Oppen rejected rhetorical build, free play, automatic writing, epiphenomenal linkages (that is, indistinguishably surrealism and dadaism), social flippancy, insouciant faking, too many words, and virtually any moralizing whatsoever. This standard simply shrivels 99 percent of what is called poetry, then and now. It was something to face this, because one could never face it down. That's obvious—I'm still talking about what Oppen's work means to me. I also know there might be a counter way of reading this essay: that Oppen was blocking for me. Let's say he had the faults of his virtues, but his virtues mattered deeply. In 1985–86 I catapulted myself into *Drafts*, incidentally writing the very first words of "Draft 1: It" in 1986 on the Pacific coast at Solana Beach having just visited the George Oppen Archive at the University of California, San Diego, in La Jolla, and just after the centenary conference on H.D. in Orono, Maine. When this long poem moment arrived and when, a month or so later, I knew it had arrived, I had to get George (who was, of course, already dead) off my back a bit—but he never said *No;* he was just too much there. You might call that "Killing the Uncle in the House."

The problem of writing for me is how to get an ethical literature without any didacticism or political forcing. How to address human issues without being trapped by the ego-, ethno-, phallo-, logocentrisms of humanism. How to honor choice in a serious way, even an existential way, while somehow allowing for mystery and transcendence (a word I use with some suspicion). And how to write poetry in brackets—meaning barred from whatever merely accomplished poetry we have in our tradition. That is, how to write: not poetry as decoration, not poetry as a recurrent symptom of problematic gender narratives and iconizations, not poetry as only expressive or simply personal, but some austere, deliberative, materialist, awestruck art in segmented language. These things—along with how to talk in a "vertical" fashion within a horizontal, extensive, and open worldview—these are things that George often did well. The first Draft I wrote vowed it, using Celan: no more sand poems. "Keine Sandkunst mehr, kein Sandbuch, keine Meister." ("No sand art anymore, no sandbook, no masters"—is how Pierre Joris translated this [1995, 106–7] in *Breathturn [Atemwende].*)

Within the term or cover word *avant-garde*—this is a finding for cultural studies—one might want now to disaggregate particular activities and practices. In the statements in poetics found in the *Selected Letters,* Oppen worked the term *avant-garde* round and round at least three different ways in his own history and in the process separated it into specific practices. He appreciated aesthetic extremism and intransigence and yet evinced a suspicion of groups and communities built solely around avant-garde claims.

In a letter to me in 1965 he claims "advanced guard" as a kind of ontological stance within poetry: "the thing that the poetry was for" (*SL* 122). In a letter to John Crawford in 1973, looking over *Discrete Series* (1928), Oppen says that the work was "avant garde alright" because the "old forms" were unusable, but that he doesn't (in 1973, and maybe in 1928) "*live* in an avant-garde." Oppen splits textual issues and questions of poetics away from the choice to live (as the surrealists did, but as the objectivists really didn't) in and as an ongoing group formation (*SL* 254). Then, in a couple of letters in 1974 to Jerome Rothenberg on the publication of *Revolution of the Word,* one of Rothenberg's crucial anthologies, Oppen implies that he was not really part of those avant-garde formations and hence didn't feel the book was a "reunion" (*SL* 291). This point is elaborated in a 1974 letter to David McAleavey in which Oppen says, "I cannot remember that I had ever set myself to enter the avant garde on the page - - - - I felt the avant-garde of time, of time itself - - - - if we would rescue love . . . etc but as for avantgardism of technique - - - - I wrote as I could   I found, if I could, and find if I can a way to say it - - - -" (*SL* 291–92). Indeed, an Oppen poem in Pound's 1934 *Active Anthology*, "Brain/All/Nuclei/Blinking/Kinetic/Electric sign," suggests that once upon a time Oppen had attempted a mild avant-gardism of technique but then stopped. Abruptly and decisively (*NCP* 292–93). This complex passage echoes his ontological textual claims—the poems are not avant-garde because this was a fashion but because they had to be.[13] Here Oppen adds a dimension—a sense of an extreme historical crisis to which he felt he responded.

Three propositions emerge, then, from Oppen's considerations of the avant-garde. First, textual, formal tactics must answer to necessity, not fashion; second, there are community formations and practices, groups of avant-garde practitioners, but to these he is agnostic. His attempted regathering of some "objectivists" and his various addresses to the "young" in the 1960s are perhaps paradoxical in this regard, but they were also eclectic and not "groupy." And third, the most essential for his practice of poetry, is his conviction of historical and political crisis—the "avant-garde of time . . . itself," to which work must respond by thought. His sense of time lurching ahead of itself, the sense of being endangered, is located in the cold war's precarious poise of atomic bomb against atomic bomb, the fear of nuclear accident, "the time of the missile" (*NCP* 70).

The impact of Oppen's poetry is not aesthetic only but is a kind of ontological arousal to thinking itself—not to knowledge as such but to the way thought feels emotionally and morally and processually in time. The way it feels is moving, aching, startling, and barely consoling. Olson's, Pound's, Williams's, even H.D.'s and Eliot's long poems are often knowledge based, written in some measure to give access to new accumulations of insight about researched (suggestive, nonscholarly) materials; they seek to present a general knowledge, one culturally useful, a new information about the way the world works, what brought us to this moment, or some analysis of the elements of culture and history. They often make you feel—even insist on—the importance of that knowledge, and they often go through a quasi-dialogic process of teaching. Oppen's serial works are based on thinking rather than knowledge (don't misunderstand this): a motivated apparently nontendentious, even random, cast into and among materials, which is open-ended and changing:

There are things
We live among 'and to see them
Is to know ourselves'.

(*NCP* 163)

His work exemplifies Blake's call to make "Mental Fight": a critique, an examination, a readiness to experience the ruptures and possibilities of our place and time.[14] A skeptical wariness combined with a kind of fervent hope—beyond reasonableness but not beyond reason. This might be summed up by Octavio Paz speaking about Republican Spain and its "desperate hopefulness. The memory will never leave me. Anyone who has looked Hope in the face will never forget it. He will search for it everywhere he goes" (quoted in Howe 1982, 352). I think of Oppen and his choices in the 1930s, and then all his later work, as searching for hope wherever he goes but never imagining it was there when it was not: the work is investigative, not self-deceived. He showed the importance of that "Mental Fight," with a muted critique by citation of Pound and an allusion to the Museum of Modern Art and what it represents of modernist aestheticization, perhaps, or the separation of the artwork from its context. "I am a man of the Thirties // 'No other taste shall change this'" (*NCP* 295). But the world being what it is, the condition of "Mental Fight" seems permanent.

It wasn't so much collage that Oppen did (though it sometimes seems to be) as gnomic aphorism pitched past thought by thinking. This is to walk the *via negativa* of poetry. It is "allegory" in Walter Benjamin's sense—that is, not seeking a totality: "allegory has to do, precisely in its destructive furor, with dispelling the illusion that proceeds from all 'given order,' whether of art or of life: the illusions of totality or of organic wholeness which transfigures that order and makes it seem endurable. And this is the progressive tendency of allegory" (Benjamin 1999, 331, 329). "Allegory holds fast to the ruins": this, precisely, the negative way: against fusion, totality, rest. If culture means affirmations only, we are doomed to those who want to manipulate us. If it means skeptical hope and secular attentiveness—we can, like Oppen, work against wholeness, positive thinking, delusive ideologies, celebratory visions. "Brush[ing] history against the grain"—a counterpoetics, a contestatory resistance, creates a stunned "conception of the present as the 'time of the now' which is shot through with chips of Messianic time" (Benjamin 1969, 257, 263).

"How this work was written: rung by rung, according as chance would offer a narrow foothold, and always like someone who scales dangerous heights," sounds as if it were written by Oppen, perhaps in reference to the poem "Song, the Winds of Downhill" or perhaps about all of his poems (*NCP* 220). However, it wasn't. The passage, by Walter Benjamin, describes the sensation of constructing his *Arcades Project* (Benjamin 1999, 460). The method of holding on, of casting one set of materials after another, the metaphor of handholds, footholds in the small words, all make one see an overlap in their concerns, the extremity of literary works negotiating the questions: what art is possible after disasters; how we can live in a world in which both Enlightenment consolations and fundamentalist consolations are horrifying, monstrous.

Benjamin brings me, by unapologetic metonymic logic, to the connections I feel between Oppen and another marked European figure. The sensation of reading George Oppen, as of reading Paul Celan, is of being propelled into a space on the edge, of being brought out about as far as one can go by a curious and unique mix of thought and language practices. Both writers offer the sensation of leaving the "poem" as made object with its conventions, of leaving the text as contained formula of words, and of leaving the poetic career as a curated artifact, in order to be in the world of statement itself, both beyond language and inside it. The only poem for our time is something that refuses poetry. Both could be called hermetic poets, yet of course both insisted that they were only writing a reality as they understood it. Both used a form of the kenning: more clearly in Celan's fused word nodules, and for Oppen in some of the odd things (I mean words) that end up together, kenninglike, on one line, like "page the magic" (*NCP* 278), or "distances the poem" (*NCP* 281), or "center of the rock   image" (*NCP* 271), riddling, mutually illuminating word clusters. Certainly both refuse to console. Both would say, as Celan did, that language in poetry "does not transfigure or render poetical; it names, it posits, it tries to measure the area of the given and the possible" (Rothenberg and Joris 1998, 155).

The January 1958 speech by Paul Celan accepting the prize of the Free Hanseatic City of Bremen offers some terms pertinent to Oppen.[15] For Oppen is, like Celan, a poet of negativity, of ontological intransigence. The final paragraph of the Celan summarizes his subject place. Even in accepting whatever honor or prize someone has decided to offer, one must be mindful of one's real exposure, an exposure that seems to increase, in modernity, not diminish.[16] Celan will refer, in this passage, to the recently launched Russian satellite *Sputnik*. Its launching was a cold war crisis moment for the West, thereupon compelled to weigh its own technological (and covertly military) prowess and "superiority," the compromises of its educational systems and values. Celan offers an even deeper crisis out of which he writes: "[These lines of thought, the poems, said Celan] are the efforts of someone who, overarced by stars that are human handiwork, and who, shelterless in this till now undreamt-of-sense and thus most uncannily in the open, goes with his very being to language, stricken by and seeking reality" (Felstiner 1995, 116).

Our political, historical time keeps sending us out, in Celan's decisive phrase, "uncannily in the open."[17] Because of this political and existential homelessness and exposure, one must undertake to find in language a strange home and in reality a subject. Celan's final phrase in German is "*wirklichkeitswund und Wirklichkeit suchend*"—in John Felstiner's close-English gloss, which I prefer for this essay, "reality-wounded and Reality-seeking" (Felstiner 1995, 117). This phrase, and its close companion, "most uncannily in the open," seem particularly germane to a meditation on George Oppen and not only because of the accidental onomastic pun. Oppen also spoke of the shelterless subject and the high stakes of the act of writing, the primary act of going to language "reality-wounded and Reality-seeking."

In the poetics and projects of Oppen there were several intransigent problems—how to achieve a saturated realism, presenting the things that had presented themselves to be comprehended, the "things on the road," the images encountered, but how to do so without what (he felt was) the taint of surrealism or willful juxtapositions. And second: how to understand the space we are in now, in this particular postwar of modernity: our exposure "uncannily in the open" without the props our civilization and other civilizations have depended on for hundreds of years: Enlightenment self-justificatory reason or vatic irrational mysticisms of the nonsecular, including religion treated as certainty, as religiosity.

Nothing is so simple, but for purposes of this argument I would say that one central instrument of his attention to these issues, in and as poetry, is a central formal mechanism: the line, which leads to and engages what I will (following Benjamin, partly) call the "dialectical image" (Benjamin 1999, 462, 464, 466, 473, 474, 475). Sometimes Oppen will use the term *prosody* for this or *music*—together these terms denominate a formal cluster that is also an intellectual, ontological, and epistemological cluster. To begin to analyze this, we have to acknowledge "line" as a crucial communicative means of poetry itself.

Something fairly straightforward, but highly distinctive, separates and distinguishes poetry from nearby modes like fiction and drama that also unroll in time and use sequencing tactics of various kinds. The word *nar-*

rativity evokes the central aspect of storytelling—making sequenced events with some point unroll in represented time. *Performativity* means making elements of coded and decodable gestures in special space and time. What, on this model, is the fundamental activity of poetry?

Both of these now-familiar neologisms (narrativity and performativity) indicate the practice of sequencing event, gesture, and image. Poetry also sequences; it is the creation of meaningful sequence by the negotiation of gap (line break, stanza break, page space). Although the other practices may have periodicities or gaps, these are more constitutive and systematic in poetry. Poetry can then be defined as the kind of writing that is articulated in sequenced, gapped lines and whose meanings are created by occurring in bounded units, units operating in relation to chosen pause or silence. The line segment creates meanings. The acts of making lines and making their particular chains of rupture, seriality, and sequencing are fundamental to the nature of poetry as a genre. Fundamental to what can be said in poetry, as poetry. To write poetry is, as Oppen said, to control the "sequence of disclosure" by segments that have a strong relation both to melos and to meaning: "separating the connections of the progression of thought" (Oppen 1984, 26; Oppen 1969, 167).[18] *Segmentivity*—the ability to articulate and make meaning by selecting, deploying, and combining segments—is the underlying characteristic of poetry as a genre. Narrativity and performativity summarize the particularities of fiction and drama, but segmentivity distinguishes poetry.

How does Oppen deploy the precise textual resources of poetry to sustain being "reality-wounded and Reality-seeking"? In Oppen matter, the substantive, the "thing" (in its sense of an object), is deeply engaged in time (with "things" in the sense of events), and the effect of all these things is to be both solid in time and streaming, broken up, interrupted with other connections in time to other objects and events. Oppen is eloquent about the line. His attention to things happening is created through the line—"a sense of the whole line, not just its ending"—including "the relation between lines, the relation in their length . . . the relation of the speed, of the alterations and momentum of the poem . . . the shape of the lines and the pulse of the thought which is given by those lines" (Oppen 1969, 167). Oppen remasters and changes the lyric, proposes a subjectivity ("reality-wounded and Reality-seeking") by historicizing (and temporalizing) not only the speaking subject of poetry but the line itself, the material practice of poetry.

To see in "the manner of poetry" is to penetrate what is primary (thus such Oppen-inflected words as *primitive, the materials, the obvious*), what presents itself as such, obdurately and irrevocably (*NCP* 198). The statement

"All that was to be thought / Yes / Comes down the road" (*NCP* 213) is the "same" as the antisurrealist statement "the image is encountered, not found" (Oppen [1963] 2003, 175). That is—it is what you cannot not see; it is not a trouvaille or wrought wit: it is the "narrative" (that is, the pedagogy) of "things."

> In the starlight things the things continue
> Narrative   their long instruction and the tide running
> Strong as a tug's wake   shorelights'
>
> Fractured dances across rough water a music
> Who would believe it
> Not quite one's own
> With one always the   black verse   the turn and the turn
>
> (*NCP* 213)

There are a number of allusions to, and metaphors for, poetry and the poetic line in this passage: "narrative" (amusingly), "long instruction," "a music," "dances,"—not the least of which is "the   black verse   the turn and the turn." This can allude to blank verse (that is, to epochal poetic form in the humanist period), to the dark ink of writing on the page, to the darkness of water at night, and the dark side of modernity's unfounded optimisms. It also alludes to the mechanism inside verse that makes it "turn," to make the next furrow of work—precisely the etymological meaning of verse. By layering the encrypted words *blank verse* underneath *black verse,* the old humanist line is alluded to and surpassed, and a new ethical and formal space for a posthumanist "black verse" line "uncannily in the open" is suggested. "Black verse" could, without too much overstatement, allude to poetic tactics chosen when one is faced with the dark events of recent history, wounded by that darkness, and yet "Reality-seeking." It is at once the prosody of and the ethical calling into the *via negativa.* "The   black verse" is always in motion, because it derives from the play of waves, the play of historical time, the play of the poetic segment. "Black verse" is Oppen's metaphor for his poetry of negativity: an unconsoled poetry of turning and searching, an unconsoling poetry of hope. That is, to go back to Adorno's terms, "black verse" is form for a poetry of commitment. To turn, as I will, to Benjamin, "black verse" constructs a dialectical image. To repeat Celan, "black verse" leaves one "uncannily in the open."

Especially in his later poetry, Oppen achieves a nonsurrealist but continuous combinatoire—a realist but destabilizing combinatory movement, by junctures along the line, openings inside the line, and by hinges created by line break. The strained, open, gnomic, and aphoristic line of his later poetry gives to him, but with a different ethics, a different epistemology, what surrealism gives to others: an investigatory tool to explore how the world may be put together differently by setting certain materials in combination. This is not a magical irrationalism in Oppen, but it does create a sense of unresolvable oddness at the core of the real.

Once upon a time I happened to use the word *dizzy,* meaning vertiginous, to George in describing the effect of his later poems on me, something I think that he misunderstood. When, in a letter to Robert Duncan, Oppen defended himself, a little proudly and happily, from the burden of my dizziness, he said something germane to this discussion: "But I thought I was simply pointing to things—and clearly enough or accurately enough" (*SL* 300). Still half-talking to the dead, let me say that I belatedly comprehend what this vertigo entailed: what Adorno in *Aesthetic Theory* called (these are Robert Kaufman's words) "a quasi-cognitive, quasi-experiential otherness in art" sensed through a "shaking of the subject in aesthetic experience" (Kaufman 2002, 49; see also Adorno 1997, 244–45).

Adorno proposed this as "a breaking through of reified consciousness" in "aesthetic experience" that allows one to "exercise . . . those faculties whose development contributes to sociopolitical critique and praxis" (Adorno 1997, 196; Kaufman 2002, 48, 49). Or even, "a liberated society . . . is enciphered in art and is the source of art's social explosiveness" (Adorno 1997, 227). The vertigo of these unrolling line turns of "black verse" propels one magnetically down the road of negativity, skepticism, and resistant hope. This is the goal of Oppen's saturated realism (the opposite of surrealism), and he achieves this not by combining image-based words but by the startling combinatoire of his line breaks. These line breaks offer a sense of another space, the space of awe and the inexpressible. For an attenuated sense of transformation enters in the turn of many of Oppen's lines. It is, as he says in "Myth of the Blaze," the "blaze // of changes" (*NCP* 248).

One aspect of the "uncanny open" is, then, Oppen's vertiginous sense of statement, syntax, and space. The spaces of the poem are like the universe of stars and of human losses. A poem swings from the smallest to the largest terms at once, a netting of the void. The open is also the historical and dialectical swing of statement, where the lines are like thesis and antithesis, and where any "synthesis" is like the beginning of a new dialectical formulation. Oppen's work is confluent with Benjamin's *Arcades Project,* which is itself a suggestive, collaged, intense, raggedy, frustrating, startling text, porous by virtue of its refusal to construct argument.

"Method of this project: literary montage. I needn't *say* anything. Merely show. I shall purloin no valuables, appropriate no ingenious formulations. But the rags, the refuse—these I will not inventory but allow, in the only way possible, to come into their own: by making use of them" (Benjamin 1999, 460). I cite this for the untoward suggestiveness of its confrontative praxis; it is more suggestive than I can say, even understanding that in its apparent refusal of anything but pointing, it has made a strange, strange claim. *The Arcades Project* was in large measure conducted exactly as these words propose. To collect and set forth scraps of insight and fact, to rupture the academic and journalistic arguments from which these facts had been gleaned, would, Benjamin claimed, allow a myriad of flashes to be generated over the whole texture of the project. This juxtaposition of deictic plenitudes made an antisystemic and antitriumphalist texture, fractally opened to a space beyond argument, to sheer suggestiveness. One of Benjamin's great ironies is how he uses positivist collection of fact against itself, for antipositivist ends. With cinematic, though not narrative, design, Benjamin proposed that a montage of images on certain topoi offered instantaneous meaning in a modernist flash, but he also modified this desire for instant epiphany by a focus on "intervals of reflection" or "distances lying between" his cited and sometimes, though rarely, glossed materials (Benjamin 1999, 456).[19] Those words ("intervals" and "distances") insist on the creation of structure by interactive space between the blocks of fact, very much the poetics of seriality, as in Oppen.

Benjamin spent some time in section "N" working through the "dialectical image" (Benjamin 1999, 462–75). "Where thinking comes to a standstill in a constellation saturated with tensions—there the dialectical image appears. It is the caesura in the movement of thought. Its position is naturally not an arbitrary one. It is to be found . . . where the tensions between dialectical opposites is greatest. Hence, the object constructed in the materialist presentation of history is itself the dialectical image" (Benjamin 1999, 475). But this is quite odd when applied to poetry, as one might immediately desire to do, led by the words *caesura,* not to speak of *image, constellation,* or even *thinking.* Benjamin seems to propose a poetics of modernist presentation (maybe applied to history)—the still moment, the held object, the formed thought emerging from a field of conflictual materials. The "dialectical image" "is dialectics at a standstill" (Benjamin 1999, 475, 462). But isn't the point of dialectics its ongoingness, its movement in time, its rejection of stasis, its situated repositioning of primary materials? It's as if Benjamin named something using a terminology that honored the play of temporality and movement, but in his descriptive definition of the constellation, he produced a modernist freeze-frame "hold." Further, for Anglo-American readers Benjamin's definition "thinking [at] a standstill in a constellation saturated with tensions" recalls Pound's famous capital *I* and quotation marked "'Image'" from 1913: "an 'Image' is that which presents an intellectual and emotional complex in an instant of time," and also recalls the methods of field and/or ideogram construction used in Poundian poetries (Pound 1954, 4).[20]

It is hard to parse this and honor its complexity. In Oppen, one might say, "thinking" never comes "to a standstill." Oppen's poetry thus offers a critique of Benjamin's modernist, freeze-frame poetics, yet it can perfectly illustrate another definition of the "dialectical image." Adorno seems to double back on Benjamin's insight when he says "the artwork is both the result of the process and the process itself at a standstill," showing how an artwork is dynamic and objectified at once, perpetually "in a process of becoming" (Adorno 1997, 179, 178). Putting words like *dialectical* and *historical* near the word *image* illuminates the poetry of Oppen and poetry in general.[21] Thus, using the same key words differently, I want to say, "Where thinking in poetry is both poised and ongoing, in a streaming of lines that one could read as a constellation, but which also embodies the experience of temporality and ceaseless questioning, there the dialectical image appears. It is the caesura in the movement of thought, a caesura paradoxically both in the full poem as a unit, and inside a line of poetry, as an actual caesura, white space or pause, in the pressure of the line break or turn of the line."

In the section of *Aesthetic Theory* called "Toward a Theory of the Artwork," Adorno comments on the dialectic of constellation as both stasis and motion. "Artworks' paradoxical nature, stasis, negates itself. The movement of artworks must be at a standstill and thereby become visible" for "it is only as finished, molded objects that they become force fields of their antagonisms"; thus stasis is necessary to the sense of transformative movement (Adorno 1997, 176). Line break in poetry—visceral and visual—expresses this lively tension between eloquent stasis and driven becoming.

One may thereby theorize Oppen's distinctive practice of hovering and enjambment, a practice achieving ethical and emotional effects from poetic segmentivity, as this dialectic constellation. These bidirectional, even multidirectional, line segments in later Oppen compel a practice of reading that makes fluid and ambiguous what part of the line segment to read with what other part. Or how to read and reckon with enjambment and *apo koinou* (syntactic hinge or pivot words) (Quartermain 1992, 93, 215). Through the various answers to the open-ended question of what line segments go with what, hovering, hinges, and bridges are created that make double or triple readings plausible. Thus from any one later Oppen poem, one has several shadowy poems (more "black verse"); and the intellectual, emotional, and structural mobility of the lines in the reading process, their modular quality, creates a sense of temporality (even historical time, large time, time in motion) inside the poem as object. These aspects make reality multidimensional and offer a sense of "occurrence," or the things we are among, and our sense of exposure "in the open" to those things. The thinking poetry achieves is created within the texture of poetry.

Oppen's poems are precisely dialectical images in this sense—in a temporal sense, not at a standstill (except insofar as they are in finished poems).[22] They are dialectical images both in individual lines and particulars and in the total poem. To say

> . . . I believe
>
> in the world
>
> because it is
> impossible
> (*NCP* 248)

is formally a constellation saturated with tensions that change temporally as you read the lines. The lines seem to have one meaning if you stop with the line breaks, another meaning if you continue. The statements (I believe in the world because it is; I believe in the world because it is impossible) propose dialectical, ongoing thought by using the deepest formal mechanisms of poetry. These kinds of moments are not the only ones in Oppen, but these tactics set the tonality and pitch for readers.

In their use of fragmented phrases, Oppen's lines are not static, but the phrases, taken as objects, seem to stream toward each other in a desire for connectedness in the "between" created by the poem. This desire is never quite fulfilled. Oppen's later poems are something between full statement and attenuated absences, plenitude in opacity, bridging between the two states in a literal demonstration of the between. One reads the potential condensation of any one thought into finality, but as more possibilities are created, the sense of a "black verse" overwritten with itself, also increases. The phrases move along on the same "speaking plane," but they turn both toward and away from each other as the stream of language moves along. There is very little settled (there is, indeed, very little final punctuation or commas), and nothing seems to end, even at the conclusion of any given poem. Yet many of the statements have the force of enormous pronouncements. This is black verse; this is the dialectical image, completeness in motion.

The statements "and the music essential" and then "clarity plain glass ray" (*NCP* 257) are final, but the statement created by line break "and the music essential // clarity plain glass ray" changes things ("essential clarity"? "essential clarity plain"?) Not to speak of the addition of the final line "of darkness ray of light" (*NCP* 257). In many (though, of course, not all) of the relationships of line to line in Oppen, there are alternative determinate meanings palimpsested as the poem releases itself into its temporality dialectically, as the lines change in relation to each other, repositioned as synthesis or as new thesis, and then antithesis. One changes or extends the statement by imagining "periods" or puncted marks after various words. One changes or extends the statement by imagining alternative relationships of apposition among the elements. But finally (something that makes later Oppen hard to read aloud, as it makes him hard to excerpt), the poem is a chain with modular links built to surround or net something ungraspable, unnettable, unassimilable. There is a relative, though not absolute, attenuation of syntax creating horizontal equality among the elements, as if they were being scanned along a changing horizon.

You are often straining for meaning as it shifts, via line break, right under your eyes. Indeed, any given line may have two centers—a completed thought and an incompleted thought (in the swing to the next line). This is a plausible condition of poetry in general, one might say, but Oppen pushed this potential of the poetic line very far. Finally, often in the later work, the poem never ends but simply stops, leaving us where we are: and by this we know we are "uncannily in the open." (I have of course, echoed both Celan's phrase and Oppen's own line, "by this we know it is the real // That we confront"; *NCP* 202). The uncanny open of Oppen exists in the tensions between surface and depth, between conclusion and endlessness; between sententia/aphorism and the breaking of those vessels not by force but by the direct continuance of thinking itself. This is Oppen's saturated realism, a mode of practicing "combination" that makes a critical answer, in form, to surrealist practices of the image, allowing for alternative combinations, pointing to real things. Oppen wants to show that claims of our materiality are the same as claims of our mystery: "I suppose it's nearly a sense of awe, simply to feel that the thing is there and that it's quite something to see" (Oppen 1969, 164). Where materiality and mystery join dialectically along the line, there is the uncanny light of his poetry.

IV
Migrated Into

10
On *Drafts*

A Memorandum of Understanding

I cannot romanticize poetry. It is hard to make up words about it. Poetry is the creation of a necessary object made in and of lines of language. As a poet, I work with language and its critique—words, their histories, the play of social materials and discourses, the twangs of nuance, neologisms, aphasias, syntax, and the construction of continuities by sequencing. I work with poetic conventions and their critique—line break, metrics, rhyme and other marked sound, sonorities and overloads, genres—their uses and undoing. I work with motivated allusions to the cadence and turbulence of past works, all the rhetorical resources I can muster, wild or tame. I work with textual conventions and their critique—punctuation, capitalization, the look on the page, the page space itself, the notion of "poem." Making poetry is work with an intractable substance and intricate social institution (language) that is at the same time a medium with which we are all too familiar, being saturated in its blandishments and banalities every day. One works in art with a manifold of conflicting traditions and in language with a manifold of exacting resources and in poetry with its histories. But also—one works out of all these categories because they may prettify, hobble, or confine. Works with the visceral surges and material densities of language. Works with excess, to excess.

What makes any writing into poetry? Poetry as a specific kind of writing is distinguished essentially by segmentivity, that is, by the choice and division of its language into lines. One makes meaningful lines by the negotiation of kinds of temporalities (speech, meter) and kinds of markers (such as rhyme, hinge, blaze, bridge, or gap) in interplay with syntax and statement. Line segments, as George Oppen proposed, construct the "sequence of disclosure" by "separating the connections of the progression of thought"

(Oppen 1984, 26). The pace of disclosure is one key to a poem's impact on the reader.

In an objectivist mode technique is the test (and text) of a person's sincerity (modifying Pound 1954, 9). This makes an ethics of writing emerge simultaneously with the making of language. The basic "rule" of technique is that every single mark, especially the merest jot and tittle, the blankest gap and space, all have meaning. "Craft" and kinds of craftiness follow the intensities of the writer's need, for the poem or the writing. At this moment, making poetry, I like best the tactile quality of moving language around, sculpting it into shapes, making bodies of syntactic manifolds that suggest . . . meaning flickering in and out of focus, within and against the enormousness, and the enormity, of silence. When a poem is finished, there is a comic, dastardly sense of satisfaction that Randall Jarrell once summed up as "The devil sold me his soul" (Jarrell [1954] 1960, 136).

The problem of memory is the largest motivation for my poetry. However, the sheer memorializing function attributed to poetry, especially as that singles out female figures to be surrounded by "the male gaze," has been an ethical and intellectual issue for me since the early 1970s. This stance, which also involves the desire to criticize and undermine the lyric, to wring its ideology out, and to envelop it in the largeness of another practice, has been consistent as a motivation for twenty-five years. It does not necessarily lead to feminist declarations in my poetry but to questions and the research of cultural materials, in short, to a feminism of critique. This commitment to analysis within the poetic act and text creates a powerful force field for me. This impulse to critique has long been joined with a tonal and structural interest in what I was calling (from about 1981 on) a "Talmud" poem, by which I innocently meant something like midrash—doubled and redoubled commentary, poetry with its own gloss built in. My idea was sidebars, visuals, anything to create "otherness inside otherness."

In 1985 I wrote a diaristic letter to myself that illustrates the mélange of feminist critique and issues in textuality that spurred *Drafts:*

> My problem with "being a poet" is stated in [my essay] "Otherhow"—I cannot believe in the perfection of lyric, the separation of lyric, the selectivity of lyric, the purity of lyric, the solitary language of lyric & cannot imagine what to "do" next. NO! I *can* understand what to do next . . . a deliberate intermingled generative midden of a voice . . . a voice which accumulates all the pressures of its situation. And it means that what will therein appear could be, generically: a poem, an

essay, a meditation, a narrative, an epigram, an autobiography, an anthology of citations, a handbill found on the street, a photograph, marginalia, glossolalia, and here we go here we go here we go again.

This note marks the beginning of *Drafts.*

I fumbled a size 8 paradun onto my 3X tippet and waded in. A businesslike boil 30 feet upstream drew my first cast. In 1986 I began, with fair abruptness, to write two intermingled canto-length works, and I recognized, stunned, that a project in the long poem had begun. Like any cast, this project had a long prehistory. The question of length, extent, duration, ambition, desire, commitment had simply combined with the calm one needs to face such a project. The claim of the long poem on myself, I recognized by virtue of establishing the title *Drafts,* a suggestive word for the title of the whole, and each. "Drafts" are never final. "Drafts" are freshly drawn and freely declared, as if a preliminary outline or sketch. In "Drafts," completion is always provisional. "Drafts" involve the pull or traction on something, a drain on something, conscription into something. Therefore "Drafts" are an examination from the ground here, not elsewhere. No matter what.

Drafts, a series of interdependent, related, canto-length poems, also began over and over for many years before 1986, and a tracking of their origins is a tracking of vectors and sources.

- *Drafts* began in 1964, when I first read *Paterson,* or a little later when I furtively and pleasurably read the whole of *Spring & All,* a work at that time available, in its entirety, only in a Rare Books Room. I was reading that at Columbia University when all the lights went off in New York City—the great blackout, November 9, 1965.
- *Drafts* began in response to the unfinished issues in my intractable dissertation, *The Endless Poem* (1970), on *Paterson* and *The Pisan Cantos.* This was an awkward and academically marginal attempt to name the objectivist poetics to which I was connected, to explain how "imagist" poetics could have generated the modern long poem. Others less in the dark than I was in the later 1960s have written very effective books on these poems, but I was then unable to write with professional maturity on a topic I nonetheless felt as vital, joyous, and festering. The impact of Pound and Williams affected me in various ways during the next decades.
- *Drafts* began in about 1981, when, after (repeatedly) teaching *The Waste Land* and seeing certain modern art, I had a vision of a text on plastic

laminate sheets, layered one over the other, which could be read through, could slide relative to each other, and thus make changeable configurations of materials. This was also like the notion of a "Talmudic" text.

- *Drafts* came from a pivotal pre-"Draft" poem, a serial work called "Writing," dated 1984–85, whose concern with the first months of a child's life was deeply influenced by the originality of Mary Kelly's *Post-Partum Document.* In this poem, which cites from Williams's "January Morning," everything was "happening on the side."[1]
- *Drafts* began in the fall of 1985, in Nijmegen, when I first read Beverly Dahlen's work *A Reading,* whose scope, passion, and design struck me with pleasure. Later I wrote about Dahlen's text and noted her "heuristic establishment of form by the reading of those words she has 'happened' to write" (DuPlessis [1990] 2006, 118). Tracking the intricate meanings of one's own accidents—a practice related to H.D.'s writing practice in *Tribute to Freud*—gives rise to a midrashic layering and linkages of interpretation, where the production and productivity of meanings is continuous.
- *Drafts* began in the nourishing brown-marbled-paper Italian notebook given to me by Kathleen Fraser, in which I (January 1986, just back from four months in Holland) "drew" or "drafted" words into the page, making a sketch pad of language. I was teaching Creeley's *Pieces.* He claimed (it was said) never to revise. But it wasn't so much that permission, as the alert, nuanced present-ing he achieved, a series of shifting weights and balances on the page, engaged in the momentary registering of emotion and response. Suddenly, even on the luscious paper, in that extraordinary notebook, I felt free simply to notate words and sounds. To set meaning down. To write stops and starts.
- *Drafts* began on Solana Beach, the other end of the States from my home, on May 17, 1986, in a notebook bought in 1980 but hardly used until that moment. It was meaningful that this notebook was bound in the work of a woman—Sonia Delaunay. I sat on the beach, a whole day, writing, continuously, but in spurts, with an intense self-consciousness that was neither paralyzing nor aggrandizing but business-like, and almost flat. I had been at La Jolla, at the Archive for New Poetry, reading George Oppen's papers for my edition of his *Selected Letters.* His words: "You have your own pencil and your own piece of paper and you're on your own word by word from scratch." It was true.

I cast myself off into "one." The first one was mixed with the second one; but once I named and separated, it was clear that I needed to write them and number them simply in the order in which they came, trusting to the fact of ongoingness. One began where "one" was. "One" was where one was writing.

At first it seemed I was going to investigate some "little words"—pronouns and pronominals *(it, she)*—the shifters. But such a conception eviscerated itself. Anyway, one had to be true to the "moving along," or ongoingness. What I learned from the first Drafts was that there was a lot of "it" out there; that it was all "it." And, one way or another, "she" was going to have to deal with "it." Those first titles were, in fact, a condensed program for the project. Then prepositions presented themselves *(of, in)*, which identified sites of participation with their vectors of direction. Still, I had no intention of writing a poem per pronoun or one for each preposition. So it began to seem as if every scheme for settling the poem, for controlling its processes of continuance, was self-devoured. Schemes became inadequate to themselves virtually at the moment of their conscious declaration. At about this time I stopped worrying about what parts of speech my titles came from, about what pattern they made, and about what I was doing in any ultimate sense.

Nonetheless, I could always point to or invent patterns of address among groups of works, and it was interesting to do so. For instance, a group of titles from 1988 to 1990 seemed to intimate the materials of writing: "The," "Page," "Letters," "Schwa"—"Letters" with the qwerty keyboard foregrounded as alphabet. After this there was a time when title words indicated genres and grammatical little words ("Haibun"—a Japanese diary form of prose mixed with haiku—and "Conjunctions"). The examination of textuality was ongoing ("Title," "Traduction," "Incipit," "Segno"), but this focus is not exclusive, for I am also interested in work, and mapping, and their results ("Working Conditions," "Cardinals," "Philadelphia Wireman," "Findings"). In the poems subsequent to "Draft X: Letters," there is an undercurrent of the sociological/poetic practice called (in the 1930s, in England) "Mass Observation." In all the works the border between the discursive and the imaginative, between the analytic and the creative, is certainly porous. I sustained continuance by being willing continually to cast myself off into it—this no longer seemed odd or awkward. I assumed it. It had advantages. The thought remains buoyant.

Let me return to memory, since I have a bad memory—maybe I haven't talked about memory yet. I have lived, for many years, with the losses of shadowy memory. Mourning for it. But in the poem I found that I was building the space of memory or a replica of its processes. There is a repressed and barely articulated grief—the extensive killing that has formed the places in which we reside. Begin with the Middle Passage or the ridding and near-extermination of many First Nations and indigenous peoples during the colonial expansion of Europe. Begin with the Armenian genocide, begin with the Belgian depredation of the Congo, or begin with the Holocaust. Begin with the accelerating firestorms of aerial bombardment, as a "good idea." Begin with the First World War or the Second. Begin with the deaths of diversity—biodiversity or linguistic diversity. Begin wherever you want, back in another century, or in ours. Begin with modernity, in any event. There is a ghost in our sociocultural house whose specific outlines depend on a particular set of identifications and histories but whose presence is palpable. Abraham and Torok's concept of the "transgenerational phantom" may explain why someone like myself, two generations removed from direct and intimate ties to European Jewry, speaks a poetry haunted by the ghosts of ghosts (Abraham and Torok 1994). It seems as if poetry is the institution (the conduit, the mouth) through which this phantom can speak. Can make sounds. It can recognize, and it can grieve.

How? Because of the thick layering of implication that words in poetry generate, because feelings are trapped in the rich matting of language, and because poetry acknowledges silence. How? Because of words that recall words used before. Words that contain the mysteries of the unspoken.

Walter Benjamin cites Georg Lukács, who proposes that "hope and memory" are "the genuinely epic experiences of time," but what happens if you have only sporadic hope and sporadic memory? (Benjamin 1969, 97). My answer is this work, written from a post-Holocaust era. The relation of this historical claim to my poetics is straightforward: I try to write so that if a single shard were rescued in the aftermath of some historical disaster, that one shard would be so touching and lucid as to give the future an idea of who we were. It is like our reading Sappho after her almost total erasure. This kind of thinking sets a standard for the work. It is, of course, an impossible standard but not the less compelling for that reason.

"Plenty of debris. Plenty of smudges" (Williams 1957, 94). These are poems challenged by—moved by—the plethora, the extent, the intricacy of the sites that seem to be at stake in their composition. Here is a typical situation: small to large, tiny to largest. It is about the plethora of stars, that vastness, and the dot or yod, the most miniscule mark. That *it is*. That we can read it. That it defines us and we barely know what or how. An absolute and ahuman sense of scale into which these works get swallowed up—a dot, a point, a little flicker. These situations—of awe and amazement—are part of what generates the poems.

In form *Drafts* is closest to collage, with its ethos of accumulation, clarity of the excerpt, preservation of edges, and juxtaposition. I think of Schwitters perpetually. And I think of the essay called "Marianne Moore" by Williams, in which the poetics of collage is analyzed. But at other times the works seem symphonic, declaring a vast performance space in which interesting sounds occur, develop, and reverberate. Structurally, the works are linked by subtle forms of repetition, presenting the reader with sets and bits of recollections, or the evanescent sensation of déjà vu, its rhythm of gap and recall. There is the sensation of forgetting and being half-reminded, as if the poem, as I said, constituted the space of memory.

Drafts could be described as heterogeneric, making allusive loops around and through concepts of genre that the poems both appropriate and disturb, genres such as midrash, elegy, ode, autobiography, and meditation. In texture they are heteroglossic—open to a range of voices, tones, verbal textures, social codes, and rhetorics. Definite motifs and thematic materials are at stake. A representative, although incomplete, list would include home and exile, writing and the scenes of writing, the minutiae of dailiness, death and the dead linked with the living, silence and speaking. And as well the question of what positions and discourses are adequate to speaking as a gendered "I" while at the same time, there is a distinct downplaying of any "I" (a word, incidentally, that rarely appears in the first thirty-eight Drafts), and no more overt discussion of gender than of anything else.

Gender issues, however, do suffuse the formal and discursive choices that underlie my resistance both to continuous narrative and to lyric. Whether or not there are, in the poems, particular comments about being a person gendered female, it is clear that gender matters for the ground of these poems. They were involved with my commitment to a critical rupture with the standpoints and ideologies of the lyric: intact "I," bounded by yearnings for female figures, climax, epiphany, desire for beauty, consumable narratives, neat length. This type of poem, to generalize briskly, offers repetitious positioning of the self in predictable poetic/political situations but via brilliant language. I have argued (both in critical prose and in poetry) that the problematic of the lyric is acute when one analyzes the female figure on whom poetry has had, historically, a number of designs. These poems are my response—an attempt to appropriate the sound, music, and nuance of the lyric but to criticize the issues of beauty, unity, finish, and female positions within these ideas and to instead articulate the claims and questions of Otherness—not as a binary to something else but rather as a seam opening inside existence.

I use the nonce word *otherhow* to indicate a space, a practice, a further distance implicit within method. I want partially to claim what narrative and lyric modes give me but otherhow, in another sense. So my resistance to lyric or narrative, my critique of their normalizing and naturalizing of gender, of causality, of trajectory, of telos, of memory is a porous resistance. It is riddled by holes through which these discourses and their rich histories of use may leak. *Drafts* comprises the sites of these struggles, the site of my wariness.

Another genre analogy is certainly the ode. Curiously the same word characterizes the political and the rhapsodic (Horatian and Pindaric). It is a genre without many guidelines (three parts about sums it up) but one that assumes some stance of commentary and exposition, but also keening, bursting, and other kinds of high feeling. I also think of my odic impulse as "ex-odic," on the analogy of Exodus—a bringing of a disparate, complaining, sloppy, backsliding, and self-suspicious set of materials into a "poem." But it's also an ex-ode in the sense of going out, a going away, a turning away from the normal blandishments of (let's say) civilization or genteel writing. An ode that exits from the ode.

As I have already made clear, *Drafts* is a large-scale project with several of the monumental works of modernism haunting the author—a work that might (with some yearning, if not total justice) be described, in Pound's words, as a "big, long, endless poem" (Stock 1970, 189). This raises the unsolved—perhaps insoluble—problem of representation and extent: for Williams, "the whole knowable world" (Williams [1951] 1967, 391). Knowing and unknowing clash interestingly in these two citations, as do termination and the interminable. Both speak of a decisive yearning to produce an encyclopedic work of grounding that explores sociopolitical and spiritual forces with collage, heteroglossia, citation, accumulation. No one could now claim anything resembling this ambition innocently, yet the question is still fresh after eighty years or more. What to do about the long poem?

Since teleology had already been taken, when I began I was not thinking about ending at all, or endlessness either, but about whatever materials come, or are figured, in the site that each poem declares. When there is some rhythmic or emotional realization, the individual "Draft" stops. There is ending for each of the poems taken individually but no end in sight for them taken collectively. The poems do not stand too far above or over anything. The vistas here are always lateral, local, immersed. I look around at the plethoras and crossings. The random strewing of debris always moves me.

But the heroic force of the artist? The sense of a poem as a *Bildung*? Any "growth of a poet's mind"? The exemplary nature of "me" in my encounter with anything? All of these were undermined both by my belatedness as a writer and (though it is amusingly self-contradictory to say it) by my humility in the face of many precursors in words. Especially when one is in the midst of a work—who can say the "I" is exemplary, historical? One just writes as best one can. The vow is simple, although it may have taken years to recognize: to work in one's time. Time and history are the situation and ground; work is the medium and the response. The ins and outs of the self are just part of the design.

At the same time, the project has its own duplicity. The "form" is ambition— not otherwise thought of structurally or as a genre. But it may well be an incitement to both. Is the very nature of ambition, no matter how constituted—biographical, literary-historical, sociopolitical, elegiac, intertextual—the nature of a claim *as* claim? Does the thing most extrinsic to the work finally make one understand that "where one is going" is to make adequate marks? This "mark of ambition" (otherwise known as work) marks the dissolution of the poet into the poem.

11
Haibun

"Draw Your Draft"

Her books on my shelf, waiting for me to attend; I had bought them, yet I didn't read them. Grove and New Directions. The photo on *Bid Me to Live,* taken at a vertiginous angle. Of a blank space. Telling the book by its cover. Telling a woman's book looking only at the surface. (For it was not blank; it was a photo of a British military monument. Could I not see?) This prereading moment is not heroic or critical but compliant, with hardly an undercurrent of real knowledge. Just the fact that I had bought her books made some kind of declaration. But not reading them—another kind. The vertigo of acceding to something limited called "woman"—I felt its danger. *Helen in Egypt* looked too "neat," too "centered." I was, instead, challenging myself with the page-space collage works of Williams *(Paterson)* and Pound *(The Cantos).* No one had yet credited the depth of H.D.'s critique of culture; hence, because I desired such a critique, I turned away from her, thinking, shamefully, that no woman could have accomplished this. That misapprehension, circa 1965, began to diminish when, thankfully, I read (certainly by the early 1970s) *The H.D. Book* chapters in *Caterpillar,* in *Stony Brook,* published in 1968 and 1969. So Robert Duncan became my first path to H.D., for he made a heterodox modernism with women's work and men's intermingled, in mutual dialogue and contestation. This—his attitude was neither gender neutrality nor gender blindness—went counter to any version of modern poetry the university or the general literate culture proposed. In his daybooks Duncan also offered a model for that "feminine" associative build, those metonymic linkages of committed argument, the interwoven projects of thought, and an insouciant, informed resistance to convention. Shock, scandal, pleasure. Indeed, his essay form—that particular form of thinking—was itself indebted to H.D., so that in hearing his essays with a wild alertness, I also started to hear hers. The essays I began writing in 1978, like "For the Etruscans," emerged via Duncan's *H.D. Book,* as well as via feminist explorations by Woolf and Rich.

During my Columbia PhD oral examination in—was it 1966?—I spoke about Williams's *Spring & All,* a work no one (I ever knew) except me had read in toto, written by a poet almost totally discounted. I also spoke critically about Dorothy Wordsworth's position as a conduit for the imagination of her brother, about the cultural meaning of the female figure in "Tintern Abbey." I had simply not understood that a central part of the study of literature was re-presenting the criticism that already existed. Therefore I had never heard anyone saying the things that were coming out of my mouth.

Prima Donna Illusion
the dreamed dreamer
my silhouette, sleep, swirled like a silver streamer
the stage is swept with shards.

At a peculiar location (time—1964 et seq., place—NYC), tamped down, insecure. I heard the New American poetry through the Donald Allen anthology, and I listened at a bubbling well where Olson, Duncan, Creeley, and also *Caterpillar* (edited by Clayton Eshleman) made sibylline sound, but, shyly or stupidly, I didn't search for any personal bond. On the other hand, I connected to the reemerging objectivists. George Oppen and I met in August 1965; I still think of him and his work insistently. Oppen is central to my sense of the seriousness and scrupulousness of poetry. He influenced my knowledge of the poetic career in its exilic, nomadic, political dimensions. By working out of a marginal place, by deploying both the leverage of critique and a sense of audacity, Oppen built himself an oeuvre in twenty-five years of intense work. These forces in poetry and poetics (all loosely related to Pound and Williams) cut perpendicular to the professional complacencies of the university as institution, in which there were a history, a library, a site of enterprise but no real or consistent training, certainly (generally? normatively? usually?) not for women. I was the uncomfortable X where these two forces crossed. I never went downtown (except to MoMA!), kept to a small but intense poetry group on 100th Street. In 1968 the radical liberatory thinking of civil rights and antiwar analyses contributed to the beginnings of a feminist movement in which I was abruptly immersed to my fibers. After a first flurry of this activity, I decamped to France for several years (1970–72) and tried to invent a feminist cultural position for myself, without immediate peers or interlocutors. Isolation is a motif. There is also no doubt I was afraid of the gift.

> hooded woman, black coat
> rigid in an
> anxious walking context
> I expect her to howl
>
> falling into the well of swallowing herself.

During the early period of my (particular/peculiar) poetic career (1963 forward) I was very good at inventing blockages. The long poem always engaged me; before 1968 I had written a serial poem called "The War Years," a long sequence called "Villa d'Este   Staten Island," and a work that was really about gender, beginning "Train journey and / journey by water," yet I found no ways for me to understand what my subjects and modes were telling me, no ways to move into a continuous and productive poetic career. During the time of writing my gnarled-up dissertation (*The Endless Poem,* on long poems by Pound and Williams), I diminished to three-line, to one-line poems. The fragment is not inconsistent with the urge to seriality, of course, but this felt like the end of my poetry. I remember with great gratitude George Oppen's looking at this work (and at this situation) and saying "Well, a good one-line poem, that's not nothing." I felt divided, wayward, underutilized, but did not know what to do.

> How many overtures
>   you gonna write
>   to yr only
>   OPERA
> "get on with it"

Yet still during the early and mid-1970s there was even more blockage, or, rather, a baroque elaboration of structures of self-resistance. No easy way to say this, it seems so scrupulously—what? (certainly undercutting). The question of beauty. I just didn't want beauty in my poetry: any hint was an invitation to a slippery slope of the feminine. Beauty was too nice, too expected, too complicit with what the feminine was in poetry, and, by extension, what the female was. The poetical poetry of the "death of the beautiful woman" (Poe's rancid idea) was the death of the woman writing (Poe [1846]

1984, 19). The death of the poet in the poetess. Of course, this became a subject of some of my literary criticism. I am so stubborn about this structure of feeling that, even now, I suspect and resist the triumphant investiture of awe and blessing in female figures made in culture and cultural products by Dante to Bréton and beyond. This is a serious blind spot, as well as part of my critical advantage. That's why I admire Lyn Hejinian's wry, recognizing line (from section—that is, age—26 of *My Life*) "The Muses are little female fellows" (Hejinian 1987, 67). This sentence takes that whole structure of feeling and flicks it away into companionship, androgyny, and drollery at about the same age-time as I also confronted, with less ability to dismiss it, the situation of woman writing. Later in *My Life* Hejinian (or someone just like her, recollecting age forty-two) proposes as "a person on paper, I am androgynous," contemporaneous with this term's appearance in second-wave feminist thinking (Hejinian 1987, 105).

In any event I tried *not* to write beauty (rhetorical staginess, lovely images, and the mellifluous) but to write language, to write syntax, to write austerely. Or to compose a beauty so hard and selective, yet in intense visionary images, as to contain its suspect presence. This urge has analogues with early H.D., but I got it via the objectivists and Pound. An unintended (but unsurprising) consequence: my poetry could not be fluid, fluent, ongoing; it could only stop and start. It (I?) was so angry about rhetorics—these are the years before *Wells*—that it (I?) became frozen and incompliant with its (my) desires for production. I thought—in the poignant jargon of the time—that "I hadn't found my voice." I'd now say (other jargon?) that the positions available for me to take up as a woman writer—inside language and inside the mechanisms of poetry, and outside it in various apparatuses and institutions of culture—were unsatisfactory and confusing to me.[1] I was writing the lyric, yet increasingly I did not want the perfection of lyric, the separation of lyric, the selectivity of lyric, the purity of lyric. This is surely a contradiction. Thus my allegiance to the objectivist realist purities, because they offered some path of skepticism and quasi refusal, some method of documentary.[2]

My ambivalent or resistant relation to "the lyric" is also a curiosity, offering, as it did, opportunities for a polemic based in part on gender analyses. These resistances are charged and meaningful, not decorative; they may be wrongheaded, but they are also, in their stubbornness, enabling. Indeed my *odi et amo* relationship to the lyric mirrors a certain erotic narrative in the lyric. But whatever did I mean by the lyric? Do I even remember? Was it a glyph for resistance to shortness, closure, beauty, and a female place inside it, and not to "it" itself? Did I resist the unitary tone, the coherent speaking subjectivity, the sense of elegant closure when all I saw were loose ends and openings? Did I want to deconstruct the genre, to say there is no "the lyric," as a single item, to resist thinking that the construction of Western subjectivity in Sappho—the frankness, the emotional climaxes and stakes, the high intensity ("akra"), the sensual intimacy, the subjective center—could be thought of as leaping forward to our time, as if nothing had changed? Was I taking all this for granted, not honoring the critical origins of lyric, its tremendous cultural achievement?[3]

Perhaps as a fallback position, I resisted the designator *the* in that phrase "the lyric," for this little article nonetheless evokes particular historical assumptions, bringing along other problems. Is this about some canon list of "the lyric"? because so much specific definition depends precisely on what works are so called. Was it a suspicion of the universalizing topoi of poetry constructed by literary criticism, its theoretical resistance to identifying the historical subjectivities that spoke poetry, and those it addresses? To understand this mode of writing, I want what Theodor Adorno calls "an aesthetic historiography that does not yet exist" (Adorno 1997, 56). That is, discussions of the historically/situationally different uses, functions, or even characteristics of a specific aesthetic mode of practice, such as the "short, nonnarrative poem" a.k.a. "the lyric."[4]

The most extreme version of resistance is the tendentious claim that there is virtually no such thing as "the lyric," but there are short poems used variously in various historical moments, including now, as teachable items. We (nineteenth- through twenty-first-century readers, critics, teachers, poets, anthologists) have selected for our own uses from the vast archive of works of poetry to emphasize this mode and its themes—"the lyric" is like a reading effect—and a historical one with political and pedagogic agendas. Adalaide Morris reminds us of the degree to which "fetishizing the lyric" was, in recent times, a post–World War II act; she cites John Guillory's incisive presentation of the ideal New Critical poem as one "uncontaminated by links with politics, history, and ideology" (Morris 2003, 5).

Another, less extreme, idea is that disaggregated elements or scraps of lyric praxis can be found distributed in contemporary poems ("the lyric valuables"—Hank Lazer cites George Oppen here), even works that encircle or resist the lyric (Lazer 1997, 25).[5] The context of his argument is firm resistance to the contemporary U.S. personal, prizewinning lyric. Lazer's consideration is deft and suggestive: not the "personal lyric" but the "voiceless lyric" (this from Susan Schultz); not a monomelodic music but in the rhythmic syncopation of shifting discourses, odd vocabularies, and social stuttering; not fluidity but moments of intensification, cognition, and rupture; not focused singularity but "impassioned (and ethically engaged) ambivalence" (Lazer 1997, 39). This last term, in Lazer's consideration of George Oppen, makes his work into a model for the contemporary lyric. By disaggregating the lyric, Lazer succeeds in reconstituting the lyrical.

A third idea fuses the suspicion of lyric with lyric to achieve "lyric of critique," "analytic lyric," "critical lyric." These similar terms have been used variously by myself in a 1979 essay on Rich, Rukeyser, and Levertov; by Michael Palmer in a talk in 1986; and by Robert Kaufman in a 2000 article on Barbara Guest, proposing to "make lyric itself critical" (Kaufman 2000, 11). These clustered terms have clearly been evocative for those who desire to deploy lyric as a leverage against social and ideological structures and language as the carrier of ideology. To write a lyric of critique is to call ideological frames into question, making a critique of consciousness and myth, within the lyric, using lyric against itself (DuPlessis 1979, 280). To write an analytic lyric is to attempt "recovering the meanings of words in a time when words have lost their meaning" (Palmer 1987). Palmer goes on to suggest a way of "taking over the condensation of lyric emotion and focusing it then on the mechanics of language . . . as a critique of the discourse of power" (Palmer 1987).

For me, various thoughts on the lyric culminated in an attempt to define poetry "coolly," as a language practice conducted in line segments and hypersaturated with its own evocativeness, rather than defining it through its subjectivities (the "I") and its emotions. That is, poetry consists of saturated segmentivities. Poetry is hypersaturated because of the multiplicity of filiated, but (paradoxically) not completely speakable, impacts emerging from the depths of language and discourse themselves. The word pools through which poems work as they move between the axes of selection and the axes of combination are deeply, saturatedly social, and it is social auras and effects, the organization of particular emotions and anxieties, at which poetry excels. I am innocently pluralizing Roman Jakobson's now-classic definition of poetry via key choices to try to reconcile his neoformalist sense that the poem is a self-referring message about itself (a later Jakobson) with the earlier "Prague Linguistic Circle" Jakobson that emphasized "the social context of the phenomena under study rather than the question of their [universalizing] invariants" (Steiner, quoted in Attridge 1987, 26).[6]

Louis Zukofsky's essay-textbook *A Test of Poetry* teaches how poetry pushes dimensions of language to a maximum evocativeness, and this involves assessing what is barely comprehensible about the effects of a poem or passage of poetry; his view parallels Jean-Jacques Lecercle's later proposal of "the remainder"—evocations from the mix of language elements that nonetheless cannot be pinned down (Lecercle 1990, 47). At the same time, Zukofsky joins this sense of richness with a concern with poetic form as a way of presenting, representing social materials, even of proposing social ideas and debates (Zukofsky [1948] 2000, 19; paraphrased here). For this reverberant sense of poetry I think the term *lyric* was, for me, "too simple"—I felt flooded with the plethora; I had, eventually, to work out another relationship with extent and with the overwhelming.

> blank-bud book
> not even certain
> which way to o-
>   pen it.

But in 1973–74 I still wrote the lyric—a work called "Eurydice," which emerged (like its companion "Medusa") out of an early feminist critique of culture—a redirection of mythopoesis: telling the "other side" of the Orphic story. That gender binarism was an important invention of the time, for it allowed us to bring women as a socially formed entity up to concerted scrutiny. My sense of the potential of feminist critique was imagining the whole world differently. It was no accident that this poem concerned the female figure who, turning away from the one whose very name is a synonym for poetry, chooses to go back underground. It was myself who said she turns—she resisting the power of him and his song; she turning back, turning away, having to become her own singer—instead of being inside his song (DuPlessis 1980, n.p.). This was my attempt to turn away from culture as it had structured the female figure in the lyric.

The lightning flash of this resistance to the myth—the power of it for me at one point in my career—was matched by the stun I felt when later I stumbled on H.D.'s "Eurydice"—a poem from fifty years before that made a parallel argument with similar means—the serial poem, the reanimation of myth. Eurydice's resistance, her sullen bitterness, her minority, led her to take the risk of her own dark light. The discovery, after completing my "Eurydice," that H.D. had written a poem called "Eurydice" was a talismanic, a talis-mantic, moment of connection between myself and H.D. Because I had written my poem, I suddenly could read and recognize her poem and her project: it became culturally legible. I understood that we were involved in parallel examinations of female figures in deeply hegemonic cultural stories. That this myth provides an allegory of the female artist at a moment of tremendous pain and struggle seems proven (at least to me!) by this eerie conjuncture. This oddity of two different female poets fifty years apart, motivated to reread myth, to trek down the Orphic road, this uncanny coincidence, suggests that there are still-recurrent cultural conditions in which a female poet must invent her routes to agency and authority. The intertwined turn of reading and writing, the reading of the writing created a bond between this poetic mind and my own, a spiral of recognition. Without exaggeration, this moment opened my poetry as it opened my literary criticism and my essays. H.D. was enabling for my poetic career.

"I needed a woman, a poet, and a modernist and I needed her badly." (This reminder from "Reader, I married me.") H.D. was this figure.

"What, then, must a woman do with the reactionary sexual ideology of high art?" Gayatri Spivak posed this penetrating question whose devastating élan at the same time suggested a program of both exodus and confrontation (Spivak 1987, 26). Her answer is "re-read"—"an immense genealogical investigation awaits us" (ibid.)

I wanted to start modernism again, all over, from the beginning.

"finally, a woman on paper"
"I'll paint it big"
"with flowers on my flower"
"I brought home the bleached bones"[7]

The revision. The reassessment. The reconsideration. I began to read, study, teach and write on H.D. Had this person ever been read before? Well, yes. A few scholars were reading H.D. voraciously. I heard Susan Stanford Friedman talk about H.D., read her first work (in 1975), bonded with her over a new, an extended, sense of modernism infused with feminist discovery. The confrontation she postulated between H.D. and Freud—the deep intellectual and spiritual engagement and the deep resistance—resonated with my relations to (loosely) the patriarchs. Feminist thinking about literary texts vibrated with questions about myth (that is, the spiritual and ideological stories culture tells to announce, investigate, and explain itself). It resonated with questions about the nature of the poetic career for women, with ideas about production, dissemination, reception, with materialist scrutiny of the ideologies and institutions that organize the poetic career and the reception of individuals.

Bizarrely, I had different temporalities of my relationship with H.D. as a scholar/critic and as a poet. As a poet I invented my own "H.D.-like" attitude toward mythopoesis while briefly remaining innocent of her own achievement. The shock of that recognition, when it came, propelled me into scholarship on her work. Speaking as a scholar, it's not so much the belatedly understood influence of H.D. on me but (don't get me wrong) my influence on H.D.[8] This peculiar position is true of several other feminist critics who wrote on H.D. very early—around 1979 and for a few years after, notably Susan Stanford Friedman, Adalaide Morris, and Alicia Ostriker.[9] These people in some ways worked on, worked out, and worked out of H.D. to accomplish the very, very first years of her rediscovery. We were inventing an H.D. We influenced her work—how it was read, what parts of it were read, why it was interesting. We made it matter for this generation. It is astonishing to make this claim, yet it is simply true. Not arrogant; it is a statement of fact, the fact of our reading of H.D. and our engagements.

But it is odd: wasn't she there before? Weren't there a few books in print? Hadn't I been blind to her, too, and once compliant to reject her? Later there would be criticisms and modifications of our critical work, extensions and reassessments of our work, maybe even the (un?)motivated disparagements—but our work putting H.D. forward as a twentieth-century poet of grandeur is there in its commitment and its subtlety—quite the opposite of crudeness. Yet, as I've already suggested, it's not as if no one had noticed before.[10] This critical situation was the story of a conjuncture. Here were the components: feminism in general; plus an incontestably "major" woman writer (so none of us had to fight the paradigms of major/minor right away nor change other mechanisms of critical recognition); a new sense of cultural legibility for issues and motifs that may occur in the writing of women; with an audience ready to understand that [patriarchal] structures of recognition had blocked and filtered any vision of her career, as they had intervened and been a condition of her employment and her own self-scrutiny for many, many decades.[11] She was a big dolphin ridden by desirous feminists who needed to find her and to be buoyed in her ocean of texts. And she was a haunting presence: we had conjured her; she had conjured us. *Dux femina facti.*

Her whole work was answering questions we had just begun to formulate; we were hot with it, and in that heat H.D. emerged, like a secret, encrypted, and invisible writing that could be read when it got hot-light enough. We had sought the story of modern female cultural position, the portrait of the artist as a struggling and investigative woman. We had sought women's contributions, women's intervention in the Western cultural compact. At every moment that the bucket went down into her vast and capacious oeuvre, it came up full, full, full. That metaphor suggests that we still need the theoretical (that is ideological) capacity to understand the matter of Mater—the "matriarchal" figure standing at the wellsprings of cultural generation. Was it Irigaray who told us about a real second sex? about the despisement of and desire for the Mother? about Western philosophy being the economy of the same? (Irigaray [1974] 1985). It was also H.D., with her grand psychoanalysis of culture and society. We found a magisterial work, intense and passionate, cunning and generous in the most nuanced turns of her language, an author austere in her knowledge of the past and fierce in her will to interpret modernity. Reading, teaching *Trilogy, Helen in Egypt,* the short poems, some of the novels (as I have done since the mid-1970s)—one can also use the archaeological metaphors that H.D. would, perhaps, have appreciated. We had started with a shard, a scrap, a mark on a piece of stone or papyrus: we had ended by commencing a multigenerational dig at an enormous city-temple complex. We had opened [Queen Tut's] tomb.

such *avis* in dreams
do the strange-handed "draw" or "read" the lines?
ombre'd on rich riven rock.

Reading the then-unpublished *HERmione,* reading *The Gift* at the Beinecke Library, where H.D.'s manuscripts were housed (indeed, helping to provoke their publication as books), like a train I was riding, speeding the tracks: clacked this is good, this is good, this is really really good. The shock of her multifaceted career, and our negotiating inside the pressure of detail to understand her scope. Open the boxes. Hatchlings. Open the cardboard hutches, the archival acid-free boxes. I am sitting in a library staring at the white underground sculpture court of Isamu Noguchi and on the plaza outside the monuments to Yale men killed in the Great Wars. The floor was carpeted; the tables were large and solid. The chairs were elegant and capacious. A portrait of Gertrude Stein hung on the wall to the ladies room. It was luxury, the luxe, calme, volupté of supported work. Open the trunk. Reading H.D. letters: gender and sexuality emerge everywhere in the desire to search for response, to give response: H.D. eroticizes the reader. The erotic radiance and the pleasure of finding, knowing, unveiling, being absorbed, being nourished, being taught, reading—like food—breathless. She was aware of the power and necessity of those archives. Indeed, one of the works of her later years was to arrange them, to organize them, and once again to consider her own career in one of the most brilliant essays she wrote—"H.D. by Delia Alton" (H.D. 1986). She exercised Control (as all poets do). She spoke into our future, it seemed. Her voracity and control became noble to me.

The facts and activities of this rediscovery had a deep influence on my

papers were housed, for I was also working on *The Selected Letters of George Oppen,* which would be published in 1990. I sketched "Draft 1: It" (without knowing quite what it was, yet) by following the instruction to

write
writings
that.

all the materials ARE there here
the ocean changed to lines.

I worked into the page that had called me. The first two poems of *Drafts* emerged together and were separated during the summer of 1986. That act of disengaging these two works was crucial for discovering that I had begun a long poem, apparently in "cantos." I was sure of no more than that (I mean I hadn't predetermined this work's "rules" or strategies), but for the moment that was certainly enough. I knew, from all my struggles before this, that one central impulse of *Drafts* was the critique of the lyric. Instead I was seeking the authority of the multiple. Willing to follow the track of making. And to think about the implications of the poesis as furthering. To read the writing. But a cultural project—making something of extent. Casting myself into that sea. No matter what one touches, the ongoingness of language demands more writing.[12]

No plan, no design, no schemata. Just a few procedures: placing works on the big stage of the page, making each be itself intact and autonomous but connected to each other as they emerged. No continuous narrative. No myth as explanation or evocation. Here *Drafts* is very different from H.D.'s long poems and quite related to objectivist ethos and poetics. The works are influenced by objectivist argument and propositions about reality. That "the image is encountered, not found," as Oppen proposed in his one essay (Oppen [1963] 2003, 175). That *the* and *a* (said Zukofsky testily) are words of the fullest implication (Zukofsky 2000, 10, paraphrased).

Draft. 1) current of air in an enclosed area 2) pull or traction of a load / that which is pulled / traction power 3) depth of a vessel's keel 4) heavy demand upon resources 5) document or instrument for transferring money 6) gulp, swallow, inhalation / a measured portion or dose 7) drawing of liquid from a keg 8) selection of personnel / conscription 9) drawing in of a net 10) preliminary outline or plan of a document or picture 11) a narrow line chiseled on a stone to guide the mason in leveling the surface 12) a slight taper given a die to ease the removal of a casting 13) an allowance made for loss in weight of merchandise.

full & empty
the more marks
the larger emptiness

generative

One first idea about individual "Drafts" was that they pretend to be informal, "unfinished"—that is self-questioning and processual, a rhetorical texture one might describe as a flow of interruption across a surface. Another idea was that they pretend to be real "drafts"—that is certain lines, images, or materials can be (as if) provisionally placed at a number of different positions. Hence certain lines or phrases repeat across poems. This tactic is central and continues. Another part of the idea of "drafts" is the interest in marks or marking. I had a number of textual markers in early drafts. The instruction "CUT" that begins "Draft 3: Of" created the predictable difficulties when the book *Drafts (3–14)* went to the printer.

At one point in this exploration of the rhetorics of "drafting," I realized that I was constructing a texture of déjà vu—a set of works that mimicked the productions and losses of memory—and that the works were my own response both to the memorializing function of poetry and to my own bad memory. "An exploration of the chaos of memory (obscured, alienated, or reduced to a range of natural references) cannot be done in the 'clarity' of a linear narrative" (Glissant 1989, 107). The poem replicates (but neither reconstructs nor represents) a space of memory.

I am no one to say. When I began *Drafts,* I thought of it as "an endless poem, of no known category, . . . all about everything" (Pound 1967, 102). My way of interpreting the "no known category" (which for Pound and Williams was the encyclopedic poem) was a kind of playful heterogenreity—heteroingeniousness of genre. For instance, "Draft 3: Of" sounds off against the "meditative derivative" while its little feet are stuck in precisely that meditative descriptive tar. But midrash became extremely important as a genre: the continuous practice of examination, gloss, and reinterpretation. This draws on H.D., Freud, and a tradition of Hebrew textuality all at once. Once the line or word or turn of phrase is stated, once the material exists as the stuff of language (and means what it claims to mean), any particle can open out to more. The generative principles of *Drafts* are repetition, recontextualization, reconsideration, returns that are not returns to the same. The "same/—different—" negative dialectic of *Trilogy*—places the emphasis at once on recurrence and universals but also on the particularities of their specific emergence (H.D. 1998a, 105). This creates a tension in my response to claim that things would recur by deeply structured patterns—to me that was mysticism, and I parted intellectual company with H.D. over the issue of "origins" and recovery.

H.D. looked at her own files. H.D. reworked elements of her life and her mythoi over and over. Studied the traces. If a photo was blurred, there was a reason. If a line was made, it could be understood and reinterpreted. A Freudian poetics: that there is no wasted mark, no unmotivated gesture. Reading the reading was writing the writing. Not just talking the talk but walking the walk. Not just reading the written but writing the wrote. Not the rote. That's how it first felt, when one could reject it—resist H.D. But it was not rote but road. Ever enough rope. In her method was pleasure and also obsession, "obsessing," as we say, hissing sounds like an airlock. The film was run, rerun, spliced, reshot. Palimpsested, so that scrim-films of one picture are superimposed, underposed. Taking what you are given (she was given a lot, but a lot was taken also) and mulling it.

> Shimmer spectra of intercut;
> waves rays way
> the page is never blank

I must say her ear, her ear, her magnificent Ear, the subtle netting of phonemes across her poems. The way a sound map of H.D. can be revelatory of subplots of sound, of pool words into which important phonemes gather and are held, of the tone-leading so phonemes and sound clusters track each other and are caught up, split, and engage again.[13] The sound—it was not "beauty" as a limit term, but the language leading itself to more language. Thus the issue of "beauty" could be encircled and contained by the fullness of, the tremendousness of, sound. What can sound do? It can create relational linkages among words, thematic materials, semantic armatures, and random nonsemantic links. It can, in classic analyses of poetry, undergird semantic meaning or float, in less classic analyses, beyond meaning into an elsewhere. It can create patches of sonority rippling out from key words and collected in pool words (my term for repeated phonemes from different words collecting or "pooling" in a specific word notable for thematic force). Sound can set up charms, formulae for control that are themselves indications of the uncontrollable. It can get in tune with the body or tune the body to it. It can beat and murmur. Music, as Nathaniel Mackey argues, "bears witness to what's left out"—to acuteness of senses beyond ours, to sounds we cannot hear, to those, like the dead, beyond the boundary of our apprehension (Mackey 1993, 232). Mackey argues that poetry, as an articulate music, gathers and redistributes ineffable events, evoking buried, denied, and obscured social materials, materials of pain, hurt, and yearning.

Keats said that a poem "surprises" by a "fine excess," appearing "almost a Remembrance"; I think this phenomenon can be attributed to sound (Keats 2002, 96–97). Sound can create a substratum of phonemic repetition so that poetry feels, in Keats's terms, like a "Remembrance." A remembrance of what? Of the reader's own thoughts, Keats says. Thus the sound on the page, apprehended before any semantic meaning, sets up a sound tunnel wherein things when understood (the semantic meaning) give the illusion of being what you already "knew"—since these things echo the nonsemantic sounds that you have just heard, a brief second before. That delay creates Remembrance. Thus sound acts as a rhetorical persuader of the rightness or aptness of any statement. Semantic meaning, in this analysis, is the echo chamber of an already apprehended sound. Remainder precedes Statement. H.D. is a master at creating this complex of remembrance through sound.

The poetics of Mass Observation (in which H.D.—astonishingly—briefly participated, writing about the coronation of George VI in 1937) became important to me as a democratic ethics of invested examination in my long poem (Collecott 1989). What is it like to live through the texture of our days? There is always a documentary aspect to my poetics. Trying to live in historical time and give some testimony, to bear some (direct or indirect) witness. This means bringing the unspeakable into words, or to the edge of words. Leaving it be mystery, but now in words. Words and the real are heroes of the poem-without-a-hero: "not hero, not polis, not story, but it" ("Draft 15: Little"). "It" speaks.

Drafts has a "midrashic" element: that means the generative processes of continuous rereading and marking. The poetry works by the endless elaboration of a practice of gloss, including self-gloss. The impulse to analysis, and doubled, redoubled commentary. Writing (by study and certainly by authority claims) commentary adequate to the text that has been set, on which there are many prior comments. The concentration on (the concatenation of) the small—the detail of the letter. Yod. Any tiny mark. Any thing can open out to meaning and be connected to other things. The way a toddler will pick up a speck of dust. Every detail could in a particular light have meaning. Error has meaning. Slips have meaning. Anything could be glossed. Gloss generates more text. Text and gloss exist in a permanent, continuous, generative relationship. Gloss on text is more text to be glossed. One makes gloss to comment on loss, against the loss of loss, but there is always more loss. "Even the loss is lost." Preserving has its antonym. Every dot cannot open for everyone, but after many years on task I could finally say: I found the opening and I wrote into it.

Think of the tit
The tit and the title
and the entitlement
think of the jot and tittle.

Drafts constructs the space of memory; each Draft also faces the breast of the mother. They bring back the cut-off breast of the mother: a work of fake restoration, of impossible milk. The hidden maternal presence: the gift that is also poison ("gift" is poison in German, she says in *The Gift*) have analogues with H.D. My mother died of cancer of the breast in May 1990; ten days after, Mary Oppen died. My mother's predeath words of bemusement and anger occur in "Draft X: Letters." And my father had already died, in December of 1986. His death is spoken of in "Draft 5: Gap" and "Draft 6: Midrush." Elegy, and not simply for two people, is a part of what the poem concerns (DuPlessis 2001). The poem is a letter, a stranger (a low flame on the grate in Coleridge's conversation poem). It is a folding over in time, of time at the mercy of its thinking. And the thoughtlessness of time.

At the beginning of *Drafts* I cited Virgil. Cano. Arms and the man cano:

CANO, can o   yes   no
conno-
tations of impurities fill the fold.
("Draft 1: It")

Motive for me from the very beginning. All the Can's and Can no's, and the way I used to Freudian-slip the Cantos (into Canots) while writing my dissertation. I typed Canots over and over whenever I referred to Pound. I guess now I'd have to say "Can too." Plus Arma virumque cano. H.D. meditates this passage in her work *Paint It To-Day* (1920) (H.D. 1992). I felt kinship, kindship: another link, among the many that set me going.

that bilingual
hip-hop talk
a creature/écriture's

langdscape
of anguage

I wanted exodus, the ex-odic, watchfulness into departures. H.D. wanted to return to plenitude, postulated as origins. I quarrel with the nonpresence. "El" and the loss of *L* means oss, a bony site. She builds a space in which presence can reemerge. I want (and this from David Carroll's exploration of J.-F. Lyotard) community without "mythical origin or end" in which to represent "the forgotten that was never part of any memory" (Carroll 1990, xxiii, xi–xii). Lyotard calls this almost forgotten element by a scandalous lowercase form, "the jews," and by this evocation of Shoah and of features in Western tradition and in contemporary philosophies of Being that helped lead to it or that supported it, "Lyotard makes the unrepresentable what all representation must strive to represent and what it must also be aware of not being able to represent; he makes the forgotten what all memory must strive to remember but what it cannot remember" (Carroll 1990, xiii). In *Drafts* as an inflected project, I return to a ground that "constitutes a demand for forms of thinking and writing that do not forget 'the fact' of the forgotten and the unrepresentable" (Carroll 1990, xiii).

I was convinced I had entered a letter and was traveling thru its uncontrollable tunnels.

This is the gift.

December 30, 1997–January 1, 1998
Revisions 2003–4

12
Inside the Middle of a Long Poem

Halfway through *Drafts.*[1] A gloomy wood, politically darker and darker, without allegorical meetings or proleptic creatures. Just a stake driven into the ground, a stop to turn where I was going. Not just at the middle, but inside it, caught, curious about both pivot and ongoingness, pulled into an anxious present. (I mean a quondam coup in the United States, a terrorist strike, a scandalous war, a geopolitics in which my taxes and my country are enlisted but not me.) The undone half of the poem is the counterpart of the poems written, their veiled others, fluctuating in nonlight, poems whose dimensions I intuit but whose actual shape—who knows? I had, as of March 2003, written fifty-seven poems in this work. Wait. Fifty-seven plus.

Plus, because there is also an unnumbered Draft, called "Précis," placed after Draft 57 but before Draft 58 (DuPlessis 2004). This unnumbered poem is a text of distance and transmission, for it summarizes, in quasi sonnets, each of the fifty-seven poems that precedes it. By making this précis, I created a floater, something set half inside, half outside the work that's apart from it and a part of it. It's a doubling of the text by its pretended reduction. This commentary or gloss condenses some of what the poems said, yet, of course, no summary can ever extract the pith or gist of anything that is truly writing, for it is not the nugget of claim that is important to the poem but the whole as babble, bubbling up, the words structured as such and only those words that tell what needs to be told. And tolled. So "Précis" is a self-investigative act, changing each poem into something other to itself.

Drafts is intended to contribute to the American long poem tradition. However true, this is also a pious remark, a statement that gets to the bottom of nothing. Instead, let's say I was vaulted into an intervention of this scope and direness by a wild sense of accumulated necessity. First, the combined utopian urgencies of the 1960s and their compromises and shredding, which are ongoing. Then a cultural responsibility to the absent women. I would not say I was speaking for them—this sounds noble but relegates those others to my imperial claims of their "silence." Any work in culture that women do thinking in part about gender and changing our relationships to gender ideas creates more women in action, thinking about gender, actively transforming culture. This may be a circular or semicircular argument, but it is a condition of this period of women's cultural activism.

Further, I certainly feel my words are spoken by or from more than myself, with a sense of those buried or dispersed before they could say or do what they wanted, ashen traces, bloody traces. I am haunted by moral nightmare, ambiguities about authority, and the demand for awe made by the Abraham and Isaac story, alluded to in "Draft 25: Segno" and elsewhere. I am haunted by Unitedstatesness, given the compromises, failures, and misuses of that global privilege. I am haunted by homelessness in "Draft 24: Gap" and other ethical losses of community. I am haunted by the "outsider" artist ("Draft 22: Philadelphia Wireman"), whose powerful wire sculptures came close to being lost, thrown out with the trash. I am haunted by a spiritual yearning and awe to which I do not give the name of any existing (or future) religious formation or allegiance. Figured too are the vastness of the universe and the littleness of the dot, or letter, or self, something that appears in these works repeatedly, as a pinhole, as "any bit of fleck along the crack" (in "Draft 24: Gap"), as the (smallest) Hebrew letter, "yod," and in other guises. I am haunted by the losses of many people in the Holocaust and holocausts of modernity, represented over and over in my work, in the "hoops of unforgivable bone" in "Draft XXX: Fosse," in "ghosts of ghosts at the open fosse" in "Draft 27: Athwart." Many of these poems speak of the enormousness of the universe and of the enormities of what has happened in our milky corner of it. As haunted poems, poems of commitment, they want to move you, the reader, and evoke irreducible constellations of emotion.

I would also say something of what Dorothy Richardson noted with her overwhelming, weird, and witty eleven-hundred-page novel, *Pilgrimage*—that she needed to put a very bulky work between herself and culture as usual, between herself and the novel with its usual blandishments. So she made "a massive mountain of narrative" that marks a kind of "vengeance on culture" (DuPlessis 1985, 145). The bulk of *Drafts,* their ambition, is uncompromising but not personal; the poems are written from a cultural edge and edginess. I have always felt exiled from most poetic discourse, from the poetries rewarded in our culture. Being in exile from most agreed-on boundaries of one's own medium does not feel pleasant all the time, or, indeed, any of the time. *Drafts* creates a space in which another poetic process can occur; each Draft is a separate meditation about presence and absence, loss and wonder, about what we are doing here, and where this here is in relation to a universe of beyonds.

Being halfway through *Drafts* locates a pivot, a turn from full to empty, from the done to the undone, from the titled to the untitled, from called forth to the unformed. And in a sense emptiness, or the void, has always been present in all the poems. But how do I surmise that I am "halfway" through this work? Why the total of *Drafts* will be, could be 114—or so I now say—is a story to tell, and not only about the compulsive numerology of poetic practice. With a number like 114, I declared "term," "limit," or "borne," while at the same time evoking a number large enough to feel like an abyss. To say "114" units of a work could occur is ample, comfortable, and comforting; yet for you this statement might sound unbidden, irresponsible, and even outrageous. Not to speak of the fact that I already violated this apparent scheme and its implied shapeliness by writing the unnumbered poem, always doomed to be extra, the odd one out. The hubristic risk of saying such a number (+ one) without having achieved it, of chattering about potential endings while inside the middle of a long poem, takes some duplicity. What fates am I stalking? What coral gestures should I make to ward off the nixies lurking round this moxie?

At the pivot, I say continuance, an artistic optimism as simple as it is powerful; for the next years I will have something to do, as many poems to write as I have just (is it really almost twenty years worth?) written. No emptiness—do I fear emptiness? Is this why the project was begun? At least. And death? Well, now you've got a secret that everyone shares. So at the pivot, I say I will not stop. Yet I have stopped; I have stopped to note this moment. For it is a terrible moment, a fearsome moment in which poetry must question itself, testing its complicity with a world turning very bad, very damaging. Our individual subject presences and subjected present-tenses have been poured into a new, almost unbearable, mold or press by the political choices we must make, by the mindfulness we must sustain in the face of controlling, antisecular attacks from outside our country and from within it. Further, we—intellectuals, poets, analysts, professors, resisters, feminists, not to speak of women and homosexuals—are quite near to being (again!) constructed as an internal enemy within our own country. To this unsavory set of prospects, *Drafts* has offered its proleptic suspicion and bitter, hopeful analysis.

Drafts is already a poem of multiple mourning, of resistance and critique, of arousal to justice and desire for transformation in its form, of struggle, of beginning again and again, of both syntactic and juxtaposed linkages, taking form as "sedimented content" (Adorno 1997, 144). *Drafts* is a project into which everything could come, not fit, but be situated and take shape in relationship to other things. If every cultural work has its political origins and motivation, is this work an allegory of community? of working institutions? of affinity and affiliation? of difference and yet linked relation?[2] It is certainly a space in which to locate the effects of time and some of the contradictions between hope and fact. Making this poem is a way of standing in time, time rushing through me, time rushing around me, half a league onward, while I take its force in a strange solid mesh that I have invented as part of time, not as buffer or veil but as a parallel act.

Each poem is magnetized by a title and finds its own enclosure, its center of gravity and necessary shape. The shapes differ. But the cue or prompt into the whole project was that one word: *Draft.* There is a pun on *blew* and *blue* and *blau* in the underswirl of the genre probe. It was a way of writing both myself, as alive and posthumous at the same time, and all transformative impermanence (and impertinence) into the inception of the project. There is a name pun in this duplicity: the provisional solidity of "drafts," poems finished and incomplete, sealed and porous.

> Cutting two birds
> from one stone.

"Unfinished" is an ideological attitude toward this writing that has nothing to do with the completeness of the text but makes this text "drafts" of another work along an unimagined horizon of awakening. A totally secular messianism constitutes one powerful motivation to write, but there is always a deferral of "fulfillment." I can only agree with Maurice Blanchot in *The Writing of the Disaster* when he suggests that any "messianic hope" is also dread, especially "when political thinking becomes messianic" (Blanchot 1986, 143). We live in such a period now. The poem's "messianism" is thus construed as endless deferral and yearning.

It seems true, as Ron Silliman has suggested, that to undertake this kind of "longpoem" project, is to postulate varieties of end (Silliman 1992, 14–15). Although most of *Drafts* is very closural, the individual poems shut or end only to open again, almost immediately, as I am called again into the page. Hence, although endings exist, the whole project belies any ideological finality. This means that none of the poems is perfect, iconic, static—something that also has gender meaning as a critique of the uses of the female/feminine to offer plenitude and fullness, in some of poetic tradition. By using the all-over title, *Drafts,* I signal that these poems are open to transformation, part of ongoing processes of construction, self-commentary, and reconstruction, similar to the genre called "midrash" (endless commentary and gloss) in Hebrew textuality.

Halfway through *Drafts.* How dare I say what I do not know? It is the project that speaks. The long poem is a work of mastery during which you submit to your own powerlessness, your being swamped or swept away by procedures and continuance, failures and unorganized urgencies, or even by the prospect of not finishing what you began—despair, death, disturbances, political crisis and revulsion, loss of equilibrium, loss of the desire for *poesis,* blockage, inability. It is all possible. This powerlessness may be what Margaret Dickie saw when, in an otherwise stolid introductory chapter in her *Modernist Long Poem,* she suddenly looks up to note, shocked, "the poet's enigmatic persistence against all odds toward the impossible poem" (Dickie 1986, 4). One wants to say, right, right. How could it be otherwise? Did anyone think that craft was mastery? It is hardly anything but loss, even with the enormous gain of word upon word sent, surging, staggering into a void that the poet is as eager to enter, as (in *Purgatorio* xxvi) the spirit of Arnaut Daniel was to leap back into the refining fire. Poi s'ascose nel foco che gli affina. But it is the fire of returning to matter and ash, not to purification.

The long poem is a way of admitting hyperstimulation. Everything pulled me to that place of plethora. I wouldn't call it "the whole knowable world around me" (Williams [1951] 1967, 391) but the whole unknowable world: the links between birds and us; the dissolving of time, going where exactly? the enormities of human action (why exactly have we all found it necessary to rip and burn and destroy acres of other human beings?). Asking what is my position when any sight line, tree, street sign, ruffles of unmelted snow, the corner of a building evokes plethoras of relations. Sight lines and layers, palimpsests and material slid over and over each other; I was motivated by a sense of the loss of things simultaneous with their presence, the loss of meaning, of detail, of understanding. It would take the rest of my time even to begin to represent any of these few feelings in the matted, evocative language of poetry. So it was the fathomless, after all, that flooded me. The first poem of *Drafts* is called "It." The fathomless and the extent. Awe, grief, astonishment, skepticism and pleasure: that *this is* as such; that we are here and need to confront making something of it. I mean this is the world, a blue teardrop of luck in endless vasts of the barely understood. *Drafts* faces this. It says awe and respect for not knowing. It is an atheist poem of spiritual tripping; a monumental task suspicious of the monumental; an opening to storms and blankness, an unteleological practice that begins anywhere and ends everywhere and nowhere.

Williams wrote a section of *Paterson* using the repetend "so be it." He said "so be it" when faced with the overwhelming roar of the world, the history of individual details, weird and uncontrollable by system, the Falls of Paterson, the persons who fell into those falls, and the fire and flood of that city in 1902—everything sweeps over him. Flooded, drowned in both water and fire. Facing the inchoate in Book III of his poem, he goes, with a certain cultural logic, to "Beautiful Thing," a black female figure brutalized and raped, the muse of the unspoken and the lost. In this figure many elements of his "Practice" coincide—erotics, empathy, intensity, desire, diagnoses of how others want to possess beauty and despoil it, ethical recognitions of how he is implicated (Williams 1992, 100–128). Beautiful Thing and her fate make one summary of all the cruelty, waste, desolation of the United States landscape, a waste so intense that I feel, now, pure shame in reading his prose passages, like the one about the boiling open of freshwater mussels in the haste to get their pearls, a haste that created ruin, or the passage about the draining of the pond and the greedy smashing of the eels and fish in it, or the passage about the teasing of the mink, so like John Clare's poem "Badger." . . . Williams looks at this despoiling with implacable breadth and force.

"Beautiful Thing" is also a statement of possibility, of an exciting Otherness now brought into question by our critique of Williams's sincere, yet exoticizing, scintillations around class, race, gender, sexuality. This is not simply an ideological point, a feminist suspicion, for these issues are manifested in form. When faced with plethora, cruelty, abuse, destruction, and violation, Williams centers his work with a muse figure who has suffered all these things. It is a brilliant and traditional solution. And he settles the work again in *Paterson* V with "I, Paterson, the King-self," a passage about the unicorn and the poet and their male power of triumph and willing entrapment by virgins and other women (Williams 1992, 231). But I can't go there. This is how I construe the dilemma of myself as woman writer, one that I have spoken of before, as simply a resistance to culture as constituted. I can't go there—though it is plausible, not wrong or necessarily reductive, to go to a male figure of power, to a female figure of power, some core figure, to focus the poem. For some other women writers, constructing a female figure of power at the center of the poem was precisely their point, as H.D. did in *Trilogy* with the "Lady" carrying the blank book, or as Alice Notley did in *The Descent of Alette* with her "Headless Woman" as a central character, a figure both helper and helped. These are brilliant figures in generative poems, generative because of their ethics of mutuality and openness. But however these gender materials emerge in the long poems of others, and despite my appreciation of these choices, it was never an option for me to focus the overwhelming with gendered figures, male or female. Where, then, could I go?

In response, I found myself magnetized by two formal modes, the fold and the grid. When this project was begun in 1986, I had just one or two tactics: titling to declare a space, and randomized repetition (recurrence of lines, phrases, situations, words). When the poem shifted, around number "19" (in late 1993, early 1994), I invented a third tactic: the "folding" of one poem over another—in which any draft corresponds in some sensuous, intellectual, allusive, or even simple way to a specific "donor draft" on this periodicity of nineteen. By virtue of the fold, different poems are "drafted" to become muses for other poems; this puts the responsibility for connection not on one central figure to settle the work's fullness, nor on any particularly gendered figure, but on numerous connectors dispersed all across the texture of the work, a mesh or net to hold fullness while honoring its enormous extent, its ungraspable rush.

The fold involves repetition and crumpled touching. Repetition could be predictable, but I don't plan beforehand what aspect of a donor draft will be reopened. It's as if every work has enough in it, as it fractally articulates, to satisfy forever. Barrett Watten has proposed a parallel, if reverse, way of describing this in relation to the work of Clark Coolidge: "Any word in the text can become the enigma of the plural impasse; the act of writing is the continual querying of these impasses by words" (Watten 1985, 102). One word leads to another. One line to another; these vectors of "querying" make the simplest, most inexplicable situation—productivity, especially as my writing feels bounded on all sides by the most extreme silences—of the dead, of the void, of the inexplicable at the core of the human. So a draft at a certain place in the grid could either evoke (in some particulars) or not evoke (in other particulars) the prior drafts on which it is nominally, designedly based. What relationships are created in these "lines"?—well, any that can be imagined, from the repetition of the simple color red, along the "line of 2," to complex reconsiderations of materials and ideas—what is it to be "of"—to be in an ethical situation of intersubjectivity (along the "line of 3").

The plethora is overwhelming. Yet instead of going to a hero, muse figure, or "girl," I have gotten to a "grid." The fold around a number (19) as it played out led to the imagination of an all-over design of numbered spaces to open the whole work to myself. Yet the grid of numbers is not a surface in space but a set of engagements in time with its own pulse and enormous irregularities. The strange thing about a grid-diagram of the poem is that it allows for the simultaneity of presence (there will be a poem in That Spot) and absence or openness (no one can define that poem or preplan the fullness of its relationships to other poems). I find this a very gratifying indeterminacy. This imagined grid was tied up with my discovering, or having suddenly revealed, that I knew a number at which I could declare this work was stoppable. That is, if I wanted to stop.

When it appears you are writing a long poem, people want to know how and when you will end. This might be nervousness or simple curiosity. They are concerned about the plethora, too. How are you going to get out of such a big thing? And they are bemused by general questions about the mystery of making anything: How do you know when you are finished? Do you know the ending beforehand? Do you know where to end? how to end? why to end? Do you know how it will come out? Is there a conclusion—in the sense of final statement? These general questions are exaggerated when a multidecade project is at stake. Not to say, fate might also have its way with you. Being stopped dead is always possible. Thus ending is different from concluding, after all. Stopping is different from ending, and stopping is also different from concluding.

In a novel the force and weight of what has gone on—the pace and shape of the whole and authorial observation made by the texture of style, on the surface and in deep tonalities—all get articulated as plot and characters within a defined fictional time. Various universes of judgment are created via narrative. Solutions to problems, or conclusions to what has occurred can be invented, inventoried, and said to satisfy. In a narrative, theme is often factored into characters or voices via the temporalities of plot; closure can articulate these relationships. Notley's, H.D.'s, and Williams's poems have enough characters so there is a bit of assistance from narrative. Or to say it another way, the overwhelming quality of the reality confronted in these poems gets assimilated via characters. But characters cannot always be available for long poems, nor is their reading time the same as narrative time.[3] So the pleasures of deferral that enhance novelistic narratives become problematic in a long poem. All that deferral—without the payoff of character-based solutions at ending—can call reader pleasure into question.

Do we understand, then, what satisfies at the end of a long poem? I'm not sure, especially when poems do not map themselves on, or even submit to, teleologies and myths already culturally validated, in the way that Eliot's *Four Quartets* does. Certainly some symbolic locus of attention can emerge, and one often looks hard at endings as if they had some magic; this may be a hangover from the lyric and a way of reading the long poem as if it were a short poem. For a lot of the long poems I know have no very grand finale. An ending is notably unstressed, as if it is a coda to itself, to its whole process. Is this a theory? that Plethora is so persistent that one must be rather subdued, or even awed, at ending, zooming out, a series of moves no different, really, from the possibility of beginning. *Drafts* allows for this by multiplicity of endings; if every "canto" ends, there is still the immediate beginning of the next. Such closures partake of the ideology of "poetry" somewhat, but when there are so many of them in a long poem, the endings are more like flares set up on a gigantic field of wandering.

A poem that manages its ending with finesse, given these conditions, is Alice Notley's *The Descent of Alette,* and of course, this is a narrative, with characters, a poem very conscious of its allegorical plot. It, too, has endings all over the work (because of its being constructed in short poem units). It ends with a scene very like the Last Judgment but made to depict a major ideological shift in the secular world, for the buried, politically enchained folks who have been compelled endlessly to ride the subway now emerge into the sane light aboveground:

> "Whatever," "whoever," "could be," "was possible," "or
> had been" "forgotten" "for long ages" "now joined us," "now
> joined us once more" "Came to light" "that morning"
>
> (Notley 1996, 148)

With the carefully executed and justified killing, by the female hero, of the Tyrant who had oppressed people ideologically and in material ways, the riders on the subway may now band together to found a new society. Notley does not narrate how her shadowy characters will bring that about, although, in this notably ethical poem, she is quite clear about the anti-Enlightenment values considered vital: resistance to any mind-body split, rage at conditions of poverty and disenfranchisement, and, positively, humor, curiosity, persistence, courage, and other moral weapons. She ends just where she must, at the beginning of an unspoken beginning—a new world still to be made.

Ending H.D.'s *Trilogy* is the epiphanic vision of a very humble girl, yet a Bona Dea goddess, holding a bundle of myrrh, enveloped in sweetness. The whole poem is structured around recurrent epiphanies of female Presence. This girl-figure refuses worship, just as H.D. (earlier in the poem) had refused to depict another Lady figure as hieratic. The purpose of this part of *Trilogy* is to add a gospel to the Gospels and thus is a culture-shattering act, as massively critical of the closed book—the Bible—as it is of any non-polytheistic Christianity that does not worship the mother-force or acknowledge the intensity of female analytic and emotional power. Yet the understressed ending is an ethical generosity on H.D.'s part, despite being narrated, in a temporally intricate plot involving prolepsis, prophesy, and fulfillment, by one of the three mages, Kaspar, as a flashback confession to Mary Magdalene. That is, the cultural purpose of H.D.'s meditative long poem is enormous and critical, but the ending makes only the gentlest of statements, as if to allow waves of suggestiveness to vibrate outward, not to insist in an absolutist way on her claims, however dearly she believed them.

Paterson has at least one "character" and the voices of many others, including historical people like Marcia Nardi, Edward Dahlberg, and Allen Ginsberg, self-represented in their epistolary words. The poem is not mono-narrative; plural, fragmented narratives go coursing through it, criss-crossing with various vignettes and stories, many unresolved. *Paterson* curiously adheres to two contradictory modes of ending, first, to multiplicity without heroes and without worshipped females, and second, hedging its bets, to an older set of satisfactions. For Beautiful Thing and Paterson, unicorn King-self, can be said to play the rescued female and the hero. But its other end is a hunting cry "Yo ho! ta ho!" and a refusal of knowledge ("we know nothing"), but an acceptance of continuance and responsiveness:

> We know nothing and can know nothing
>   but
> the dance, to dance to a measure
> contrapuntally,
>   Satyrically, the tragic foot.
>   (Williams 1992, 235–36)

That triple-genre allusion—satire, tragedy, lyric-dance—corresponds at once to Smaro Kamboureli's contention that a long poem is not monogeneric but multiple. The Canadian works she discusses combine epic, lyric, narrative, and documentary. The long poem is arguably always a genre collage, or a set of multiple genre discourses, and is defined by a "generic restlessness" that, curiously, she calls "lawlessness" rather than, for example, generic negative capability (Kamboureli 1991, xiv).[4]

For the long poems that reject master genres and are heterogeneric, one might derive a theory of endings. Simply put, there must be multiple endings for such long poems, because multiple genres have been alluded to. The pluralizing of endings changes our reception and the poem's impact; one is confronted with a constellation of contradictory materials that can never be seen as a totality. One might acknowledge this in the famous five-language ending of Eliot's *The Waste Land,* from "London Bridge" through "shantih," alluding to quite a number of genres activated in the poem, from quest and purgatorial nekuia, to lyric, to ritual, to dramatic monologue. As genres proliferate in a long poem, especially away from narrative, ending will get harder to locate in one spot. A single ending may become less and less textually plausible, and one might talk of a large field of various overtures and motions toward end. Perhaps one might even say that during the last pages of a long poem one might find stopping, concluding, settling, giving up, ending, solution, and perhaps even opening, beginning again (and again).

The work of *Drafts* is not yet finished, and discussion about its way or ways of ending is speculative only. But inside the middle, I can confess where I got the number 114, even though when I began, I had no plan to declare any potential terminus. Somewhere during the exfoliation of *Drafts,* I think in around 1993, but possibly just after *The Trouble with Genius* appeared in 1994, Bob Perelman asked me, not quite casually, "how many of them there would be." I hadn't considered the question consciously, but unconsciously I was ready. So I answered, "100, like Pound's *Cantos.*" We both sort of gasped. I am grateful that he asked, because his question (he is always interestingly curious) catapulted me into facing my actual ambition. It was the first time I had said a number aloud. Been allowed to say that number. What are the implications of this revealing remark? What stopped it (or maybe not!) from being just sheer bravado, the work of the blurter in me, a stagy, confrontative claim to which I had no right? Well, to say this project was involved with and against Pound from the start is almost tautological.

First off, "100, like Pound's *Cantos*" means many things, but one thing is immediately clear—the number is wrong; I was fusing Pound and Dante, something Pound himself always encouraged in comments about his project. *The Cantos* actually go along an infinite line of numbers, for Pound's last title numbers were *CXVII et seq.* suggesting unmistakably that even more Cantos could emerge. So the number 114 offers a total approximately parallel to the *Cantos* but also just a usefully large number, a number that might be said both to challenge Pound and to let him alone, a number for which there are no guarantees in the world of chance and accident. And a number that happens to equal six times nineteen. Hence 114 was a result of the turn at nineteen; it followed that turn to one logical end by choosing a convenient multiplier that gives an allusive, and interestingly Poundian, sense of extent.

Everyone who writes a long poem has probably attended to that damaged, powerful, generative case of contradictions between goal and outcome. Facing *The Cantos* one sees a masterful, distressing poem of scope and daring, urgency and desire, that embraced repugnant values, not only social and political values but repugnant textual and literary values. What I finally acknowledge in Pound, when all else is burned away or turned from in sadness and anger, is his political rage and despair, and his hyperstimulation, for he is literally overwhelmed, drowned in data, in the storm of history, in the floods of mud, water, in the dangerous pools in the early cantos: a person "in the water up to his neck" like Malatesta (Pound [1948] 2003 [Canto IX], 34) or a voice considering "the osmosis of persons" (Pound [1948] 2003 [Canto XXIX], 143, 145). Perhaps this feminine position of being swamped with too many stimuli called forth his rigid phallic compensation. Rage and plethora plus an apocalyptic urgency set him aswirl down paths that are unfollowable. And unforgivable.

While I comprehend one key feature—his abyssal rage and sense of lacerating disgust at political and economic damage—what is impossible to understand is the fascist anti-Semitism—perhaps most evident in titles from his *Meridiano di Roma* articles from 1940 to 1943 in *Orientamenti* of 1944, titles such as "l'Ebreo, patologia incarnata" [the Jew, pathology incarnate], evident as well in contributions through the 1930s to the fascist *British-Union Quarterly* or in the salaried radio broadcasts of 1940 to 1943.[5] After the war, *"I Cease Not to Yowl"* offers a window on his opinions from 1937 through 1959—with the bulk of letters from the postwar period: gnarled, allusive, opinionated, cryptic, know-it-all writing that is again pro-Axis, pro-Fascist, and anti-Semitic. Pound's defense of Hitler in 1953 is characterized, by the editors, as both an "intellectual" and a "moral failure of the greatest magnitude" (Pound 1998, xviii). *The Pisan Cantos,* which was composed in the uncertainty of his imprisonment in Pisa and pending his trial for treason, became in its final revisions "a requiem for Italian Fascism" (Pound [1948] 2003 [Sieburth drawing on Bush], xxxvi).

Pound eventually said, in general, that he was a

> . . . pitiless stone—
> stone making art work
> and destroying affections.
>
> (Pound 2002, 256)

Yet this, and some other parallel statements, full of self-pity, are more than a curiosity given his former announcement (in Canto XXX) of pitilessness against the allegorized "rot" of society. A *Rock-Drill* reference to the same material refers a little differently to pity but maintains the metaphor of cleansing:

> pity, yes, for the infected,
>   but maintain antisepsis,
> let the light pour.
>
> (Pound 1957, 95)

Even taking Pound's "pitiless stone" comment at face value, still it softens the political allegiances into personal qualities ("pitiless") and individual choices ("making art works") that destroyed personal relationships. The comment sentimentalizes artworks, for it insists sotto voce on the singular artist destroying himself and others so that an art object be born. The comment makes bad relationships the price while art is the gain. However, it is not just bad relationships but bad politics that Pound produced. He was not only making artworks; he was writing seriously meant propaganda articles and fascist apologetics out of conviction in the late 1930s through 1944, encouraging social-ethnic cleansing ("antisepsis"). Far from rethinking his position, he encouraged kinds of white supremacist and soft fascist thought in the United States, when he was incarcerated in St. Elizabeths. It was not just his own personal relationships that were destroyed but all those killed and tortured systematically by a fascist policy with which he was complicit, about which he was fairly well-informed. That is, Pound was a cultural activist for fascism until his death. Period. One looks in a kind of horror at the moments and historical junctures when he could have said "no" to all this and yet didn't.[6]

One must stare down these politics—his anti-Semitism and unstoppable fascist allegiances, his fantasmal cathexis to Mussolini. This was so astonishing and deeply felt that by parading Mussolini's superficial, society-chatter comment about how "divertente" the Cantos are ("amusing, entertaining, enjoyable, fun"), Pound actually undercuts his own goal for the work, which was to model the flash of intense, transformative insight beyond diversion or pleasure (Pound [1948] 2003 [Canto XLI], 52). As he said, "It may be even that the serene flow of sentence is more exciting to the reader than are words set down in anger. But when one is not narrating? When one specifies the new life or the new temple? When one talks to the capo maestro, that is to the building foreman as distinct from making architectural pictures that one knows will remain for ever (or for ages) unrealized, one may have other criteria [of understandability]?" (Pound 1937, 55). His desire to communicate instantaneously to the men on the ground and to the "capo maestro" implicates us, through his rhetoric, in his fantasies about Mussolini, for Il Capo, Boss, was Mussolini's nickname. Pound thought he could be the éminence grise of the new culture brought about by Mussolini's politics, given this rhetorical tactic of the "detached phrase."[7]

Pound (in one student's malapropism) is "anti-Semantic." Well, that too. His brilliant, nerve-wracking semireadability arouses and frustrates the reader with its deferrals and displacements of meaning. For it is not just Pound's politics, but his senses of text and culture, that are problematic. One must reject his desire for a total work that would replace other works, cleansing or condensing cultural products and traditions and erasing multiple paths for cultural access. The desire to narrow culture to a book of "sacred odes" to teach a new elite brought into being by the mechanism of the poem was more than benign syllabus. It might even be possible to say that the incessant notational and fragmented materials, by radically decontextualizing sources and erasing syntax, created a reader who was perpetually evacuated of ways of knowing and, by being perpetually baffled, was made ignorant.[8] Yet Pound attracts because, as Perelman argues, his theory of language seems to rest on a totally transparent relation between word and thing—thus a person does not "read" but "sees" in a perpetual white-light illumination. Pound's whole thrust toward condensation, getting only the nugget on the page, is a resistance to language as exchange, social, contaminated. There was no purity in language, a fact that enraged Pound. Perelman eloquently shows the ways this sociality of language associated with Jews as shorthand for all the filth and disorder that he reviled. So there was a major binarist split in Pound between "the pure and the impure: light, health, hierarchy, the phallus, nature, the classics . . . and darkness, sickness, swamps, sodomy, Jews, usury . . . , an endless chain of opposing forces" (Perelman 1994, 46). His is one model of writing out of a sense of permanent emergency; it is necessary to invent other models even when emergency is patent.

A comment by Maurice Blanchot on aphorism is pertinent to Pound's detached phrase, his rhetoric of choice for the emergency he felt: "The isolated aphoristic sentence is attractive because it affirms definitely, as if nothing besides this sentence spoke anymore in its vicinity" (Blanchot 1986, 133). This rhetorical choice was, thereby, asocial and solipsistic. Yet contractors and builders—"the men on the ground"—are not, in fact, anything as Pound would have them; building is all discussion, negotiation, articulating the probable possible. Pound's desire to build the new city by the oblique shorthand instruction of *The Cantos*—the "detached phrase" was the fantasy of political and social action in a vacuum (Pound 1960b, 50). Pound had a view of language without sociality, language as pure force beamed into the brains of others, the ruthless fantasy that interpretation, discussion, partial understanding, patient unfolding are all contemptible.

However much I would continue this critique and identify Pound's paradoxical, embittering contradictions, it is also true that *Drafts* was involved with Pound from its inception, but as a critical resistance to the impact of the work. That is, I wanted to make an alternative *Cantos,* a counter-*Cantos.* This is not so much a fantasy of oedipal replacement (well, you tell me!) as it is a desire to place a counterweight inside culture and history, a poem with parallel ambitions that comes to thoroughly different conclusions by different literary means.[9] This fact of investigation without allegiance is signaled by my use of the title *Drafts,* a direct echo of Pound's 1930 collection *A Draft of XXX Cantos* and the 1969 work *Drafts & Fragments of Cantos CX–CXVII.*

Why even say Pound? Given all this, why admit to Pound? Well, who among us of our generation who thinks at all of the literary has not been hailed into Pound's secretum (or perhaps to Olson's)—the sense that you were one of the cultural elite of knowers? Perelman speaks of this, quite accurately and with an evocative fortitude, in *The Trouble with Genius;* my experience was parallel, and I am paralleling his argument here. This was, perhaps, the final delusion of ideologies of modernism. As an elite knower, you could do what needed to be done; you could articulate values without dialogue, in cadres, not in communities. Who has not been hailed into the band of knowers by Pound only to find that one was actually unable to read but only to parrot versions of Pound's unforgiving binaries? One could learn his language—that Pound-speranto—only to find one was without hope. Besides, one was a woman, one was more or less a Jew (certainly was nothing else); the implications are overwhelming.

So we can take *Drafts* as a response to a scandalous remark Pound made in "A Visiting Card" in one hyperabsolute, slashing moment. About T. S. Eliot, actually, but of literature in general, he said, "Not a jot or tittle of the hebraic alphabet can pass into the text without danger of contaminating it" (Pound 1973, 320).[10] Given this, *Drafts* is pleased to be an unclean, female-penned poem filled with jots and tittles and thoroughly contaminated by traces of the Hebraic. *Drafts* is a poem filled with debris, rot, fragment, corners in which collages of trash collect. *Drafts* is precisely based on the rot that was not "clene slayne" as Pound says in Canto XXX, a rot that Pound laments and excoriates. There is rot all over nature, a composting and transformation, yet the paradox of Pound's "organicism" is the rejection of such organic processes. Mine is a poem that—how to say this right—speaks of the dilemma of writing upon, or after, the deaths of those to whom Pound addressed the possibility of "antisepsis" or a "cleansing" social purgation. My work begins in the long aftermath of the destructive underside of modernity. Therefore, my work is inflected with, it considers, it knows, and cannot ignore those facts of extreme proportions, genocides enormous with their own enormity, a variety, not only one, not totally isolated and alone in the history of modernity, but accompanied, so to speak, with other parallel manifestations of social organization for injustice. This is the world we are. Needing to look at it was my necessity.

Halfway through *Drafts*, I stopped, I paused . . .

Spring–Summer 2003
Revised 2004

Notes

Introduction

1. My title's blue thus parallels Joan Retallack's "blue" essay in *The Poethical Wager* but is not related; I wanted blue to correspond to, and differ from, the pink of *The Pink Guitar,* just as the essays are related but different.

2. A statement from Paola Masi, told to me by Paola Bono in regard to Bono's translation into Italian of "For the Etruscans" (e-mail, Nov. 2004).

3. This statement triangulates a speech made by Thai poet Chiranan Pitpreecha at the Fifth International Encounter of Poets, Coimbra, Portugal, May 2004; a discussion in Watten 2002, 146–49, of subjectivity and movements of emancipation; and a discussion in Butler 2004, 216–17, of "resignification" and "being in the mode of becoming." See also Heuving (2002).

4. Greene and Kahn quote Elizabeth Ermarth in their anthology: "To say 'I' . . . is to say something profoundly social, as distinct from merely 'individual'" (Greene and Kahn 1993, 237).

5. Retallack's argument occurs in the context of her insistence on a "pragmatic realism" of open systems, imitations of fractal, dynamic "interactive responsiveness" (Retallack 2003, 191), synchronicities, and anti Aristotelian flows (without be ginning, middle, end), what she sometimes, triumphantly and wittily, calls the "mess" (Retallack 2003, 189). The interest in plot, narrative endings, and their feminist transformation is covered in DuPlessis 1985. For defenses of feminist rewriting of narrative but a clear formal preference for the force of plot see Felski 2003, 95–133; and Friedman 1998, 228–42.

Chapter 1. Reader, I married me

1. This essay concerns the making of academic feminist criticism and therefore talks from "inside" the university. Many social, cultural and political institutions

were changed by feminism. The expression "paradigm shift" is from Kuhn 1970; it was applied to feminism by Catharine Stimpson and others. Kuhn's model of growing contradictions and discontinuities in the way one's knowledge holds together, issuing in major intellectual discomforts, provoking a sudden conversion experience that changes the shape of knowledge and then gets institutionalized, is echoed in my experience and my narrative.

2. I am not proud of this; I record it as a datum of the time: mid-1960s. A feisty, energetic woman with trouble entering the heterosexual marital economy "feared" she was a lesbian. Homophobia and sexism rampant on a field of green. I hung a copy of Pontormo's "Three Graces" on my wall; these were young men duplicitously drawn as women, breasts stuck on male bodies: this was one vow of androgyny—to not be consumed in emotional ground wars, to not be colonized by men.

3. From the first, the Lessing intrigued me formally; the notebooks, separate and fused, were like a structural coup expressing my sense of the multiple dimensions of being situated as a woman politically, sexually, artistically, relationally.

4. Except—when I profile us, I see we were all, at least then—please forgive me—Daddys' Girls and possibly had certain elements of psychic safety and reassurance to the appointers, aside from whatever credentials we possessed. Luckily, I was in France that first year, and my replacement was Lillian Robinson, not one, I believe, to have fallen, then or at any time, under the "paternal" rubric.

5. In the interests of the sociology of knowledge, it is also worth listing the number of feminist critics who emerged from that Columbia matrix—I don't mean Columbia Women's Liberation but the English and French departments: my unsystematic count reveals in English Nina Auerbach, Louise Bernikow, Carolyn Burke, the late Barbara Christian, myself, Kate Ellis, Judith Kegan Gardiner, Sandra Gilbert, Myra Jehlen (as junior faculty), Nancy Milford, Kate Millett, Lillian Robinson, Catharine Stimpson (also faculty), Louise Yelin. And Alice Jardine, Nancy Miller, and the late Naomi Schor were in the same academic generation in the French Department. The late Carolyn Heilbrun, on the faculty during this ferment, was herself becoming a notable and influential feminist critic; in her citation of this list she added Susan Suleiman, Gayle Greene, Constance Jordan, Alice Kaplan (Heilbrun, in Greene and Kahn 1993, 269; see also Kress 1997, 196–202, on Heilbrun's relation to Columbia University culminating in her 1992 resignation).

6. I could have written "I was born again, a feminist." However, I feel more than somewhat uncomfortable, and even campy, in invoking this New Testament structure of feeling. There was, for instance, no messiah. Luckily. No "fulfillment," which implies orthodoxy and heresy (unfortunately, this was a characteristic of some feminism, to my astonishment). Also "born again" implies a first baptism prior to the renewal, but for a long time we thought we were engaged in the invention of feminism. Later, with scholarship and study, we understood the degree to which many historical feminisms had already occurred and had to a large degree been erased or distorted.

7. Someone recently asked me whether Columbia Women's Liberation was an

"official" university committee; I simply laughed and laughed. The answer is "no." Ann Sutherland Harris was proudly sent off to represent Columbia Women's Liberation in June 1970 to provide testimony before the House Special Subcommittee on Education (91st Cong.) during hearings on Section 805 of H. R. 16098 to prohibit discrimination against women in federally assisted programs and in employment in education; her testimony is in the Congressional Record (*Discrimination against Women* 1:237–60). So, too, is our ad hoc committee report from December 1969 (see *Discrimination against Women* 1:260–66) with its demands on the university. An incisive account of the impact of this Columbia Women's Liberation report occurs in McCaughey 2003, 513–16. He sums up the argument this report made in its comparison of the number of PhDs awarded to women (from one-fourth to one-half of the total especially in the humanities and social sciences) as opposed to the miniscule numbers of female faculty members. "The inference that Columbia willingly took the tuition money of women wishing to pursue graduate studies and just as readily certified their competence by awarding them Ph.D.s but resolutely declined to consider them for faculty appointments was not hard to draw" (McCaughey 2003, 514).

8. Echols 1989, 195–97, helped me date the events in which I participated; see also the chronology in DuPlessis and Snitow 1998. I am insisting, here, on the integration of political and social arousals into the cultural work of feminist literary criticism. Theory and praxis were integrated; at any rate, this was a goal.

9. "68er" is Meredith Tax's coinage from French usage.

10. Therefore I responded strongly to the Marxist work of Fredric Jameson and Raymond Williams, the latter a real influence on *Writing Beyond the Ending.*

11. I was in France, not at the Modern Language Association's convention in 1971, and did not hear firsthand either Adrienne Rich or Tillie Olsen's essays. They nonetheless became central, definitional statements when I read them in *College English* (1972), contributing much to my formulation of feminist cultural projects. The subtle layers of personal and political thinking characteristic of the work of both writers has been exemplary to me.

12. Another instructor, Paulette Williams, stayed one semester. We had lunch. She said, "I dream of a work, a work of many women speaking a kind of poetry, with many colors, like a rainbow, and dancing and singing." I said, "O it sounds wonderful—you should do it." She went off to San Francisco and, as Ntozake Shange, did it. Indeed she did.

13. The professor of the course was feminist classicist Froma Zeitlin. I was an adjunct on yet another one-year terminal contract (1973–74) at Douglass College, replacing Elaine Showalter, whose women writers course was, happily, already on the books. Teaching my version of a "Women in Literature" course further spurred my desire to write about women's writing.

14. Women do not necessarily have a revisionary relationship to culture, of course, but it was clear why this interpretation emerged at this historical juncture of the women's movement.

15. I had the pleasure of working in H.D.'s manuscripts and archives, always, I

would argue, a vital move for an enriched understanding of figures whom one is trying to recontextualize and put on the critical agenda. My work on H.D. appears in DuPlessis 1986; Friedman and DuPlessis 1990; and essays in DuPlessis [1990] 2006.

16. The introduction to *The Feminist Memoir Project* analyzes this phenomenon: "Earlier on [in second-wave feminism] women could bear to name themselves as victims because the end of victimization was in sight—through feminist politics. In contrast, the word 'victim' today is like a heavy stone; no one expects victimhood to budge soon, so once again, few want to acknowledge a 'sisterhood' of timeless pain and sorrow. And those who enshrine victim status run the risk of seeming to claim that such status is in itself a source of power" (DuPlessis and Snitow 1998, 20).

17. A member of the central Editorial Collective until 1982, the associate editor for creative work from 1982–87. I am still affiliated with the journal as a consultant and reader. I was convinced that feminist artistic, creative, and visual work was a central component of our intellectual revolution. So I was the artistic member of the board, with an eye for covers (which I chose until there was an art editor), who fought for a more open, "voicey," essay style as part of the canon of acceptable work, who insisted that poems and fiction be represented.

18. In a letter to Tillie Olsen, Jan. 4, 1978.

19. I was not directly influenced by Cixous's "Laugh of the Medusa," but I might as well have been, as there is no doubt that this is the great manifesto of maenadic writing.

20. In many ways *Writing Beyond the Ending* began with the example of Showalter's *A Literature of Their Own.* I was critical of the dismissive readings Showalter had given of Woolf and Richardson but intrigued by the question of how to define what women writers had in common and committed to the cultural studies that have always been the distinguishing marks of Showalter's criticism. As well, my central finding of a critique of heterosexuality would not have been possible without lesbian-feminist criticism, which I knew then through such little magazines as *Amazon Quarterly.*

21. Thus, I feel situated in what Susan Stanford Friedman called Post/post-structuralist feminist criticism, a criticism that (like Nancy Miller's) does not scant intention, agency, thematics, and the impact of material conditions, while it makes nuanced readings of language and linguistic play, the partial and interested claims of any reality, and the careers of master narratives (Friedman 1991). This is what it now (1990) meant to me to be a "feminist reader."

Chapter 2. *f*-words

1. Goldwater 1989, 47–48, 152. When they first met, Magritte gave Broodthaers a talismanic copy of Mallarmé's poem (Goldwater 1989, 17).

2. Readers should note that the original publication of this essay in 1996, in a special issue of *American Literature* reviewing contemporary U.S. writing, contained

a number of informative references to contemporary writers of essay, both male and female. Here I will not provide this survey of practitioners.

3. In the U.S. context the movement for African American civil rights came before and during 1968, as did a number of peace and antinuclear war movements.

4. Of course, academic feminist criticism was born from this impulsion. People will quickly remember Adrienne Rich, Tillie Olsen, Joanna Russ, Alice Walker, and Mary Daly as offering influential examples of this arousal for U.S. practice; Virginia Woolf is, of course, a central model of anglophone essay work, work that had as well to be recovered from dismissal and minoritization in order to be of influence. Ruth-Ellen Boetcher Joeres and Elizabeth Mittman argue that the essay by women has very often manifested a political valence; of course this is true of work from other groups as well, which tends to modify the point, though not change it (Joeres and Mittman 1993, 14).

5. Nancy Miller makes a parallel point about the upsurge of personal critical writing in the United States, currently: that it makes a critique of that mode of Theory that "depended finally on the theoretical evacuation of the very social subjects producing it" (Miller 1991, 20).

6. More systematic studies are Adorno, "The Essay as Form" (1991); Atkins (1992); Bennett (1989); Bensmaïa (1987); Butrym (1989); Caserio (1992); Good (1988); Joeres and Mittman (1993); Lukács, "On the Nature and Form of the Essay" (1971); Mailhot (1983).

7. Graham Good points out that Montaigne's use of citation was not intended to provide authorities but to bring new voices "into a conversation." Thus citation strategy created a collective, not an academic, texture (Good 1988, 1).

8. Smith argues, drawing on Bakhtin, that "the 'self' that autobiography inscribes is constituted from the polyphonic voices of discourse" (Smith 1987, 48).

9. I may be twisting Miller somewhat; what she actually says is "that the personal and the positional . . . are both the same and different. Or, that what feminist theory is about is the effort to analyze that relation" (Miller 1991, 16).

10. But see, as a counter to my piece of intransigence, the important, unimpeachable point: "In light of the essay's history, subjectivity, for example, becomes a political issue if we view the expressed presence of a subject—most often an explicitly present narrative 'I'—in terms of the problem of author/authority" (Joeres and Mittman 1993, 18).

11. Thus, some attempts at, or gestures toward, plural authorship, such as I made in "For the Etruscans" may occur to signal intersubjectivity inside form. Réda Bensmaïa speaks about a sense of collectivity in the genre of essay, stating that "'subjects' other than the Author people the Essay" and that the nature of the specific excess or boundlessness of the essay, has to do with "an exoteric object: the multiple body of the 'Society of Friends of the Text'" (Bensmaïa 1987, 55, 91). The desire to invoke a matted field of [social] vectors is clear.

12. When I composed "For the Etruscans" I tried to use the most up-to-date ma-

terial available on the Etruscans, particularly on their language and writing. These formed the basis of my imaginative projection: arguing that the Etruscans are (metaphoric) descendents of the wife of Aeneas, lost in the smoke as the three generations of Trojan men exited the burning city to found Rome. This binarist allegory in which men were Romans and women were Etruscans depended on the relatively unknown nature of the Etruscans, one of the pre-Roman civilizations on the Italic peninsula and one with a very sophisticated cultural development. Etruscans provided a metaphor for women, taking "women" in binarist fashion as an underknown, highly developed, colonized "civilization" (that was polemic) with an unread writing. For the Etruscan language was not decipherable in the 1970s; it is now. Revisiting Etruria, we can now understand that in their own cultural mythology, Etruscans thought of themselves as the heroic Greeks in the Trojan War and considered that their enemies, the Romans, were like the defeated Trojans. At least this is the allegory of the famous Etruscan frescoes of the Tomb of François outside of Vulci, Italy. This is almost the flat opposite of my speculative argument (which held that Trojan women "became" the Etruscans, while Trojan men "became" the Romans). So much for artful gender binarism. Revisiting Etruria, it is striking, if also totally coincidental, that as feminist criticism and critique have grown in power and scope in these twenty-five years, so, too, the Etruscan language is now relatively more understood and deciphered by specialists than it was in the 1970s. Incidentally, many of its statements deal with naming (funerary inscriptions of name and family), possession (this cup belongs to So-and-So), and boundary markers (Rix 2000).

13. More recently Irigaray proposes the eradication of stereotypical binaries of masculine and feminine and the articulation of what she has argued is missing in culture to date, a positive and articulate play of nondichotomized value that she calls "a sexuate dimension of discourse"—filled with sexual energy, and the energy of gender, but neither gender treated as negative. There seems, in this work, to be a resistance to the term *feminine* as too limiting for the project (Irigaray [1987] 1991, 143).

14. Or again: "Can one say that the Feminine (wherever it may find itself—in woman, man, hermaphrodite) is the experimental principle that projects its vision outside limiting structures? The active 'Experimental Feminine' is a necessary update to Goethe's passive 'Eternal Feminine'" (Retallack 2003, 109).

15. See my essay "Manifests." Marianne DeKoven's comment is germane. Feminist critics should "acknowledge the antipatriarchal potential of form in historical, male-signed avant-garde writing, but at the same time acknowledge the self-canceling counter-move of that writing toward male supremacism and misogyny" (DeKoven 1989, 78).

16. Although the "feminine" aspects of the essay might indeed be easily recuperable for feminist projects (as Joeres and Mittman suggest, as visible, sometimes, here), the crossing of feminine writing with feminist agendas, with female-type interests, or with a woman's signature has, until quite recently, often been a toxic combination in terms of reception (Joeres and Mittman 1993, 19–20). Retallack also makes this point.

Chapter 3. Blue Studio

1. Barbara Cole's complete essay-letter appears in *Open Letter: A Canadian Journal of Writing and Theory,* a journal committed to staging epistolary exchanges.

2. In a frank answer to the question of women and editing practices in a poll conducted for *Chain* no. 1, Marjorie Perloff notes the degree to which, after feminism, people expect all women to be feminists (an error of judgment, certainly) and, further, still seem to slot women critics as "subaltern" (not taking on the big issues), a term from postcolonial criticism about power relations that indeed criticizes assumptions about female intellectual subordination. The remark is thus infused with feminism while overtly disinterested in this position.

3. "In . . . assertions [like 'I am not a feminist poet'] there is a clear concern with archive/biography/history; how the career will be recorded by the biographers; whether the work ultimately will be canonized or forgotten" (Cole 2002, 33).

4. In a penetrating book published after I first wrote this essay, Rita Felski makes parallel points—that it is poor logic to fault feminist critics for flaws that many critics share. It is callow to claim that feminists are "political" but that better critics are simply "disinterested" and/or upholding literary and aesthetic value (Felski 2003, 8–13). Felski argues that a critic does not "bring" the social and political into the study of literature; such materials are already palpably present.

5. More Spahr: "Or if the women poets were all about their own identity, which was not uncommon, because women too have a tendency to talk excessively about themselves, then that was a problem also. The heroism liked only heroic identity. Heroism felt that the woman poets couldn't help it; it wasn't their fault. They had to deal with the bad society. But it was sad about their work. . . . [The heroic attitudinal heritage] dismissed their work as being too much about women, or gender specific as it might be said" (Spahr 2002).

6. Felski's discussion of female authorship situates various "allegories" (madwoman, masquerading women, and home girls), proposing that "pluralistic, pragmatic, piecemeal" examinations can prevent the reductiveness of overeager, partial, monocausal gender analyses (Felski 2003, 89).

7. Rich presents the 1976 changes as "a few revisions, mainly updating" in the headnote to the essay (Rich 1979, 33).

8. Linda Russo's dissertation (2004) tries to track the "becoming-subject of women" in relation to Joanne Kyger, Rosmarie Waldrop, Bernadette Mayer, and others, but these poets do not exactly see themselves engaged in feminist inflected "becoming." This is an illustration of how a critic constructs the feminist reception of women writers relatively skeptical of feminism.

9. In this survey about the cultural work of editing and gender they find wildly variable attitudes, from Rosmarie Waldrop's entire disinterest in thinking about the gender of whom she published, to Kathleen Fraser's committed desire to clear a space in which women doing experimental work could exfoliate "that which had not yet been uttered." (Fraser 1994, 45).

10. There are many women writers whose gender basically controlled the comments critics made about them (Showalter 1971; Ellmann 1968).

11. See at minimum Bernstein 1999; Davidson 2004; Keenaghan 2002; Middleton 1992; Mossin 2005; Rifkin 2000; Watten 1998.

12. Ostriker made a taxonomy of themes that emerged in some poetry as "the women's movement" both spoke in poetry and was spoken in the critics who constructed poetic reception (Ostriker 1986, 8). Her thematic readings and synopses of poetry crystallize various female positions in a differential relationship to culture.

13. But this "feminism of reception," as David Buuck reminds us, will need to position the recovery of women artists as events in the general history of literature, not solely or narrowly as an act for women (Buuck 1999, 31). Note—the "feminism of reception" will also be alert to the issue of erasure. As Elizabeth Treadwell pointed out, "The problem of erasure is *everreal.* It is never, I've found, that women weren't there [in literature], but that they were there and it takes us forever to re-figure it out." And later: "Those of us who find ourselves figured as Other—in whatever era, in whatever way: *We are never silent to ourselves*" (Treadwell 2000–2001, 180, 181).

14. "I am not proposing that you formulate a hypothetical Feminist Nexus"; later Cole uses the term "nexus of feminism" (Cole 2002, 40).

15. The idea of "nexus" seems apropos, even allowing for the fact that not one set of linked terms in one seminal essay is the propellant (which was the case for the objectivists). In Zukofsky's 1931 essay the terms are *objectivist, sincerity,* and *objectification* in relation to the materialist political/cultural movement of communism, socialism, and the progressive left.

16. In the past decades an accelerating number of critical and speculative works (for ease of handling, my list is U.S. only) have broached the question of how to acknowledge and discuss the upsurge in experimental or innovative work in poetry by women writers, some loosely affiliated with specific formations and *scuole,* some not. This upsurge lies behind Barbara Cole's queries here. Did the fact that people were women matter at all, and how? How to define feminist or feminine or women's writing? Are production, reception, and dissemination gendered, and what are the implications? This upsurge is so striking a phenomenon that any enumeration will be embarrassingly incomplete, suggestive only. The poets include at least (listing people whose various critical works are not noted below) Harryette Mullen, Leslie Scalapino, Rae Armantrout, Fanny Howe, Johanna Drucker, Hannah Weiner, Cecilia Vicuña, Rosmarie Waldrop, Erica Hunt, Bernadette Mayer, Myung-Mi Kim, Beverly Dahlen, Norma Cole, Chris Tysh, and Ann Lauterbach. Many are visible in Sloan 1998; Rankine and Spahr 2002; and Dienstfrey and Hillman 2003 (an anthology about a specific "female" issue—motherhood). These questions had been fueled by important works of critical speculation by some of the poets; a sampling includes DuPlessis [1990] 2006; Fraser 2000; Harryman 1995; Hejinian 2000; Howe 1985; Notley 1980; Retallack 2003; Waldman 2001. This interest was signaled in the academy by the broadening of attention to varieties of poets in Hollenberg 2000; Keller and

Miller 1994; Prins and Shreiber 1997; and correspondingly the attention to gender analysis in experimental modes, as in Beach 1998; capped by a rich anthology that shows whole fields of inquiry have opened, Hinton and Hogue 2001. Critics now often analyze innovative women writers, and gender and the avant-garde; a partial list includes Evans, 2001; Frost 2003; Keller 1997; Kinnahan 1994, 2004; Russo 2001–2; Sloan 2001–2; Vickery 2000. Important acts of reception of female authors do not, of course, have to focus particularly on gender; see Perloff 1991, 2004; and Lazer 1996.

17. Alice Notley, in conversation, has called all the women writing in this period "the group without a name." A similar argument about "that sudden generation of strong women poets" is in Notley and Foster 2001–2, 534.

Chapter 4. Manifests

1. See Judith Butler's incisive critique of Lacanian theory as a "theological impulse," countering that "the symbolic itself is the sedimentation of social practices" (Butler 2004, 46, 44).

2. In "A"-12 Louis Zukofsky calls his wife Celia "My one reader / Who types me," situating her at both ends of the scale—an assistant to production and reception (Zukofsky 1978, 246). Yet as a collagist-composer, she coproduced the final canto of "A"—juxtaposing Zukofsky's words with work of Handel to complete his long poem.

3. Svetlana Boym uses Marie Tsvetaeva as a test case of these kinds of questions under the rubric "The duel between the woman-poet and her female pedigree. . . . Can she in her writing escape the ghosts of cultural metaphors of femininity? How does she redefine her literary identity against (or rather, together with and against) the cultural myth of female creativity? Can she escape that touch of a 'bad taste' that marks the discourse of a poetess?" (Boym 1991, 200).

4. Boym argues for "aesthetic obscenity" to counter the notion of the "aesthetic dignity" of paradigmatic male poets; she thereby produces a defense of contradictory, polyphonic, fragmented, parenthetical, multigeneric rhetorics (Boym 1991, 196–97, 203, and 216).

5. *Residual* is one of Raymond Williams's terms for sociocultural practices (Williams 1977, 122–23).

6. The poems that follow in this essay were not written in my voice but by me, as interested experiments in theorizing.

7. Younger women may reject that they are ultimately figured in culture "like" the mother; thus the alliance of young women and all men against the mother is a central way to continue the cultural disempowerment of women. Men reading this analysis might be embarrassed by these two examples and thereupon say that Grossman and Olson are not typical examples. They are, however, rather influential. They are also important here because both visibly struggle with gender and poesis.

8. In "Summa Lyrica" Grossman credits speakers in poems as female, but writers of poems are, generally, not (Grossman 1992, 237, 259).

9. In his analysis of the two fundamental, gendered paradigms for poetry in essays that just precede "Summa Lyrica" but are not incorporated in it, Grossman proposes two transhistorical poetic positions for all humans—"Orpheus" and "Philomela"—that symbolize, respectively, the power of memory and the "pain of experience without memory" (Grossman 1989–90, 239). Poets can find themselves in either of these positions, not necessarily along binary gender lines yet tending toward such binary assignment. Grossman's transhistorical archetypalist analysis uses many gender stereotypes to describe positions said to be flexible in practice.

10. Possibly a tendentious example. It may be that she and the women will then echo or re-sing the song that Moses sang, adding their nonverbal, unrecordable art—dance. But it is as plausible that Miriam will sing or invent a new song beginning with the same verse as did Moses—as if this were a song fest or ode contest to "sing unto the Lord, for he hath triumphed gloriously." Her invention would be consistent with her status as prophetess.

11. This symptomatic anecdote, which, of course, need not be true, is from Pausanius, *Description of Greece* (Campbell 1992, 21–23). In this stew of gender materials it is interesting to observe the hectoring criticism Pindar mounts of other men's judgment for their act of rewarding a woman.

12. Made orally at the 1995 conference at Cornell University, where this essay was presented in its original form.

13. This is particularly striking when Frances Boldereff's intellectually and poetically inspiring role for this manifesto is acknowledged; its first draft, emerging from the Olson-Boldereff interchange, was sent by Olson in a letter to her (Maud and Thesen 1999, xv, 163–67).

14. Kathleen Fraser shows how Olson's spatial poetics became crucial to women who wanted to break with the tidy, domesticated page in order to visualize their expansive thinking in works of visual scope. Women painters of the artistic movements of abstraction and expressionism were a parallel source for this enriched graphic use of the page (Fraser 2000, 175–83).

15. Susan Winnett (1990) offers a significant overview of this issue.

16. This position of female ambivalence prefaced Catharine Stimpson's early consideration of Olson but is not discussed at length (Stimpson 1973–74).

17. The correspondence as published runs from 1947 to 1950; the introduction alludes to some later letters and exchanges up to a few months before Olson's death, but these are not included; the focus of the book is the contribution of Boldereff to the making of Olson's poetic career.

18. In the double-digit volumes of the Olson-Creeley correspondence (dated hourly in the early 1950s), Boldereff is not indexed under any of her surnames—whether Ward, Motz, Boldereff, or her given name, Frances.

19. Meret Oppenheim's 1974 recapitulation of the artistic career for women analyzes some of these pressures and strategies: "They project their male tendency on

to men because they are forced to suppress it in themselves," an observation germane to Boldereff, even its binarist absolutes (Curiger 1989, 130).

20. Boldereff calls the readers of *Harper's Bazaar,* where one of Olson's first poems was published, "servant girls," saying, "I am extremely pleased that it [the poem] should make a public appearance among the servant girls," perhaps differentiating herself (Maud and Thesen 1999, 20); Olson was awkwardly amused by the gendered space, making "boobie" puns on the name of the magazine: "Boozoomzar" "or Bra-sar/or Bubsie-zar/or Boob-zar/or any equally brazen offence" and seemed to be proudly abashed at his appearance near an ad for "MODESS."

21. Thesen remarks that Boldereff constantly resisted the public authority of authorship, working through anonymity, several pseudonyms, and modes of self-effacement.

22. Children are implicit—Boldereff's daughter was six in 1949.

23. Dana Polan's critique is echoed here: "Most especially, as Alice Jardine has pointed out, the lines of escape [in political transformations] tend to be especially open to privileged male figures: for all their talk of a *devenir-femme,* a becoming-woman, Deleuze and Guattari tend to abstract the process away from any tie to the historically specific situation and struggle of women" (Polan, in Deleuze and Guattari 1986, xxvi).

24. Olson also has, in "Human Universe" (an essay with a firm criticism of American imperial materialism), a rather Lawrencian section insisting that contemporary Mayan peoples have gentle flesh (Olson 1997, 158). They are warmer, more human, more earthy, nicer to touch, more whole. If I were Mayan, I would regard this with a queasy mixture of embarrassment and temptation. While flattering, still, romantic primitivism undercuts Olson's observations. Being "closer to nature" ends people up in the timeless, ahistorical dioramas in Museums of Natural History.

25. This is a finding parallel to James Breslin's: "The essay may propound openness in a bullying tone, its ideas may or may not be derivative, but 'Projective Verse' did make available to younger writers alternative ways of measuring the line and shaping the poem" (Breslin 1984, 66).

Chapter 5. Marble Paper

1. Extending the analysis of American Africanism from Morrison 1992.

2. This material expands the discussion of Easthope in DuPlessis 2001, 15–17.

3. Johnson's reading is also culturally located at a moment of feminist criticism influenced by a Richean sense of struggle between the life of the mother and the life of the child, and at a moment of poetic canon-formation from what Alicia Suskin Ostriker has called "the women's poetry movement" (Ostriker 1986, 13). By using Anne Sexton, Lucille Clifton, and Gwendolyn Brooks, in which "each of these poems exists because a child does not," Johnson has chosen (with some acknowledgment of their "randomness" but thematic coherence) a specific set of poems (Johnson 1986, 197). If she had selected poems about young children by Alice Notley,

Kathleen Fraser, Bernadette Mayer, or Rae Armantrout written at about the time of Johnson's article (1986), or the pioneering poem about childbirth by Mina Loy that makes the parturient body a problem in thought—in philosophy, really—as well as physically, quite different conclusions about the nature of poetry might have emerged.

4. The poem, written on November 5, 1805, and published in 1807 in *Poems in Two Volumes,* was among lyrics indirectly inspired by the 1803 Scotland tour taken by Wordsworth, Dorothy, and, for a time, Coleridge. During this tour Wordsworth and his sister met Walter Scott on very friendly terms. Wordsworth acknowledged him as a fellow worker in ballads yet became jealous at the success of "Lay of the Last Minstrel" (Gill 1989, 216–18).

5. Incidentally, the word *single* in the first line extends and anticipates the words *singing* and *sings;* indeed, in a manuscript the word *single* was used instead of the word *singing* (Wordsworth 1946, 77). Further, the number of times in the poem that the words *singing, song,* or *sang* occur is remarkable. This fact is also noted by Hartman 1987. In addition, there are numerous synonyms for *song (strain, sound, chaunt, notes, numbers, lay, music).*

6. Even if this line is taken as a rhetorical question, our interest must be provoked by its failure to agree with two main conditions of rhetorical questions: that it should not be a genuine searching for information, and that there should be an "obvious answer" (Baldick 1991, 189).

7. Jones argues that Wordsworth "exercises his gender and class prerogatives" to appropriate the "essence" of the Reaper's song (Jones 1991, 267, 271). The reference to "essence" may make any analytic rejoinder unarguable.

8. "[Wagner's oeuvre, like nineteenth-century consumer goods,] knew no greater ambition than to conceal every sign of the work that went into them, perhaps because any such traces reminded people too vehemently of the appropriation of the labour of others, of an injustice that could still be felt. A contradiction of all autonomous art is the concealment of the labour that went into it" (Adorno 1981a, 83).

9. "In the seventeenth century, women came for the first time to occupy a place as poets in the Gaelic bardic tradition, helping to shape the subject matter of the verses" (Houston 1989, 140).

10. See Wordsworth 1946, 444–45.

11. *Erse* is "the term used for Irish Gaelic." "The term is the Lowland Scots word for Irish," sometimes "inaccurately" used for Scots Gaelic, according to Drabble 1985, 324.

12. For the 1807 version (with all the sweetness) see Wu 1998, 384–85; for the 1827 version (sans "sweet" words) see Ferguson et al. 1996, 424–25. On the excision of "sweet" see Moorman 1965, 450. In the later version the allegorical capitalization of *Highland Lass* and *Vale,* for example, suggest to the reader that this is no simple incident but has symbolic status. The punctuation changes are somewhat more neutral.

13. I am grateful for the one word *Erse* that piqued my imagination and helped provoke this essay.

14. Gill suggests that cultural difference was something strongly impressed on the Wordsworths from their Scottish tour in 1803 (Gill 1989, 215).

15. Bridget Hill is talking about England, but since some of her observations about a labor shortage in agriculture apply to the north, they help construct a portrait of the Scottish or Highland reaper.

16. Many contemporaneous commentators who heard Gaelic song, especially seventeenth-century "waulking songs"—sung during the collectively done process of fulling handwoven cloth—were a little condescending to the wildness and exoticism of the singing, the rhythm of the feet hitting the cloth. See Campbell and Collinson 1981, 2–5.

17. The barriers are traced by Symonds as personal or ideologically maintained modesty, in the case of Anna Gordon Brown, who "would sing but was not comfortable with publishing" (Symonds 1997, 16), and later critical reception that theorized collective, not individual, makers of ballads and male bards, not female singers (Stewart 1991). Symonds also traces gender divisions in topic and therefore in gender of singer (warfare and courtship) but notes crossover topics such as bride stealing (Symonds 1997, 18).

18. In terms of social origin, though, none of these was an agricultural worker—one was a retainer of a clan chief, one was a daughter of a clan chief, and the third has no biography in the Watson anthology.

19. There was a significant division between boys and girls in Scottish education in the eighteenth century. "SSPCK Schools [Society in Scotland for Propagating Christian Knowledge; responsible for repressing the many pagan religious forms] . . . [gave] . . . males the opportunity to speak English and Gaelic while leaving females as monoglots. If men used English and literate forms more commonly over time, women's status as transmitters of traditional oral culture may have been enhanced. Yet the standing of the whole cultural form was being eroded" (Houston 1989, 134).

20. My sense of ballad topics also from Symonds 1997, 9, although these ballads are in Scots, not Gaelic; and from Houston 1989, 138.

21. Ward (1997) offers a discussion of the functions of female figures in Wordsworth's poetry. Judith W. Page's "Shakespeare's Scottish Sister" discusses Wordsworth's occlusion of his literary indebtedness to the Scots writer Joanna Baillie in his "Preface to the Lyrical Ballads" (Page 1994, 39–44). Page remarks on "Wordsworth's implicit denial of his connection with women writers," often "his competitors. He deliberately constructs a view of literary history without women," despite his own documentable relationships with their work (Page 1994, 39).

22. In neither poet is this effort completely self-consistent; Wordsworth praises Anne Finch in 1815; Pound praises Mary Bernard in 1933—and takes her potential seriously (Page 1994, 40; Pound 1950, 248).

23. For Boldereff see Maud and Thesen 1999, 292–97. For Nardi see Williams 1992; and O'Neil 1994.

Chapter 6. Propounding Modernist Maleness

1. This sentence is indebted to Jonathan Culler's remarks about an argument by Steven Knapp: "a text has literary interest insofar as our interest in it exceeds our interest in figuring out what the author intends" (Culler 2000, 280).

2. "Women are the 'Muses' whom genius has kissed, just as man, the genius, has been 'kissed by the Muse,'" notes Meret Oppenheim carefully, trying to analyze the impact of just such a stolid convention on herself as woman artist (Curiger 1989, 130). Lisa Rado observes that "the ways in which writers have portrayed the source of their inspiration can serve in part as a reflection of literary and cultural history"; she links "third-sex" theories in sexology and what she calls the androgyne muse (Rado 2000, 2).

3. One can hardly avoid seeing this poem as similar to Eliot's "Portrait of a Lady," which expresses the speaker's desire to separate from a maternal and genteel figure of entrapment and apparently amateur status. However, it is unlikely that Pound knew of this Eliot poem when he wrote his; in 1912 the Eliot poem existed only in manuscript. The two poets did not meet until 1914. Marianne Moore's 1917 "Monkeys"—with its puma or lynx speaking bitterly about animal-human power relations (possibly a gender allegory), and its ending about the sea's shocking deposits of debris—seems to be an oblique commentary on Pound's "Portrait d'une Femme."

4. For Farr see also www.modjourn.brown.edu/mjp/Bios/Farr.html (accessed June 7, 2005). Although this is not my subject, there is also a small depiction of Farr in Pound's Canto XXVIII, in which she appears as Loica (really Louka—from a character in Shaw's *Arms and the Man*), a five-line depiction of her trip to Sri Lanka, and a summary epitaph.

5. Cullingford (1993, 40–41) argues that while patriarchal religion had one male deity, a male priesthood, gender inequality, and asexual or relatively powerless female cult objects like the Virgin Mary, in contrast occult religions offered female deities, female adepts, and priestesses of high status, and a sense of gender equality with a potentially sexualized and power-laden aura; thus, "the attraction of occult societies for rebellious women is obvious" (Cullingford 1993, 40).

6. Or, conversely, Pound, the great mind, sought her lacking someone else (Yeats). In either case she is "second always." It is also possible to "translate" this line in ways suggested by Richard Ellmann: Yeats had an affair with Farr, because Maud Gonne (the "someone else") was not available (Ellmann 1961, 182).

7. Yeats refers to Farr by her married name although she was divorced from her husband in 1895; as for the word *queer:* I take it to mean amusing, odd, spritely, needy.

8. Pound also notes that Yeats can't sing (Pound 1960a, 197–98).

9. Similarly, a provoking split in memories of Farr between her pre-Raphaelite look and her professional activities as capable performer and organizer is articulated in Yeats's final summary in *A Vision* (1938): "A certain actress [Farr] is typical [of

Phase 19], for she surrounds herself with drawings by Burne-Jones in his latest period, and reveres them as [if] they were holy pictures, while her manners are boisterous, dominating, and egotistical. They are faces of silent women, and she is not silent for a moment" (Yeats [1938] 1961, 150). The New Woman subjectivity is disparaged in these remarks and viewed as a deception. The consensus is, better silent pre-Raphaelite women than demanding modern ones who have opinions and claims. In the case of Yeats this judgment is the more striking given Cassandra Laity's argument in her unpublished dissertation that Yeats was indebted to the New Woman in general and to Farr in particular in his changed depictions of warrior queens in his drama: decisive, masculine, female figures of agency and force (Laity 1985b).

10. We don't know who initiated this metaphor. This novel appeared in 1912; in the same year Farr departed for Sri Lanka (in August), and Pound wrote his poem in the spring, apparently. On *The Solemnization of Jacklin* Dorothy wrote to Ezra: "Just read a new book by 'Florence Farr'. Such a Sargasso Sea muddle. Every body divorced several times, & in the end going back to their originals: & a young man called 'Dorus Callando' who lay among lilies all night & is Oscar [Wilde] without the bitter-sweetness" (Pound and Litz 1984, 132).

11. A study by Kumari Jayawardena sketches European, mainly British, women who contributed in a variety of ways to South Asian life, whether as reformers, educators, or spiritual seekers. Jayawardena discusses Farr's end-career commitment to education for Hindu girls in Sri Lanka; Farr served as principal of a Ramanathan College in Jaffna for several years until just before her death in 1917, a role that became increasingly unsatisfying, as her guru turned out to have rather retrograde ideas about the education of girls into wife and motherhood. Jayawardena depicts Farr as "misrepresented" by the various men in her life and uses the *Modern Woman* briefly to trace Farr's feminist politics, although the book's racial politics are not mentioned (Jayawardena 1995, 146).

12. On aspects of Marinetti's program see Perloff 1986, 86–92; for gender interpretations of that program see Burke 1996, 156–57; Lyon 1999, 92–123; and Nicholls 1995, 84–92.

13. I am extending this argument about Marinetti's spur to imagism to apply to "Portrait d'une Femme."

14. For more gender materials in Pound see Bush 1990.

Chapter 7. Lorine Niedecker, the Anonymous

1. In comments to Zukofsky, Niedecker parses the final line as "Was enough to have carried me thru," noting that "folk don't say that, they slur it over into simply what I did say." Her comments on an Ian Finley translation of the poem into Scots show how seriously she took her witty word *carry* as indicating "*carry* pail or in pail, and *carry* me thru life," that is, as both literal and figurative/idiomatic (Niedecker 1993, 290). This version has an exclamation point after the third line. Peter Middle-

ton discusses how and in what senses Niedecker used folk materials and social stances in her work. By comparing "Granite Pail" with Williams's red wheelbarrow poem from *Spring & All* (1923), Middleton argues that Niedecker differed from objectivist and avant-garde practices, showing how her words demand readings that are specific, local, nonuniversal, responsive to idiom and usage distinctive to particular settings. The essay proposes that Niedecker "seems oddly suspended between the apparently incompatible worlds of the avant-garde and folk poetry" (Middleton 1999, 186).

2. Until the important University of California Press edition and the devotion of its editor, Jenny Penberthy, Niedecker was published by the Press of James A. Decker (Prairie City, Illinois); Wild Hawthorn Press (Edinburgh); Fulcrum Press (London); Jargon Society (North Carolina); Elizabeth Press (New Rochelle); North Point Press (San Francisco); Pig Press (Durham, U.K.); in *Origin* magazine (Boston and Kyoto); there were two collections of essays from Truck Press (North Carolina); and Interim Press (Devon). In the fifth edition of the *Norton Anthology of Poetry,* advertised in 2004, she is not included. Nor are Oppen or Zukofsky.

3. Niedecker instructed her second husband, Al Millen, that her journals be destroyed at her death (a demand loyally and unfortunately executed), thus pulling her back from posthumous personal revelations.

4. Glenna Breslin reports that after a two-year marriage that ended in 1930, Niedecker met Zukofsky, lived with him briefly in New York, became pregnant, and terminated the pregnancy of twin fetuses. This account is sometimes contested but seems accurate. They sustained, after that, a rich relationship in correspondence (Breslin 1990, 146).

5. The ambiguity of this strategy may be surmised from a letter by Carl Rakosi to George Oppen:

> I was shaken by the sudden death of Lorine Niedecker. I met her for the first time last spring in her house on the edge of a creek, a house so small that if there had been one more person than the four of us there [probably Al Millen, Leah Rakosi, Carl, and Lorine], it would have been impossible to sit down to table. She had been described as having some strange ailment and of refusing to see anyone, but she was *delighted* to see me and I found her as fresh and wide-awake as a daisy. I jolted her when I didn't go along with her adulation of Zukofsky. When she saw I was serious, she beamed and looked relieved. She said she found it refreshing. All in all, a very *healthy* person." (Letter of Jan. 18, 1971, UCSD [University of California, San Diego], Mandeville Collection, Archive for New Poetry, George Oppen Papers, Box 9, Folder 35)

6. Niedecker married Al Millen in May 1963. The Cuban missile crisis occurred in 1962. Niedecker (who wrote the poem in 1967) described this poem as coming "from a folk conversation and I suppose some of my own dark forebodings"

(Niedecker 1986, 129). It is not clear whether the forebodings are personal, political/historical, borrowed from another speaker, or her own.

7. Jenny Penberthy notes that Niedecker's first haiku appeared in a "For Paul" manuscript in 1953. Niedecker owned the Peter Pauper Press "gift" edition of *Japanese Haiku* (1955) and *One Hundred Poems from the Japanese* (1955). The latter, edited by Rexroth, contains a small sampler of twelve famous haiku. *Origin* series 2 (July 1964) featured Bashō. See Niedecker 1986, 49–50, 33, 145.

8. A letter to Charles Reznikoff from Lorine Niedecker, Nov. 23, 1959 (University of California, San Diego, Mandeville Collection, Archive for New Poetry, Charles Reznikoff Papers, Box 4, Folder 1).

9. Niedecker to Gail Roub, 1981, in *Origin* 16 (July 1981). This letter is a statement of her poetics, accomplished, she suggests, and realized in "My Life by Water." This letter also reveals her ambiguous relation to the Zukofskian version of "objectivist" practice: "I used to feel that I was goofing off unless I held only to the hard, clear image, the thing you could put your hand on but now I dare do this reflection."

10. Letters to Cid Corman: "folky," Oct. 13, 1966 (Niedecker 1986, 102); "blues" [identified as probably a collection of blues lyrics] Nov. 2, 1968 (Niedecker 1986, 180).

11. "A ballad is a folk song that tells a story with stress on the crucial situation, tells it by letting the action unfold itself in event and speech, and tells it objectively with little comment or intrusion of personal bias" (Bold 1979, 97, citing Gerould 1932). It probably should be added that there is a stock stanza—of 4,3,4,3 stresses and b rhymes. Ballads often feature dialogue.

12. Lingering occurs with the use of stanzas identical except for several pivotal words; the tactic of incremental repetition of ballads is a version of "lingering."

13. "I'm Nobody! who are you?" Johnson #288, and the reference to "chanticleer of dew" also Dickinson; the earlier reference could be to "I Felt a Funeral, in My Brain," Johnson #280 (Dickinson 1960).

Chapter 8. The Gendered Marvelous

1. Articulating this Benjaminian proposition, Adorno summarizes the argument in the aphorism "Expression is the gaze of artworks" (Adorno 1997, 112). On aura and "recognition" see Bernstein 1997, 204.

2. In Robert Kaufman's "Aura, Still," a learned and suggestive article on aura in contemporary poetry and in Frankfurt School theory and its debates, the gender issue at the heart of Benjamin's analysis is not mentioned (Kaufman 2002). Kaufman's (following Adorno's) project to extend the idea of aura in Benjamin does, nonetheless, have this gender dimension to contend with. How can "auretic works contribute to sociopolitical critique" if aura's gender normativity is not considered? (Kaufman 2002, 49). In another article, on Guest read particularly in relation to Adorno's theories, Kaufman simultaneously investigates her work in the lyric and proposes that lyric in general is emphatically the site of critique in poetry, this be-

cause poetic form indicates "modern social complexity," offering by virtue of "aesthetic thought" a freedom "from pre-existent concepts or cognitive rules" and imagining "positions and experiences" new to the subject (Kaufman 2000, 12, 14, 16). Thus for both Benjamin and Adorno, the lyric has a "historical relation to critical thought and emancipatory possibility" (Kaufman 2000, 16). Kaufman situates Guest at the center of a "critical lyric Modernism" (Kaufman 2000, 11).

3. The artists and writers in collaboration are Pablo Picasso (with *The Woman in Green Costume*) and Lewis Galantière; George Braque and Benjamin Péret; Fernand Léger and Clement Greenberg; William Baziotes and Harold Rosenberg; Romere Bearden and William Carlos Williams; Byron Browne and Barry Ulanov; Adolph Gottlieb and Victor Wolfson; David Hare and J.-P. Sartre; Hans Hofmann and Tennessee Williams; Carl Holty and Paul Goodman; Robert Motherwell and Weldon Kees.

4. The portfolio is not paginated. The controversy over the Picasso may have centered on the "sow's snout" prominent on her face; at least this is what Lewis Galantière calls it in his commentary in the portfolio.

5. Ulanov made a polemical, dismissive survey of the depiction of female figures in Manet, Monet, Cassatt, Renoir, Degas, Van Gogh, Toulouse-Lautrec, Gauguin, Modigliani, Matisse, Leger. Since, despite his claims, females had hardly "blanked out" as a subject for painting, the works treating them had to be disparaged.

6. Sara Lundquist (1997, 262) includes editor David Shapiro's fervent joint apology in a note.

7. Robert Belton solves this contradiction by proposing that female surrealism ("post-Surrealism") is not the same as male surrealism (Belton 1995, 12), since "*Woman*" was essential to surrealism, but "*women's* concerns" only emerged in a "post-Surrealist phase" (Belton 1995, 273). Mary Ann Caws and Gwen Raaberg call for a rereading of surrealism with female visual artists as central and problematic, discussing how such artists developed their "work within the context of surrealist principles" and in what ways they are marked by contradictions given that poetics (Caws, Kuenzli, and Raaberg 1991, 16; Raaberg 1991, 2). Facing the question of how surrealist women produced their works, Susan Suleiman proposed the Irigarayan concept of mimicry, through which women artists imitated the image of Woman offered by surrealists, giving this a mocking or parodic twist that compromised the image, critiqued it, torqued it (Suleiman 1990, 27). She also noted the historical delay in the entrance of women artists, proposing that "as the movement grew weaker and more embattled, it became more welcoming to women" (Suleiman 1990, 31). This interest in examining how a woman artist touched by surrealism faced the contradictions and, in critique, "subverted, inverted, and extended—that discourse" has analogues with my task here (Raaberg 1991, 4). Caws's later claim of a "surrealist feminism" might be a correct, if sometimes counterintuitive position, given the binding down of female figures in surrealist visual art (Caws 1997, 20). Made critique/mad critique would be the appropriate typo.

8. Let me invoke Michael Davidson's incisive remark (made about an even more

homosocial set of artists) that "Vision . . . purchased at the expense of women" is a problematic stance "even when her gender . . . is invoked as a positive value" (Davidson 1995, 198, 199). Nonetheless, not all women affected by surrealism would credit this critique.

9. Mary Ann Caws proposes this attention, not to specific, perhaps dated surrealist techniques but to the philosophic premises of surrealism—to "rethink the self" (Caws 1997, 21) by attention to a boundary-crossing, baroque sensibility, and an erotic scintillation. The political charge of surrealism is underplayed here in favor of spiritual shock, but this position seems pertinent to Guest's work.

10. Liberation, freedom, mystery, and the escape from your own limitations via surrealism were motifs that repeated in this conversation as Guest talked about herself and about Dora Maar as surrealist. See also Lundquist 2002. Work by Guest forthcoming as I write this includes an "exploration into Surrealist poems" and poems on paintings by surrealists in *The Red Gaze,* announced with the subtitle *Surrealism and Other Poems,* 2005 (see Hejinian 2004, 255), but listed in the Wesleyan University press catalogue without the subtitle.

11. Sara Lundquist circulated this material to me in typescript; I am grateful for her in-depth discussions, now in Lundquist 1997, which also reproduces the Miró and the Balla paintings.

12. Guest's work thereby is a prime example of "lyric abstraction" for Robert Kaufman, philosophical and critical works that embody aura (Kaufman 2002, 50). In my reading, Guest's "critical lyric" (Kaufman 2002, 77) is concerned with examining gender materials central to lyric as a formation.

13. In Guest's 2003 collection, *Forces of Imagination: Writing on Writing,* there are some significant revisions of the essays published under the same titles as those I received in typescript form through the courtesy of Barbara Guest. This is reflected in some of the citations of Guest given here.

14. Guest's *Fair Realism* contains "The Cradle of Culture" in which the artist Miró draws a work called "The Poetess" (Guest 1989, 76–77). "The Cradle of Culture" alludes to this earlier work called "The Poetess" (after Miró's painting of that name), which appeared in *Moscow Mansions* (Guest 1973, 46) about twenty years earlier.

15. Compare "The silk was turned into curtains and thus began to lead a tamed, domestic existence, its history asleep in our house, much as a poem enters into an anthology" in the 1986 version of *HOW(ever).*

16. The periodical publication of this essay included Dickinson and Moore on the list.

17. Though incidentally Guest says, "all poetry is confessional," a statement that can be read as absolutely confessional and also as wry, given the interests of a certain cadre of poets under that rubric (Guest 1992, 23).

18. We know that for Brandt the artist is male since he is depicted as such in a few of these works.

19. Mary Ann Caws has written a lucid, well-illustrated, and comprehensive

study of Maar (1907–97), focusing on Maar's career as a visual artist, poet, and working photographer, on her proud erotic presence, on her dynamic intelligence. Caws points out that when Picasso painted her as a "weeping woman," Maar did parallel self-portraits alluding to these works that reclaimed her image; a less empathetic interpretation would claim she was simply imitating him (Caws 2000, 126–31).

20. This in response to a question from interviewer Sarah Rosenthal about the political nature of the surrealist movement and about the political response to McCarthyism in the New York School. Guest goes in another direction in her response (Guest 2004a, 31).

21. John Richardson comments that *Guernica* "is permeated by Dora's presence. She not only photographed it at different stages of completion, but she actually painted part of it, and the figure holding a lamp is unquestionably a likeness of Dora. (So far as I know, nobody has published the fact that Dora Maar worked on *Guernica*. Many of the vertical strokes on the horse's body were painted by her.)" (Richardson 1982, 281–82). Caws remarked that the strokes Maar painted on *Guernica*'s horse were "a minor but symbolic contribution" (Caws 2000, 103).

22. When Picasso left Maar (in 1943–44), she suffered a collapse. She then had therapy with Jacques Lacan, who had been part of the surrealist circles both Picasso and Maar frequented. After, she became a recluse.

Chapter 9. "Uncannily in the open"

1. Written originally as a lecture for my receipt of the Roy Harvey Pearce Archive for New Poetry Prize (2002). In the citations of Oppen, *SL* refers to *Selected Letters* (Oppen 1990); and *NCP* refers to *New Collected Poems* (Oppen 2002).

2. He agrees, for example, with the critique of his absolute position offered by Hans Magnus Enzensberger, "that literature must resist precisely this verdict, that is, be such that it does not surrender to cynicism merely by existing after Auschwitz" (Adorno 1992, 88). He further argues that it is unthinkable to engineer "transfiguration": "By this alone an injustice is done the victims, yet no art that avoided the victims could stand up to the demands of justice" (Adorno 1992, 88). However, turning the victims into "works of art, [they are] tossed out to be gobbled up by the world that did them in," an ethical nightmare of the aesthetic. Furthermore, he rejects the "dreary metaphysics" of a humanism (and presumably journalism) that "shows us humanity blossoming in so-called extreme situations"—a "cozy existential atmosphere" whose implications are happier for "the executioners" than the victims. The impulse to make such literature would then be—intransigent self-questioning and lacerating judgment unto blockage.

3. On the silence see DuPlessis 1987; on its impact on others see Weinberger (*NCP* vii–viii). Charles Bernstein has also commented on Riding's and Oppen's stopping writing: how political grief and thinking about human social disasters, a grief so strong it is almost blocking, affected them obliquely (Bernstein 1999, 257–59).

4. I will bracket the issue of the translation of these works as interpretive practices and any reader's dependence on translations.

5. With a number of literary historical models possible (from George Oppen to Langston Hughes), serial poems are sectional or modular works whose argument is built by the order of the parts, by the nature and montage cut of the parts (image, phrase, line, word), by the shape of blankness or space in relation to the parts, and by the varied intellectual and emotional relations of suture and leap among these parts. Seriality proceeds by vectors, adjusting to pressures on all sides and coming out with a situational path.

6. Eliot Weinberger notes Oppen's "obstinate blindness to all forms of surrealism, which he saw as an escape from, and not a way into, current realities" (*NCP* x). In an important set of comments in an email of May 6, 2003, the poet and critic Andrew Joron notes the degree to which surrealism "haunts" my essay, first by virtue of the fact that surrealism serves as a "constitutive moment" for both Benjamin and Celan, as Margaret Cohen argued in *Profane Illumination* (1993), and second by virtue of the terms I come to use: *vertiginous* and the *uncanny,* both of which have serious uses in surrealist thought. Third—and here I will cite Joron, whose defense of surrealism deconstructs Oppen's resistance: "At the same time I remain convinced of the French movement's relevance and vitality, especially with regard to a negative poetics (aren't Oppen's valorizations, for example, of austerity and clarity conditioned by their relations to opposites, their repressed others, namely jouissance and obscurity? Poetic meaning, at some level, must conjure and agonistically embrace its repressed Other, a contradiction that cannot be resolved or thought through, perhaps, so much as lived through, 'uncannily in the open')." I thank Joron for these penetrating remarks and for permission to cite them.

7. For a corrective view of the career of John Cage see Joan Retallack's essays in *The Poethical Wager.*

8. In the year of his second book Oppen wrote on Olson, McClure, and Ginsberg, praising Ginsberg's *Kaddish* in strong terms for its lack of "preciousness" and its breadth. But he takes issue with the overdone quality of "declamatory form" in the shorter poems, with the temptation of "riding 'no hands'" in that poetics, and finally with Ginsberg's putting opinions into poetry without subjecting them to "rigorous thought" (Oppen 1962). The review, which always tempers criticism with allusions to the better work of those poets, frankly criticizes his serious and well-received peers.

9. The stakes were very high, and his sense of isolation from "Bohemia" is patent in his 1963 essay "The Mind's Own Place" (see Oppen [1963] 2003).

10. This is the point—poems tracking the graph of thought—at which a "projective" poetics as in Olson, Creeley, and, differently, Duncan and Blaser meet the "objectivist" tendency.

11. For his part, Oppen told me repeatedly I should leave the university, something I also ignored.

12. In a remarkable letter (1976) Oppen enunciates the "principle" of working to connect each word at BOTH ENDS" (which in his view demands a major cutting of superficial syntactic connections)—and indicates thereby how, out of a purely horizontal and paratactic poetics, he achieves the "vertical dimension" (*SL* 316).

13. In a striking article written after this essay was completed, Peter Nicholls traces Oppen's (1969) meditations on the scandals of The Living Theater's confrontational theatrics and Oppen's critique of the concept avant-garde for its military metaphor, its stylistic pretensions, and its failure to offer serious challenges to the status quo (Nicholls 2005).

14. Blake's poem "from Milton" beginning "And did those feet in ancient times." That Oppen is a kind of meditative poet about class might explain why he (mis)cites George Herbert's anti-Platonic pastoral "Jordan (I)" ("Shepherds are good people let them sing" [*NCP* 250] for "Shepherds are honest people; let them sing"); that he is a kind of revolutionary poet suggests why he miscites Shelley (?) (Oppen's "of the world's deed this is the young age" [*NCP* 240] derives possibly from *Hellas:* "The world's great age begins anew"); that he is a poet of essences of insight explains his Western Wind citation; that he has a scrupulous, brilliant aphoristic quality and a social vision might explain why Blake was so important to him. These were talismans.

15. There is even a curious coincidence of dates, for 1958 was a turning point: Oppen returned to poetry after interior and exterior exile, after choices of other work.

16. This is akin to Oppen's refusal to commodify himself immediately after winning the Pulitzer Prize for Poetry in 1969, although that prize offered the potential for some fame.

17. The twentieth-plus century keeps on exposing us. The satellite, a stunning and moderately positive event, is just one more of the events of the twentieth century that Celan explicitly says have made him shelterless—exposed. Those "called" to look upward in earlier times could look at the stars without ambient light, without airplanes, without the (evocative) satellites of human science and militarism. Oppen was quite stunned by the moon landing, by the threats of military prowess he saw immediately in it.

18. All of Oppen on prosody is about this. See "note by note the prosody carries the relation of things and the sequence" (Oppen 1984, 26). Important remarks on prosody and the line occur in the Dembo interview:

> I do believe in a form in which there is a sense of the whole line, not just its ending. Then there's the sense of the relation between lines, the relation in their length; there is a sense of the relation of the speed, of the alterations and momentum of the poem, the feeling when it's done that this has been rounded. . . . The meaning of a poem is in the cadences and the shape of the lines and the pulse of the thought which is given by those lines. The meaning of many lines will be changed—one's understanding of the lines will be

> altered—if one changes the line-ending. It's not just the line-ending as punctuation but as separating the connections of the progression of thought in such a way that the understanding of the line would be changed if one altered the line division. And I don't mean [line break as] just a substitute for the comma; I mean with which phrase the word is most intimately connected—that kind of thing. (Oppen 1969, 167)

19. Benjamin 1999, 462. The material is rather similar to the sense of the image that Pound offered in 1913 but adds a temporal aspect that does rather transform it. "It's not that what is past casts its light on what is present, or what is present its light on what is past; rather, image is that wherein what has been comes together in a flash with the now to form a constellation." Image is the crystallization of historical forces or temporal forces otherwise in movement.

20. In the same way the Benjaminian word *constellation* offers the interplay between elements in a field poetics or a multiple array of a thicket of materials.

21. "Only dialectical images are genuine images (that is, not archaic); and the place where one encounters them is language" (Benjamin 1999, 462). *Not archaic* means "genuinely historical" (Benjamin 1999, 463).

22. Here one could comment how in later Oppen the modular movement of lines and materials from site to site (keeping the poems experimentally unfinished or open) is a kind of indication of the force of thinking temporally with the words for Oppen. Thus, at the end of his career poems float into each other, something discussed by Michael Davidson at several junctures (see *NCP* xl; Davidson 1997).

Chapter 10. On *Drafts*

1. Hank Lazer's acute consideration of "Writing" in the context of my turn toward *Drafts* proved presciently accurate (Lazer 1996, 34–59).

Chapter 11. Haibun

1. Fraser penetratingly names these issues of "authority and fluency" (Fraser 2000, 2).

2. Many of the objectivist poets whom I was reading also did something odd to "the" lyric, at least via seriality—its arguments by vector and its deferral of closure, and as well with their social arousals and complex responsibilities to those arousals.

3. Page duBois sums up the argument about the "invention" of nontribal, non-oikos, nonheroic individual subjectivity in Sappho, for she and her contemporaries "are among the first to inhabit fully the first person singular" with emphasis on the play of consciousness, sexual desire, and pleasure (duBois 1995, 6). For duBois this invention of the lyric is accomplished in a critical relationship to the Attic culture of discipline, austerity, masculinity, drawing on rhetorics and interests known as

"Asiatic"—from the East (duBois 1995, 26, 170–77). Her discussion of "akra"—"high moments" rupturing normal time occurs on 66.

4. In the course of planning for a set of seminars on "The Lyric," held at the American Comparative Literature Association 2005 Annual Meeting, Jonathan Culler made the carefully limiting claim that the "short non-narrative poem is an identifiable form" (email, Sep. 2, 2004).

5. The Oppen citation, unidentified in the essay, comes from the early poem called "From Disaster," whose first stanza reads:

> Ultimately the air
> Is bare sunlight where must be found
> The lyric valuables.
>
> (Oppen 2002, 50)

6. Derek Attridge quotes Steiner (1978) in the course of a penetrating critique of the universalizing, ahistorical tendencies in later Jakobson. Jakobson's indelible formulation is as follows:

> What is the indispensable feature inherent in any piece of poetry? To answer this question we must recall the two basic modes of arrangement used in [all] verbal behavior, *selection* and *combination.* If "child" is the topic of the message, the speaker selects one among the extant, more or less similar nouns like child, kid, youngster, tot, all of them equivalent in a certain respect, and then, to comment on this topic, he may select one of the semantically cognate verbs—sleeps, dozes, nods, naps. Both chosen words combine in the speech chain. The selection is produced on the basis of equivalence, similarity and dissimilarity, synonymity and antonymity, while the combination, the build-up of the sequence, is based on contiguity. *The poetic function projects the principle of equivalence from the axis of selection into the axis of combination.* (Jakobson 1987, 71)

This is certainly a shorthand way of understanding that X marks the spot of any given word in a poem, but it scants the creation of a mesh or network or set of calibrated balances of such X-spots as the whole poem, which is another set of tasks and judgments undertaken in writing poetry. It seems pertinent to make plural the famous word *axis* in Jakobson because the notion that there is one axis of selection, instead of a braid of multiple decisions and influences on selections (personal, regional, theoretical, etymological, ideological, discursive), and the sense that there is one axis of combination, instead of a variety of braided judgments (e.g., syntactic, asyntactic, conventional, forensic, generic, modal) making combinations, seems inaccurate to the continuous pressure of calibrated choices and the push-pull within one "axis" made in writing a poetic text.

7. The first of these quotations was said by Alfred Stieglitz in 1915, when he first

saw the work of Georgia O'Keeffe. The next three are excerpted from "About Myself," a catalogue statement that O'Keeffe made in 1939. All are recorded in Pollitzer 1988, xiii, 226, 229.

8. This formulation plays with the assignment of the earlier version of this essay as a contribution to the book *H.D. and Poets After,* concerning "H.D.'s influence on contemporary American poetry" (Hollenberg 2000, xiv).

9. Also Lucy Freibert, Susan Gubar—and other feminist poets or poet critics—Denise Levertov, Beverly Dahlen, Adrienne Rich, and then Barbara Guest.

10. Robert Duncan and Lawrence Dembo had noticed, as well as Vincent Quinn, Joseph Riddel, Norman Holmes Pearson, and Denise Levertov. And they knew the H.D. of majority.

11. Some years after, Adalaide Morris has this to say about the carping, fallback position denouncing the plausibility of H.D.'s importance: that the desire to claim a writer as "great" is a useful and strategic move "to those attempting to get a writer back into print, into select anthologies, or, more simply, into . . . the conversation" (Morris 2003, 13). It is (pace Rainey 1991) not a calibratible measurement. The issue is to what conversations does thinking about H.D. contribute? What cultural meanings and stances does her work foreground? What, in Morris's words, are "the cultural links generated within her poetic language"? (Morris 2003, 13).

12. To track the origins of *Drafts* justly, I want to note that I was reading not only the modernists but certain of my contemporaries: the *HOW(ever)* cohort: Beverly Dahlen, Kathleen Fraser, Frances Jaffer, and some others at various times in the early-to-mid-1980s and forward: Rae Armantrout, Michael Palmer, Robert Duncan, Ron Silliman, Susan Howe, Bob Perelman, Robin Blaser, Charles Bernstein, Lyn Hejinian, Clayton Eshleman.

13. Two striking studies of H.D.'s sound occur in Ostriker 1983 and Morris 2003.

Chapter 12. Inside the Middle of a Long Poem

1. I would like to acknowledge Chris McCreary, Dan Featherston, and Jeanne Heuving for their desires to conduct interviews about my project; graduate students in a spring 2003, Temple University course on the long poem, including Emily Abendroth, Matt Chambers, Jo Grudziak, Jennifer Lowenthal, and Sharon Nowak; Kim Bernstein for a letter in which she said "are you literally midbook? I'm curious about your relationship to the concept of the 'whole' thing of it"; Burt Hatlen, who said, "Pound!?" Ron Silliman for his example; and Bob Perelman for his question.

2. Barrett Watten has traced the relationship between aesthetic and political choices for the emergence of Language poetry in the 1960s in ways that puts the question of "a political genealogy" squarely on the critical agenda for all poets, not just for movements, and not simply for poets choosing explicitly political messages as their mode (Watten 2002, 139).

3. Ron Silliman's paper "'As to Violin Music'" opened the issue of time in long poems for me.

4. To have generic mix—contradictions among genres, cunning and commenting self-consciousness about genres, hybridity, the heterogeneric—is simply to have a lot of "laws" (conventions of use, histories of poems in which certain tasks are taken up). This is not lawlessness except if one is uncomfortable with contradictions and multiple, even competing, genres. That Kamboureli's list of genres is also more limited than it need be can be attributed to the specific contemporary texts she sets in her taxonomy.

5. See Pound 2004.

6. This is the meaning of Oppen's challenge, concerning the use of poetry as a mode of thought and a way to evaluate its conclusions, in a note about Pound that ends with a direct address to him: "Pound, the encyclopedic, didn't speak of the gas chambers. Why not? Possible to imagine that he approved them. But why did he not speak of them?? . . . TEST it by poetry, Ezra: write about the gas chambers, write of the children in the gas chambers" (Oppen 1989, 22).

7. "Pound . . . grew [over the years] to justify his uses of juxtaposition and fragmentation—tactics after all used by many modernists—by their political usefulness to select and train [fascist] cadres. Therefore the tragedy of Pound, who staked too little on his poem as poem and too much on [his] narrow understanding of the historical realities with which he was confronted" (DuPlessis 1981, 141).

8. The reader of Pound, finding moments of austere, lyric language amid encoded unclarity, hypercathects to this understandable material in ways that parallel the impact of the emperor on the peasants, in "gratitude and obedience" (Perelman 1994, 62).

9. *Drafts* is certainly more than an act of disidentification, but it may certainly be that. In several particular poems there are direct allusions to Pound: "Draft XXX: Fosse," "Draft 57: Workplace: Nekuia," and "Draft 61: Pyx." In these particular works *Drafts* explicitly positions itself as not-Cantos.

10. This is cited from the version of "A Visiting Card" in Pound's *Selected Prose*, arguments and aperçus written and published in Italian in 1942 and then in a translation by Peter Russell in 1952. This sentence and four other paragraphs have been excised in Pound 1960b, 58. That is, the version of "A Visiting Card" published in *Impact* excises four paragraphs criticizing Eliot's *After Strange Gods* and includes several anti-Semitic remarks, such as the statement I cited about the "hebraic alphabet" (Pound 1973, 320; see Pound 1960b, 58).

References

Abraham, Nicolas, and Maria Torok. 1994. *The Shell and the Kernel: Renewals of Psychoanalysis.* Vol. 1. Trans. and ed. Nicholas T. Rand. Chicago: University of Chicago Press.

Adorno, Theodor. 1974. *Minima Moralia: Reflections from Damaged Life.* Trans. E. F. N. Jephcott. London: Verso.

———. 1981a. *In Search of Wagner.* London: Verso.

———. 1981b. *Prisms.* Trans. Samuel Weber and Shierry Weber. Cambridge, MA: MIT Press.

———. 1991. *Notes to Literature.* Vol. 1. Trans. Shierry Weber Nicholsen. New York: Columbia University Press.

———. 1992. *Notes to Literature.* Vol. 2. Trans. Shierry Weber Nicholsen. New York: Columbia University Press.

———. 1997. *Aesthetic Theory.* Trans. Robert Hullot-Kentor. Minneapolis: University of Minnesota Press.

———. 2000. *The Adorno Reader.* Ed. Brian O'Connor. Oxford: Blackwell.

Allen, Donald, ed. 1960. *The New American Poetry, 1945–1960.* New York: Grove Press.

Allen, Donald, and Warren Tallman, eds. 1973. *The Poetics of the New American Poetry.* New York: Grove Press.

Atkins, G. Douglas. 1992. *Estranging the Familiar: Toward a Revitalized Critical Writing.* Athens: University of Georgia Press.

Attridge, Derek. 1987. "Closing Statement: Linguistics and Poetics in Retrospect." In *The Linguistics of Writing: Arguments between Language and Literature,* ed. Nigel Fabb, Derek Attridge, Alan Durant, and Colin MacCabe, 15–32. New York: Methuen.

Baldick, Chris. 1991. *The Concise Oxford Dictionary of Literary Terms.* Oxford: Oxford University Press.

Barthes, Roland. 1975. *The Pleasure of the Text.* Trans. Richard Miller. New York: Hill and Wang.

Beach, Christopher, ed. 1998. *Artifice and Indeterminacy: An Anthology of New Poetics.* Tuscaloosa: University of Alabama Press.

Beauvoir, Simone de. 1953. *The Second Sex.* Trans. and ed. H. M. Parshley. New York: Knopf.

Belsey, Catherine. 2000. "Writing as a Feminist." In *Feminisms at a Millennium,* ed. Judith A. Howard and Carolyn Allen, 158–61. Chicago: University of Chicago Press.

Belton, Robert J. 1995. *The Be-Ribboned Bomb: The Image of Woman in Male Surrealist Art.* Calgary: University of Calgary Press.

Benjamin, Walter. 1969. *Illuminations.* Trans. Harry Zohn. New York: Schocken Books.

———. 1989. "N [Re: The Theory of Knowledge, Theory of Progress]," trans. Leigh Hafrey and Richard Sieburth. In *Benjamin: Philosophy, Aesthetics, History,* ed. Gary Smith, 43–83. Chicago: University of Chicago Press.

———. 1999. *The Arcades Project.* Trans. Howard Eiland and Kevin McLaughlin. Cambridge, MA: Harvard University Press.

Bennett, James. 1989. "The Essay in Recent Anthologies of Literary Criticism." *SubStance* 18, no. 3:105–11.

Bensmaïa, Réda. 1987. *The Barthes Effect: The Essay as Reflective Text.* Trans. Pat Fedkiew. Minneapolis: University of Minnesota Press.

Benveniste, Emil. 1966. *Problems in General Linguistics.* Trans. Mary Elizabeth Meek. Coral Gables: University Press of Florida.

Bernstein, Charles. 1986. *Content's Dream: Essays, 1975–1984.* Los Angeles: Sun & Moon Press.

———. 1992. "The Second War and Postmodern Memory." In *A Poetics,* 193–217. Cambridge, MA: Harvard University Press.

———. 1999. *My Way: Speeches and Poems.* Chicago: University of Chicago Press.

Bernstein, J. M. 1997. "Why Rescue Semblance? Metaphysical Experience and the Possibility of Ethics." In *The Semblance of Subjectivity: Essays in Adorno's Aesthetic Theory,* ed. Tom Huhn and Lambert Zuidervaart, 177–212. Cambridge, MA: MIT Press.

Blanchot, Maurice. 1986. *The Writing of the Disaster.* Trans. Ann Smock. Lincoln: University of Nebraska Press.

Bloch, Ernst, Georg Lukács, Bertolt Brecht, Walter Benjamin, Theodor Adorno. 1977. *Aesthetics and Politics.* London: New Left Books.

Bold, Alan. 1979. *The Ballad.* London: Methuen.

Boym, Svetlana. 1991. *Death in Quotation Marks: Cultural Myths of the Modern Poet.* Cambridge, MA: Harvard University Press.

Braidotti, Rosi. 1994. *Nomadic Subjects: Embodiment and Sexual Difference in Contemporary Feminist Theory.* New York: Columbia University Press.

Brandt, Warren. 1986. *Nudes.* New York: The Arts Publisher.

Breslin, Glenna. 1990. "Lorine Niedecker: Composing a Life." In *Revealing Lives:*

Autobiography, Biography, and Gender, ed. Susan Groag Bell and Marilyn Yalom, 141–53. Albany: State University of New York Press.

Breslin, James. 1984. *From Modern to Contemporary: American Poetry, 1945–1965.* Chicago: University of Chicago Press.

Breton, André. 1969. *Manifestoes of Surrealism.* Trans. Richard Seaver and Helen R. Lane. Ann Arbor: University of Michigan Press.

Buchloh, Benjamin H. D., ed. 1988. *Broodthaers: Writings, Interviews, Photographs.* Cambridge, MA: MIT Press.

Burke, Carolyn. 1996. *Becoming Modern: The Life of Mina Loy.* New York: Farrar, Straus and Giroux.

Bush, Ronald. 1990. "Ezra Pound." In *The Gender of Modernism*, ed. Bonnie Kime Scott, 353–59. Bloomington: Indiana University Press.

Butler, Judith. 2004. *Undoing Gender.* New York: Routledge.

Butrym, Alexander, ed. 1989. *Essays on the Essay: Redefining the Genre.* Athens: University of Georgia Press.

Buuck, David. 1999. "Against Masculinist Privilege." *Tripwire* 3 (summer): 24–35.

Campbell, David A., ed. 1982. *The Greek Lyric.* Vol. 4. Cambridge, MA: Harvard University Press.

Campbell, J. L., and Francis Collinson, eds. 1981. *Hebridean Folksongs.* Vol. 3. Oxford: Clarendon Press.

Carroll, David. 1990. Foreword to Lyotard, *Heidegger and "the jews,"* vii–xxix.

Caserio, Robert. 1992. "The Novel as a Novel Experiment in Statement: The Anticanonical Example of H. G. Wells." In *Decolonizing Tradition: New Views of Twentieth-Century "British" Literary Canons*, ed. Karen Lawrence, 88–109. Urbana: University of Illinois Press.

Caws, Mary Ann. 1991. "Seeing the Surrealist Woman: We Are a Problem." In Caws, Kuenzli, and Raaberg 1991:11–16.

———. 1997. *The Surrealist Look: An Erotics of Encounter.* Cambridge, MA: MIT Press.

———. 2000. *Picasso's Weeping Woman: The Life and Art of Dora Maar.* Boston: Little, Brown.

Caws, Mary Ann, Rudolf Kuenzli, and Gwen Raaberg, eds. 1991. *Surrealism and Women.* Cambridge, MA: MIT Press.

Celan, Paul. 1995. *Breathturn [Atemwende].* Trans. Pierre Joris. Los Angeles: Sun & Moon Press.

Chadwick, Whitney. 1985. *Women Artists and the Surrealist Movement.* Boston: Little, Brown.

Chambers, Anne. 1986. *The Practical Guide to Marbling Paper.* New York: Thames and Hudson.

Cixous, Hélène. 1980. "The Laugh of the Medusa," trans. Keith Cohen and Paula Cohen. In *New French Feminisms*, ed. Elaine Marks and Isabelle de Courtivron, 245–64. Amherst: University of Massachusetts Press.

———. 1986. "Sorties: Out and Out: Attacks/Ways Out/Forays." In *The Newly Born*

Woman, by Hélène Cixous and Catherine Clément, 63–132. Trans. Betsy Wing. Foreword by Sandra Gilbert. Minneapolis: University of Minnesota Press.

Clark, Tom. 1991. *Charles Olson: The Allegory of a Poet's Life*. New York: Norton.

Cole, Barbara. 2002. "Open Letters: Feminism From & To." *Open Letter: A Canadian Journal of Writing and Theory*. 11th ser., no. 4 (spring): 33–43.

Collecott, Diana. 1989. "H.D. and Mass Observation." *Line* 13: 153–61.

Corman, Cid, trans. 2003. *One Man's Moon: Poems by Bashō and Other Japanese Poets*. Frankfort, KY: Gnomon.

Creeley, Robert. 1989. *The Collected Essays*. Berkeley: University of California Press.

Culler, Jonathan. 1981. *The Pursuit of Signs*. Ithaca, NY: Cornell University Press.

———. 1995. "Deconstruction and the Lyric." In *Deconstruction is/in America: A New Sense of the Political*, ed. Anselm Haverkamp, 41–51. New York: New York University Press.

———. 2000. "The Literary in Theory." In *What's Left of Theory*, ed. Judith Butler, John Guillory, and Kendall Thomas, 273–92. New York: Routledge.

Cullingford, Elizabeth Butler. 1993. *Gender and History in Yeats's Love Poetry*. Cambridge, UK: Cambridge University Press.

Curiger, Bice. 1989. *Meret Oppenheim: Defiance in the Face of Freedom*. Cambridge, MA: MIT Press.

Davidson, Michael. 1989. *The San Francisco Renaissance: Poetics and Community at Mid-Century*. Cambridge, UK: Cambridge University Press.

———. 1995. "Compulsory Homosociality: Charles Olson, Jack Spicer, and the Gender of Poetics." In *Cruising the Performative: Interventions into the Representation of Ethnicity, Nationality, and Sexuality*, ed. Sue-Ellen Case, Philip Brett, and Susan Leigh Foster, 197–216. Bloomington: Indiana University Press.

———. 1997. *Ghostlier Demarcations: Modern Poetry and the Material Word*. Berkeley: University of California Press.

———. 2004. *Guys like Us: Citing Masculinity in Cold War Poetics*. Chicago: University of Chicago Press.

DeKoven, Marianne. 1989. "Male Signature, Female Aesthetic: The Gender Politics of Experimental Writing." In *Breaking the Sequence: Women's Experimental Fiction*, ed. Ellen Friedman and Miriam Fuchs, 72–81. Princeton, NJ: Princeton University Press.

De Lauretis, Teresa. 1987. *Technologies of Gender: Essays on Theory, Film, and Fiction*. Bloomington: Indiana University Press.

Deleuze, Gilles. 1988. *Spinoza: Practical Philosophy*. Trans. Robert Hurley. San Francisco: City Lights Books.

Deleuze, Gilles, and Félix Guattari. 1986. *Kafka: Toward a Minor Literature*. Trans. Dana Polan. Foreword by Réda Bensmaïa. Minneapolis: University of Minnesota Press.

Dent, Peter, ed. 1983. *The Full Note: Lorine Niedecker*. Devon, UK: Interim Press.

DeSalvo, Louise. 1989. *Virginia Woolf: The Impact of Childhood Sexual Abuse on Her Life and Work*. Boston: Beacon Press.

DiBattista, Maria, and Lucy McDiarmid, eds. 1996. *High and Low Moderns: Literature and Culture, 1889–1939*. New York: Oxford University Press.

Dickie, Margaret. 1986. *On the Modernist Long Poem*. Iowa City: University of Iowa Press.

Dickinson, Emily. 1960. *The Complete Poems of Emily Dickinson*. Ed. Thomas H. Johnson. Boston: Little, Brown.

Dienstfrey, Patricia, and Brenda Hillman, eds. 2003. *The Grand Permission: New Writings on Poetics and Motherhood*. Middletown, CT: Wesleyan University Press.

Diggory, Terence. 1993. *Grace Hartigan and the Poets: Paintings and Prints*. Saratoga Springs, NY: Schick Art Gallery, Skidmore College.

Diggory, Terence, and Stephen Paul Miller, eds. 2000. *The Scene of My Selves: New Work on New York School Poets*. Orono, ME: National Poetry Foundation.

Dinnerstein, Dorothy. 1976. *The Mermaid and the Minotaur: Sexual Arrangements and Human Malaise*. New York: Harper & Row.

Discrimination against Women. 1970. Hearings before the Special Subcommittee on Education of the Committee on Education and Labor, House of Representatives, 91st Cong., 2nd sess., on Section 805 of H.R. 16098, to prohibit discrimination against women in federally assisted programs and in equal employment in education. June 17, 19, 26, 29, 30, 1970. 2 vols. Washington: U.S. Government Printing Office.

Doane, Mary Ann. 1982. "Film and the Masquerade: Theorising the Female Spectator." *Screen* 23, nos. 3–4 (Sep.–Oct.): 74–87.

Drabble, Margaret. 1985. *Oxford Companion to English Literature*. 5th ed. Oxford: Oxford University Press.

Drucker, Johanna. 1992. "Visual Pleasure: A Feminist Perspective." *M/E/A/N/I/N/G/*, no. 14 (May): 3–11.

duBois, Page. 1995. *Sappho Is Burning*. Chicago: University of Chicago Press.

Duncan, Robert. 1967. "*The H.D. Book*, Part One: Chapter 6. Rites of Participation." *Caterpillar* 1 (Oct.): 6–29.

———. 1968a. "*The H.D. Book*, Part One: Chapter 5. Occult Matters." *Stony Brook Poetics Journal* 1/2 (fall): 4–19.

———. 1968b. "*The H.D. Book*, Part One: Chapter 6. Rites of Participation." *Caterpillar* 2 (Jan.): 124–54.

———. 1969. "*The H.D. Book*, Part Two: Nights and Days, Chapter 2." *Caterpillar* 6:16–38.

———. 1979. "*The H.D. Book*, Part Two: Nights and Days, Chapter 9." *Chicago Review* 30, no. 3 (winter): 37–88.

———. 1983. "Nights and Days: Part II, Chapter 10 [1961]." In *The H.D. Book. Ironwood* 11, no. 2 (#22) (fall): 43–64.

DuPlessis, Rachel Blau. 1979a. "Psyche, or Wholeness." Massachusetts Review 20, no. 1 (spring): 77–96.

———. 1979b. "The Critique of Consciousness and Myth in Levertov, Rich, and Rukeyser." In Gilbert and Gubar, *Shakespeare's Sisters*, 280–300.

———. 1980. *Wells.* New York: Montemora. Duration Press Online Out of Print Book Archives, 1999. http://www.durationpress.com/archives/rduplessis/wells.pdf (accessed Aug. 20, 2005).

———. 1981. "Objectivist Poetics and Political Vision: A Study of Oppen and Pound." In *George Oppen: Man and Poet,* ed. Burton Hatlen, 123–48. Orono, ME: National Poetry Foundation.

———. 1985. *Writing Beyond the Ending: Narrative Strategies of Twentieth-Century Women Writers.* Bloomington: Indiana University Press.

———. 1986. *H.D.: The Career of That Struggle.* Bloomington: Indiana University Press.

———. 1987. "'The familiar / becomes extreme': George Oppen and Silence." *North Dakota Quarterly* 55, no. 4 (fall 1987): 18–26; special issue ed. Sherman Paul.

———. [1990] 2006. *The Pink Guitar: Writing as Feminist Practice.* New York: Routledge. Repr. Tuscaloosa: University of Alabama Press.

———. 2001. *Drafts 1–38, Toll.* Middletown, CT: Wesleyan University Press.

———. 2004. *Drafts. Drafts 39–57, Pledge, with Draft, Unnumbered: Précis.* Cambridge, UK: Salt Publishing.

DuPlessis, Rachel Blau, and Peter Quartermain. 1999. Introduction to DuPlessis and Quartermain, eds., 1999:1–22.

DuPlessis, Rachel Blau, and Peter Quartermain, eds. 1999. *The Objectivist Nexus: Essays in Cultural Poetics.* Tuscaloosa: University of Alabama Press.

DuPlessis, Rachel Blau, and Ann Snitow. 1998. *The Feminist Memoir Project: Voices from Women's Liberation.* New York: Three Rivers Press.

Easthope, Antony. 1983. *Poetry as Discourse.* London: Methuen.

Echols, Alice. 1989. *Daring to Be Bad: Radical Feminism in America, 1967–1975.* Minneapolis: University of Minnesota Press.

Edmunds, J. M., ed. 1922. *Lyra Graeca.* Vol. 3. Cambridge, MA: Harvard University Press.

Eliot, T. S. 1963. *Collected Poems, 1909–1962.* London: Faber and Faber.

Ellmann, Mary. 1968. *Thinking about Women.* New York: Harcourt Brace and World.

Ellmann, Richard. 1961. *Yeats: The Man and the Masks.* London: Faber and Faber.

Evans, Steve. 2001. "Introductory Note: After Patriarchal Poetry: Feminism and the Contemporary Avant-Garde." *differences* 12, no. 2 (summer): i–v.

Farr, Florence. [1907–8] 1996. "Ibsen's Women [Six Essays]." In DiBattista and McDiarmid 1996:91–106.

———. 1910. *Modern Woman: Her Intentions.* London: Frank Palmer.

——— [a.k.a. Emery]. 1912. *The Solemnization of Jacklin: Some Adventures on the Search for Reality.* London: A. C. Fifield.

Feldman, Jessica R. 2001. "Modernism's Victorian Bric-à-Brac." *Modernism/Modernity* 8, no. 3 (Sep.): 453–70.

Felski, Rita. 1989. *Beyond Feminist Aesthetics.* Cambridge, MA: Harvard University Press.

———. 1995. *The Gender of Modernity.* Cambridge, MA: Harvard University Press.

———. 2003. *Literature after Feminism.* Chicago: University of Chicago Press.

Felstiner, John. 1995. *Paul Celan: Poet, Survivor, Jew.* New Haven, CT: Yale University Press.

Ferguson, Margaret, Mary Jo Salter, Jon Stallworthy, eds. 1996. *The Norton Anthology of Poetry.* 4th ed. New York: Norton.

Fraser, Kathleen. 1993. "The Tradition of Marginality." In *Where We Stand: Women Poets on Literary Tradition,* ed. Sharon Bryan, 52–66. New York: Norton.

———. 1994. "The Jump: Editing HOW(ever)." *Chain* 1 (spring/summer): 43–45.

———. 2000. *Translating the Unspeakable: Poetry and the Innovative Necessity.* Tuscaloosa: University of Alabama Press.

Friedan, Betty. 1963. *The Feminine Mystique.* New York: Norton.

Friedman, Susan Stanford. 1975. "Who Buried H.D.? A Poet, Her Critics, and Her Place in 'The Literary Tradition.'" *College English* 36 (March): 801–14.

———. 1981. *Psyche Reborn: The Emergence of H.D.* Bloomington: Indiana University Press.

———. 1991. "Post/Post Structuralist Feminist Criticism: The Politics of Recuperation and Negotiation." *New Literary History* 22, no. 2 (spring): 465–90.

———. 1998. *Mappings: Feminism and the Cultural Geographies of Encounter.* Princeton, NJ: Princeton University Press.

Friedman, Susan Stanford, and Rachel Blau DuPlessis, eds. 1990. *Signets: Reading H.D.* Madison: University of Wisconsin Press.

Frost, Elisabeth A. 2003. *The Feminist Avant-Garde in American Poetry.* Iowa City: University of Iowa Press.

Frye, Marilyn. 1992. *Willful Virgin: Essays in Feminism.* Freedom, CA: Crossing Press.

Gallop, Jane. 1982. *The Daughter's Seduction.* Ithaca, NY: Cornell University Press.

Gedo, Mary Mathews. 1980. *Picasso: Art as Autobiography.* Chicago: University of Chicago Press.

Gerould, Gordon Hall. 1932. *The Ballad of Tradition.* Oxford: Clarendon Press.

Gilbert, Sandra, and Susan Gubar. 1979. *The Madwoman in the Attic: The Woman Writer and the Nineteenth-Century Literary Imagination.* New Haven, CT: Yale University Press.

———, eds. 1979. *Shakespeare's Sisters: Feminist Essays on Women Poets.* Bloomington: Indiana University Press.

Gill, Stephen. 1989. *William Wordsworth: A Life.* Oxford: Clarendon Press.

Glissant, Edouard. 1989. *Caribbean Discourse: Selected Essays.* Trans. J. Michael Dash. Charlottesville: University Press of Virginia.

Godard, Barbara, ed. 1994. *Collaboration in the Feminine: Writings on Women and Culture from Tessera.* Toronto: Second Story Press.

Goldwater. Marge. 1989. Introduction to *Marcel Broodthaers.* Minneapolis: Walker Art Center; and New York: Rizzoli.

Good, Graham. 1988. *The Observing Self: Rediscovering the Essay.* London: Routledge.

Greene, Gayle, and Coppélia Kahn. 1993. *Changing Subjects: The Making of Feminist Literary Criticism.* London: Routledge.

Grossman, Allen. 1989–90. "Orpheus/Philomela: Subjection and Mastery in the Founding Stories of Poetic Production and in the Logic of Our Practice." *TriQuarterly* 77 (winter): 229–48.

———. 1992. "Summa Lyrica: A Primer of the Commonplaces in Speculative Poetics." *The Sighted Singer: Two Works on Poetry for Readers and Writers.* Baltimore: Johns Hopkins University Press.

Guest, Barbara. 1973. *Moscow Mansions.* New York: Viking.

———. 1984. "Working Notes." *HOW(ever)* 1, no. 3 (Feb.): 7.

———. 1986. "In the Shadow of Surrealism." Typescript.

———. 1989. *Fair Realism.* Los Angeles: Sun & Moon Press.

———. 1992. "Barbara Guest: An Interview by Mark Hillringhouse." *American Poetry Review* 21, no. 4 (July/August): 23–30.

———. 1995. *Selected Poems.* Los Angeles: Sun & Moon Press.

———. 1996. *Quill, Solitary APPARITION.* Sausalito, CA.: Post-Apollo Press.

———. 2003a. *Forces of Imagination: Writing on Writing.* Berkeley: Kelsey St. Press.

———. 2003b. *Dürer in the Window: Reflexions on Art.* New York: Roof Books.

———. 2004a. "Clearing the Ordinary from the Room: An Interview with Barbara Guest." Conducted by Sarah Rosenthal. *Rain Taxi* 9, no. 2 (summer 2004): 30–31.

———. 2004b. "Barbara Guest and Kathleen Fraser in Conversation with Elisabeth Frost and Cynthia Hogue." *Jacket* 25 (Feb.): http://jacketmagazine.com/25/guest-iv.html (accessed June 1, 2005).

Gummere, Francis B. 1907. *The Popular Ballad.* Boston: Houghton, Mifflin.

Harryman, Carla. 1995. *There Never Was a Rose without a Thorn.* San Francisco: City Lights Books.

Harshav, Benjamin. 1990. *The Meaning of Yiddish.* Berkeley: University of California Press.

Hartman, Geoffrey H. 1987. *Wordsworth's Poetry: 1787–1814.* Cambridge, MA: Harvard University Press.

Hatlen, Burton, ed. 1981. *George Oppen: Man and Poet.* Orono, ME: National Poetry Foundation.

H.D. 1960. *Bid Me to Live (A Madrigal).* New York: Grove Press.

———. 1974. *Tribute to Freud.* Boston: David R. Godine.

———. 1981. *HERmione.* New York: New Directions.

———. 1983. *Collected Poems, 1912–1944.* Ed. Louis L. Martz. New York: New Directions.

———. 1986. "H.D. by Delia Alton." *Iowa Review* 16 (fall): 174–221.

———. 1992. *Paint It To-Day.* Ed. Cassandra Laity. New York: New York University Press.

———. 1998a. *Trilogy.* New York: New Directions.

———. 1998b. *The Gift: The Complete Text.* Ed. Jane Augustine. Gainesville: University Press of Florida.

Hejinian, Lyn. 1987. *My Life.* Los Angeles: Sun & Moon Press.

———. 2000. *The Language of Inquiry.* Berkeley: University of California Press.

———, ed. 2004. *The Best American Poetry, 2004*. New York: Scribner Poetry.

Heller, Michael. 1993. "Oppen and Stevens: Reflections on the Lyrical and the Philosophical." *Sagetrieb* 12, no. 3 (winter): 13–32.

Heuving, Jeanne. 2002. "'A Dialogue about Love [. . . in] the Modern World'/Tracking Leslie Scalapino." *How2* 1, no. 7 (spring): http://www.scc.rutgers.edu/however/v1_7_200/current/readings/heuving.shtm (accessed March 25, 2005).

Hill, Bridget. 1989. *Women, Work, and Sexual Politics in Eighteenth-Century England*. Oxford: Basil Blackwell.

Hillman, Brenda. 1996. "The Artful Dare: Barbara Guest's *Selected Poems*." *Talisman* 16 (fall): 207–20.

Hinton, Laura, and Cynthia Hogue, eds. 2001. *"We Who 'Love to Be Astonished'": Experimental Women's Writing and Performance Poetics*. Tuscaloosa: University of Alabama Press.

Hollenberg, Donna Krolik, ed. 2000. *H.D. and Poets After*. Iowa City: University of Iowa Press.

Homans, Margaret. 1980. *Women Writers and Poetic Identity: Dorothy Wordsworth, Emily Brontë, and Emily Dickinson*. Princeton, NJ: Princeton University Press.

———. 1985. "'Syllables of Velvet': Dickinson, Rossetti, and the Rhetorics of Sexuality." *Feminist Studies* 11, no. 3 (fall): 569–93.

hooks, bell. 1989. *Talking Back: Thinking Feminist, Thinking Black*. Boston: South End Press.

Houston, R. A. 1989. "Women in the Economy and Society of Scotland, 1500–1800." In *Scottish Society, 1500–1800*, ed. R. A. Houston and I. D. Whyte, 118–47. Cambridge, UK: Cambridge University Press.

Howe, Irving. 1982. *A Margin of Hope: An Intellectual Autobiography*. San Diego: Harcourt Brace Jovanovich.

Howe, Susan. 1985. *My Emily Dickinson*. Berkeley: North Atlantic Books.

———. 1993. *The Birth-Mark: Unsettling the Wilderness in American Literary History*. Hanover, NH: Wesleyan University Press.

Hubert, Renée Riese. 1994. *Magnifying Mirrors: Women, Surrealism, and Partnership*. Lincoln: University of Nebraska Press.

Hunt, Erica. 1990. "Notes for an Oppositional Poetics." In *The Politics of Poetic Form: Poetry and Public Policy*, ed. Charles Bernstein, 197–212. New York: Roof Books.

Irigaray, Luce. [1974] 1985. *Speculum of the Other Woman*. Trans. Gillian Gill. Ithaca, NY: Cornell University Press.

———. [1977] 1985. *This Sex Which Is Not One*. Trans. Catherine Porter with Carolyn Burke. Ithaca, NY: Cornell University Press.

———. [1987] 1991. "The Three Genres," trans. David Macey. In *The Irigaray Reader*, ed. Margaret Whitford, 140–53. Cambridge, UK: Basil Blackwell.

Jakobson, Roman. 1971. *Word and Language*. Vol. 2 of *Selected Writings*. The Hague: Mouton.

———. 1987. *Language in Literature*. Ed. Krystyna Pomorska and Stephen Rudy. Cambridge, MA: Harvard University Press.

Jameson, Fredric. 1981. *The Political Unconscious: Narrative as a Socially Symbolic Act.* Ithaca, NY: Cornell University Press.

Jarrell, Randall. [1954] 1960. *Pictures from an Institution: A Comedy.* New York: Meridian Books.

Jayawardena, Kumari. 1995. *The White Woman's Other Burden: Western Women and South Asia during British Rule.* New York: Routledge.

Jeffreys, Mark. 1995. "Ideologies of the Lyric: A Problem of Genre in Contemporary Anglophone Poetics." *PMLA* 110, no. 2 (March): 196–205.

Jehlen, Myra. 1990. "Gender." In *Critical Terms for Literary Study,* ed. Frank Lentricchia and Thomas McLaughlin, 263–73. Chicago: University of Chicago Press.

Joeres, Ruth-Ellen Boetcher, and Elizabeth Mittman, eds. 1993. *The Politics of the Essay: Feminist Perspectives.* Bloomington: Indiana University Press.

Johnson, Barbara. 1986. *A World of Difference.* Baltimore: Johns Hopkins University Press.

———. 1998. *The Feminist Difference: Literature, Psychoanalysis, Race, and Gender.* Cambridge, MA: Harvard University Press.

Johnson, Josephine. 1975. *Florence Farr: Bernard Shaw's "New Woman."* Totowa, NJ: Rowman and Littlefield.

Jones, Nancy A. 1991. "The Rape of the Rural Muse: Wordsworth's 'The Solitary Reaper' as a Version of Pastourelle." In *Rape and Representation,* ed. Lynn A. Higgins and Brenda R. Silver, 263–77. New York: Columbia University Press.

Joyce, Patrick, ed. 1987. *The Historical Meanings of Work.* Cambridge, UK: Cambridge University Press.

Kamboureli, Smaro. 1991. *On the Edge of Genre: The Contemporary Canadian Long Poem.* Toronto: University of Toronto Press.

Kaplan, Carla. 1996. *The Erotics of Talk: Women's Writing and Feminist Paradigms.* New York: Oxford University Press.

Kaplan, Cora. 1986. *Sea Changes: Culture and Feminism.* London: Verso.

Kaplan, E. Ann. 2000. "Is the Gaze Male?" (1983). In *Feminism and Film,* ed. E. Ann Kaplan, 119–38. Oxford: Oxford University Press.

Kaufman, Robert. 2000. "A Future for Modernism: Barbara Guest's Recent Poetry." *American Poetry Review* 29, no. 4 (July/August): 11–16.

———. 2002. "Aura, Still." *October* 99 (winter): 45–80.

Keats, John. 2002. *Selected Letters of John Keats.* Ed. Grant F. Scott, on texts of Hyder Edward Rollins. Rev. ed. Cambridge, MA: Harvard University Press.

Keenaghan, Eric. 2002. "A Virile Poet in the Borderlands: Wallace Stevens' Reimagining of Race and Masculinity." *Modernism/Modernity* 9, no. 3 (Sept.): 439–62.

Keller, Lynn. 1997. *Forms of Expansion: Recent Long Poems by Women.* Chicago: University of Chicago Press.

Keller, Lynn, and Cristanne Miller, eds. 1994. *Feminist Measures: Soundings in Poetry and Theory.* Ann Arbor: University of Michigan Press.

Kelly, Mary. 1985. *Post-Partum Document.* London: Routledge and Kegan Paul.

Kinnahan, Linda A. 1994. *Poetics of the Feminine: Authority and Literary Tradition in William Carlos Williams, Mina Loy, Denise Levertov, and Kathleen Fraser.* Cambridge, UK: Cambridge University Press.

———. 2004. *Lyric Interventions: Feminism, Experimental Poetry, and Contemporary Discourse.* Iowa City: University of Iowa Press.

Krauss, Rosalind. 1985. "Grids." In *The Originality of the Avant-Garde and Other Modernist Myths,* 151–70. Cambridge, MA: MIT Press.

Kress, Susan. 1997. *Carolyn G. Heilbrun: Feminist in a Tenured Position.* Charlottesville: University Press of Virginia.

Kristeva, Julia. 1981. "Women's Time." *Signs* 7, no. 1 (autumn): 13–35.

Kugelberg, John. 2001. Comments for the Damian Loeb Exhibit (April). New York: Mary Boone Gallery.

Kuhn, Thomas. 1970. *The Structure of Scientific Revolutions.* Chicago: University of Chicago Press.

Laity, Cassandra. 1985a. "W. B. Yeats and Florence Farr: The Influence of the 'New Woman' Actress on Yeats's Changing Images of Women." *Modern Drama* 28 (Dec.): 620–37.

———. 1985b. "From Fatal Woman to New Woman: Yeats's Changing Image of Woman in His Art and Aesthetics." PhD diss., University of Michigan.

Langer, Lawrence L. 1998. *Preempting the Holocaust.* New Haven, CT: Yale University Press.

Lazer, Hank. 1996. *Opposing Poetries.* Vol. 1, *Issues and Institutions;* Vol. 2, *Readings.* Evanston, IL: Northwestern University Press.

———. 1997. "The Lyric Valuables: Soundings, Questions, and Examples." *Modern Language Studies* 27, no. 2 (spring):25–50.

Lecercle, Jean-Jacques. 1990. *The Violence of Language.* London: Routledge.

Lessing, Doris. [1962] 1971. *The Golden Notebook.* New York: Simon and Schuster.

Levitsky, Rachel. 2000. Statement in Belladonna pamphlet.

Litz, A. Walton. 1996. "Florence Farr: A 'Transitional Woman.'" In DiBattista and McDiarmid 1996:85–90.

Litz, A. Walton, and Lawrence Rainey. 2000. "Ezra Pound." *The Cambridge History of Literary Criticism.* Vol. 7, *Modernism and the New Criticism.* Ed. A. Walton Litz, Louis Menand, and Lawrence Rainey. Cambridge, UK: Cambridge University Press.

Longenbach, James. 1988. *Stone Cottage: Pound, Yeats, and Modernism.* New York: Oxford University Press.

Lord, James. 1993. *Picasso and Dora: A Personal Memoir.* New York: Farrar, Straus and Giroux.

Lukács, Georg. 1971. *Soul and Form.* Trans. Anna Bostock. Cambridge, MA: MIT Press.

Lundquist, Sara. 1997. "Reverence and Resistance: Barbara Guest, Ekphrasis, and the Female Gaze." *Contemporary Literature* 38, no. 2 (summer): 260–86.

———. 2002. "Implacable Poet, Purple Birds: The Work of Barbara Guest." In Rankine and Spahr 2002:191–221. Middletown, CT: Wesleyan University Press.

Lyon, Janet. 1999. *Manifestoes: Provocations of the Modern.* Ithaca, NY: Cornell University Press.

Lyotard, Jean-François. 1990. *Heidegger and "the jews."* Trans. Andreas Michel and Mark S. Roberts. Foreword by David Carroll. Minneapolis: University of Minnesota Press.

Mackey, Nathaniel. 1993. "Sound and Sentiment, Sound and Symbol." In *Discrepant Engagement: Dissonance, Cross-Culturality and Experimental Writing,* 231–59. New York: Cambridge University Press.

Mailhot, Laurent. 1983. "The Writing of the Essay," trans. Jay Lutz. In *The Language of Difference: Writing in QUEBEÇ(ois),* ed. Ralph Sarkonak, 74–89. New Haven, CT: Yale University Press.

Mallarmé, Stéphane. 1965. *Mallarmé.* Trans. Anthony Hartley. Baltimore: Penguin.

Marinetti, Filippo Tommaso. 2001. "The Founding and Manifesto of Futurism." In *Manifesto: A Century of Isms,* ed. Mary Ann Caws, 185–89. Lincoln: University of Nebraska Press.

Maud, Ralph, and Sharon Thesen, eds. 1999. *Charles Olson and Frances Boldereff: A Modern Correspondence.* Middletown, CT: Wesleyan University Press.

McCaffery, Steve. 1986. *North of Intention: Critical Writings, 1973–1986.* New York: Roof Books.

———. 1991. *Theory of Sediment.* Vancouver: Talonbooks.

———. 2001. *Prior to Meaning: The Protosemantic and Poetics.* Evanston, IL: Northwestern University Press.

McCaughey, Robert A. 2003. *Stand, Columbia: A History of Columbia University in the City of New York, 1754–2004.* New York: Columbia University Press.

McGann, Jerome. 1991. *The Textual Condition.* Princeton, NJ: Princeton University Press.

Mellor, Anne K. 1995. "British Romanticism, Gender, and Three Women Artists." In *The Consumption of Culture, 1600–1800: Image, Object, Text,* ed. Ann Bermingham and John Brewer, 121–42. London: Routledge.

Middleton, Peter. 1992. *The Inward Gaze: Masculinity and Subjectivity in Modern Culture.* London: Routledge.

———. 1999. "Lorine Niedecker's 'Folk Base' and Her Challenge to the American Avant-Garde." In DuPlessis and Quartermain, eds., 1999:160–88.

Miller, Nancy K. 1991. *Getting Personal: Feminist Occasions and Other Autobiographical Acts.* New York: Routledge.

Millett, Kate. 1970. *Sexual Politics.* Garden City, NY: Doubleday.

Moorman, Mary. 1965. *William Wordsworth, a Biography: The Later Years, 1803–1850.* Oxford: Clarendon Press.

Morris, Adalaide. 2003. *How to Live / What to Do: H.D.'s Cultural Poetics.* Urbana: University of Illinois Press.

Morrison, Toni. 1992. *Playing in the Dark: Whiteness and the Literary Imagination.* Cambridge, MA: Harvard University Press.

Morrison, Yedda, and David Buuck. 1999. "Editors' Notes." *Tripwire* 3 (summer): 1.

Morrisson, Mark. 1996. "Performing the Pure Voice: Elocution, Verse Recitation, and Modernist Poetry in Prewar London." *Modernism/Modernity* 3, no. 3 (Sep.): 25–50.

Mossin, Andrew. 2005. "'In Thicket': Charles Olson, Frances Boldereff, Robert Creeley, and the Crisis of Masculinity at Mid-Century." *Journal of Modern Literature* 28, no. 4 (summer): 13–39.

Mulvey, Laura. [1975] 2000. "Visual Pleasure and Narrative Cinema." In *Feminism and Film,* ed. E. Ann Kaplan, 34–47. Oxford: Oxford University Press.

Myers, John Bernard, ed. 1969. *The Poets of the New York School.* Philadelphia: Graduate School of Fine Arts, University of Pennsylvania; and New York: Gotham Book Mart and Gallery.

Nicholls, Peter. 1995. *Modernisms: A Literary Guide.* Berkeley: University of California Press.

———. 1999. "Of Being Ethical: Reflections on George Oppen." In DuPlessis and Quartermain, eds., 1999:240–53.

———. 2005. "George Oppen: The New or the Avant-Garde?" *Journal of Modern Literature* 28, no. 4 (summer): 1–12.

Niedecker, Lorine. 1946. *New Goose.* Prairie City, IL: Press of James A. Decker.

———. 1981. [Niedecker materials], ed. Cid Corman. *Origin* 16 (July).

———. 1986. *"Between Your House and Mine": The Letters of Lorine Niedecker to Cid Corman, 1960–1970.* Ed. Lisa Pater Faranda. Durham, NC: Duke University Press.

———. 1993. *Niedecker and the Correspondence with Zukofsky, 1931–1970.* Ed. Jenny Penberthy. New York: Cambridge University Press.

———. 2002. *Collected Works.* Ed. Jenny Penberthy. Berkeley: University of California Press.

Nochlin, Linda, and Ann Sutherland Harris. 1976. *Women Artists, 1550–1950.* Los Angeles: Los Angeles County Museum.

Notley, Alice. 1980. *Dr. Williams' Heiresses.* Berkeley, CA: Tuumba.

———. 1996. *The Descent of Alette.* New York: Penguin.

———. 1998. "The Poetics of Disobedience." http://epc.buffalo.edu/authors/notley/disob.html (accessed June 2, 2005).

Notley, Alice, and Edward Foster. 2001–2. "An Interview with Alice Notley." In *The World in Time and Space: Towards a History of Innovative American Poetry in Our Time,* ed. Edward Foster and Joseph Donahue, 526–35. Jersey City: Talisman House.

Olsen, Tillie. [1971] 2003. "One Out of Twelve Women Who Are Writers in our Century." In *Silences,* 22–46. New York: Feminist Press.

Olson, Charles. 1966. *Selected Writings.* Ed. Robert Creeley. New York: New Directions.

———. 1997. *Collected Prose.* Ed. Donald Allen and Benjamin Friedlander. Berkeley: University of California Press.

O'Neil, Elizabeth Murrie. 1994. *The Last Word: Letters between Marcia Nardi and William Carlos Williams.* Iowa City: University of Iowa Press.

Oppen, George. 1962. Review of Ginsberg, Olson, McClure. *Poetry* 110, no. 5 (Aug.): 329–30.

———. [1963] 2003. "The Mind's Own Place." In *The Selected Poems of George Oppen,* ed. Robert Creeley, 173–82. New York: New Directions.

———. 1969. "Interview with George Oppen." Conducted by L. S. Dembo on April 25, 1968. *Contemporary Literature* 10, no. 2 (spring): 159–77.

———. 1984. "Statement on Poetics." *Sagetrieb* 3, no. 3 (winter): 25–27.

———. 1989. "The Circumstances." Ed. Rachel Blau DuPlessis. *Sulfur* 25 (fall): 10–43.

———. 1990. *The Selected Letters of George Oppen.* Ed. Rachel Blau DuPlessis. Durham, NC: Duke University Press.

———. 2002. *New Collected Poems.* Ed. Michael Davidson. Preface by Eliot Weinberger. New York: New Directions.

Ostriker, Alicia Suskin. 1983. *Writing like a Woman.* Ann Arbor: University of Michigan Press.

———. 1986. *Stealing the Language: The Emergence of Women's Poetry in America.* Boston: Beacon Press.

———. 2000. *Dancing at the Devil's Party: Essays on Poetry, Politics, and the Erotic.* Ann Arbor: University of Michigan Press.

Padgett, Ron, and David Shapiro, eds. 1970. *An Anthology of New York Poets.* New York: Random House.

Page, Judith W. 1994. *Wordsworth and the Cultivation of Women.* Berkeley: University of California Press.

Palmer, Michael. 1987. "Lyric Practice (Analytic Lyric?)." Cited by David Levi Strauss. *Acts* 7, copyright page.

Penberthy, Jenny, ed. 1996. *Lorine Niedecker: Woman and Poet.* Orono, ME: National Poetry Foundation.

Perelman, Bob. 1994. *The Trouble with Genius: Reading Pound, Joyce, Stein, and Zukofsky.* Berkeley: University of California Press.

Perloff, Marjorie. 1986. *The Futurist Moment: Avant-Garde, Avant Guerre, and the Language of Rupture.* Chicago: University of Chicago Press.

———. 1991. *Radical Artifice: Writing Poetry in the Age of Media.* Chicago: University of Chicago Press.

———. 2004. *Differentials: Poetry, Poetics, Pedagogy.* Tuscaloosa: University of Alabama Press.

Poe, Edgar Allan. [1846] 1984. "The Philosophy of Composition." In *Poe: Essays and Reviews.* New York: Library of America.

Pollitzer, Anita. 1988. *A Woman on Paper: Georgia O'Keeffe.* New York: Simon and Schuster.

Pollock, Griselda. 1993. "The Politics of Theory: Generations and Geographies: Feminist Theory and the Histories of Art History." *Genders* 17 (fall): 97–120.

———. 1999. *Differencing the Canon: Feminist Desire and the Writing of Art's Histories.* London: Routledge.

Pound, Ezra. 1926. *Personae.* New York: New Directions.

———. 1937. *Polite Essays.* London: Faber and Faber.

———. [1948] 2003. *The Pisan Cantos*. Ed. Richard Sieburth. New York: New Directions.

———. 1950. *The Letters of Ezra Pound, 1907–1941*. Ed. D. D. Paige. New York: Harcourt, Brace & World.

———. 1954. *Literary Essays of Ezra Pound*. London: Faber and Faber.

———. 1957. *Section Rock Drill, 85–95 de Los Cantares*. New York: New Directions.

———. 1960a. *ABC of Reading*. New York: New Directions.

———. 1960b. *Impact: Essays on Ignorance and the Decline of American Civilization*. Chicago: Henry Regnery.

———. 1967. *Pound/Joyce: The Letters of Ezra Pound to James Joyce*. Ed. Forrest Read. New York: New Directions.

———. 1969. *Drafts & Fragments of Cantos CX–CXVII*. New York: New Directions.

———. 1971. *The Cantos*. New York: New Directions.

———. 1973. *Selected Prose*. Ed. William Cookson. New York: New Directions.

———. 1984. *Ezra Pound and Dorothy Shakespear: Their Letters, 1909–1914*. Ed. Omar Pound and A. Walton Litz. New York: New Directions.

———. 1991. *The Selected Letters of Ezra Pound to John Quinn, 1915–1924*. Ed. Timothy Materer. Durham, NC: Duke University Press.

———. 1998. *"I Cease Not to Yowl": Ezra Pound's Letters to Olivia Rossetti Agresti*. Ed. Demetres P. Tryphonopoulos and Leon Surette. Urbana: University of Illinois Press.

———. 2002. *Canti postumi*. Ed. Massimo Bacigalupo. Milan: Mondadori.

———. 2004. *World War II Radio Speeches. Draft Text/Prototype CDs*. Transcribed by Ben Friedlander with Stefani Bardin and Carla Billitteri. Personal circulation.

Pound, Omar, and A. Walton Litz. 1984. *Ezra Pound and Dorothy Shakespear: Their Letters, 1909–1914*. New York: New Directions.

Preminger, Alex, and T. V. F. Brogan, eds. 1993. *The New Princeton Encyclopedia of Poetry and Poetics*. Princeton, NJ: Princeton University Press.

Prins, Yopie, and Maeera Shreiber. 1997. *Dwelling in Possibility: Women Poets and Critics on Poetry*. Ithaca, NY: Cornell University Press.

Quartermain, Peter. 1992. *Disjunctive Poetics: From Gertrude Stein and Louis Zukofsky to Susan Howe*. New York: Cambridge University Press.

Raaberg, Gwen. 1991. "The Problematics of Women and Surrealism." In Caws, Kuenzli, and Raaberg 1991:1–10.

Rado, Lisa. 2000. *The Modern Androgyne Imagination: A Failed Sublime*. Charlottesville: University Press of Virginia.

Rainey, Lawrence S. 1991. "Canon, Gender, and Text: The Case of H.D." In *Representing Modernist Texts: Editing as Interpretation*, ed. George Bornstein, 99–123. Ann Arbor: University of Michigan Press.

Rankine, Claudia, and Juliana Spahr, eds. 2002. *American Women Poets in the 21st Century: Where Lyric Meets Language*. Middletown, CT: Wesleyan University Press.

Rasula, Jed. 1994. "Gendering the Muse." *Sulfur* 35:159–75.

———. 2002. *This Compost: Ecological Imperatives in American Poetry.* Athens: University of Georgia Press.

Retallack, Joan. 2003. *The Poethical Wager.* Berkeley: University of California Press.

Rexroth, Kenneth, ed. 1955. *One Hundred Poems from the Japanese.* New York: New Directions.

Rich, Adrienne. 1975a. *Adrienne Rich's Poetry and Prose.* Ed. Barbara Charlesworth Gelpi and Albert Gelpi. New York: Norton.

———. 1975b. *Poems Selected and New, 1950–1974.* New York: Norton.

———. 1979. *On Lies, Secrets, and Silence: Selected Prose, 1966–1978.* New York: Norton.

———. 1986. *Bread, Blood, and Poetry: Selected Prose, 1979–1985.* New York: Norton.

Richardson, John. 1982. "Picasso: A Retrospective View." In *A Picasso Anthology: Documents, Criticism, Reminiscences,* ed. Marilyn McCully, 278–84. Princeton, NJ: Princeton University Press.

Rifkin, Libbie. 2000. *Career Moves: Olson, Creeley, Zukofsky, Berrigan, and the American Avant-Garde.* Madison: University of Wisconsin Press.

Riley, Denise. 1988. *"Am I That Name?" Feminism and the Category of 'Women' in History.* Minneapolis: University of Minnesota Press.

———. 1993. *Mop Mop Georgette: New and Selected Poems, 1986–1993.* London: Reality Street.

Rix, Helmut. 2000. "La scrittura e la lingua." In *Etruschi: Una nuova immagine,* ed. Mauro Cristofani, 199–227. Florence: Giunti Gruppo Editoriale.

Ross, Kristin. 1988. *The Emergence of Social Space: Rimbaud and the Paris Commune.* Minneapolis: University of Minnesota Press.

Rothenberg, Jerome, and Pierre Joris, eds. 1998. Introduction to *Poems for the Millennium: The University of California Book of Modern and Postmodern Poetry.* Volume 2, *From Postwar to Millennium,* 1–18. Berkeley: University of California Press.

Russo, Linda. 2001–2. "'F' Word in the Age of Mechanical Reproduction: An Account of Women-Edited Small Presses and Journals." In *The World in Time and Space: Towards a History of Innovative American Poetry in Our Time,* ed. Edward Foster and Joseph Donahue, 285–320. Jersey City: Talisman House.

———. 2004. "Becoming Poetic: Women, Gender, and Innovation in 20th-Century Avant-Garde Poetry and Poetics." PhD diss., SUNY-Buffalo.

Said, Edward. 1983. "Opponents, Audiences, Constituencies, and Community." In *The Anti-Aesthetic: Essays on Postmodern Culture,* ed. Hal Foster, 135–59. Port Townsend, WA: Bay Press.

Schor, Mira. 1997. *Wet: On Painting, Feminism, and Art Culture.* Durham, NC: Duke University Press.

Scully, James. 1988. *Line Break: Poetry as Social Practice.* Seattle: Bay Press.

Shange, Ntozake. 1977. *For Colored Girls Who Have Considered Suicide When the Rainbow Is Enuf: A Choreopoem.* New York: Macmillan.

Showalter, Elaine. 1971. "Women Writers and the Double Standard." In *Woman in*

Sexist Society: Studies in Power and Powerlessness, ed. Vivian Gornick and Barbara Moran, 452–79. New York: New American Library.

———. 1976. *A Literature of Their Own: British Women Novelists from Brontë to Lessing*. Princeton, NJ: Princeton University Press.

———. 1987. "Women's Time, Women's Space: Writing the History of Feminist Criticism." In *Feminist Issues in Literary Scholarship*, ed. Shari Benstock, 30–44. Bloomington: Indiana University Press.

Shreiber, Maeera Y. 1998. "The End of Exile: Jewish Identity and Its Diasporic Poetics." *PMLA* 113, no. 2 (March): 273–87.

Silliman, Ron. 1985. "Interview with Tom Beckett." *Difficulties* 2, no. 2:34–46.

———. 1992. "I Wanted to Write Sentences: Decision Making in the American Longpoem." *Sagetrieb* 11, nos. 1 and 2 (spring and fall): 11–20.

———. 2005. "'As to Violin Music': Time in the Longpoem." *Jacket* 27 (April): http://jacketmagazine.com/27/silliman.html (accessed June 17, 2005).

Sloan, Mary Margaret, ed. 1998. *Moving Borders: Three Decades of Innovative Writing by Women*. Jersey City: Talisman House.

———. 2001–2. "Of Experience to Experiment: Women's Innovative Writing, 1965–1995." In *The World in Time and Space: Towards a History of Innovative American Poetry in Our Time*, ed. Edward Foster and Joseph Donahue, 498–525. Jersey City: Talisman House.

Smith, Sidonie. 1987. *A Poetics of Women's Autobiography*. Bloomington: Indiana University Press.

Smout, T. C. 1969. *A History of the Scottish People, 1560–1830*. New York: Charles Scribner's Sons.

Solomon-Godeau, Abigail. 1997. *Male Trouble: A Crisis in Representation*. London: Thames and Hudson.

Spahr, Juliana. 2002. "Editing and Community." http://people.mills.edu/jspahr/editing.htm (accessed June 17, 2005).

Spitzer, Leo. 1948. *Linguistics and Literary History: Essays in Stylistics*. Princeton, NJ: Princeton University Press.

Spivak, Gayatri Chakravorty. 1987. "Finding Feminist Readings: Dante-Yeats." In *In Other Worlds: Essays in Cultural Politics*, 15–29. New York: Methuen.

Steiner, Peter. 1978. "The Conceptual Basis of Prague Structuralism." In *Sound, Sign, and Meaning: Quinquagenary of the Prague Linguistic Circle*, ed. Ladislav Matejka, 353–56. Ann Arbor: University of Michigan Department of Slavic Languages and Literatures.

Stevens, Wallace. 1957. *The Collected Poems of Wallace Stevens*. New York: Alfred A. Knopf.

Stewart, Susan. 1991. "Scandals of the Ballad." *Representations* 32 (fall): 134–56.

———. 1993. "The State of Cultural Theory and the Future of Literary Form." In *Profession 93*, 12–15. New York: Modern Language Association.

Stimpson, Catharine R. 1973–74. "Charles Olson: Preliminary Images." *Boundary 2* II, nos. 1–2 (fall-winter): 151–72.

Stock, Noel. 1970. *The Life of Ezra Pound.* New York: Pantheon.

Suleiman, Susan Rubin. 1990. *Subversive Intent: Gender, Politics, and the Avant-Garde.* Cambridge, MA: Harvard University Press.

Symonds, Deborah A. 1997. *Weep Not for Me: Women, Ballads, and Infanticide in Early Modern Scotland.* University Park: Pennsylvania State University Press.

Treadwell, Elizabeth. 2000–2001. "Letter to the Editor." *Tripwire* 4 (winter): 180–81.

Varèse, Edgar. 2001. As cited by James Freeman, program notes, Orchestra 2001, May 6. Concert Program.

Vickery, Ann. 2000. *Leaving Lines of Gender: A Feminist Genealogy of Language Writing.* Middletown, CT: Wesleyan University Press.

Waldman, Anne. 1993. *IOVIS.* Minneapolis, MN: Coffee House Press.

——. 1994–95. Interview by Ed Foster. *Talisman* 13 (fall/winter): 62–78.

——. 2001. *Vow to Poetry: Essays, Interviews, & Manifestoes.* Minneapolis, MN: Coffee House Press.

Waldrop, Rosmarie, trans. 2003. Introduction to *Collected Prose,* by Paul Celan, vii–x. Manchester: Carcanet Press.

Ward, John Powell. 1997. "'Will No One Tell Me What She Sings?'" *Studies in Romanticism* 36, no. 4 (winter): 611–33.

Watson, Roderick, ed. 1995. *The Poetry of Scotland: Gaelic, Scots, and English, 1380–1980.* Edinburgh: Edinburgh University Press.

Watten, Barrett. 1985. *Total Syntax.* Carbondale: Southern Illinois University Press.

——. 1998. "What I See in 'How I Became Hetty Jones.'" *Poetics Journal* 10 (June 1998): 98–121.

——. 2002. "The Turn to Language and the 1960s." *Critical Inquiry* 29 (autumn): 139–83.

——. 2003. *The Constructivist Moment: From Material Text to Cultural Poetics.* Middletown, CT: Wesleyan University Press.

Watts, Charles, and Edward Byrne, eds. 1999. *The Recovery of the Public World: Essays on Poetics in Honour of Robin Blaser.* Vancouver: Talonbooks.

Whyte, Ian D. 1997. *Scotland's Society and Economy in Transition, c. 1500–1760.* New York: St. Martin's.

Williams, Raymond. 1977. *Marxism and Literature.* Oxford: Oxford University Press.

Williams, William Carlos. [1951] 1967. *The Autobiography of William Carlos Williams.* New York: New Directions.

——. 1954. *Selected Essays.* New York: Random House.

——. 1957. *Selected Letters.* Ed. John C. Thirlwall. New York: McDowell, Oblensky.

——. 1978. *A Recognizable Image: William Carlos Williams on Art and Artists.* Ed. Bram Dijkstra. New York: New Directions.

——. 1992. *Paterson.* Ed. Christopher MacGowan. New York: New Directions.

Winnett, Susan. 1990. "Coming Unstrung: Women, Men, Narrative, and Principles of Pleasure." *PMLA* 105, no. 3 (May): 505–18.

Wolfson, Susan. 1997. *Formal Charges: The Shaping of Poetry in British Romanticism.* Stanford, CA: Stanford University Press.

Women: A Collaboration of Artists and Writers. 1948. New York: Samuel M. Kootz.

Woods, Tim. 2002. *The Poetics of the Limit: Ethics and Politics in Modern and Contemporary American Poetry.* New York: Palgrave Macmillan.

Woolf, Virginia. [1925] 1962. "The Modern Essay." In *The Common Reader, First Series,* 267–81. London: Hogarth.

———. [1929] 1957. *A Room of One's Own.* New York: Harcourt, Brace & World.

———. 1979. "'Anon' and the Reader." *Twentieth Century Literature* 25, nos. 3/4 (fall/winter): 397–98; special issue on Virginia Woolf, ed. Brenda Silver.

Wordsworth, William. 1946. *The Poetical Works of William Wordsworth.* Volume 3. Ed. E. de Selincourt and Helen Darbishire. Oxford: Clarendon Press.

Wu, Duncan, ed. 1998. *Romanticism: An Anthology.* Oxford: Blackwell.

Yeats, W. B. [1938] 1961. *A Vision.* New York: Macmillan.

———. 1955. *The Letters of W. B. Yeats.* Ed. Allen Wade. New York: Macmillan.

Zukofsky, Louis. [1948] 2000. *A Test of Poetry.* Middletown, CT: Wesleyan University Press.

———. 1978. "A." Berkeley: University of California Press.

———. 2000. *Prepositions +: The Collected Critical Essays.* Middletown, CT: Wesleyan University Press.

Index

Abraham, Nicolas, and Maria Torok, 214
Adorno, Theodor, 1, 4, 5, 7, 10, 34, 40, 61, 76, 97–101, 105, 110, 169, 186–187, 188, 200, 201, 203, 222, 239, 264n8, 272n2

Balla, Giacomo, 175, 178
Barnard College, 18, 27, 165
Bashō, 152
Baudelaire, Charles, 162, 163
Beauvoir, Simone de, 56, 166
Beinecke Library, Yale University, 227, 228
Bellamy, Dodie, 63
Belsey, Catherine, 3
Benjamin, Walter, 38, 140, 162–164, 170–171, 175, 186, 196, 197, 200, 201–203, 214, 275n19, 275n20, 275n21
Bensmaïa, Réda, 38, 257n11
Bernstein, Charles, 3, 186, 188, 272n3
Bible, 245; Abraham and Isaac, 237; Miriam, 82, 262n10; Moses, 82
Blake, William, 174, 196, 274n14
Blanchot, Maurice, 5, 10, 239, 249
Boldereff, Frances, 77, 87–92, 94, 113, 120, 165, 262n13, 262n17, 262n18, 262n19, 263n20, 263n21, 263n22
Boym, Svetlana, 75, 123, 261n3, 261n4
Braidotti, Rosi, 58
Brecht, Bertolt, 9
Breton, André, 166, 167–168, 169, 170, 177, 221
Broodthaers, Marcel, 34, 35, 256n1
Brooks, Gwendolyn, 107, 157, 263n3
Brown, Sterling, 157, 158
Browning, Robert, 133, 134
Butler, Judith, 4, 94, 261n1
Buuck, David, 54
Byrd, Don, 84

Cage, John, 190, 273n7
Cahun, Claude, 169
Caws, Mary Ann, 270n7, 271n9, 271n19
Chadwick, Whitney, 168
Celan, Paul, 186, 194, 197–198, 200
Char, René, 10
Cixous, Hélène, 42, 44, 92–93, 256n19
Cole, Barbara, 48, 52, 68, 259n1, 260n14
Coleridge, Samuel Taylor, 107, 234
Columbia University, 20, 21, 22, 188–189, 211, 219, 254n5, 254n7
Coolidge, Clark, 242
Cooper, Jane, 192
Corinna, 83
Corman, Cid, 142, 144, 147, 152, 153
Crawford, John, 188, 194
Creeley, Robert, 80, 87, 88, 212, 219, 262n28
Cullen, Countee, 64
Culler, Jonathan, 105, 107, 266n1, 276n4

Dahlen, Beverly, 212, 228
Daly, Mary, 58, 257n4
Dante, 6, 74, 221, 240, 246
Darwin, Charles, 148
Davidson, Michael, 270n8

DeKoven, Marianne, 258n15
Delaunay, Sonia, 212
De Lauretis, Teresa, 3, 102, 122
Deleuze, Gilles, 92
Dickinson, Emily, 145, 161, 228, 269n13, 271n16
Diggory, Terence, 170
Dinnerstein, Dorothy, 75, 123
Dolmetsch, Arnold, 128
Doane, Mary Ann, 104, 119
Donne, John, 106
Drucker, Johanna, 119
Duchamp, Marcel, 169
Duncan, Robert, 2, 24, 27, 167, 201, 218–219
DuPlessis, Rachel Blau: *Drafts,* 10, 193–194, 210–213, 214–217, 228, 230–232, 233–235, 236–241, 242–243, 246, 250–251, 277n12, 278n9; "For the Etruscans," 26, 27–29, 40, 43, 66, 257n11, 257n12; *The Pink Guitar,* 3, 5, 30, 32, 41; *Writing Beyond the Ending,* 24, 29, 30

Easthope, Antony, 102–103, 105
Eliot, T. S., 6, 50, 76, 86, 195, 211–212, 243, 246, 250, 266n3
Eluard, Paul, 181
Ernst, Max, 169
Eshleman, Clayton, 219
Ethical Culture Movement, 16, 18
Eurydice (and Orpheus), 24, 224–225
Evans, Steve, 5

Farr, Florence, 126–133, 135–136, 266n4, 266n7, 266n9, 267n10, 267n11
Feldman, Jessica, 126, 134
Felski, Rita, 122, 127, 136, 253n5, 259n4, 259n6
Feminist Studies, 26, 256n17
Foster, Ed, 58
Fraser, Kathleen, 3, 61, 63, 167, 212, 259n9, 262n14, 263n3, 275n1
Freud, Sigmund, 40, 44, 79, 83, 225, 231, 232
Friedman, Susan Stanford, 25, 57, 60, 225, 226, 228, 253n5, 256n21
Frye, Marilyn, 81

Gaelic song, 115–116, 264n9, 265n16
George, Stefan, 98–99, 105
Gilbert, Sandra, 228
Ginsberg, Allen, 190, 193, 245, 273n8
Glissant, Edouard, 231
Good, Graham, 73
Grossman, Allen, 77–83, 94, 262n8, 262n9
Gubar, Susan, 228
Guest, Barbara, 9, 166–184, 271n10, 271n13, 271n14, 271n15, 271n16, 271n17
Guillory, John, 222

Harris, Ann Sutherland, 22, 255n7
Harryman, Carla, 63
H.D., 3, 9, 11, 24, 27, 30, 31, 40, 167, 194, 195, 212, 218, 221, 224–229, 230, 231–234, 241, 243, 244, 255n15
Hejinian, Lyn, 3, 9, 10, 61, 63, 221
Hill, Bridget, 114
Holocaust (Shoah), 17, 186–187, 213–214, 235, 237, 250–251, 278n6
"hooks, bell," 41
Howe, Susan, 3, 228
Hubert, Renée Riese, 168–169
Hughes, Langston, 106
Hunt, Erica, 3

Ibsen, Henrik, 126, 127, 128, 130, 132, 133, 136
Irigaray, Luce, 8, 44–45, 80, 83, 227, 258n13, 270n7

Jakobson, Roman, 102–103, 223, 276n6
James, Henry, 124–125, 126, 172
Jane Eyre, 16
Jarrell, Randall, 210
Jehlen, Myra, 60
Johnson, Barbara, 107, 123
Jones, Nancy, 109
Joris, Pierre, 186, 194
Joron, Andrew, 273n6
Joyce, Patrick, 120

Kaplan, Cora, 78
Kaufman, Robert, 201, 223, 269n2
Keats, John, 6, 105, 130, 153, 157, 173, 174, 175, 233
Kelly, Mary, 212
Kootz, Samuel, 164
Kristeva, Julia, 94, 228–229
Kuhn, Thomas, 254n1

Lazer, Hank, 222–223, 275n1
Lecercle, Jean-Jacques, 223–224
Lessing, Doris, 19, 23, 254n3
Levertov, Denise, 191, 223
Levitsky, Rachel, 53, 63
Litz, A. Walton, 126, 128, 134
Lorde, Audré, 61
Loy, Mina, 62, 263n3
Lukács, Georg, 214
Lundquist, Sara, 170, 175–176, 271n11
Lyon, Janet, 135

Maar, Dora, 178, 180–184, 271n19, 272n21, 272n22
Mackey, Nathaniel, 233
Mac Low, Jackson, 190
Mallarmé, Stephane, 34, 35, 174, 184
Marinetti, Filippo, 134, 135, 136, 267n12, 267n13
Marx, Karl, 120
Mass Observation, 213, 233
Matisse, Henri, 48, 184
McAleavey, David, 195
McCaffery, Steve, 10, 41
McGann, Jerome, 103
McIntosh, Millicent Carey, 18
Mellor, Anne K., 109
Midrash, 212, 231, 233–34, 240
Middleton, Peter, 267n1
Miller, Nancy, 41, 42, 256n21, 257n5, 257n9
Millett, Kate, 21, 22, 49
Miró, Juan, 171, 172, 178
Monroe, Harriet, 133
Moore, Marianne, 85, 266n3, 271n16
Mörike, Eduard, 99
Morris, Adalaide, 222, 226, 277n11, 277n23
Morrison, Yedda, 54
Mulvey, Laura, 104
Myers, John Bernard, 167

Nardi, Marcia, 76, 120, 245
New American Poetry, 19
New Criticism, 122
New Yorker, The, 123
Niedecker, Lorine, 9, 11, 139–161, 267n1, 268n3, 268n4, 268n5, 268n6, 269n8, 269n9, 269n10
Notley, Alice, 63, 241–242, 243, 244, 261n17, 263n3

Olsen, Tillie, 255n 10, 256n18, 257n4
Olson, Charles, 46, 62, 77, 84–93, 94, 113, 120, 169, 195, 219, 250, 262n13, 262n14, 262n16, 262n17, 262n18, 263n20, 263n24
Oppen, George, 6, 9, 11, 32, 67, 140, 186–205, 209–210, 212, 219, 220, 222–223, 229–230, 273n8, 273n9, 274n12, 274n13, 274n 14, 274n15, 274n16, 274n18, 276n5, 278n6
Oppen, Mary, 234
Oppenheim, Meret, 262n19, 266n2
Osman, Jena, 54, 58
Ostriker, Alicia Suskin, 61, 62, 226, 260n12, 263n3, 277n23

Padgett, Ron, 167
Palmer, Michael, 223
Paz, Octavio, 196
Penberthy, Jenny, 143, 268n2
Perelman, Bob, 246, 249, 250
Perloff, Marjorie, 259n2
Petrarchan tropes, 74, 192
Picasso, Pablo, 164, 178, 180–184, 270n3, 270n4, 272n21, 272n22
Pindar, 83, 262n11
Plath, Sylvia, 61
Poe, Edgar Allan, 76, 220
Polan, Dana, 92
Pollock, Griselda, 7, 8, 57, 102
Pound, Ezra, 8, 11, 24, 32, 113, 120, 124–126, 128–131, 133–136, 147, 152, 161, 175, 188–189, 192, 195, 196, 203, 210, 211, 216, 218, 219, 220, 221, 231, 234, 246–251, 265n22, 267n10, 278n6, 278n7, 278n8, 278n9, 278n10
Praxilla, 83

Quartermain, Peter, 203

Rainey, Lawrence, 134
Rakosi, Carl, 32, 268n5
Rasula, Jed, 36, 123–124
Retallack, Joan, 3, 9, 32, 45–46, 253n1, 253n4, 258n14, 258n16, 273n7
Reznikoff, Charles, 11, 153, 269n8

Rich, Adrienne, 20, 26, 57–58, 61, 145, 219, 223, 255n11, 257n4, 259n7
Richardson, Dorothy, 30, 237, 256n20
Riley, Denise, 7, 56, 73, 94
Rilke, Rainer Maria, 76
Rothenberg, Jerome, 186, 194
Roub, Bonnie and Gail, 142

Sappho, 192, 214, 222, 275n3
Sartre, Jean-Paul, 187
Scalapino, Leslie, 61, 63
Schultz, Susan, 222
Schwerner, Armand, 192
Schwitters, Kurt, 214
Shakespear, Dorothy [Dorothy Pound], 131, 267n10
Shakespear, Olivia, 127
Shakespeare, William, 125–26, 140
Shapiro, David, 167, 270n6
Shapiro, Karl, 167
Shaw, George Bernard, 126, 127, 130, 133, 136
Shreiber, Maeera, 112
Showalter, Elaine, 255n13, 256n20
Silliman, Ron, 11, 239, 277n3
Sociopoesis, 2
Spahr, Juliana, 54, 58, 259n5
Spitzer, Leo, 77
Spivak, Gayatri, 79, 80, 225
Stein, Gertrude, 54, 227
Stevens, Wallace, 75, 180
Stewart, Susan, 77, 157
Symonds, Deborah A., 115, 117

Thoreau, Henry, 41, 42

Ulanov, Barry, 165–166, 270n5

Vietnam War, 17, 21
Virgil, 226, 234

Waldman, Anne, 3, 58–59, 66, 69
Ward, John Powell, 118
Watten, Barrett, 6, 124, 242, 277n2
Weinberger, Eliot, 193, 273n6
Wilbur, Richard, 167
Wilkinson, Thomas, 110, 114
Williams, Jonathan, 147
Williams, Raymond, 30, 82, 255n10, 261n5
Williams, William Carlos, 24, 32, 62, 85, 120, 152, 155, 165, 177, 188–189, 195, 210, 212, 214, 215, 216, 218, 219, 220, 240, 241–242, 243, 245
Wollstonecraft, Mary, 60
Woolf, Virginia, 19, 23, 30, 33, 34–35, 38, 51, 59, 75, 142, 166, 219, 229, 256n20, 257n4
Wordsworth, Dorothy, 109, 219, 264n4
Wordsworth, William, 8, 106, 107–119, 121, 180, 219, 264n4, 264n5, 264n12, 265n21, 265n22

Yeats, W. B., 126, 127, 128, 129, 130, 133, 136, 266n6, 266n8, 266n9

Zukofsky, Louis, 5, 11, 67, 142, 143, 153, 155, 161, 223–224, 230, 261n2, 268n4, 268n5
Zukofsky, Paul, 143